MENASHA RIDGE PRESS
Birmingham, Alabama

60 HIKES WITHIN 60 MILES

ALBUQUERQUE

INCLUDING
SANTA FE,
MOUNT TAYLOR, AND
SAN LORENZO CANYON

STEPHEN AUSHERMAN

DISCLAIMER

This book is meant only as a guide to select trails in the Albuquerque area and does not guarantee hiker safety in any way—you hike at your own risk. Neither Menasha Ridge Press nor Stephen Ausherman is liable for property loss or damage, personal injury, or death that result in any way from accessing or hiking the trails described in the following pages. Please be aware that hikers have been injured in the Albuquerque area. Be especially cautious when walking on or near boulders, steep inclines, and drop-offs, and do not attempt to explore terrain that may be beyond your abilities. To help ensure an uneventful hike, please read carefully the introduction to this book, and perhaps get further safety information and guidance from other sources. Familiarize yourself thoroughly with the areas you intend to visit before venturing out. Ask questions, and prepare for the unforeseen. Familiarize yourself with current weather reports, maps of the area you intend to visit, and any relevant park regulations.

Copyright © 2008 by Stephen Ausherman

All rights reserved

Printed in the United States of America

Published by Menasha Ridge Press

Distributed by Publishers Group West

First edition, first printing

Library of Congress Cataloging-in-Publication Data

Ausherman, Stephen.

60 hikes within 60 miles : Albuquerque, including Santa Fe, Mount Taylor, and San Lorenzo Canyon / Stephen Ausherman.—1st ed.

   p. cm.

Includes index.

ISBN-13: 978-0-89732-590-5

ISBN-10: 0-89732-590-7

1. Hiking—New Mexico—Albuquerque Region—Guidebooks. 2. Albuquerque Region (N.M.)—Guidebooks. I. Title. II. Title: Sixty hikes within sixty miles.

GV199.42.N62A434 2008

796.5109789—dc22

2007049409

Cover and text design by Steveco International

Cover photos by Stephen Ausherman

Author photo by Stephen Ausherman

Cartography and elevation profiles by Chris Erichson and Scott McGrew

Menasha Ridge Press

P.O. Box 43673

Birmingham, AL 35243

www.menasharidge.com

TABLE OF CONTENTS

DEDICATION

to Chuck & Nancy, Judy & Aimee, the Boerigters, Dave Shapiro,

Scout Lisagor, Señor Hawley, Mr. Smith, Mr. Death,

Jim Bo, Elzbieta, Scial, Shay, and Betsy (especially Betsy)

for enduring hikes with me when I was less familiar with these trails

and for Gurdin Chapin

(Pasó por aquí)

—STEPHEN AUSHERMAN

FOREWORD

Welcome to Menasha Ridge Press's *60 Hikes within 60 Miles.* Our strategy was simple: First, find a hiker who knows the area and loves to hike. Second, ask that person to spend a year researching the most popular and very best trails around. And third, have that person describe each trail in terms of difficulty, scenery, condition, elevation change, and all other categories of information that are important to hikers. "Pretend you've just completed a hike and met up with other hikers at the trailhead," we told each author. "Imagine their questions, and be clear in your answers." An experienced hiker and writer, author Stephen Ausherman has selected 60 of the best hikes in and around the Albuquerque metropolitan area. From the greenways and urban hikes that make use of parklands to flora- and fauna-rich treks along the cliffs and hills in the hinterlands, Ausherman provides hikers (and walkers) with a great variety of hikes—and all within roughly 60 miles of Albuquerque.

You'll get more out of this book if you take a moment to read the Introduction explaining how to read the trail listings. The "Topographic Maps" section will help you understand how useful topos will be on a hike, and will also tell you where to get them. And though this is a "where-to," rather than a "how-to" guide, those of you who have hiked extensively will find the Introduction of particular value. As much for the opportunity to free the spirit as well as to free the body, let these hikes elevate you above the urban hurry.

All the best,
The Editors at Menasha Ridge Press

ABOUT THE AUTHOR

STEPHEN AUSHERMAN has worked as a public health assistant in Iraq, Nigeria, Kenya, and Tanzania, a teacher in Korea and China, and a journalist in India and the United States. He was a Writer-in-Residence at Buffalo National River in Arkansas, Devils Tower National Monument in Wyoming, and Bernheim Forest in Kentucky, and an Artist-in-Residence for Cornucopia Art Center in Minnesota. His books include *Restless Tribes,* an award-winning collection of travel stories, and *Fountains of*

Youth, a novel. Born in China and raised in North Carolina, Ausherman took an unscheduled detour to Albuquerque in 1996. He has lived there ever since. Check out Stephen's Web site: www .restlesstribes.com.

PREFACE

*May your trails be crooked, winding, lonesome, dangerous,
leading to the most amazing view.*
—EDWARD ABBEY

Sometime in the mid 1920s, New Mexico Governor Arthur T. Hannett placed a ruler on a map and conceived an idea for a shorter Route 66. He drew a straight line connecting Santa Rosa to Gallup, with Albuquerque lying near the halfway point. The planned shortcut was met with less enthusiasm than protest, particularly among those living in the towns it would have bypassed. When Hannett lost the 1926 gubernatorial election, he spent his final month in office executing a retaliatory farewell to the capital city. Without regard for land ownership or what stood in the way, he ordered a new road cut between Santa Rosa and Moriarty. And despite boundary fences, dense piñon forests, blizzard conditions, and sabotaged equipment, road crews completed the unwavering 69-mile roadway in just 31 days. This new segment of Route 66 soon brought travelers to Albuquerque in record time by eliminating the old winding route through Santa Fe.

In the summer of 2007, I put a ruler on the map and drew straight lines, each a 60-mile spoke radiating from the hub of Albuquerque. With the addition of a rim, my diagram resembled a wagon wheel, and it effectively illustrated that the scope of this book was bigger than I'd initially guessed.

Within 60 miles of Albuquerque, you'll find six national forest ranger districts, four national monuments, four federally designated wilderness areas, a national wildlife refuge, a national preserve, and at least three state parks. You'll also hit upon equally fascinating, but lesser-known tracts under the stewardship of the Bureau of Land Management, the State Land Office, and the Middle Rio Grande Conservancy District.

Architectural details on Central Avenue
(Historic Route 66)

With the hub and rim established, I erased the spokes. The sections they created were useless for any pragmatic arrangement, as few roads serve Albuquerque with the linear efficiency Hannett might have hoped for. But crooked as they are, the primary highways do contribute to a straightforward approach for organizing such widespread hikes. They'll not only point you in the right direction, but also reveal something about those who've gone that way before. And though you may end up driving farther than 60 road miles to reach a trailhead (46 miles on average), every hike featured in this book is well within the bounds of a reasonable daytrip.

THE DUKE CITY

Named for the Duke of Alburquerque, minus the superfluous *r*, our focal city is fairly easy to spell when you consider its Navajo name: *Bee'eldííldahsinil*. With more than 25 percent of its land protected as public open space, Albuquerque tops the national list of largest city park systems. In the Duke City section of this book, you'll find quick access to 10 routes, starting with an urban hike in the heart of the historic district. Irrigation ditches, or acequias, and the Rio Grande provide settings for shaded waterside walks, whereas Petroglyph National Monument is so exposed that even the rocks are sunburned. Open Space in the Northeast Heights serves as a gateway to the Sandia Mountains, which rise a mile above this mile-high city.

THE SALT MISSION TRAIL

Take a look at the Sandia Ranger District map, and you'll spot 60 hikes in 60 seconds. Extending south from the Sandias, the Manzanita and Manzano ranges continue the possibilities for nearby mountain hikes. Despite their proximity to the urban center of New Mexico, only one road manages to pierce the 60-mile span of these three ranges. The I-40 corridor traverses Tijeras Canyon, which separates the Sandias from the Manzanitas. Once you drive east through the canyon, you face a choice between two historic routes: south on the Salt Mission Trail or north on the Turquoise Trail.

Early Spaniards established Franciscan missions to lord over the Salinas Province and its salt-driven economy. Colonial influences are still apparent in the centuries-old land grants along the scenic highways south of Tijeras. Ruins of the mission at Quarai stand near the last hike in this section, the southernmost loop in the Manzano Mountain Wilderness. All three hikes on this side of the Manzanos feature crest views from 8,700 feet or higher. Closer to Albuquerque, two canyons in the Manzanitas are better suited for quick getaways. The first and nearest hike in this group is one of the southernmost in the Sandia Mountain Wilderness. True, it seems to belong in the next section, but then you'd never find the trailhead if you started north on NM 14, the Turquoise Trail.

THE TURQUOISE TRAIL

The east side of the Sandias is gentler and shadier than its stark west face, as you'll notice in this section's first two hikes. The next two hikes originate near the same point on a country road, but they explore two vastly different aspects of the same juniper savanna. The last pair takes you into the legendary mining territory of Cerrillos Hills, where mystic blue stones are still the object of a thousand-year quest. An unofficial story behind the Turquoise Trail refers to a gaffe in the initial construction of the highway. Road crews allegedly scooped gravel from the wrong mine. The error went largely unrealized until local residents were seen fervently combing the newly graveled road and pocketing their finds. For that brief time, it was quite literally a trail of turquoise.

EL CAMINO REAL

El Camino Real de Tierra Adentro (The Royal Road of the Interior Land) was the primary route between the colonial Spanish capital of Mexico City and the provincial capital of Santa Fe. This 1,600-mile corridor still reflects the diverse heritages of Native America, the Old World, and the modern societies of the United States and Mexico. A 404-mile segment of El Camino Real was designated a National Historic Trail in 2000. (For details on the official route, visit **www .nps.gov/elca.**)

El Camino Real's nearest modern alignment is I-25, and you won't drive more than 50 miles of it to reach the hikes in this northern group. The section begins with Tunnel Spring, our sixth and final hike in the Sandias. Farther north you'll explore three relatively unknown areas that are rich in archaeological and paleontological features. Getting back to more familiar terrain, you'll visit a national monument and a wilderness area that are famous for rock formations and forest fires, respectively. Also included in this group is La Bajada. Once considered the most perilous hill on the Camino Real, "the descent" now serves as the starting point for a pleasant hike along the Santa Fe River.

THE CITY DIFFERENT

Conceived in response to the City Beautiful movement of the 1900s, this self-inflicted nickname underscores the idea that Santa Fe is, well . . . *different*. In New Mexico's tale of two cities, she plays the eccentric spinster, whereas Albuquerque is the tart with a heart of gold, and together they endure the love-hate relationship of inseparable sisters. In this group you'll find five hikes on the cusp of the Santa Fe National Forest. The first two are a popular couple, each just a short drive from the Santa Fe Plaza. The last two head from Buckman, an obsolete town on the east bank of the Rio Grande. The odd one in the middle, Glorieta Canyon, ventures into the Pecos/Las Vegas Ranger District for a cool hike in aspen forest.

THE CUBA ROAD

The road between Bernalillo and Cuba was once known as a two-lane suicide run. That's all changed since a $312-million upgrade in the late 1990s, but the land you'll access via US 550 remains very much the same. It's unforgiving desert from the barrancas at La Ceja to the burned-out coal seams on Deadman Peaks. On this convergence of the Rio Grande rift and the Colorado Plateau, you'll find slot canyons, sandstone hoodoos, volcanic plugs, banded mesas, and other classic features that contribute to the irresistible allure of the American Southwest. The recent designation of the Ojito Wilderness has renewed attention to three recreational areas southwest of San Ysidro. From San Ysidro to Cuba, US 550 squeezes between the volcano fields in the San Juan Basin and the southernmost uplift in the Rocky Mountains. This inspiring stretch of road also accounts for nearly a third of the 132-mile Jemez Mountain Trail National Scenic Byway.

THE JEMEZ MOUNTAIN TRAIL

Eight of America's 99 National Scenic Byways are in New Mexico, including the Turquoise Trail, El Camino Real, Historic Route 66, and the Jemez Mountain Trail (JMT). About 60 miles of NM 4, nearly its entire length, have been incorporated into the JMT, and it's as much a scenic drive as an erratic trip through time. It starts at the pastoral 19th-centry villa of San Ysidro, traverses a mountainous landscape reshaped by a massive volcanic eruption 1.2 million years ago, and finally arrives at a corner of the technological frontier known as Los Alamos National Laboratories. Here upon the slopes of a slightly dyspeptic supervolcano, the world's top nuclear eggheads have converged to expand on the pioneering work of J. Bob Oppenheimer, papa of the atomic bomb. Hikes accessed from this stretch of the Jemez Mountain Trail visit a marvelous collection of stone goblins, historic ruins, mountain rivers, red rock canyons, cliff dwellings, and the gigantic caldera of the aforementioned volcano.

THE CHIHUAHUA TRAIL

As mentioned earlier, I-25 roughly follows El Camino Real, but then every main road of commerce under the Spanish crown was a camino real. The 550-mile segment of El Camino Real from Santa Fe to the capital city of Chihuahua was once distinguished as the Chihuahua Trail. Forged millennia ago as an Indian trade route, the corridor has since rumbled with the traffic of conquistadors, oxcarts, wagon trains, and cattle drives. To reach the distant trailhead in this wildly diverse group, you'll motor it 50 miles south of the last exit to Albuquerque. Features on hikes along the way include a mysterious rock, a sacred hill, and two wooded canyons in the Manzano Mountain Wilderness. A couple of easy strolls near Bernardo are followed by a potentially arduous ridgeline ascent in the notorious Sierra Ladrones. The final three hikes examine a few of the widely varied ecosystems in the Sevilleta National Wildlife Refuge.

THE MOTHER ROAD

The last group brings us back to Route 66. In his 1939 novel *The Grapes of Wrath,* John Steinbeck dubbed it "the mother road." I-40 now assumes the bulk of its heavy load, but remnants of this song-worthy highway still stand. As you travel to Herrera, you might recognize the Rio Puerco Bridge from its cameo role in the 1940 cinematic adaptation of Steinbeck's book. As with the hikes near Herrera, two excursions in the Greater Petaca Pinta visit lonesome landscapes of rugged beauty. Gorgeously hostile badlands are the big attraction at El Malpais. To top it all off, the highest and final hike passes through aspen woodland to reach the summit of Mount Taylor.

INTRODUCTION

Welcome to *60 Hikes within 60 Miles: Albuquerque*. If you're new to hiking or even if you're a seasoned hiker, take a few minutes to read the following introduction. We explain how this book is organized and how to use it.

HOW TO USE THIS GUIDEBOOK

THE OVERVIEW MAP AND OVERVIEW MAP KEY

Use the overview map on the inside front cover to find the exact locations of each hike's primary trailhead. Each hike's number appears on the overview map, on the map key facing the overview map, and in the table of contents. Flipping through the book, a hike's full profile is easy to locate by watching for the hike number at the top of each page. The book is organized by region as indicated in the table of contents. A map legend that details the symbols found on trail maps appears on the inside back cover.

REGIONAL MAPS

The book is divided into regions and prefacing each regional section is an overview map of that region. The regional provides more detail than the overview map, bringing you closer to the hike.

TRAIL MAPS

Each hike contains a detailed map that shows the trailhead, the route, significant features, facilities, and topographic landmarks such as creeks, overlooks, and peaks. The author gathered map data by carrying a Garmin eTrex Legend GPS unit while hiking. This data was downloaded into the digital mapping program Topo USA and processed by expert cartographers to produce the highly accurate maps found in this book. Each trailhead's GPS coordinates are included with each profile.

ELEVATION PROFILES

Corresponding directly to the trail map, each hike contains a detailed elevation profile. The elevation profile provides a quick look at the trail from the side, enabling you to visualize how the trail rises and falls. Note the number of feet between each tick mark on the vertical axis (the height scale). To avoid making flat hikes look steep and steep hikes appear flat, height scales are used throughout the book to provide an accurate image of the hike's climbing difficulty.

GPS TRAILHEAD COORDINATES

To collect accurate map data, each trail was hiked with a Garmin eTrex Legend GPS unit. Data collected was then downloaded and plotted onto a digital USGS topo map. In addition to highly specific trail outlines, this book also includes the GPS coordinates for each trailhead in two formats: latitude/longitude and UTM. Latitude/longitude coordinates tell you where you are by locating a point west (latitude) of the 0° meridian line that passes through Greenwich, England, and north or south of the 0° (longitude) line that belts the Earth, a.k.a. the equator.

Topographic maps show latitude/longitude as well as UTM grid lines. Known as UTM coordinates, the numbers index a specific point using a grid method. The survey datum used to arrive at the coordinates in this book is WGS84 (versus NAD27 or WGS83). For readers who own a GPS unit, whether handheld or on board a vehicle, the latitude/longitude or UTM coordinates provided on the first page of each hike may be entered into the GPS unit; just make sure your GPS unit is set to navigate using WGS84 datum. Now you can navigate directly to the trailhead.

Most trailheads, which begin in parking areas, can be reached by car, but some hikes still require a short walk to reach the trailhead from a parking area. In those cases a handheld unit is necessary to continue the GPS navigation process. That said, however, readers can easily access all trailheads in this book by using the directions given, the overview map, and the trail map, which shows at least one major road leading into the area. But for those who enjoy using the latest GPS technology to navigate, the necessary data has been provided. A brief explanation of the UTM coordinates from South Valley: Montessa Park (page 65) follows.

UTM Zone   13S
Easting   0354109
Northing   3876205

The UTM zone number 13 refers to one of the 60 vertical zones of the Universal Transverse Mercator (UTM) projection. Each zone is 6 degrees wide.

The UTM zone letter S refers to one of the 20 horizontal zones that span from 80 degrees south to 84 degrees north. The easting number 0354109 indicates in meters how far east or west a point is from the central meridian of the zone. Increasing easting coordinates on a topo map or on your GPS screen indicates that you are moving east; decreasing easting coordinates indicate you are moving west. The northing number 3876205 references in meters how far you are from the equator. Above and below the equator, increasing northing coordinates indicate you are traveling north; decreasing northing coordinates indicate you are traveling south. To learn more about how to enhance your outdoor experiences with GPS technology, refer to *GPS Outdoors: A Practical Guide For Outdoor Enthusiasts* (Menasha Ridge Press).

HIKE DESCRIPTIONS

Each hike contains seven key items: an "In Brief" description of the trail, a Key At-A-Glance box, directions to the trail, trailhead coordinates, a trail map, an elevation profile, and a trail description. Many also include a note on nearby activities. Combined, the maps and information provide a clear method to assess each trail from the comfort of your favorite reading chair.

IN BRIEF

A "taste of the trail." Think of this section as a snapshot focused on the historical landmarks, beautiful vistas, and other sights you may encounter on the hike.

KEY AT-A-GLANCE INFORMATION

The information in the Key At-A-Glance boxes gives you a quick idea of the statistics and specifics of each hike.

LENGTH AND CONFIGURATION The length of the trail from start to finish (total distance traveled). There may be options to shorten or extend the hikes, but the mileage corresponds to the described hike. Consult the hike description to help decide how to customize the hike for your ability or time constraints. A description of what the trail might look like from overhead. Trails can be loops, out-and-backs (trails on which one enters and leaves along the same path), figure eights, or a combination of shapes.

DIFFICULTY The degree of effort an "average" hiker should expect on a given hike. For simplicity, the trails are rated as "easy," "moderate," or "difficult."

SCENERY A short summary of the attractions offered by the hike and what to expect in terms of plant life, wildlife, natural wonders, and historic features.

EXPOSURE A quick check of how much sun you can expect on your shoulders during the hike.

TRAIL TRAFFIC Indicates how busy the trail might be on an average day. Trail traffic, of course, varies from day to day and season to season. Weekend days typically see the most visitors. Other trail users that may be encountered on the trail are also noted here.

SHARED USE Indicates the types and levels of use from non-hikers.

TRAIL SURFACE Indicates whether the trail surface is paved, rocky, gravel, dirt, boardwalk, or a mixture of surfaces.

HIKING TIME The length of time it takes to hike the trail. A slow but steady hiker will average 2 to 3 miles an hour, depending on the terrain.

DRIVING DISTANCE One way, measured from the Big I (the I-40 and I-25 exchange)

ACCESS A notation of any fees or permits that may be needed to access the trail or park at the trailhead. Also may include park hours and sesonal closings.

LAND STATUS Indicates which agency manages the land.

MAPS Here you'll find a list of maps that show the topography of the trail, including 7.5–minute USGS topo maps.

FACILITIES What to expect in terms of restrooms and water at the trailhead or nearby.

LAST CHANCE FOOD/GAS A bonus feature for those who set out not quite fully prepared for the journey.

DIRECTIONS

Used in conjunction with the overview map, the driving directions will help you locate each trailhead. Once at the trailhead, park only in designated areas.

GPS TRAILHEAD COORDINATES

The trailhead coordinates can be used in addition to the driving directions if you enter the coordinates into your GPS unit before you set out. See page 2 for more information on GPS coordinates.

DESCRIPTION

The trail description is the heart of this book. Here, the author provides a summary of the trail's essence and highlights any special traits the hike has to offer. The route is clearly described, including landmarks, side trips, and possible alternate routes along the way. Ultimately, the hike description will help you choose which hikes are best for you.

NEARBY ACTIVITIES

Look here for information on nearby activities or points of interest. This includes nearby parks, museums, restaurants, or even a brew pub where you can get a well-deserved beer after a long hike. Note that not every hike has a listing.

WEATHER

My initial field research for this book coincided with the onset of an epic heat wave and what seemed like another endless drought. Then the rain came, and no one had guessed that it would bring the 100-year floods. Winter followed suit with record snowfall—26 inches in 24 hours. Spring brought more of it, and Cinco de Mayo just wasn't the same with snow blustering through the fiestas. Tornados are a rarity in north-central New Mexico, but a single afternoon storm in June spawned three landspouts near La Bajada. In short, weather can be unpredictable from year to year or season to season.

With a base elevation of 5,000 feet, Albuquerque usually enjoys a high desert climate. Days are generally sunny and warm; but as the sun sets, the temperature falls. The city experiences an average change of 27 degrees from day to night all year. An average year here includes 310 days of sunshine and about 9 inches of rain, with relative humidity normally around 44 percent.

Summer is hot, of course, but low humidity helps keep it cooler than just about anywhere else south of the 36th parallel. And even when daytime temperatures soar into triple digits, you can always count on cool nights. In July and August, afternoon monsoons break the heat with sudden and furious thunderstorms.

Autumn can bring sunshine, thunderstorms, snow, or all of the above at once. Generally, warm temperatures still linger in September and early October, with sweater days firmly established by November.

Winter requires extra layers, though a light jacket often suffices on sunny days. Snow seldom lasts more than a day or two in town. However, deep canyons, north-facing slopes, and elevations above 8,000 feet can take weeks or months to fully defrost.

Spring often begins with high winds that can blow for days. Whether gusting off the West Mesa or howling through Tijeras Canyon, they create miserable conditions for outdoor recreation. On the plus side, it's a sure sign that perfect weather is right around the corner.

Before you go out, check the forecast with the National Weather Service: www.srh.noaa.gov/abq or call (505) 821-1111.

And no matter what they say, be prepared for anything.

ALBUQUERQUE MONTHLY CLIMATE SUMMARY

Period of Record: 1/1/1914 to 12/31/2005

Average Temperature by Month

	Jan	Feb	Mar	Apr	May	Jun
High	47.2°	53.2°	60.6°	70.0°	79.4°	89.3°
Low	23.4°	27.8°	33.0°	40.8°	50.1°	59.2°
Precipitation	0.37"	0.40"	0.52"	0.54"	0.63"	0.61"

	Jul	Aug	Sep	Oct	Nov	Dec
High	91.7°	88.9°	82.4°	71.0°	56.9°	47.7°
Low	64.6°	62.9°	56.0°	44.0°	31.4°	24.4°
Precipitation	1.38"	1.46"	0.96"	0.88"	0.46"	0.46"

WATER

How much is enough? Well, one simple physiological fact should convince you to err on the side of excess when deciding how much water to pack: A hiker working hard in 90-degree heat needs approximately 10 quarts of fluid per day. That's 2.5 gallons—10 quart-sized water bottles or 16 20-ounce ones. In other words, pack along one or two bottles even for short hikes.

Some hikers and backpackers hit the trail prepared to purify water found along the route. This method, while less dangerous than drinking it untreated, comes with risks. Purifiers with ceramic filters are the safest. Many hikers pack along the slightly distasteful tetraglycine-hydroperiodide tablets to purify water (sold under the names Potable Aqua, Coughlan's, and others).

Probably the most common waterborne "bug" that hikers face is Giardia which may not hit until one to four weeks after ingestion. It will have you living in the bathroom, passing noxious rotten-egg gas, vomiting, and shivering with chills. Other parasites to worry about include E. coli and Cryptosporidium, both of which are harder to kill than Giardia.

For most people, the pleasures of hiking make carrying water a relatively minor price to pay to remain healthy. If you're tempted to drink "found water," do so only if you understand the risks involved. Better yet, hydrate prior to your hike, carry (and drink) six ounces of water for every mile you plan to hike, and hydrate after the hike.

THE TEN ESSENTIALS

One of the first rules of hiking is to be prepared for anything. The simplest way to be prepared is to carry the "Ten Essentials." In addition to carrying the items listed below, you need to know how to use them, especially navigation items. Always consider worst-case scenarios like getting lost, hiking back in the dark, broken gear (for example, a broken hip strap on your pack or a water filter getting plugged), twisting an ankle, or a brutal thunderstorm. The items listed below don't cost a lot of money, don't take up much room in a pack, and don't weigh much, but they might just save your life.

WATER: durable bottles and water treatment like iodine or a filter

MAP: preferably a topo map and a trail map with a route description

COMPASS: a high-quality compass

FIRST-AID KIT: a high-quality kit including first-aid instructions

KNIFE: a multi/tool device with pliers is best

LIGHT: flashlight or headlamp with extra bulbs and batteries

FIRE: windproof matches or lighter and fire starter

EXTRA FOOD: you should always have food in your pack when you've finished hiking

EXTRA CLOTHES: rain protection, warm layers, gloves, and a warm hat

SUN PROTECTION: sunglasses, lip balm, sunblock, and a sun hat

FIRST-AID KIT

A typical first-aid kit may contain more items than you might think necessary

Ace bandages or Spenco joint wraps

Antibiotic ointment (Neosporin or the generic equivalent)

Aspirin, ibuprofen, or acetaminophen

Band-Aids

Benadryl or the generic equivalent diphenhydramine (in case of allergic reactions)

Butterfly-closure bandages

Epinephrine in a prefilled syringe (for people known to have severe allergic reactions to such things as bee stings)

Gauze (one roll)

Gauze compress pads (a half dozen 4 x 4-inch pads)

Hydrogen peroxide, Betadine, or iodine

Insect repellent

Matches or pocket lighter

Moleskin/Spenco "Second Skin"

Sunscreen

Whistle (It's more effective in signaling rescuers than your voice.)

HIKING WITH CHILDREN

No one is too young for a hike in the outdoors. Be mindful, though. Flat, short, and shaded trails are best with an infant. Toddlers who have not quite mastered walking can still tag along, riding on an adult's back in a child carrier. Use common sense to judge a child's capacity to hike a particular trail, and always count that the child will tire quickly and need to be carried.

When packing for the hike, remember the child's needs as well as your own. Make sure children are adequately clothed for the weather, have proper shoes, and are protected from the sun with sunscreen. Kids dehydrate quickly, so make sure you have plenty of fluid for everyone. To assist an adult with determining which trails are suitable for children, a list of hike recommendations for children is provided on page 19.

GENERAL SAFETY

To some inexperienced hikers the deep woods can seem perilous and at times scary. But with proper planning and the following tips, your trip can be fun, easy, and above all else safe.

- **Always hike with a buddy. While most of these areas are safe, you should have someone else with you while hiking.**

- **Always carry food and water whether you are planning to go overnight or not. Food will give you energy, help keep you warm, and sustain you in an emergency situation until help arrives. You never know if you will have a stream nearby when you become thirsty. Bring potable water or treat water before drinking it from a stream. Boil or filter all found water before drinking it.**

- **Stay on designated trails. Most hikers who get lost do so because they leave the trail. Even on the most clearly marked trails, there is usually a point where you have to stop and consider which direction to head. If you become disoriented, don t panic. As soon as you think you may be lost, stop, assess your current direction, and then retrace your steps back to the point where you went awry. Using map, compass, this book, and keeping in mind what you have passed thus far, reorient yourself, and trust your judgment on which way to continue. If you become absolutely unsure of how to continue, return to your vehicle the way you came in. Should you become completely lost and have no idea of how to return to the trailhead, remaining in place along the trail and waiting for help is most often the best option for adults and always the best option for children.**

- Be especially careful when crossing streams. Whether you are fording the stream or crossing on a log, make every step count. If you have any doubt about maintaining your balance on a foot log, go ahead and ford the stream instead. When fording a stream, use a trekking pole or stout stick for balance and face upstream as you cross. If a stream seems too deep to ford, turn back. Whatever is on the other side is not worth risking your life.

- Standing dead trees and storm-damaged living trees pose a real hazard to hikers and tent campers. These trees may have loose or broken limbs that could fall at any time. When choosing a spot to rest or a backcountry camp-site, look up.

- Know the symptoms of hypothermia. Shivering and forgetfulness are the two most common indicators of this insipid killer. Hypothermia can occur at any elevation, even in the summer, especially when the hiker is wearing light-weight cotton clothing. If symptoms arise, get the victim shelter, hot liquids, and dry clothes or a dry sleeping bag.

- Take along your brain. A cool, calculating mind is the single most important piece of equipment you'll ever need on the trail. Think before you act. Watch your step. Plan ahead. Avoiding accidents before they happen is the best recipe for a rewarding and relaxing hike.

- Ask questions. Park employees are there to help. It's a lot easier to gain advice beforehand and thereby avoid a mishap than to try to amend an error far away from civilization. Use your head out there.

SAFETY ADVICE FOR HIKERS IN THE SOUTHWEST

The trails are generally safer than the roads you'll drive to reach them, provided of course that you adhere to common sense.

Unfortunately, even experienced hikers suffer an occasional lapse in judgment, as I was reminded recently while hanging upside down by a strap snagged on a dead pine about 80 feet above the floor of Sanchez Canyon. Exactly how I ended up in that awkward position isn't important now. Suffice to say one of the biggest potential hazards on the trail is gravity. Many hiking injuries result from falling rocks, but even more result from falling hikers. Use caution near cliff edges, whether you're above or beneath them. New Mexico is the fifth highest state. With five peaks over 13,000 feet, there's no shortage of opportunities for a spectacular fall.

ALTITUDE SICKNESS

Elevations for hikes in this book range from 4,700 to 11,200 feet. A serious case of altitude sickness is unlikely, though lowlanders do occasionally experience shortness of breath, headaches, dizziness, and nausea. Take a day or two to accli-matize before attempting a strenuous hike.

EXPOSURE

Most of these hikes occur in the high desert, where there's precious little shade and less atmosphere to shield you from the sun. Protective clothing and sunscreen are essential, especially for gringos. Also be prepared for sudden drops in temperature. Lost hikers have been known to suffer from heat exhaustion and hypothermia in the same day. Of the two extremes, cold weather is by far the greater danger in New Mexico.

DEHYDRATION

In 1944, several German sailors almost perished from dehydration as they hauled their makeshift raft 20 miles down a dry streambed in the Sonoran Desert. These Nazi POWs had made a potentially fatal mistake in an otherwise flawless escape plan when they assumed that they'd find water in rivers they'd seen on a map. Sure, it sounds hilarious now, but it's not so funny when it happens to you. Always bring enough drinking water for the entire hike, and save your great rafting escape for snowmelt season.

THUNDERSTORMS

Rain is rare, but it can come with a fury. Many of these hikes follow canyon routes and drainages, where flash flooding can be a serious hazard. High ridges are just as dangerous when lightning strikes.

Always check the forecast before heading out. Stay aware of cloud conditions, especially during monsoon season (July and August).

HUNTERS

Seasonal hunting is permitted on most public lands. Wear bright colors if hiking in active areas. For more specifics on where and when hunting is permitted, consult the annual game proclamations, which are available free from most sporting goods retailers and from the New Mexico Department of Game and Fish (505) 476-8000, **www.wildlife.state.nm.us**.

PLANT AND ANIMAL HAZARDS

POISON IVY

Recognizing poison ivy and avoiding contact with it is the most effective way to prevent the painful, itchy rashes associated with these plants. Poison ivy ranges from a thick, tree-hugging vine to a shaded groundcover, three leaflets to a leaf. Urushiol, the oil in the sap of this plant, is responsible for the rash. Usually within 12 to 14 hours of exposure (but sometimes much later), raised lines and/ or blisters will appear, accompanied by a terrible itch. Refrain from scratching because bacteria under fingernails can cause infection, and you will spread the rash to other parts of your body. Wash and dry the rash thoroughly, applying calamine lotion or other product to help dry the rash. If itching or blistering is severe, seek medical attention. Remember that oil-contaminated clothes, pets, or hiking gear can easily cause an irritating rash on you or someone else, so wash not only any exposed parts of your body but also clothes, gear, and pets.

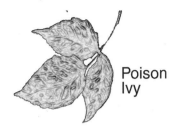

Poison Ivy

YUCCA AND CACTI

Steer clear of spiny plants. A casual bump against a yucca hurts worse than a flu shot. Cactus needles easily penetrate canvas shoes. Sturdy footwear is essential. For more drastic encounters, use tweezers to pluck thick needles. Then remove the finer ones with careful applications of adhesive tape or school glue.

HANTAVIRUS, BUBONIC PLAGUE, AND WEST NILE VIRUS

The plague is usually transmitted from infected rodents to humans via fleas. Most cases in the U.S. occur in New Mexico, Arizona, Colorado, and California. Hunters, hikers, and campers are listed among the risk groups. Incidents are rare but can be fatal if untreated. From 1949 to 2006, a total of 250 human plague cases, 32 fatal, were reported in New Mexico.

Tularemia, also known as rabbit fever, is a zoonotic disease caused by the bacterium *Francisella tularensis.* Typically, humans become infected through tick or deerfly bites, or by handling infected animals. Seven human cases of tularemia were reported in New Mexico in 2006.

Deer mice are the primary carriers of the viruses that cause hantavirus pulmonary syndrome, a rare but often fatal infection. Rodents shed the virus in their urine, droppings, and saliva. The virus is mainly transmitted to people when they breathe in air contaminated with the virus. From 1993 to 2007, 75 cases, 31 fatal, were reported in New Mexico.

Hikers should take precautions to reduce the likelihood of their exposure to infectious materials. Avoid coming into contact with rodents and rodent burrows, or disturbing dens, such as pack rat nests. Also avoid confined spaces such as caves and abandoned structures that contain evidence of rodent activity. Always keep kids and pets a safe distance from wild animals.

For more information, check with the New Mexico Department of Health: **www.health.state.nm.us**

MOSQUITOES

Although it's not a common occurrence, individuals can become infected with the West Nile virus by being bitten by an infected mosquito. Culex mosquitoes, the primary varieties that can transmit West Nile virus to humans, thrive in urban rather than in natural areas. They lay their eggs in stagnant water and can breed in any standing water that remains for more than five days. Most people infected with West Nile virus have no symptoms of illness, but some may become ill, usually 3 to 15 days after being bitten.

Late spring and summer are the times thought to be the highest risk periods for West Nile virus. At this time of year—and anytime you expect mosquitoes to be buzzing around—you may want to wear protective clothing, such as long sleeves, long pants, and socks. Loose-fitting, light-colored clothing is best. Spray clothing with insect repellent. Remember to follow the instructions on the repellent and to take extra care with children when using a repellent with DEET.

SCORPIONS

The New Mexico Scorpions are a chippy breed of pucksters in the Central Hockey League. But if you're seeking clawed arachnids, you probably won't find any unless you look at night. As many desert ravers have learned, scorpions glow under black light. Though a sting from most scorpions is painful, none of the dangerous species, such as the bark scorpion, commonly range within 60 miles of Albuquerque. (The last scorpion-related death in the U.S. was reported from Arizona in 1968.) If camping, shake out your shoes, sleeping bags, and any clothes left on the ground. If stung, gently cleanse and elevate the wound, and apply a cold compress to reduce swelling.

TICKS

Ticks like to hang out in the brush that grows along trails. Though rare in this region, you should be tick-aware during all months of the year. Ticks, which are arthropods and not insects, need a host to feast on in order to reproduce. The ticks that light on you while hiking will be very small, sometimes so tiny that you won't be able to spot them. Primarily of two varieties, deer ticks and dog ticks, both need a few hours of actual attachment before they can transmit any disease they may harbor. Ticks may settle in shoes, socks, hats, and they may take several hours to actually latch on. The best strategy is to visually check every half hour or so while hiking, do a thorough check before you get in the car, and then, when you take a post-hike shower, do an even more thorough check of your entire body. Ticks that haven't attached are easily removed, but not easily killed. If you pick off a tick in the woods, just toss it aside. If you find one on your body at home, dispatch it and then send it down the toilet. For ticks that have embedded, removal with tweezers is best.

SNAKES

The most important preventative measure is to watch your step. Like most hikers in snake country, I've developed a habit of continuously scanning the ground ahead. However, one thing I learned while standing nose-to-nose with a viper in the forest: rattlesnakes can climb trees. Don't hike during times of peak rattlesnake activity, which is usually at night. Wear high-top hiking boots and long pants for additional protection. If bitten, gently cleanse the area and apply a clean dressing. If bitten on the arm or hand, splint the limb. Do not use pressure dressings, tourniquets, or make incisions. Remain calm and seek transport to a medical facility. If you need to walk to reach help, do so as soon as possible. Severe reactions

from a venomous snakebite may not occur for several hours. Rattlesnakes rarely strike hikers, and when they do, it's usually a dry bite. They don't want to kill you. They just want you to leave them alone.

LIVESTOCK

Cows encountered on the trail are generally skittish, but there are a few exceptions. For example, bovine thugs near the Ojito Wilderness recently proved themselves more hostile than any I ever faced in the bullring. And though my stint as a matador was ill advised and short-lived, I can offer this sage advice: if it doesn't run away, steer clear.

BEARS AND MOUNTAIN LIONS

In May 2007, a 200-pound black bear wandered into a medical office in Rio Rancho. Three months later, a 100-pound mountain lion broke into a jewelry store on the Santa Fe Plaza. Yes, New Mexico is still quite wild, but chances are you won't see any either of these animals on the trail. Still, to be on the safe side, there are a few things you should know, just in case.

Black Bears Unlike unpredictable and fearsome grizzly bears, black bears are North America's smallest bear (although still weighing in at 300 to 400 pounds!) and are more interested in your food than anything else. It is extremely rare for a black bear to act aggressively toward humans, and it is almost always due to human provocation. That's not to say that black bears can't be destructive. They will go to great lengths to secure a free meal—everything from tearing the door off a car to raiding a carelessly maintained camp. If any of these hikes are planned as overnighters, it is no longer a viable option to hang your food, as bears have learned to undo your handiwork. Instead bear-proof food canisters are recommended.

If you do see a bear on the trail or in your camp, it is best to back away slowly while shouting loudly and making noise to scare off the animal. Never try to wrestle food away from a bear, and never get between a mother and her cub!

Mountain Lions   Mountain lions are the largest cats found in North America, but your chances of seeing one are extremely small (most hikers are content to simply look for the cat's four-toed print on the trail). Sometimes called cougars or pumas, they are shy, solitary creatures that hunt (mostly deer) alone and are masters at camouflage with their tawny coats and preference for wooded cover. They can grow up to eight feet in length, including their distinctively long tails. In the unlikely instance that you should come across a mountain lion, you should make eye contact, try to appear larger by spreading your arms, and make noise. Do not run from a mountain lion as this may trigger its natural instinct to chase you.

Here are a few helpful guidelines for handling potential mountain lion encounters:

- **Keep kids close to you. Observed in captivity, mountain lions seem especially drawn to small children.**

- **Do not run from a mountain lion. Running may stimulate the animal's instinct to chase.**

- **Don't approach a mountain lion—give him room to get away.**

- **Try to make yourself look larger by raising your arms and/or opening your jacket if you're wearing one.**

- **Do not crouch or kneel. These movements could make you look smaller and more like the mountain lion's prey.**

- **Try to convince the mountain lion you are dangerous—not its prey. Without crouching, gather nearby stones or branches and toss them at the animal.**

Slowly wave your arms above your head and speak in a firm voice.

- **If all fails and you are attacked, fight back. People have successfully fought off attacking mountain lions with rocks and sticks. Try to remain facing the animal, and fend off its attempts to bite your head or neck—the lion's typical aim.**

That may sound a bit alarmist in nature to some people, but it's always best to be prepared just in case. That said, you probably will never see a mountain lion on any of these hikes.

DOGS

A more common hazard than any of the above animals is another hiker's unrestrained dog. Pets are allowed on most public lands, but taking one along is rarely recommended. Encounters between domestic and wild animals rarely end well for anyone. If you do bring your dog, note that Canine Fecal Coliform is one of the biggest problems facing local water supplies. Collect your pet's waste and dispose of it properly to keep these bacteria from being washed into our aquifers.

TOPO MAPS

The maps in this book have been produced with great care and, used with the hiking directions, will direct you to the trail and help you stay on course. However, you will find superior detail and valuable information in the United States Geological Survey (USGS) 7.5-minute series topographic maps. Topo maps are available online in many locations. A well-known free service is located at **www .terraserver.microsoft.com,** and another free service with fast click-and-drag browsing is located at **www.topofinder.com.** You can view and print topos of the entire United States from these Web sites, and view aerial photographs of the same area at TerraServer-USA. Several online services such as **www.trails.com** charge annual fees for additional features such as shaded relief, which makes the topography stand out more. If you expect to print out many topo maps each year, it might be worth paying for shaded-relief topo maps. The downside to USGS topos is that most of them are outdated, having been created 20 to 30 years ago. But they still provide excellent topographic detail.

Digital topographic map programs such as Delorme's Topo USA enable you to review topo maps of the entire United States on your PC. Gathered while hiking with a GPS unit, you can also download GPS data onto the software and plot your own hikes.

If you're new to hiking, you might be wondering, "What's a topographic map?" In short, a topo indicates not only linear distance but elevation as well, using contour lines. Contour lines spread across the map like dozens of intricate spider webs. Each line represents a particular elevation, and at the base of each topo, a contour's interval designation is given. If the contour interval is 20 feet, then the distance between each contour line is 20 feet. Follow five contour lines up on the same map, and the elevation has increased by 1,000 feet.

Let's assume that the 7.5–minute series topo reads "Contour Interval 40 feet," that the short trail we'll be hiking is two inches in length on the map, and that it crosses five contour lines from beginning to end. What do we know? Well, because the linear scale of this series is 2,000 feet to the inch (roughly 2.75 inches representing 1 mile), we know our trail is approximately four-fifths of a mile long (2 inches are 2,000 feet). But we also know we'll be climbing or descending 200 vertical feet (five contour lines are 40 feet each) over that distance. And the elevation designations written on contour lines will tell us if we're heading up or down.

TRAIL ETIQUETTE

Whether you're on a city, county, state, or national park trail, always remember that great care and resources (from nature as well as from your tax dollars) have gone into creating these trails. Treat the trail, wildlife, and fellow hikers with respect:

- **Hike on open trails only. Respect trail and road closures (ask if not sure), avoid possible trespassing on private land, and obtain all permits and authorization as required. Also, leave gates as you found them or as marked.**

- **Leave only footprints. Be sensitive to the ground beneath you. This also means staying on the existing trail and not blazing any new trails. Be sure to pack out what you pack in. No one likes to see the trash someone else has left behind.**

- **Never spook animals. An unannounced approach, a sudden movement, or a loud noise startles most animals. A surprised animal can be dangerous to you, others, and themselves. Give them plenty of space.**

- **Plan ahead. Know your equipment, your ability, and the area in which you are hiking—and prepare accordingly. Be self-sufficient at all times; carry necessary supplies for changes in weather or other conditions. A well-executed trip is a satisfaction to you and others.**

- **Be courteous to other hikers, bikers, equestrians, and other people you encounter on the trails.**

RECOMMENDED HIKES

HIKES 1–3 MILES

HIKES 3–6 MILES

HIKES 3–6 MILES (CONTINUED)

HIKES 6–10 MILES

HIKES 6–10 MILES (CONTINUED)

HIKES MORE THAN 10 MILES

TOP 12 PLACES FOR . . .

KIDS

DOGS

SUMMER HIKES

SNOWSHOE HIKES

MARKED TRAILS

INTERPRETIVE TRAILS AND EDUCATIONAL EXHIBITS

21 Cerrillos Hills Historic Park (page 134)
47 Tome Hill (El Cerro Tomé) (page 277)
01 Historic District: Old Town–Downtown–BioPark (page 30)
02 Rio Grande Nature Center State Park (page 35)
10 Elena Gallegos: Cottonwood Springs (page 75)
26 Kasha-Katuwe Tent Rocks National Monument (page 163)
31 Hyde Memorial State Park (page 191)
45 Bandelier National Monument Visitors Center (page 264)
53 Sevilleta National Wildlife Refuge Visitors Center (page 306)
59 El Malpais Visitors Centers (page 337)
04 Corrales: Acequias–Bosque Preserve (page 45)
05 Petroglyph National Monument Visitors Center (page 50)

SACRED SITES

47 Tome Hill (El Cerro Tomé) (page 277)
60 Mount Taylor (page 342)
26 Kasha-Katuwe Tent Rocks National Monument (page 163)
05 Petroglyph National Monument (pages 50, 55)
01 Historic District: Old Town (page 30)
04 Corrales: Acequias (page 45)
30 Bishop's Lodge (page 186)
39 Cabezon Peak (page 232)
45 Bandelier National Monument (page 264)
29 La Cienega and La Cieneguilla (page 178)
43 San Diego (page 254)
46 Hidden Mountain (page 272)

GHOST TOWNS AND RUINS

20 La Madera Road (page 129)
45 Bandelier National Monument (page 264)
21 Cerrillos Hills Historic Park (page 134)
42 Stable Mesa (page 249)
59 El Malpais (page 337)
28 La Bajada (page 173)
37 Ojito Wilderness (page 222)
58 Greater Petaca Pinta (page 332)
39 Cabezon Peak (page 232)
27 Dome Wilderness (page 168)
32 Glorieta Canyon (page 196)
08 South Valley: Montessa Park (page 65)

SOLITUDE

57 Greater Petaca Pinta (pages 327, 332)
25 Ball Ranch (page 158)
49 Monte Largo Canyon (page 286)
52 Cerro Montoso (page 301)
56 Herrera (pages 318, 322)
51 Sierra Ladrones (page 296)
40 Continental Divide Trail (page 236)
43 San Diego (page 254)
49 Monte Largo Canyon (page 286)
27 Dome Wilderness (page 168)
37 Ojito Wilderness (page 222)
60 Mount Taylor (page 342)

PEOPLE WATCHING

01 Historic District: Old Town–Downtown–BioPark (page 30)
45 Bandelier National Monument (page 264)
02 Rio Grande Nature Center State Park (page 35)
05 Petroglyph National Monument (pages 50, 55)
07 South Valley: Arenal and Atrisco Ditch Trails (page 60)
10 Elena Gallegos Picnic Area (page 75)
11 Canyon Estates–Faulty Trails (page 82)
18 Tree Spring–Crest Trail (page 119)
26 Kasha-Katuwe Tent Rocks National Monument (page 163)
30 Bishop's Lodge–Big Tesuque Creek (page 186)
32 Glorieta Canyon (page 196)
47 Tome Hill (El Cerro Tomé) (page 277)

BIRD WATCHING

15 Capilla Peak (page 102)
26 Kasha-Katuwe Tent Rocks National Monument (page 163)
02 Rio Grande Nature Center State Park (page 35)
50 Bernardo (page 291)
53 Sevilleta National Wildlife Refuge (page 306)
04 Corrales: Acequias–Bosque Preserve (page 45)
30 Bishop's Lodge–Big Tesuque Creek (page 186)
10 Elena Gallegos: Cottonwood Springs–Nature Trail (page 75)
13 Mars Court (page 92)
21 Cerrillos Hills Historic Park (page 134)
24 Placitas: Las Huertas Creek (page 153)
44 Valles Caldera National Preserve: Coyote Call Trail (page 259)

REPTILIAN ENCOUNTERS

ROCK FORMATIONS

WATER FEATURES

WOODLAND

WILDFLOWERS

EQUESTRIANS

MOUNTAIN BIKERS

36 White Mesa Bike Trails Area (page 217)
13 Mars Court (page 92)
21 Cerrillos Hills Historic Park (page 134)
12 Chamisoso Canyon (page 87)
41 Paliza Canyon Goblin Colony (page 244)
32 Glorieta Canyon (page 196)
03 Rio Grande Valley State Park (page 40)
53 Sevilleta National Wildlife Refuge (page 306)
20 La Madera Road (page 129)
06 Petroglyph National Monument: The Volcanoes (page 55)
38 San Ysidro Trials Area (page 227)
60 Mount Taylor: Gooseberry Spring Trail (page 342)

OTHER RECOMMENDATIONS:

WHEELCHAIR TRAVERSABLE TRAILS

10 Elena Gallegos: Cottonwood Springs (page 75)
21 Cerrillos Hills Historic Park (Village View Trail) (page 134)
03 Rio Grande Valley State Park (Paseo del Bosque) (page 40)
45 Bandelier National Monument (Main Loop Trail) (page 269)
53 Sevilleta National Wildlife Refuge (page 306)
50 Bernardo Waterfowl Area (page 291)
01 Historic District: Old Town–Downtown–BioPark (page 30)
26 Kasha-Katuwe Tent Rocks National Monument (page 163)
59 El Malpais (page 341)

RUNNING/JOGGING

03 Rio Grande Valley State Park (page 40)
04 Corrales: Acequias–Bosque Preserve (page 45)
07 South Valley: Arenal and Atrisco Ditch Trails (page 60)
10 Elena Gallegos: Cottonwood Springs–Nature Trail (page 75)
20 La Madera Road (page 129)
53 Sevilleta National Wildlife Refuge (page 306)
12 Chamisoso Canyon (page 87)

VISTAS

60 Mount Taylor: Gooseberry Spring Trail (page 342)
59 El Malpais: Narrows Rim Trail (page 337)
23 Tunnel Spring–Agua Sarca (page 148)
26 Kasha-Katuwe Tent Rocks National Monument (page 163)
36 White Mesa Bike Trails Area (page 217)

VISTAS (CONTINUED)

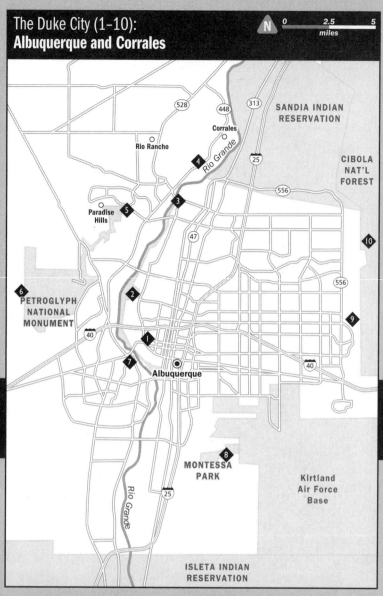

The Duke City (1–10):
Albuquerque and Corrales

N

0   2.5   5
miles

528   448   313

SANDIA INDIAN
RESERVATION

Corrales

Rio Rancho

Rio Grande

25

CIBOLA
NAT'L
FOREST

4

556

3

5

Paradise
Hills

47

10

6

PETROGLYPH
NATIONAL
MONUMENT

2

9

40

556

1

7

Albuquerque

40

8

MONTESSA
PARK

Kirtland
Air Force
Base

Rio Grande

25

ISLETA INDIAN
RESERVATION

THE DUKE CITY

HISTORIC DISTRICT:
Old Town–Downtown–BioPark

KEY AT-A-GLANCE INFORMATION

LENGTH: 5.8-mile loop plus optional detours

DIFFICULTY: Easy

SCENERY: City parks and plazas, historic architecture, and Route 66 Americana

EXPOSURE: Half shade

TRAIL TRAFFIC: Bustling

SHARED USE: Urban traffic

TRAIL SURFACE: Pavement

HIKING TIME: 3–5 hours

DRIVING DISTANCE: 3 miles (one way) from the I-40/I-25 exchange

ACCESS: Year-round. Hours and admission fees vary at museums and BioPark sites. No fee to access to Old Town and Tingley Beach.

LAND STATUS: City of Albuquerque

MAPS: USGS Albuquerque West

FACILITIES: Shops and restaurants

SPECIAL COMMENTS: For the grand tour, pick up these five brochure maps: *Old Town: A Walking Tour of History and Architecture; Historic Albuquerque Plaza to Plaza Self-Guided Walking Tour; Albuquerque Tricentennial Pueblo Deco Tour; West Park Neighborhood Tour;* and *Raynolds Neighborhood Tour.* These free publications can be obtained from the Visitor Information Center on Don Luis Plaza.

IN BRIEF

Equal parts *volksmarch,* sightseeing tour, and civic orientation, this urban hike offers a crash course in Albuquerque's 300-year history. Spanning from the Rio Grande to the railroad, it covers the heart of the Historic District and features many of the city's biggest attractions, in addition to a few unique residential areas.

DESCRIPTION

Start by heading west on Mountain Road, turn left on San Felipe Street. Coming up on the left is a quick detour that isn't mentioned in the brochures. Hidden in the back end of the Patio Escondido is the **Chapel of Our Lady of Guadalupe,** which is more on the scale of a grotto shrine, but nonetheless captivating in its simple reverence.

Return to San Felipe Street and continue south. Then turn right on Church Street, left on Romero Street, and right into Plaza Don Luis. There you'll find the **Visitor Information Center,** where you can score the brochure maps listed. Use the *Old Town: A Walking Tour* brochure to learn about the variety of historic edifices in Albuquerque's premier neighborhood. A self-guided tour should take about 20 minutes but can drag on for hours with shoppers in tow. Highlights include the

GPS Trailhead Coordinates

UTM Zone 13S

Easting 0347951

Northing 3885234

Latitude 35° 05' 54"

Longitude 106° 40' 05"

Directions

From I-40, take Exit 157A, and go 0.5 miles south on Rio Grande Boulevard to Mountain Road. Turn left, and go 0.15 miles east to 20th Street. Turn left, andthen take another left into the lot behind the parking garage. Walk back to Mountain Road. The hike begins on the south side of the parking garage.

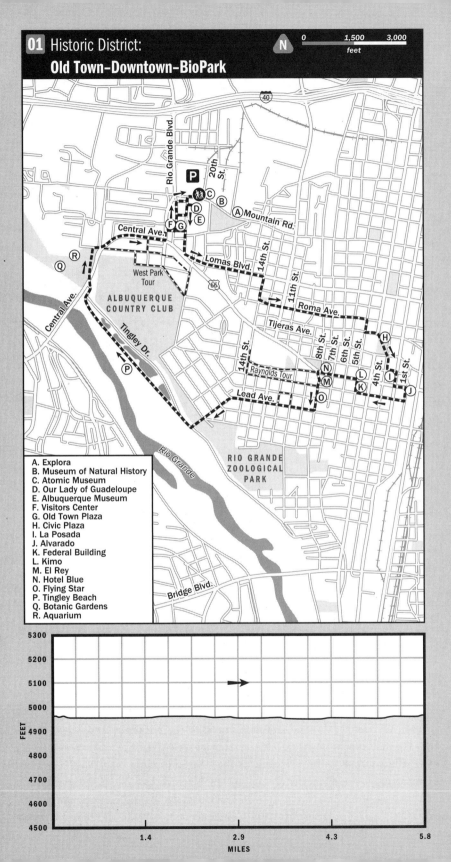

N

0   1,500   3,000
feet

Rio Grande Blvd.

20th St.

P 👣 Ⓒ Ⓑ

Ⓐ Mountain Rd.

Ⓓ

Ⓕ Ⓖ Ⓔ

Central Ave.

14th St.

Lomas Blvd.

11th St.

66

West Park Tour

ALBUQUERQUE COUNTRY CLUB

Ⓡ

Ⓠ

Central Ave.

Tingley Dr.

Ⓟ

Roma Ave.

Tijeras Ave.

8th St.
7th St.
6th St.
5th St.

Ⓗ

4th St.

1st St.

14th St.

Reynolds Tour

Ⓝ
Ⓜ
Ⓞ

Ⓛ
Ⓚ

Ⓘ
Ⓙ

Lead Ave.

Rio Grande

RIO GRANDE ZOOLOGICAL PARK

Bridge Blvd.

A. Explora
B. Museum of Natural History
C. Atomic Museum
D. Our Lady of Guadeloupe
E. Albuquerque Museum
F. Visitors Center
G. Old Town Plaza
H. Civic Plaza
I. La Posada
J. Alvarado
K. Federal Building
L. Kimo
M. El Rey
N. Hotel Blue
O. Flying Star
P. Tingley Beach
Q. Botanic Gardens
R. Aquarium

5300
5200
5100
5000
4900
4800
4700
4600
4500

FEET

1.4   2.9   4.3   5.8
MILES

Pueblo Deco details on the Kimo Theater

San Felipe de Neri, an 18th-century church with folk Gothic spires and fascinatingly morbid interior decor, and the **Rattlesnake Museum,** home to the world's largest collection of rattlesnake species. End your Old Town tour at the **Bottger Mansion** (listed as the Charles A. Bottger House), a B&B near the south end of San Felipe Street.

At the end of the block, break out the *Plaza to Plaza* map and begin the second self-guided tour. The 1.3-mile trail leads downtown, visiting historic buildings en route. Markers embedded in the sidewalk at street corners point the way, but just in case you have difficulty spotting these little brass squares: Walk east on Lomas Boulevard. Turn right on 14th Street, left on Roma Avenue, right on 5th Street, and left on Marquette Avenue. This segment concludes on 4th Street at **Civic Plaza.** Officially known as the Harry E. Kinney Civic Plaza, the outdoor venue can hold more than 20,000 people and often hosts free concerts and cinema events.

Walk to the southeast corner of Civic Plaza and head south on 3rd Street. Turn left on Copper Avenue and stop ahead at the corner of 2nd Street in front of **La Posada de Albuquerque.** This Territorial-style high-rise first opened in 1939 as the Albuquerque Hilton. Notable as the first building in New Mexico with air-conditioning, it was the fourth hotel built by New Mexico native Conrad Hilton.

Turn right on 2nd Street, left on Central Avenue, and right on 1st Street to reach the **Alvarado Transportation Center (ATC).** Built in the Mission Revival style in 2002, the ATC stands on a site formerly occupied by the Alvarado Hotel (demolished in 1970) and the Albuquerque train station (burned in 1993). A brass plaque near the main entrance provides more details. Service for the Rail Runner started in 2006. The commuter line currently runs between Belen and Bernalillo, with service expected to reach Santa Fe by 2009.

Continue south and turn right on Gold Avenue, an oft-bypassed corridor of hip little shops, cafés, and bars. **Burt's Tiki Lounge** (motto: "Never a Cover. Ever.") is a recommended live-music venue. (For current listings of downtown nightlife, pick up a copy of the *Weekly Alibi,* available free citywide.) A block ahead, locate the **Albuquerque Federal Building.** Directional patterns on this former federal courthouse are sometimes mistaken for swastikas. The motif was borrowed from the Navajo, as page 6 of the *Albuquerque Tricentennial Pueblo Deco Tour* brochure explains. To be sure, you can check with the **New Mexico Holocaust & Intolerance Museum,** one block north at 415 Central Avenue NW.

To continue with the deco tour, take a right turn on 5th Street to head north to Central Avenue, formerly Route 66. On the northeast corner, the **Kimo Theater** stands as the quintessential example of Pueblo Deco. Head west on Central Avenue for more designs that emerged in the era of Route 66, including **Maisel's Indian Trading Post** and the **El Rey Theater.**

Sporting a 21st-century Deco makeover, the ultra-hip **Hotel Blue** stands at Central Avenue and 8th Street and overlooks **Robinson Park,** a triangular green with a modest memorial to an otherwise forgotten hero, John Braden. During a fiesta parade here in 1896, someone threw a firecracker into Braden's horse-drawn wagon, which was packed with ammunition. Braden bravely steered the runaway horses away from the crowd before the wagon exploded. (No mention of why he brought a wagon full of ammunition to a fiesta parade.)

Central and 8th also marks the halfway point in the 5.8-mile route. Nearby, to the south, the 800 block of Park Avenue SW shows up as (15) on the *Raynolds* map. Use this map to locate murals and ornamental gardens in this pleasant neighborhood, finishing at Lead Avenue and 14th Street. If you strategically combine the east and west loops on the Raynolds map, this detour will add 1 mile to the overall hike.

Or to abbreviate the Raynolds tour, go south two blocks to Silver Avenue, where you'll find the **Flying Star Café,** a great place to refuel on coffee and pastries. It's indicated as (1) on the Raynolds map. Continue south another block and turn right on Lead Avenue. Follow it to its west end, where it bends left and becomes Alcalde Place. Go to the southwestern end of Alcalde Place, cross Tingley Drive, and turn right.

The Albuquerque Biological Park, better known as the BioPark, includes the Rio Grande Zoo, Rio Grande Botanic Garden, Albuquerque Aquarium, and the next feature on this hike. Ahead on the left, **Tingley Beach** first opened in 1931 as Conservancy Beach and quickly became a popular boating and swimming area. In response to the polio scare of the 1950s, the city dismantled its marina and bathhouse and reduced the lake to a duck pond, which it then left to stagnate for the next few decades.

Since 2004 Tingley Beach has undergone major renovations, including the restoration of 9 acres of wetland and 48 acres of riparian woodland, and the reconstruction of ponds for fishing, pedal boats, and remote-control model boats. Fishing licenses, tackle, and boat and bike rentals are available at **Tingley Beach Outfitters and Café.** This quaint red house also serves as a station on the Rio Line, a narrow-gauge railroad that shuttles visitors among the BioPark attractions.

Tingley Beach shows as (B) on the *West Park* map. Refer to the map for more information on other upcoming features. If you want to explore the funky West Park neighborhood (1–15), you'll access it more easily later from New York Avenue. For now, continue to the end of Tingley Beach Drive and cross Central Avenue. Straight ahead, at the far end of the parking lot, is the ever-growing **Rio Grande Botanic Garden.** A walk through its thematic oases and greenhouses could easily add a mile or more to your hike. The main feature at the adjacent **Albuquerque Aquarium** is the shark tank. You can get a free peek at it from the Shark Reef Café, located near the main entrance.

The first cross street past the aquarium is New York Avenue. The legendary **El Vado Motel,** (H) on the *West Park* map, was built on the southeast corner in 1937. The motel lodges now have the charm of old tube socks, but its neon sign and front office are classic Route 66 landmarks. Despite its placement on the National Register of Historic Places, the nostalgic tourist court was slated for demolition in 2007. A more recent proposal calls for building townhomes on the property but preserving the portion of the motel facing the street.

From here, a detour through the West Park residential area adds less than 1 mile to the overall hike if you start the loop at (9) and return to Central Avenue via Clayton Street. Otherwise, stay on Central until you reach the southwestern corner of Old Town at Rio Grande Boulevard. Then enjoy another stroll through Old Town as you return to the parking lot.

NEARBY ACTIVITIES

Hit the museums on Mountain Road. The Albuquerque Museum, straight across from the parking garage, features an impressive array of traveling and permanent exhibits. To the east, the National Atomic Museum chronicles the state's role in nuclear weaponry. (The growing collection is slated for an uptown relocation in October 2008.) A short block east is the New Mexico Museum of Natural History and Science, which houses the Lockheed Martin DynaTheater, the LodeStar Astronomy Center, and the oddly mesmerizing STARTUP Gallery of Personal Computers. All museum Web sites are linked at **itsatrip.org/activities/museums culture.** You can also call (800) 284-2282, or just dial 311 from any local phone.

For more local urban routes and *volksmarches,* contact the Albuquerque Double Eagle Hike and Bike Club at (505) 298-1256, or online at **members.aol .com/abqdoubleeagles.**

RIO GRANDE NATURE CENTER STATE PARK

02

IN BRIEF

Cottonwood-shaded interpretive trails to the banks of the Rio Grande offer a quick escape from the urban desert and a thorough introduction to the state's most vital ecosystem.

DESCRIPTION

Rio Grande Nature Center State Park is a 270-acre preserve in the heart of Rio Grande Valley State Park, a narrow, 4,300-acre multiuse area along the river from the Sandia Pueblo to the Isleta Pueblo (Albuquerque's northern and southern neighbors, respectively). But unlike Rio Grande Valley State Park, the preserve *is actually* a state park.

Most people simply refer to any given point in the area as "the bosque" (BOHS-kay, though it is often mispronounced BAH-skee). Adding to the confusion is the fact that the bosque actually extends well beyond the park boundaries and runs nearly 100 miles along the banks of the Rio Grande.

Such vagueness adds to the mystique of the bosque, a nebulous riverside forest where you don't have to stray far from the beaten path for encounters with coyotes, hobo camps, and (according to local lore) witches known as *brujas*.

KEY AT-A-GLANCE INFORMATION

LENGTH: 1.8-mile figure eight with spur

DIFFICULTY: Easy

SCENERY: Riparian habitat, cottonwood forest, ponds, and wetlands

EXPOSURE: Mostly shade

TRAIL TRAFFIC: Popular

SHARED USE: Low (no dogs or vehicles)

TRAIL SURFACE: Packed dirt, gravel

HIKING TIME: 1 hour

DRIVING DISTANCE: 4 miles (one way) from the I-40/I-25 exchange

ACCESS: Visitor center: 10 a.m.–5 p.m. daily, except Thanksgiving, Christmas, and New Year's days; trails: April–October, 7 a.m.–9 p.m., and November–March, 7 a.m.–7 p.m.

LAND STATUS: State park

MAPS: Available in visitor center and at www.emnrd.state.nm.us; USGS Los Griegos

FACILITIES: Wildlife blinds, picnic area, visitor center, wheelchair-accessible restrooms

SPECIAL COMMENTS: Check at the visitor center for special events and guided tours. The more popular activities, like the Full Moon Hike, often require reservations days in advance.

Directions

From I-40 west, take Exit 157A to Rio Grande Boulevard. Drive north 1.4 miles, and turn left onto Candelaria Road. Go west 0.6 miles, and turn right at the park entrance. Note that if you park your car inside, the 5 p.m. gate closure can force you to rush an otherwise leisurely hike. To avoid the worry (and the $3 parking fee), go back one block, and park on Trellis Drive.

GPS Trailhead Coordinates

UTM Zone (WGS 84) 13S

Easting   0346728

Northing   3888697

Latitude   35° 07' 46"

Longtitude 106° 40' 56"

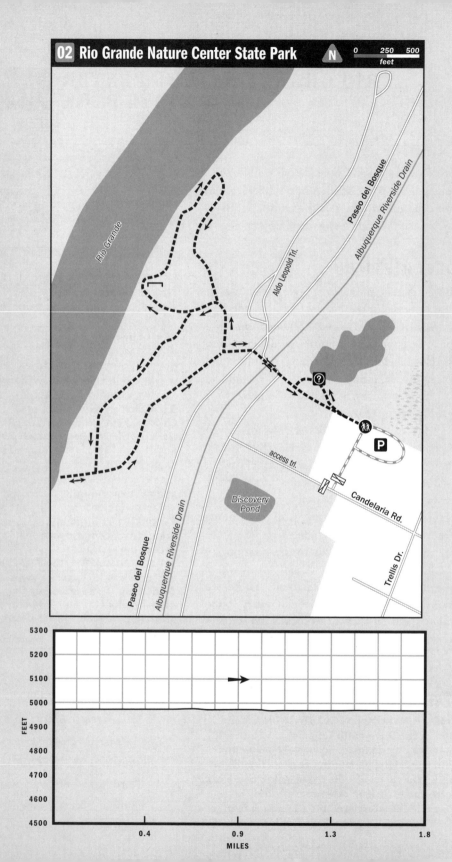

02 Rio Grande Nature Center State Park

N

0   250   500
feet

Rio Grande

Paseo del Bosque

Albuquerque Riverside Drain

Aldo Leopold Trl.

access trl.

Discovery Pond

Paseo del Bosque

Albuquerque Riverside Drain

Candelaria Rd.

Trellis Dr.

P

5300
5200
5100
5000
4900
4800
4700
4600
4500

FEET

0.4   0.9   1.3   1.8

MILES

Residents of the wildlife pond, as seen from the glass-walled library.

One of the bigger draws is the reconstructed wetland on the northeast side of Rio Grande Nature Center. The ponds and cattail swamp attract thousands of Canada geese and sandhill cranes during the late fall and winter, and about as many bird-watchers show up to ogle them. But if you miss the migratory season, there's plenty more to do here, including hiking two trails—the Riverwalk and the Bosque Loop—that work best as one continuous hike.

The hike: You have two ways to reach the trailhead. If the parking lot gate is closed, take the Candelaria Access Trail, a narrow corridor that begins at the yellow pylons at the end of Candelaria Road. Turn right at the far end and follow the path to a wooden footbridge.

Otherwise, start down the path on the west side of the parking lot. The left fork leads straight to the footbridge. The right one detours into what appears to be a half-buried drainage pipe jutting from a hill. This is the entrance to the visitor center. Inside, you'll find natural history exhibits, a gift shop, restrooms, and a glass-walled library overlooking a wildlife pond. Exit through the back door and proceed to the aforementioned footbridge.

The bridge spans the Albuquerque Riverside Drain. Stairs ahead and a ramp to the right climb the levee. Both the drain and levee are part of an elaborate flood-control and irrigation system in the Rio Grande Valley. The paved path atop the levee is Paseo del Bosque, a 16-mile recreation trail. As you cross it, stay alert for high-speed cyclists and skaters.

Beavers' appetites result in trees gnawed
down to nubs.

The ramp leads to the Aldo Leopold trailhead, described below; the **Bosque Loop** trailhead is opposite the stairs. The trail traverses a gap in a tangle of flood-control fences, or jetty jacks. Apparently inspired by designs from the beaches of Normandy, the Army Corps of Engineers installed these giant iron crosses throughout the bosque shortly after World War II to protect the levee from flood debris.

The trail is well groomed, clearly marked, and edged with fallen cotton-wood limbs. Follow the arrow to the right. You'll soon find an unmarked trail on your right; ignore it—it soon ends at a locked gate. The second right is the return path from **Riverwalk Trail,** so bypass that as well. A sign at the junction ahead offers a choice of staying on Bosque Trail (left arrow) or picking up Riverwalk Trail, a 0.8-mile loop through denser stands of cottonwood.

Turn right to follow this shaded path to a pair of park benches—front-row seats on the Rio Grande. Yes, the river smaller than its name implies. For this, people come to mock it. Will Rogers once remarked that he'd never before seen a river in need of irrigation. Mark Twain quipped that our dear Rio Grande is too thick to drink and too thin to plow. Albuquerque mayor Harry Kinney joined the fun in 1983, presenting a set of keys for a new Rolls Royce to the commanding officer of the USS *Albuquerque* and promising the car to the first skipper to pilot this 360-foot nuclear submarine up the Rio Grande to its namesake. The offer still stands.

From the clearing on the riverbank, trails run off in five directions, with those closest to the river always the most tempting. Riverwalk Trail, the one directly behind the benches, resumes northeast, heading back into the woods, where a series of stairs will help you negotiate contours in the terrain.

As you walk upriver, you'll have few chances to see the water. Vegetation grows thick along the river's edge, where native species contend with invasive ones—such as the thorny Russian olive and tamarisk, a salt cedar imported to control riverbank erosion.

Once blamed for guzzling the river, cottonwoods faced annihilation in 1969 when the Bureau of Reclamation proposed clearing them from the bosque in an effort to provide more water to farmlands. They later determined that the tamarisk was by far the heavier drinker. Adding to the native trees' disadvantages is the beavers' appetite for local wood, as evidenced in the hefty cottonwoods they topple throughout the bosque.

Riverwalk Trail hooks right, turning away from the river and into an open meadow. Tufts of alfalfa are all that remain of a long-ago farm field where rattlesnake weed and young cottonwoods are now slowly reclaiming the land. The trail soon rejoins Bosque Loop via the return path you bypassed earlier. Turn right. A brief overlapping segment of the two trails brings you back to the junction with the sign. This time, follow the left arrow.

Those creatures you hear scattering at the sound of your footsteps are bark lizards and whiptails. They grow up to 9 inches long and can create a racket in dry underbrush. They're easy to spot during the warmer months, running for their lives or dangling from the beaks of roadrunners. Snakes are said to be common as well, but I've ventured into the bosque at least a hundred times and have yet to find one.

Summer brings downy blizzards of cottonwood seeds and a high risk of fire. The latter can result in blackened swaths as stark and bare as the dead of winter. In these times of drought, the Rio Grande breaks down into muddy pools and narrow channels. You could hop sandbars to cross it in places. Your last chance to see it along this trail is from a short spur on the southern end of Bosque Loop. Turn right for a panoramic view of the elevated west bank and the pricey houses perched atop it.

Turn back and follow the gravel trail straight to Paseo del Bosque. From here, you can return to the parking area or extend your hike on the **Aldo Leopold Trail.** This paved out-and-back runs about 1 mile round-trip. It falls short of a river view, but a sandy, 100-yard extension does visit the riverbank. A few dirt paths split off from there and stray through the bosque. Webbing the wooded corridor between the river and the levee, these interior trails offer an opportunity for miles of further exploration with no chance of getting lost. (If you do get disoriented, just remember that Paseo del Bosque is never more than 0.25 miles east.)

NEARBY ACTIVITIES

Visit the Flying Star Café and Bookworks, both located in Dietz Farm Plaza. From Candelaria Road, turn left (north) onto Rio Grande Boulevard. The plaza is 1 mile on the right. Visit **www.bkwrks.com** or **www.flyingstarcafe.com**.

03 RIO GRANDE VALLEY STATE PARK

KEY AT-A-GLANCE INFORMATION

LENGTH: 3.4-mile loop, with a 9-mile option

DIFFICULTY: Easy

SCENERY: Wooded riparian habitat, exemplary recreational trails, and camels

EXPOSURE: Mostly sunny

TRAIL TRAFFIC: Heavy

SHARED USE: Heavy (bicycles, equestrians, skaters, and joggers; dogs must be leashed)

TRAIL SURFACE: Asphalt, packed dirt, sand

HIKING TIME: 1.5 hours

DRIVING DISTANCE: 10 miles (one way) from the I-40/I-25 exchange

ACCESS: April–October, 7 a.m.– 9 p.m.; November–March, 7 a.m.– 7 p.m.

LAND STATUS: Open Space Division; Middle Rio Grande Conservancy District

MAPS: USGS Los Griegos

FACILITIES: ADA-compliant trail and picnic area

SPECIAL COMMENTS: The Albuquerque Bicycle Map shows most access points and major trails in the Rio Grande Valley Park system. Call (505) 768-2680 or visit www.cabq.gov/openspace/trailmaps.

GPS Trailhead Coordinates

UTM Zone (WGS 84) 13S

Easting 0350684

Northing 3895916

Latitude 35° 11' 43"

Longitude 106° 38' 25"

IN BRIEF

Hikes along the Rio Grande can be pieced together from any combination of natural-surface trails, levee roads, pedestrian-friendly bridges, and a paved recreation trail. This route samples all four on a loop at the northern end of Rio Grande Valley State Park.

DESCRIPTION

Established by the state legislature in 1983, Rio Grande Valley State Park isn't a state park—go figure. At 4,300 acres, and with a land area seldom exceeding 0.5 miles in width, it's one of the skinnier parks in the city's Open Space inventory. This wooded riparian environment flanks Albuquerque's segment of the Rio Grande, stretching from Sandia Pueblo to Isleta Pueblo—a good 22 miles. And for every mile of river, you'll find up to 6 miles of trails where motorized vehicles are not allowed.

You can start this hike from any access point between Alameda Boulevard and Paseo del Norte or embark on an extended-route option from any access point between Alameda Boulevard and Montano Road.

Alameda/Rio Grande Open Space is currently the northernmost access area and is the

Directions

From I-25, take Exit 233 and drive 3.4 miles. Turn left after crossing Rio Grande Boulevard (and before the bridge).

From I-40, take Exit 157A. Go north 6.8 miles on Rio Grande Boulevard. Turn left on Alameda Boulevard, and then turn left into the parking area.

Westside Access: From Coors Boulevard, go east on Alameda Boulevard. Cross the bridge, and turn right into the parking area.

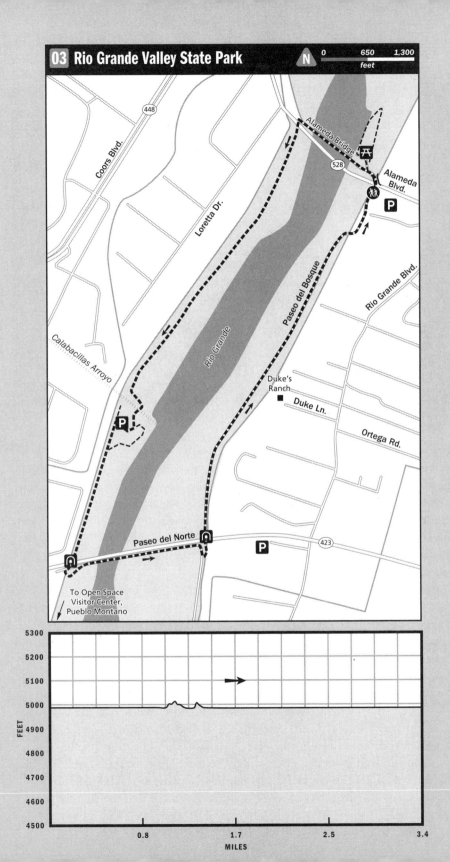

03 Rio Grande Valley State Park

N

0   650   1,300
feet

448

Coors Blvd.

Loretta Dr.

Calabacillas Arroyo

P

Alameda Bridge

528

Alameda Blvd.

P

Rio Grande

Paseo del Bosque

Rio Grande Blvd.

Duke's Ranch

Duke Ln.

Ortega Rd.

Paseo del Norte

P

423

To Open Space
Visitor Center,
Pueblo Montano

FEET

5300
5200
5100
5000
4900
4800
4700
4600
4500

0.8   1.7   2.5   3.4
MILES

Healthy lichens are a good indication of clean air.

starting point for this hike. Here you'll find a parking lot big enough to accommodate RVs and horse trailers. The area is also popular among bird-watchers, who flock to the Alameda Wetland for views of waterfowl and other wildlife. The wetland is a reconstruction of otherwise naturally occurring ponds and marshlands that had once occupied the Rio Grande floodplain. Projects to further rehabilitate the river habitat will continue on islands and sandbars upriver over the next several years.

Start the hike on the west side of the parking lot and turn right on the paved path. It runs along the east side of the Albuquerque Riverside Drain as it crosses beneath the Alameda Boulevard Bridge. Use the bicycle–pedestrian bridge ahead to cross the drain, and then walk to the top of the levee. The old Alameda Bridge, straight ahead, has been preserved to accommodate pedestrians, skaters, cyclists, and equestrians. You'll find great views of the river along the right side of the bridge.

When you reach the west bank, turn left and cross over to the south side of Alameda Boulevard. There you'll find a drain with a dirt road on each side. However, for this segment of the hike, try a path that runs through the bosque.

You will find natural-surface trails, also called **interior trails,** on both sides of the river. These unmarked paths meander erratically, as though blazed by toddlers, and usually arrive at nothing in particular. Often, the destination is a riverbank clearing just wide enough to cast a line (permitted with a New Mexico fishing license). As informal and often ephemeral paths, these trails simply wind beneath the cottonwood canopy between the river and the levee. Should you happen to lose the path, just return to the levee road and look for another one.

The interior trail between Alameda and the Calabacillas Arroyo is a well-shaded dirt singletrack that's equally enjoyable on foot or bike. (I once surprised a coyote while rounding a downhill bend on this trail.) After 1 mile, it arrives at the arroyo.

The Calabacillas Arroyo is a 40-yard-wide channel that drains from Rio Rancho, carrying with it sand and silt from the West Mesa. It can be a muddy crossing at times. In worst-case scenarios, you may need to detour 0.3 miles upstream to cross it at Coors Boulevard. The Calabacillas parking area is on the south side of the arroyo. To access it by car, take Coors Boulevard 0.75 miles north from Paseo del Norte and turn right on Westside Drive. Go 0.2 miles northeast to the dirt levee road, then southeast 0.25 miles to the parking area.

Deep sand characterizes the interior trails south of Calabacillas. To stick with this hike, for the next 0.4 miles, use the **levee roads;** you'll have a few to choose from. As you approach the tunnel, switch over to the low road, which aims straight for it.

Before crossing the Paseo del Norte Bridge, see the Extended route option for points of interest farther downstream.

Paseo del Norte is a busy six-lane highway. Use the tunnel to cross beneath it, and then use the bike lane to cross the river. Hefty barricades keep cyclists and pedestrians safe from motor-vehicle traffic. This 0.25-mile span overlooks islands in the Rio Grande and jetty jacks on its shores. You can also use this vantage point to scout interior trails heading south. As you approach the eastern end of the Paseo del Norte Bridge, turn south at the end of the barrier onto the first paved trail on your right. Take the stairs or the ramp to the paved trail below.

Shining River parking area is on the southeast side of the Paseo del Norte Bridge. Car access is from Rio Grande Boulevard, which is *not* accessible from Paseo del Norte. On foot, you can reach the parking area by crossing the Albuquerque Riverside Drain and continuing 0.1 mile east.

To return to the Alameda parking area, use the tunnel to cross beneath Paseo del Norte. You're now on the **Paseo del Bosque,** a paved 16-mile recreational trail. The smooth, flat asphalt is suitable for everyone, from endurance cyclists to Sunday strollers. The trail lacks shade, and it gets too hot, an interior trailhead is usually close at hand. Plans call for extending the Paseo del Bosque north to Bernalillo and south to Belen to create a 50-mile trail. This hike uses the upper 1.2 miles to reach its current northern terminus at Alameda.

About 0.4 miles north of the tunnel, look east across the drain for Don Duke's Ranch; you'll recognize it by the camels and llamas he keeps in his backyard. Just ahead, a 7-3/4 mile marker indicates the distance from Central Avenue. From here it's just 0.5 miles back to Alameda.

OPTIONAL EXTENDED ROUTE

From the western end of the Paseo del Norte Bridge, levee roads continue 3.8 miles to an oxbow lake south of Pueblo Montano. The interior trails in this stretch also hold up well, for the most part. Distances to points of interest below were measured on the levee road.

The Open Space Visitor Center, completed in late 2006, features an art gallery, interpretive exhibits, and agricultural fields to attract wildlife. To walk there from Paseo del Norte, continue downstream 1.9 miles to the point where the Corrales Main Canal crosses the Riverside Drain. Follow the canal north 0.3 miles to the visitor center. To get there by car, take Coors Boulevard 1 mile south from Paseo del Norte, and turn east on Bosque Meadows Road.

Pueblo Montano is an Open Space project that rose from the ashes of the 2003 bosque fire. The blaze burned more than 250 acres of woodland on both sides of the river. Recovery efforts are ongoing, and many nearby interior trails are still a mess, but jetty jacks and invasive plants have been removed. Native saplings and understory shrubs were planted, and in a gesture that is at least charming for its complete lack of pragmatism, Girl Scouts volunteered to patrol the area. All of which goes to show just how much Burqueños (Albuquerqueans) love their bosque.

Chainsaw artists have since transformed the thick trunks of scorched trees into fictive images and sculptural memorials to lost wildlife. One towering work depicts a firefighter standing on the head of a slain dragon. In another, the amputated Y of charred tree limbs evolved into the wings of a bald eagle. And beneath carved owls and crows perched on high sits a howling coyote, because no Southwestern art collection would be complete without one. A 0.15-mile loop through the sculpture garden is ADA-compliant.

Pueblo Montano is on the southwest side of Montano Bridge, a 3-mile walk from Paseo del Norte. When you reach the bridge, turn left to cross beneath it. Then turn right and follow the path 0.1 mile along Montano Road to the sculpture garden.

Montano Bridge also features a protected lane for bikes and pedestrians. Cross to the east bank to pick up the Paseo del Bosque. An Alameda–Montano loop runs about 9 miles, and a Montano–Paseo del Norte loop runs about 7 miles.

CORRALES:
Acequias–Bosque Preserve 04

IN BRIEF

Follow the waterways around the village of Corrales for a display of eclectic architecture from the past and present. Groves of cottonwood and Siberian elm and plentiful waterfowl also highlight the route. You may also spot riparian creatures such as beavers, muskrats, and pocket gophers.

DESCRIPTION

The first weekend in May is Mud Day in Corrales. Yet personal experience tells me every day is Mud Day in this charming village. For some reason, I can never seem to escape without mud caked on my boots, bike, and truck. And this isn't just any kind of mud. It dries into some kind of titanium-grade adobe. I snapped the tip off a tire iron trying to pry it off my mountain bike.

Perhaps in a similar manner, the settlers of Corrales discovered how such mud might enhance the durability of their buildings. Some of these structures, most notably the Old San Ysidro Church, highlight the first half of this route.

Acequias (3.3 miles): Begin by heading toward the gate on the far side of the soccer field. The line of trees indicates where the

KEY AT-A-GLANCE INFORMATION

LENGTH: 7.4-mile loop

DIFFICULTY: Easy

SCENERY: Vineyards, historic buildings, deciduous forest, and mountain views

EXPOSURE: Half shade

TRAIL TRAFFIC: Popular

SHARED USE: Moderate (mountain bikers, equestrians; popular with dog owners; restricted motorized-vehicle access)

TRAIL SURFACE: Dirt, some asphalt

HIKING TIME: 4 hours, longer with optional detours

DRIVING DISTANCE: 13 miles (one way) from the I-40 and I-25 exchange

ACCESS: Daily, 5 a.m.–10 p.m.

LAND STATUS: Village of Corrales; Middle Rio Grande Conservancy District

MAPS: Brochure maps available at the visitor center; USGS Alameda and Bernalillo

FACILITIES: Restrooms inside and soft-drink vending machines outside the rec center

Directions

From I-25 north, take Exit 233 at Alameda Boulevard (NM 528). Turn left (west) on Alameda Boulevard, and go 4.2 miles. Turn right (north) on Corrales Road (NM 448— notorious for speed traps), and drive 2 miles. Turn left on Jones Road, (immediately after Territorial Plaza). Go 0.2 miles, and park near the Corrales Recreation Center. The hike begins at the gate to the soccer field.

GPS Trailhead Coordinates

UTM Zone (WGS 84) 13S

Easting 0352301

Northing 3898824

Latitude 35° 13' 18"

Longitude 106° 37' 23"

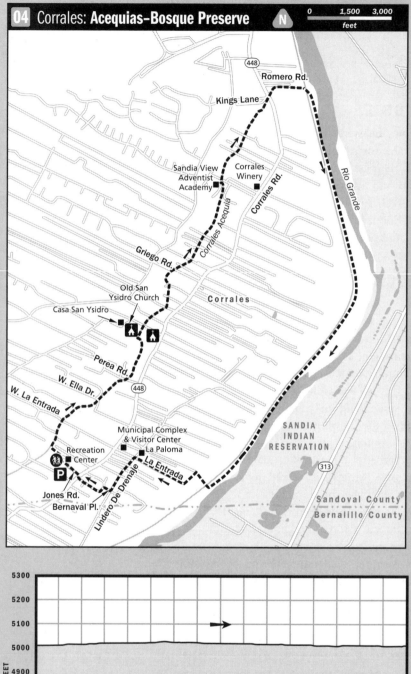

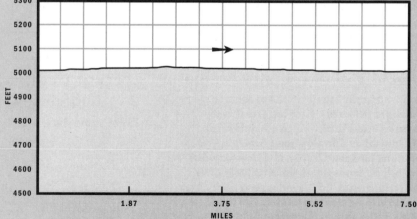

Corrales Lateral flows. This prominent acequia, or irrigation ditch, has been channeling water to local farm fields since the early 18th century. The system has since been enhanced. Currently about 17 miles of canals and ditches course through Corrales. The ditch rider, or system administrator, maintains the flow of water from early May through early November.

Service roads run along both sides of the acequia. Turn right after the gate and take the one with the least mud. Dams allow for frequent crossings in case you change your mind. You can simply follow the ditch for the first 3 miles of the loop or take a few detours for a closer look at nearby historic buildings. There are too many to list here, but those featured in the brochures are all within the first mile or so.

Often you can identify an architectural style by the roof alone. Red tiles suggest Spanish Revival. Rounded corners are indicative of the Pueblo style. Flat roofs with stepped parapets and exposed vigas (ceiling beams) indicate Spanish-Pueblo Revival, more popularly known as Santa Fe style, which in turn developed into a craze for incorporating multiple styles into a single structure for no apparent reason. You'll find numerous examples of that in Corrales.

When you reach the end of a long coyote fence, you'll see the new San Ysidro Church over on Corrales Road on the right. Ahead on the left are the pitched tin roofs of the Old San Ysidro Church's twin bell towers. The towers function as buttresses to support the old adobe walls, which are nearly 3 feet thick. Villagers apply additional layers of mud annually on Mudders' Day Weekend, or Mud Day.

The Gutiérrez-Minge House, also known as Casa San Ysidro, is across the street from the old church. This extension of the Albuquerque Museum features a replica of a 19th-century rancho and offers tours for a small fee. To visit the San Ysidro complex, turn left at the next crossroad, Old Church Road. This detour will add less than 0.4 miles to the hike.

Continuing north along the arroyo, you may notice domestic animals noticing you. Dogs see fit to alert the entire village of your presence. Horses and goats trot up to the fences and stare. Cats snap out of their bird-induced hypnosis and flee as though set afire. You may also notice No Trespassing signs posted by the Middle Rio Grande Conservancy District (MRGCD) at ditch trail entrances. These serve mainly as reminders that the MRGCD has not yet officially sanctioned the ditch roads for recreational use. (By contrast, the No Trespassing signs posted on private property should be strictly observed.)

To keep track of your pace, note that Old Church Road was 1.2 miles into the hike. Stella Lane marks the end of the second mile. Ahead you'll pass by Sandia View Adventist Academy on the left and, soon after, the Corrales Winery on the right. (For info on visiting the winery, see Nearby activities.) At the end of the third mile, you arrive at the intersection of Kings Lane and Corrales Road. The latter is often busy so use care in crossing it.

Soon the Corrales Lateral merges into the Sandoval Lateral. Cross the dam and turn right, heading toward the mountains. The mature Rio Grande Valley cottonwoods closer ahead mark the western edge of the Corrales Bosque Preserve.

There is a small parking area on the near side of a green pipe gate. The Sandoval Lateral turns right and flows south. Shady service roads running alongside it present an enticing alternate route on hot days.

Bosque Preserve (3.1 miles): To stick with the planned route, go through the gate, cross the wide Corrales Riverside Drain (also called the Clear Ditch), and climb up the levee. Turn right and follow the high road (also known as the Clear Ditch road and the dike road).

But before setting off in that direction, note two footpaths continuing down the east side of the levee. Both lead to the Rio Grande, less than 500 feet ahead. These, too, are shaded alternatives to the planned route and are part of an informal path system that spiderwebs between the road and the river throughout the cool deciduous woods.

The paths often break up or disappear under weeds and fallen trees, but this dense floodplain habitat makes for a more interesting hike than does the linear dike road. Though rare, black bears occasionally raid nearby apple orchards and leave evidence along these trails. Getting lost may look effortless in places; just remember to keep the river on your left and the levee on your right. Detours along these trails can add a few hundred feet or a couple of miles to the hike, depending on how much you want to explore the bosque.

Of course the dike road has the advantage of being remarkably easy to follow, and its elevation affords more expansive views. Overlooking the bosque, the drain, and nearby farm fields, you're more likely to spot wildlife, such as cottontails, porcupines, and any one of approximately 180 bird species—from ruby-crowned kinglets to yellow-rumped warblers. Hawks, owls, herons, and woodpeckers are also common in the area.

Opportunities to cross back over the riverside drain are few. About 1.5 miles downstream from the first crossing, the river and the road bend westward. Another mile or so past the bend, you'll see a bridge. Continue on the road another 0.5 miles, rounding a slight bend, to the second bridge. Cross that one and turn right on the lower embankment. You'll see a board over the ditch. Cross it and turn left. About 200 yards ahead, turn right and exit through the green gate.

Bosque access gate to Rec Center (1 mile): You're now on East La Entrada Road. One block west on the right is La Paloma Greenhouse. This ARCA initiative provides vocational experience and horticultural training for adults with developmental disabilities. Drop in Monday–Friday, between 7:30 a.m. and 3:30 p.m., to browse their wide selection of plants (they grow 28,000 annually) or shop online at **www.arc-a.org/services/orderinfo.**

East La Entrada Road goes straight to Corrales Road, which is not what you'd call "pedestrian-friendly." So instead, just past the greenhouse, turn left

A wintry silhouette of cottonwood in the
Corrales Bosque Preserve

on a ditchbank road marked "Lindero del Drenaje." Follow it south about 0.25 miles, and then turn right at the fourth crossroad, Bernaval Place. About 200 feet ahead it ends at a T-junction with Priestly Place. Turn left and follow it around to the right, where it becomes Coroval Road. Follow that to its end at Corrales Road; Territorial Plaza is across the street. To the immediate right is Jones Road. Follow it back to the rec center.

Note: Two brochures to enhance the first mile of this hike are *Corrales Historical Society Walking Tour* and *Walking Guide for the Old Corrales Acequia*. A booklet titled *The Corrales Bosque Preserve* is useful for the second half of this hike. All are available free from the visitor center in the Corrales Municipal Complex at 4324 Corrales Road, 0.35 miles past Jones Road. (See Directions.) Interpretive information is also posted on their outdoor display boards. For more information, visit the Village of Corrales Web site, **www.corrales-nm.org** and the Corrales Historical Society Web site, **www.corraleshistory.org.**

NEARBY ACTIVITIES

The Corrales Winery is open for free tours and wine tasting Wednesday–Saturday from noon5 p.m. Its entrance is on Corrales Road, 2.2 miles north of Jones Road. Call (505) 898-5165 or visit **www.corraleswinery.com** for more information.

05 PETROGLYPH NATIONAL MONUMENT:
Piedras Marcadas Canyon

KEY AT-A-GLANCE INFORMATION

LENGTH: 1.8 miles of interconnected loops

DIFFICULTY: Easy

SCENERY: Ancient etchings on volcanic rock, and city views

EXPOSURE: No shade

TRAIL TRAFFIC: Popular

SHARED USE: Low (dogs must be leashed; equestrians permitted; no motorized vehicles)

TRAIL SURFACE: Sand

HIKING TIME: 1 hour

DRIVING DISTANCE: 12 miles

ACCESS: Year-round, dawn–dusk

LAND STATUS: National Park Service; City of Albuquerque Open Space Division

MAPS: Basic trail map posted at trailhead and available at visitor centers); USGS Los Griegos

FACILITIES: Picnic shelter, playground

SPECIAL COMMENTS: For more information visit the Petroglyph National Monument Visitor Center online at www.nps.gov/petr. Check out the Open Space Visitor Center at www.cabq.gov/openspace. See note at the end of the chapter for more details.

GPS Trailhead
Coordinates
UTM Zone (WGS 84) 13S
Easting   0346524
Northing 3895272
Latitude 35° 11' 19"
Longitude 106° 41' 09"

IN BRIEF

Hidden in West Side suburbia, the northernmost outpost of this national monument contains an estimated 7,000 petroglyphs. Hunts for images carved into the basalt lava escarpment of Piedras Marcadas Canyon never fail to yield fascinating finds.

DESCRIPTION

Albuquerque's escarpment is a product of the volcanoes described in the next hike. This 17-mile ribbon of basalt lava winds along the base of the West Mesa, forming points, alcoves, and canyons. The flat surfaces of boulders found here are shiny and smooth, with a sheen known as "desert varnish." People figured out long ago that by pecking through this patina, they could create pictures that were, if nothing else, durable. The oldest of their squiggly lines date back to around 1000 BC.

Most works seen in Piedras Marcadas ("marked rocks") Canyon feature the elaborate designs from what was likely the largest pueblo in the Rio Grande Valley during the Pueblo IV period (AD 1300–1600). The pueblo flourished with more than 1,000 rooms before expeditionary forces under

Directions

From I-40 west, take Exit 155 and go 5.8 miles north on Coors Boulevard. Turn left on Paseo del Norte and go west 1.2 miles. (Alternate directions: From I-25 north, take Exit 232 on Paseo del Norte and go west 5.9 miles.) Turn right on Golf Course Road and go 0.6 miles north. Turn left on Jill Patricia Street. The parking lot entrance is about 100 yards ahead on the right. The trail begins on the sidewalk on the west side at the sign for Piedras Marcadas.

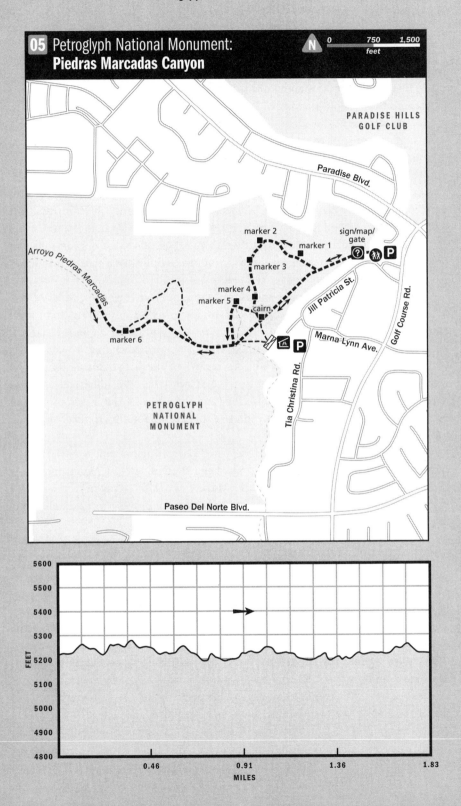

05 Petroglyph National Monument:
Piedras Marcadas Canyon

N 0   750   1,500
         feet

PARADISE HILLS
GOLF CLUB

Paradise Blvd.

marker 2
marker 1
sign/map/
gate

Arroyo Piedras Marcadas

marker 3

marker 4
marker 5
cairn
marker 6

Jill Patricia St.

Golf Course Rd.

Marna-Lynn Ave.

PETROGLYPH
NATIONAL
MONUMENT

Tia Christina Rd.

Paseo Del Norte Blvd.

Francisco Vasquez de Coronado destroyed it. Though largely unexcavated today, the Piedras Marcadas Pueblo ruins are located at the Open Space Visitor Center. (See Special Comments.)

The canyon contains about a third of the monument's petroglyphs, yet only 3 percent of the 124,000 annual visitors venture into this area. Suburban sprawl is the chief deterrent. Residential developments over the past decade have nearly sealed off this area of the park, which you'll no doubt notice as you begin your hike up a concrete alley between two houses wedged into a corner behind a Valvoline station.

It's not what you'd call the classic Attenborough expedition. Instead, Piedras Marcadas Canyon might be best appreciated as a study in contrasts. For better or worse, few places in America present such an immediate juxtaposition of ancient and modern worlds. And though you'll be reminded in every piece of tourist literature, it bears repeating: the land is a living shrine that continues to have a sacred role in contemporary Pueblo cultures.

A sign at the top end of the walkway shows a basic trail map. Most of this hike follows that map, however, the canyon contains far more trails than indicated. In fact, for every mile of designated trails within the monument, local wanderers have blazed 5 miles of "social trails." As of this writing, you can walk on any existing trail. This rule will change when the park releases its official map of designated trails, likely in 2008. For now the map illustrates a designated trail with numbers to indicate locations of a few of the more interesting petroglyphs. The rumor is that interpretive text corresponding to these numbers might be available in 2008.

From the sign, follow the trail to your left through a yellow barrier gate. Bypass any little shortcuts angling toward the south side of the escarpment. At the Y ahead, turn right on a wide path. **Marker 1,** a subtle gray post about knee high, is just around the bend. Now look up at the escarpment to find faces staring back at you.

First-time visitors share a tendency to climb up for a closer look. Park regulations aside, your time is better spent at the petroglyphs ahead, which are not only closer to the trail but also represent finer craftsmanship in terms of detail and definition. The most-revered designs include full-bodied kachina iconography and crosses and cattle brands from the Spanish colonial era.

As you follow the trail deeper into the alcove, the views and sounds of the city diminish, and it's easy to forget for a moment that just outside the walls of this basalt fortress, the suburban hordes are mustering in golf carts and SUVs. **Markers 2 and 3** are set off the main trail. Side trails allow for a closer look at nearby petroglyphs. Also keep an eye out for petroglyphs between markers. Half the fun is finding one without the assistance of trail markers.

After marker 3, you will cross a dry wash and head downhill. The trail points directly toward a prominent cluster of buildings about 8 miles to the southeast. The tall one is the Bank of Albuquerque Tower on the downtown

15th-century petroglyphs bear 20th-century bullet wounds.

Civic Plaza. Also dead ahead, **marker 4** indicates the location of five hand-prints, three of which are riddled with bullet holes. Kirtland Air Force Base, now largely contained within Albuquerque's southeastern quadrant, used these and other petroglyphs for target practice in the 1950s. (Others say it was the National Guard in the 1970s, but so far neither has claimed credit for the skilled marksmanship.)

Turnoffs for the trail into the second alcove, where you'll find **marker 5,** start about 80 feet ahead on the right. Access to this smaller trail is sometimes obscured under dense vegetation. If you stumble across a large cairn, you've gone too far. Go back and follow the trail nearest the escarpment wall. At last check, marker 5 was about 100 yards up, at the edge of a deep rut, where it is unlikely to withstand the next gulley washer. Likewise, the trail heading out of the alcove is easy to lose, but it runs parallel to the wash and stays close to the escarpment. Once out of the alcove, you'll find a perpendicular trail. Turn right and follow it around the basalt outcropping.

Unlike the trails in previous alcoves, this one bends in only slightly en route to the next marker on the far side. However, at least one park official has hinted that the path skirting the base of the escarpment is the best of the social trails and one that may likely be included in the official plan. This detour into the canyon's deepest alcove meets up with the main trail at **marker 6** and adds less than 0.25 miles to the overall hike.

A cross-town view to the Sandias

If you continue straight ahead, the trail soon becomes more of a trench, with devil's claw growing from the edges as though reaching for a handout. Park maps show this trail ending about 200 feet past marker 6, but there it arrives at another trail. To the right it climbs through a gap in the escarpment. From there the canyon widens, exposing developments along Paradise Boulevard to the north.

To return to the parking lot, follow the trail that crosses in front of the last alcove. Or, if you packed a lunch and the kids, visit the sheltered picnic table and playground 250 yards east of the outcropping.

Despite the commercial and residential encroachments, the canyon still echoes with the call of the wild. Just wait until sunset, when coyotes set off howling from the mesa's edge. Sure it's a Southwestern cliché, but it still sounds wonderful, even if they are just coming to dine on house pets.

Note: The Petroglyph National Monument Visitor Center, Las Imágenes, is best reached en route from I-40 west. Take Exit 155 and go 1.8 miles north on Coors Boulevard. Turn left on Western Trail, and go west about 1 mile. Open all year, 8 a.m. to 5 p.m.; closed Thanksgiving, Christmas, and New Year's days. Call (505) 899-0205, or visit **www.nps.gov/petr** for more information. The Open Space Visitor Center is also located en route from I-40 at 6500 Coors Boulevard, on the right about 2 miles north of Western Trail. Open Tuesday to Saturday, 9 a.m. to 5 p.m.; call (505) 897-8831, or visit **www.cabq.gov/openspace**.

PETROGLYPH NATIONAL MONUMENT: The Volcanoes

06

IN BRIEF

Walk the flanks of four scoria cones and look for lizards in the lava rock. The Albuquerque Volcanoes also boast the West Side's best views of both the city and the Sandia Mountains.

DESCRIPTION

Try counting every volcano within 60 miles of Albuquerque, and you should come up with a tally in the neighborhood of 270. They range in size from scorched dents in the earth to the towering peak of Mount Taylor.

Ten volcanoes reside within Albuquerque's city limits, with five blistering the otherwise flat western horizon. Compared to the Sandia granite that dominates the eastern vista, the spatter cones are mere babes, born in the final throes of a fissure eruption just 140,000 years ago.

Lava spilled primarily east into the Rio Grande Valley. Concealed beneath the sand and sage of Albuquerque's West Mesa, a lava crust (basalt caprock) rests upon older layers of sediments. Thousands of years of erosion undermined eastern edges of the caprock, causing it to break apart and collapse. The result is an exposed volcanic escarpment that appears from a distance as a fairly uniform black cliff.

Pueblo Indians have long considered this a sacred landscape. Later cultures developed their own interpretations, with each new generation finding unique ways to express its

KEY AT-A-GLANCE INFORMATION

LENGTH: 1.0-, 2.0- and 6.3-mile loop options
DIFFICULTY: Easy to moderate
SCENERY: Cinder cones, city views, birds, and reptiles
EXPOSURE: Full sun
TRAIL TRAFFIC: Popular
SHARED USE: Moderate (mountain bikers, equestrians; dogs must be leashed; no motorized vehicles)
TRAIL SURFACE: Packed dirt, sand, loose rock
HIKING TIME: 20 minutes–3 hours
DRIVING DISTANCE: 15 miles (one way) from the I-40/I-25 exchange
ACCESS: Daily, 9 a.m.–5 p.m.
LAND STATUS: National Park Service; City of Albuquerque Open Space Division
MAPS: Trail map posted at trailhead and at nps.gov/petr; USGS The Volcanoes
FACILITIES: Shade shelters, interpretive signage, no water, limited wheelchair access to trails, wheelchair-accessible restrooms
SPECIAL COMMENTS: For more information, contact the Petroglyph National Monument Visitor Center, Las Imágenes, at (505) 899-0205.

Directions

From I-40 west, take Exit 149, and go 4.8 miles north on Paseo del Volcan. Turn right on the access road, and follow it east 0.3 miles to the parking lot. The trailhead is near the southeastern corner of the lot.

GPS Trailhead Coordinates

UTM Zone (WGS 84)   13S
Easting   0337781
Northing   3888986
Latitude   35° 07' 50"
Longitude 106° 46' 50"

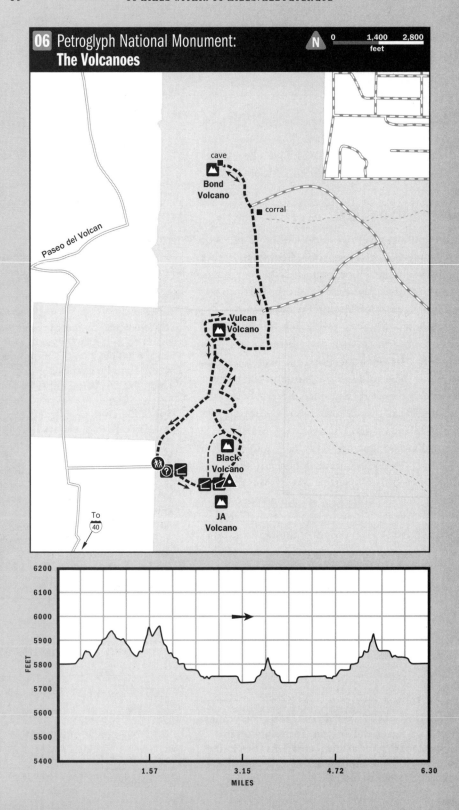

06 Petroglyph National Monument: The Volcanoes

Collared lizard

fondness for the volcanoes. The U.S. Air Force hasn't bombed them in more than 60 years, and in 2007 the U.S. Army Corps of Engineers announced plans to retrieve all the ordnances out there that have, so far, failed to detonate.

On a quiet morning in 1947, Albuquerque residents seemed to gain a new appreciation for their volcanoes when they woke to find thick black smoke billowing from the biggest cone. Citywide panic naturally ensued. A brave crew eventually assessed the fuming crater and returned to announce that the smoke was coming from strategically placed car tires, soaked in gasoline and set ablaze. The prank would be repeated over successive years with considerably less impact.

In 2002 the volcanoes park area received a few new amenities, including shade shelters and interpretive signage. But the biggest improvements came with relocating the parking lot. Visitors can no longer drive to the base of the big volcano, and many seem unwilling to attempt the 2-mile trek on foot. As a result, vegetation stands a healthy chance of reclaiming a surplus of roads and trails. Many longstanding traffic scars vanished in the persistent monsoons of 2006, and in the green eruption that soon followed, the Albuquerque Volcanoes could've passed for the hills of Ireland.

Navigating the wide-open space in the volcanoes area is easy. You'd have to go completely blind to get lost out here, however, it takes a sharp eye to discern designated trails from discontinued ones. Sometimes the best you can do is just make a good-faith effort to stay on the right ones. Also, although climbing to

View south from the slopes of Vulcan Volcano

the top of the volcanoes is not expressly prohibited, it is considered in bad form because they enjoy a sacred status among Pueblo peoples.

Most volcano visitors tend to dash to the scenic overlook at JA Volcano for a gawk before rushing back to the interstate. This 1-mile out-and-back takes about 20 minutes. Those traveling at a more leisurely pace might consider the longer options outlined below. Each begins with a visit to the overlook.

Start the hike from the gate at the southeast corner of the parking lot, take a moment to read the interpretive displays under the nearby shelter and at the trailhead, and then proceed out to JA Volcano. An arrow sign helps you stay on the right track at the intersection with a discontinued road to the southwest escarpment. Continue straight past the shelter ahead to the one at the overlook.

JA Volcano gets its name from a pair of initials painted long ago on its eastern face. They've since faded, but those who know where to look claim the letters are still visible from 8 miles away. These tend be the same people who claim to see gasses rising from the cones and insist that the city's Technicolor sunsets are due to the filtering effect of volcanic vapors.

From the overlook, turn left and head north on the main trail. It skirts around east sides of Black and Cinder volcanoes—or what's left of them. Some Burqueños still remember when six robust volcanoes stood out here, before miners cut Black down to a stump and reduced Cinder to a pit.

About 1.4 miles into the hike, you'll arrive at the junction with the return path at the base of Vulcan Volcano. Named for the Roman god of fire, it is by far the largest in the group. The old parking area was located here, which helps explain the remnants of roads and footpaths blazed in at least seven directions. Stick to the main path going up the south side of the cone. About a third of the way up the slope, the trail curves to the left and crosses over a saddle between the main volcano and a baby cone. Continuing clockwise to the north, it passes by a half-domed outcrop. From here the path tends to fade as it rounds the steepest flank. Stick to the base of Vulcan until you reach the hollowed-out area of a former quarry. From here you can finish the loop and head back to the parking lot via the old access road, which runs southwest to a fence, and then straight south. The Vulcan loop totals 2 miles and takes about an hour.

To visit Bond Volcano, follow the road south–southeast from the Vulcan quarry. Refrain from taking any shortcuts as you may disturb birds and snakes nesting in the grassy areas. The trail soon curves left and goes roughly north about 1.2 miles to the remains of an old corral at the junction of five roads. (At last check, two of the roads on the left were being overrun by tall grass and winterfat.) Take the road heading northwest about 0.25 miles to Bond's southern flank. There you'll find a cave that sometimes smells ripe with musk, depending on the season.

The best time of year to visit the volcanoes is debatable. Certainly the cooler weather in fall and spring make hiking more pleasant. Fresh snow on the West Mesa has its own mystical allure. But my favorite time is in the fierce heat of summer, in the days following a heavy rain. The crowds are thin and the craters are thick with insects. These combined factors draw the resident wildlife out in full force. Collared lizards do their push-ups on every other slab of basalt. (*Warning:* They bite.) Blister beetles fat as lug nuts display shiny black carapaces with brilliant red pinstripes. (*Warning:* Do not touch. They're called *blister bugs* for a reason). And although I have yet to greet any of the three species of rattlesnake, I've spotted numerous nonvenomous cousins and a horned lizard or two. The vast majority of my reptilian encounters occurred on the road between the old corral and Bond Volcano.

Return to Vulcan the same way you came. From there you can return to the parking lot via the old access road.

Note: For every mile of designated trails within the monument, local explorers have blazed 5 miles of "social trails." As of this writing, you can walk on any existing trail. However, closures are expected when the park releases the official trail plan, tentatively slated for the summer of 2008. For updates, check with the Petroglyph National Monument Visitor Center, Las Imágenes, at (505) 899-0205.

07 SOUTH VALLEY:
Arenal and Atrisco Ditch Trails

KEY AT-A-GLANCE INFORMATION

LENGTH: 3-mile loop

DIFFICULTY: Easy

SCENERY: Irrigation canals; old-growth cottonwoods; a residential area with both urban and agrarian characteristics

EXPOSURE: Half shade

TRAIL TRAFFIC: Moderate

SHARED USE: Moderate (bicycles, joggers, equestrians; popular with dog owners; restricted motorized-vehicle access on ditch trails)

TRAIL SURFACE: Mostly dirt, some pavement

HIKING TIME: 1–2 hours

DRIVING DISTANCE: 4.25 miles (one way) from the I-40 and I-25 exchange

ACCESS: Not recommended after dark

LAND STATUS: Middle Rio Grande Conservancy District; City of Albuquerque

MAPS: USGS Albuquerque West

FACILITIES: None

SPECIAL COMMENTS: For more information on ditchbank hikes in Albuquerque, visit the Ditches with Trails Project Web site at www.ditcheswithtrails.com

IN BRIEF

Walk along a centuries-old system of working irrigation ditches for a unique cultural study of one of Albuquerque's first neighborhoods.

DESCRIPTION

The mystery legend and Los Ranchos resident Tony Hillerman has been known to muse at length on his serene walks along the ditches around his neighborhood, particularly in colder months, when flocks of sandhill cranes descend upon harvested fields. By no coincidence, recent years have seen a surge in the popularity of ditchbank walks in the North Valley, with the trend spreading all the way up to the foothill arroyos. Fortunately, there's no shortage of waterways in the Rio Grande Valley.

Formed in 1925 to control flooding and reclaim farmland, the Middle Rio Grande Conservancy District now operates more than 1,200 miles of canals, laterals, and drains. The irrigation system helps sustain 30,000 acres of bosque and delivers water to 70,000 acres of cropland in a greenbelt that stretches 150 miles from Cochiti to the Bosque del Apache National Wildlife Refuge.

In 2007 the district put out an open call for recreational-trail proposals for the

----

GPS Trailhead
Coordinates
UTM Zone (WGS 84)   13S
Easting   0346466
Northing   3883501
Latitude   35° 04' 57"
Longitude   106° 41' 03"

Directions ———————————►

From I-40, take Exit 157A, and go 0.7 miles south on Rio Grande Boulevard. Turn right on Central Avenue, and go 1.1 mile. Turn left on Atrisco Drive (the third left after the bridge). Continue south one block on Atrisco Drive, then turn right and park at Atrisco Park.

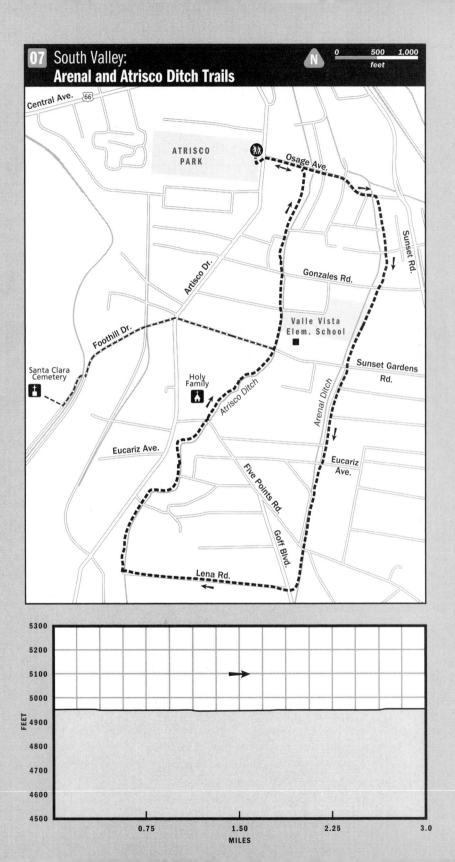

N

0   500   1,000
feet

Central Ave. 66

ATRISCO PARK

Osage Ave.

Sunset Rd.

Artisco Dr.

Gonzales Rd.

Foothill Dr.

Valle Vista Elem. School

Santa Clara Cemetery

Holy Family

Atrisco Ditch

Arenal Ditch

Sunset Gardens Rd.

Eucariz Ave.

Eucariz Ave.

Five Points Rd.

Goff Blvd.

Lena Rd.

5300
5200
5100
5000
4900
4800
4700
4600
4500

FEET

0.75   1.50   2.25   3.0
MILES

Venerable cottonwood on the Atrisco Acequia

"Ditches with Trails" project. The first studies on formal ditch-trail corridors occurred along the Arenal and Atrisco acequias in the Atrisco neighborhood of Albuquerque's South Valley.

Spanish settlers first arrived in the South Valley with Juan de Oñate's 1598 expedition. According to one version of local history, Nahuatl Indians later referred to the area of settlements on the west bank of the Rio Grande as *Atlixo,* meaning "across the water." The earliest known record of its name comes from a 1662 government document that describes the valley of Atrisco as "the best site in all New Mexico."

In 1692 the Spanish crown awarded the 41,000-acre Atrisco Land Grant to Fernando Durán y Chávez for his services in the reconquest of New Mexico. It would be the first of 300 such grants in the province. By 1896, heirs of the grant successfully petitioned to incorporate additional lands, expanding the Atrisco Land Grant to nearly 83,000 acres.

The South Valley maintained its agrarian character well into the 20th century. Its small farm economy boomed during World War II but began to falter in the following decades. The Atrisco neighborhood, with its proximity to Route 66 (Central Avenue), was among the first to experience the ensuing pressures for rapid development and the consequences of it.

Despite hardships, descendants of the original settlers retained possession of the land grant for well over 300 years. That legacy came to an abrupt end in 2006, when Atrisco heirs transferred their ancestral lands to developers in a controversial $250-million deal. How that might affect the Atrisco neighborhood remains to be seen. Most of its fields were carved into subdivisions years ago, yet enough endure to keep the acequias flowing.

Atrisco still seems to have a spirited sense of community that's sorely lacking in suburbia. Warm weekends and the long afternoons of summer buzz with games in the park, church picnics, and backyard family gatherings. A chance to glimpse the lively customs and traditions of Atrisqueños is what draws *gabachos* like me out on hikes like this.

Start the hike by exiting the parking lot the same way you drove in. Cross Atrisco Drive and proceed east on Osage Avenue. The first ditch, Atrisco Acequia, crosses under this street near the end of the first block. You'll follow it on the return segment of this loop. Note the house with the green tin roof on your right so you'll know where to turn when you get back to this point.

Stay on Osage Avenue another three short blocks. Just past Stella Drive you'll see the second ditch, Arenal Acequia. Turn right and follow it south. After a couple of cross streets, you'll see the Valle Vista Elementary schoolyard on the right. A primary reason for establishing formal trails along the Arenal and Atrisco ditches was to provide the students with a safe walking route to and from school. (Nearby signs reading "Ditches Are Deadly—Stay Away" are another one of the district's campaigns for kids.)

Continue south, crossing Sunset Gardens Road and then Eucariz Avenue. Along the way, residential properties alternate with Atrisco's few remaining orchards and crop fields. Backyards often feature interesting details, from folk shrines in a manicured garden to a dirt lot full of cannibalized Cadillacs. Yard animals include sheep, goats, and gamecocks. The centuries-old tradition of cockfighting was finally outlawed in New Mexico in March 2007. Though loose dogs are fairly uncommon, stay alert; pit bulls are quite popular here.

About 100 yards or so past Five Points Road, a diagonal cross street, you'll see a second diagonal street. Look to the right for the street signs marking the junction of Goff Boulevard and Lena Road. When you see it, cut across the dirt lot and head down Lena Road.

Take Lena Road west about 0.4 miles to its end at the Atrisco Acequia. Turn right and follow this winding ditch north. You'll see the Holy Family Church before you reach Five Points Road. Be careful at the crossing—there's a blind curve on your right. Continue north, passing an assembly of refrigerators at the back end of the spacious church grounds.

Optional detour: The next intersection, Sunset Gardens Road, presents an opportunity for a side trip to the historic Santa Clara Cemetery. Be warned, however, that the streets are a bit narrow for a comfortable stroll. If you're up for the challenge, turn left and cross Atrisco Drive, and then proceed southwest on Foothill Drive to the Arenal Main Canal, which runs along the base of the escarpment. Go south one block, and look for the angelic murals on the walls and gate on the right. A small graveyard extends up the face of the escarpment. Walk up to the mesa rim to see the rest of the hand-scrawled markers and elaborate monuments in this sprawling cemetery. You'll also get an excellent view over the neighborhood. Return to the Atrisco Acequia the way you came, and proceed north. This detour will add about 1.3 miles to the hike.

The path continues past the other side of the schoolyard and back up to Osage Avenue. You won't see a road sign from the ditch trail, so keep an eye out on your left for the house with the green tin roof. The road in front of it is where you turn left for Atrisco Park. If you encounter a metal guardrail across the ditch, you've gone a block too far.

There are plenty more canals and drains to explore throughout the South Valley, but moving between them isn't always as easy as a walk down Lena Road. Rights-of-way are few, and private-property boundaries should be strictly observed. A simple guideline to remember: when in doubt, stay out.

NEARBY ACTIVITIES

Visit the art museum at the National Hispanic Cultural Center (NHCC), take a guided tour of its attractive campus, and enjoy lunch at La Fonda del Bosque, rated by *Hispanic Magazine* as one the 50 best Hispanic restaurants in the country. To get there from Atrisco Park, go 1.25 miles south on Atrisco Drive. Turn left on Bridge Boulevard and go 2 miles east to cross the Barelas Bridge. The first right after the bridge leads into the NHCC parking lot. For hours, fees, and event schedules call (505) 246-2261 or visit **www.nationalhispaniccenter.org.**

For a wine-country alternative to the South Valley's urban vibrancy, consider a ditchbank hike from Los Ranchos de Albuquerque. From I-40, take Exit 157A and go 4 miles north on Rio Grande Boulevard. Turn right and park at Harnett Park. Locate the irrigation ditch behind the playground, and follow it south 0.5 miles to the northwest corner of Los Poblanos Fields, a 138-acre Open Space Farmland with miles of ditch trails. For more information on ditchbank hikes in Albuquerque, visit the Ditches with Trails Project Web site at **www .ditcheswithtrails.com.**

SOUTH VALLEY: Montessa Park 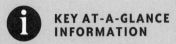 08

IN BRIEF

For those who enjoy hiking unusual environments, this route uses an abandoned railroad spur and a major arroyo for a mostly flat hike through roller-coaster terrain. Despite its reputation for high-flying motorbikes and low-flying aircraft, this semi-urban area along the lower Tijeras Arroyo is often quieter than most city parks.

DESCRIPTION

The Tijeras ("scissors") Arroyo, Bernalillo County's largest, is a conduit for runoff from the mountains to the east, draining into the Rio Grande to the west. To the south is Mesa del Sol, site of imminent residential developments. And to the immediate north are the runways of Kirtland Air Force Base and the Albuquerque International Sunport, the state's primary airport. The arroyo floodplain spans more than 1,000 feet, with embankments on either side rising up to 300 feet. City planners considered damming the arroyo for a recreational reservoir, but more-recent proposals call for restoring it as a natural corridor to facilitate wildlife traffic between the mountains and the river.

Erosion of the embankments has created steep, hilly terrain well suited for the antics

(i) KEY AT-A-GLANCE INFORMATION

LENGTH: 6-mile figure-8 or 4.4-mile loop

DIFFICULTY: Easy

SCENERY: Desert wildlife, abandoned railroad tracks, aircraft, postmodern landscaping

EXPOSURE: Minimal shade

TRAIL TRAFFIC: Low

SHARED USE: Moderate (Frisbee golfers, motorized vehicles)

TRAIL SURFACE: Gravel, sand

HIKING TIME: 2–3 hours

DRIVING DISTANCE: 11 miles (one way) from the I-40 and I-25 exchange

ACCESS: Daylight hours

LAND STATUS: Albuquerque Open Space and other city land; State of New Mexico

MAPS: USGS Albuquerque East and Albuquerque West

FACILITIES: Off-leash dog park, disc golf course

SPECIAL COMMENTS: Heed military boundary notices, trespassing convictions carry a potential 6-month jail term and a $5,000 fine.

Directions ➞

From I-25 south, take Exit 220 and go 0.4 miles west on Rio Bravo Boulevard. Turn left onto Broadway Boulevard and go 1.8 miles south. Turn left on Bobby Foster Road and cross over I-25. Turn left on Los Picaros Road and follow it 3 miles. Park next to the green gate on the left side of the road. The hike begins on the right side of the gate.

GPS Trailhead Coordinates

UTM Zone (WGS 84) 13S

Easting 0354109

Northing 3876205

Latitude 35° 01' 05"

Longitude 106° 35' 57"

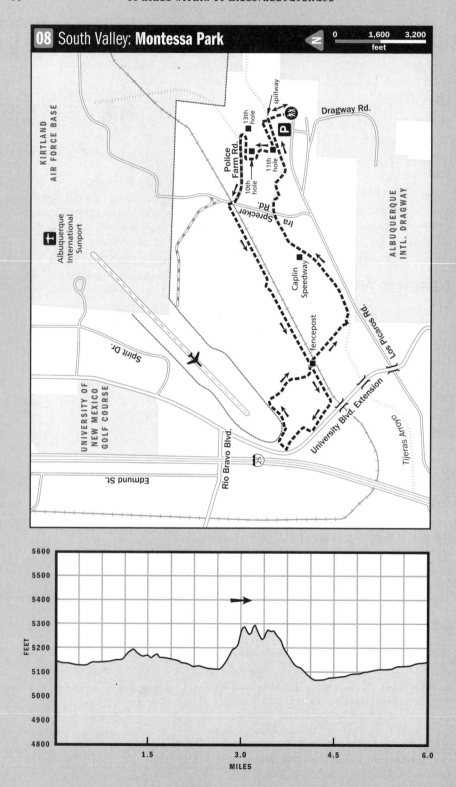

of vehicular daredevils. Accordingly, the 577-acre Montessa Park, located along the lower arroyo, is currently the only area in the Open Space system available for off-road driving. Dirt bikes, quads, and other all-terrain vehicles have ripped a hundred trails in and around the park. It's a sacrificial land; without it, these ersatz Knievels would surely tear up more property elsewhere.

From some perspectives, Montessa Park seems a place where communion with nature could get ugly. Neighboring facilities include the Bio-Disease Management Unit, which monitors the state for outbreaks of hantavirus, rabbit fever, bubonic plague, and other critter-borne illnesses. Another neighbor, the Zia Pistol and Rifle Club, boasts a 600-yard shooting range for high-powered rifle competitions. You might hear the crackle of their M–16s. And, of course, there's the occasional jet screaming overhead. Keep an eye out for the new CV–22 Ospreys, capable of vertical take-offs and landings.

From other perspectives, the landscape is a fascinating study on the urban–wildlife interface at the southern fringe of the state's biggest city.

Begin the hike by exploring the grounds of the Brent Baca Memorial Disc Golf Course, accessed by slipping through the pedestrian gateway to the right of the green gate. If you have time and a Frisbee, toss a few rounds. This challenging 7,805-foot course has four par-four holes, in addition to short tees for novices. Maps and scorecards are in a mailbox near the first tee. Or just follow the path straight past the 15th tee and down to a concrete spillway.

The return leg of this hike runs about 1.5 miles up the arroyo streambed to return to this point, so note conditions beneath the spillway. If there's water, you'll need to consider alternate return routes. Also note the depth of the channel—15 to 20 feet in places. Debris wrapped around tree trunks growing above the rim should give you a good idea of what to expect in the event of a flash flood.

After crossing the spillway, make your way to the tenth hole in the northwestern corner of the course. The easiest route involves turning right by the stacks of metal frames that comprise the hazard on the 11th hole.

Behind a solitary tree on the tenth hole, a rutted doubletrack runs between two wire fences. Follow it to the north end, then turn right at the fence ahead. The road widens into a dry wash. Once you reach the end of the fence on your left, you're in undesignated motorcross country. Stay alert. Airborne bikes don't brake for anything.

The railroad tracks lie to the north on the far side of the nearest hill. The easiest way to reach them is by taking the dirt road northwest (it shows up on some maps as Police Farm Road, named for the City Police Prison and Farm that was located here in the 1950s). The road crosses the tracks just before reaching Ira Sprecker Road. For a slightly more challenging approach to the railroad tracks, follow a motorcross trail straight up the hill, and then scramble down into the cut on the other side.

Once on the railroad tracks, it's a straight shot to the southern extension of University Boulevard, about 1.5 miles southwest. By this point, you may have

Abandoned tracks seem to aim straight for
South Sandia Peak.

noticed black trucks with tinted windows prowling the ridge that marks the airbase
perimeter. They may even park there until you leave. You might also encounter
"T-hunters" lurking about the hills. They're the ones with devices that resemble
rooftop TV antennae. Transmitter hunting, or radio direction finding, is the ham
operator's version geocaching, and this area seems to be a popular place for it.

After crossing Ira Sprecker Road, you'll pass north of the Harvey Caplin
Memorial Speedway, a 0.2-mile dirt oval track used primarily for kart racing. Illegal dumping is evident around the speedway. Black-tailed jackrabbits dart through
a debris field of shot TVs, matching recliners, and major kitchen appliances.

A gap in the tracks ahead indicates where flash flooding washed out a
trestle. Pick up the tracks on the other side of the wash. About 0.5 miles ahead,
you'll see a wooden post wrapped in barbed wire—a landmark for your return
route. (To cut 1.6 miles and a steep climb from this hike, turn left here, and follow the old dirt road straight down to the arroyo.)

You'll arrive at another trestle 0.25 miles past the post, just before the
tracks go under University Boulevard. Jump off the tracks here, and follow the
boulevard easement uphill. At the bus stop near the crest of the hill, turn right,
and then angle down to the dirt road below to the left. Follow it up to this hike's
destination at the mesa top. (*Note:* New developments may eventually obstruct
access at this point. In that case, follow the boulevard around the bend and
access the mesa top from the north side.)

Once on the mesa top, you won't see the runway, but you'll get a good sense of its proximity when an 80-ton Airbus A320 comes in for a landing. As you might expect, a sturdy fence prevents folks from wandering onto the tarmac. A well-worn path along this perimeter fence is popular for dog walking. Follow it 0.25 miles, keeping the fence on your left, until you reach a high point, where the airport comes into view.

Break away from the perimeter trail, and take the path going south along the ridge. Pause a moment to enjoy the view, and scout your return route. Look for the old dirt road cutting straight down to the Tijeras Arroyo. If the streambed seemed too muddy earlier, now is the time to locate alternate routes. A few options should come into plain view, keeping in mind that the easiest points to cross the arroyo are at Ira Sprecker Road and the spillway at the 15th tee.

At the Y on the ridge ahead, bear left, and head down to the wash below. It shallows as it approaches the railroad tracks. Turn left on the tracks. The barbed-wire fencepost is about 100 yards ahead on the right. Leave the tracks to pick up the old dirt road. You'll cross under two sets of power lines. Hawks and falcons often perch on the crossbeams of the utility poles.

The descent from the road to the streambed is easy, but as you walk upstream, the walls are higher, and you'll soon notice limited opportunities to exit. The environment along the streambed is much different from the dry expanse above the rim. Vegetation grows thick with gourds and devil's claw. Jimsonweed often sprouts pods that resemble medieval flails. River rock adds color, with greenstone, red jasper, and glassy chunks of obsidian. Fossils found in the Tijeras Arroyo include ancient species of land tortoise, camel, llama, and mammoth.

Illegal dumping becomes more noticeable as you approach Ira Sprecker Road. The inventory of artifacts found here includes Christmas lights, shopping carts, and the overturned wreckage of what might have been a Pinto or a Gremlin. Airplane parts occasionally turn up, adding credibility to rumors of small aircraft falling short of their designated runways.

Cross Ira Sprecker Road, and continue up the arroyo. You might find pockets of quicksand in this section, so choose your steps carefully. When you reach the spillway, climb up, and turn right. Follow the path back to the parking area at the green gate. If returning at dusk, watch for great horned owls; you may find one perched above the rope swing in the old cottonwood by the gate.

09 PIEDRA LISA CANYON

KEY AT-A-GLANCE INFORMATION

LENGTH: 2.8-mile loop

DIFFICULTY: Moderate to difficult

SCENERY: City overlooks, canyons, rock features

EXPOSURE: Some canyon shade

TRAIL TRAFFIC: Heavy near trailhead

SHARED USE: Moderate (mountain biking and equestrians on Foothills Trail; dogs must be leashed)

TRAIL SURFACE: Sand, bedrock, packed dirt

HIKING TIME: 2 hours

DRIVING DISTANCE: 12 miles (one way) from the I-40 and I-25 exchange

ACCESS: April–October, 7 a.m.– 9 p.m., and November–March: 7 a.m.–7 p.m.

LAND STATUS: Open Space Division

MAPS: Sandia Ranger District; USGS Tijeras

FACILITIES: None

IN BRIEF

In this informal route in the Sandia foothills, nontechnical rock climbing leads to great opportunities for bouldering, in addition to unrivaled city and sunset views. Wildlife includes quail, mule deer, and cottontail among dense stands of cholla cacti.

DESCRIPTION

Not to be confused with Piedra Lisa Trail at the northern end of the Sandias, this route comprises sections of a designated trail, an arroyo, a boundary-fence trail, and an informal trail. I first plotted this course a few years back while seeking quick access to some light rock-climbing and bouldering spots. It has since become one of my favorite late-afternoon excursions.

The steep ascending and descending segments are visible from the Foothills Trail. Previews tend to surprise uninitiated hiking companions, who invariably respond: No @*# way! But they try it anyway and soon learn that although the route is strenuous in places, it's not nearly as difficult or dangerous as it first looked.

From the parking lot, the descent appears as a natural dam wedged high into the canyon.

GPS Trailhead Coordinates

UTM Zone (WGS 84) 13S

Easting 0364370

Northing 3886518

Latitude 35° 06' 45"

Longitude 106° 29' 18"

Directions

From I-40, take Exit 167. Drive 3.1 miles north on Tramway Boulevard. Turn right on Candelaria Road and go 0.5 miles. Turn right on Camino de la Sierra and go 0.25 miles to the Piedra Lisa Canyon parking area on the left.

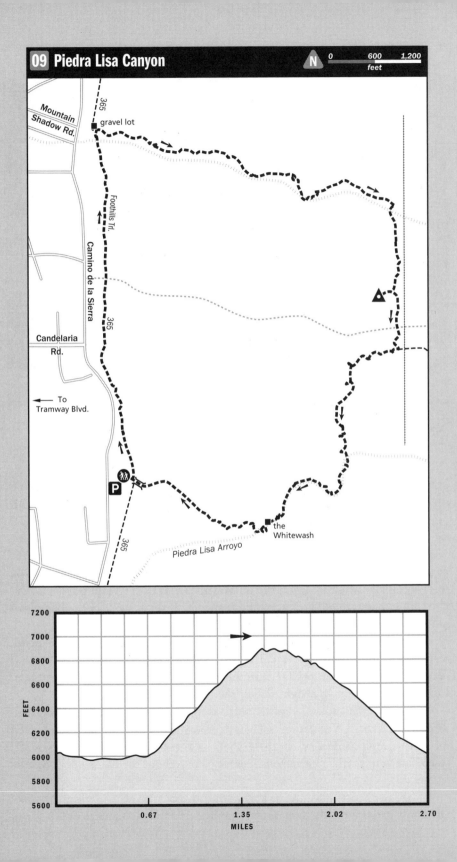

The Two Tenors: holes form when softer rock erodes faster than the harder coarse-grained granite.

Known locally as "the Whitewash," the sheer face of the light-gray cliff suggests insurmountability. Add to that its name—Piedra Lisa ("slick rock")—and the potential for nasty falls soon becomes all too obvious. Most visitors to this popular Open Space area flock straight to the cliff. This hike, however, saves the best for last.

The hike: Find the footbridge at the top of the stairs on the east side of the parking lot. Immediately before the bridge, turn left and begin hiking north on the Foothills Trail (365). Upon the hillside ahead sit hundreds of boulders that, if set in motion, could blaze a few hiking trails through the subdivisions down to the west.

Throughout most of the year, every other footstep along the path incites scaled quail to burst from the tall grass. Farther along, the path narrows as it squeezes between steep foothills and the backyard fences built up against them. Continue north along the right side of the wire fence.

Channels that drain from the ridge on your right flow into South Glenwood Hills Arroyo. Vegetation, such as dense patches of stink gourds, so named for their armpit aroma, often grows thick in these watercourses. The gourds' resemblance to small watermelons recalls a story about the name of the Sandia Mountains.

The Tiwa people have always known the range as Bien Mur—"big mountain." Spaniards arriving in the late 1500s renamed it Sandia—"watermelon"—after mistaking a crop of gourds for a watermelon patch. Once realizing their mistake, they recognized the little gourd as *calabazilla,* as it is still commonly known in the region today. The mountains and the nearby pueblo, however, remain stuck with the fruity misnomer—or so goes one cynical theory.

A far more popular explanation credits the peaks' sunset blush as the inspiration behind the conquistadors' rosy christening. In the early evening hours, the otherwise stark west face can take on every shade of watermelon flesh. By extension, the pine-forested crest and pale-limestone caprock represent the outer and inner rind, respectively, and piñon trees that dot the face are supposed to be the seeds.

A 0.6-mile stroll along the Foothills Trail brings you to a gravel lot with scattered flood debris. Ruts up to 6 feet deep cut through the sediment, further illustrating the work of the rare rains. If there's a chance of precipitation, save this hike for a sunny day.

A quick overview of the scramble ahead: Your current elevation is about 6,000 feet. About halfway up the arroyo, a large slab of pale rock that marks a 500-foot gain in elevation. This hike crests just under 6,900 feet.

The best strategy for the ascent is to stay in the arroyo. Climbing along the embankment above leads only to annoying encounters with prickly brush. Most of the arroyo is classic Sandia granite. Its coarse grain provides excellent traction, particularly in the steepest areas. The mineral composition includes pink quartz, which some credit for the Sandias' rosy alpenglow.

Be aware, however, that spots throughout the arroyo are worn smooth and that the slightest moisture activates a slick film of algae, essentially transforming an otherwise grippy slope into a Slip 'n Slide.

At 6,700 feet, the grade lessens, and the arroyo becomes a sandy path. Follow it up about 400 feet to a barbed-wire fence, which roughly defines the boundary between the City of Albuquerque and the Sandia Mountain Wilderness. Turn right, and follow the fence south. This hike reaches its highest point about 300 yards ahead. An outcropping of boulders to the right provides an excellent view of the city. For reference, the east–west thoroughfare slightly to the south is Candelaria Road.

Continue following the fence trail south, and cross a shallow drainage. About 100 yards farther south, at a break in the fence, the intersecting path is the northernmost part of the old Piedra Lisa Canyon Trail. A left turn here would lead to another 200-foot gain in elevation before the descent into the upper canyon, adding about 0.8 miles to this hike.

To stay on this hike, turn right and aim for the next pile of boulders. From there, turn south to continue your descent. The trail splits into competing footpaths, with increasingly prominent boulder piles effectively serving as giant cairns. The space beneath some of these precariously balanced goliaths is roomy enough for you to pitch a tent. (Note: overnight camping in Open Space areas requires a permit.)

Soon the streambed of Piedra Lisa Canyon comes into view. The challenge now is in picking the least destructive path to reach it. One way is to head slightly eastward and down into a fabulously pink tributary channel. You'll have to climb out once or twice to get around clumps of shrub live oak and other spiny plants, but otherwise it's a direct route to the Piedra Lisa Canyon streambed below.

Turn right and follow the sinuous canyon down successively higher drops. A sudden flourish in graffiti indicates that the popular trailhead area is near. The streambed briefly levels out as it passes through a green tunnel of willows. However, there's one last drop to negotiate, and it's a big one.

If you brought enough rope, you could rappel down, but I can't vouch for the integrity of the bolts in the rock except to say they've held their places for years. Otherwise, flip a coin to decide which side to scramble down. Most hikers would agree that the south side is easier because a stone corridor slopes down to the base. I generally prefer the terraced descent on the north side.

Once back on terra firma, pick up the path on the north side of the streambed, and follow it back to the footbridge.

NEARBY ACTIVITIES

Hungry? Reward yourself with a two-pound porterhouse steak at The Great American Land & Cattle Co. They're on the northeast corner of Indian School Road and Tramway Boulevard and can be reached at (505) 292-1510; their Web site is **steakandwine.com**.

ELENA GALLEGOS:
Cottonwood Springs–Nature Trail

IN BRIEF

Artistic enhancements along an all-access interpretive trail and the old nature loop provide a stylish introduction to the cultural history and abundant wildlife in the Sandia Mountain foothills.

DESCRIPTION

What is the Elena Gallegos? The short answer defines it as a 1694 Spanish land grant that stretched from the Sandia Mountains to the Rio Grande. However, interpretations of its original boundaries have entered disputes in matters ranging from President Lincoln's 1864 land patent to the T'uf Shur Bien Preservation Trust Area Act of 2003.

Although New Mexico governance passed from Spain to Mexico (1821) to the United States (1848) to the Confederacy (1862, albeit briefly) before New Mexico achieved statehood (1912), the Elena Gallegos Land Grant remained in the possession of one family. State claims and realty demands have since carved up the estate beyond recognition. From this vast parcel, once estimated at 35,084 acres, all that officially bears the

KEY AT-A-GLANCE INFORMATION

LENGTH: 1.4-mile balloon, with longer options

DIFFICULTY: Easy

SCENERY: Open foothills, continuous mountain views

EXPOSURE: Minimal shade

TRAIL TRAFFIC: Popular

SHARED USE: Moderate (mountain bikes and equestrians permitted on one short trail segment; dogs must be leashed)

TRAIL SURFACE: Pavement, fine gravel

HIKING TIME: 1 hour

DRIVING DISTANCE: 17 miles (one way) from the I-40 and I-25 exchange

ACCESS: April–October, 7 a.m.–9 p.m., and November–March, 7 a.m.–7 p.m.; $1 per car weekdays, $2 weekends; free with Open Space annual pass

LAND STATUS: Open Space Division

MAPS: cabq.gov/openspace; Sandia Ranger District; USGS Sandia Crest

FACILITIES: Interpretive trail, picnic areas, group reservation areas with barbeque grills, restrooms. Drinking water near parking areas is shut off in winter months but available at information center year-round.

Directions

From I-40, take Exit 167 and go 6 miles north on Tramway Boulevard. (Or from I-25, take Exit 234 and go 7.5 miles east and then south on Tramway Boulevard.) Turn east on Simms Park Road and go 1.5 miles to the fee station at Elena Gallegos Picnic Area/Albert G. Simms Park. Take a hard left around the station, toward the Kiwanis Reservation Area. At the end of this 0.3-mile drive, just past the reservation area, is the Cottonwood Springs Trail parking area.

GPS Trailhead Coordinates

UTM Zone (WGS 84) 13S
Easting 0365866
Northing 3892430
Latitude 35° 9' 57"
Longitude 106° 28' 22"

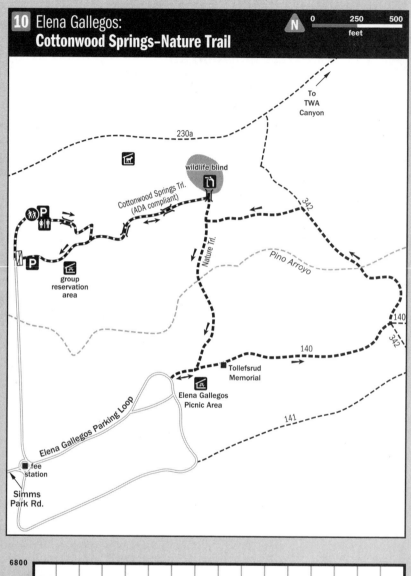

10 Elena Gallegos:
Cottonwood Springs–Nature Trail

N

0   250   500
feet

To
TWA
Canyon

230a

wildlife blind

Cottonwood Springs Trl.
(ADA compliant)

342

Nature Trl.

Pino Arroyo

140

342

group
reservation
area

140

Tollefsrud
Memorial

Elena Gallegos
Picnic Area

141

Elena Gallegos Parking Loop

fee
station

Simms
Park Rd.

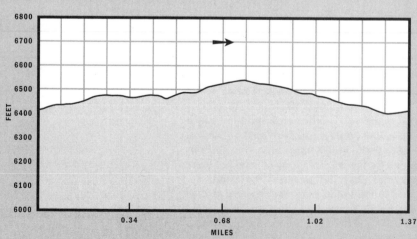

Pino Arroyo in a good monsoon season

name of Elena Gallegos today is an 11-acre picnic area in Albert G. Simms Park. But most people who are familiar with this 640-acre city park refer to it by the more lyrical name, Elena Gallegos.

Situated in a buffer zone between pricey suburban developments and Sandia Mountain Wilderness, the popular recreation area often rumbles with equestrians and mountain bikes. By contrast, the 0.25-mile **Cottonwood Springs Trail** leads through a relatively quiet corner of the park. Created in response to the Americans with Disabilities Act and dedicated in April 2000, the trail has since been nurtured into a secret garden of sorts.

A broad cement walkway, tinted to match the pinkish shades of desert rock, leads to a wooden bridge over a (usually) dry wash. Thick stands of juniper thrive on both sides despite the scarcity of water. A latilla shelter on the far side of the bridge shades the first of six interpretive stations. Each is a work of art, with sculptural steel and ceramic tiles illustrating snippets of information on local geology, cultural history, and ecology. The one on the first bridge highlights a few animals that share the Sandia habitat. A more complete list would include 200 bird, 34 mammal, and 23 snake and lizard species.

The path takes two sharp curves to avoid too steep a grade within the first 400 feet. Landscaping details along the trail blend seamlessly into these natural surroundings. Gravel accents keep wildflowers from spilling over the pavement. Globemallow and verbena flourish with the slightest summer rain, painting the Upper Sonoran life zone with splashes of orange, yellow, red, and lavender.

A bridge and shelter on Cottonwood Spring Trail

At the intersection ahead, a right turn would take you to the Kiwanis Reservation Area, worth exploring later. For now, turn left and continue to the next bridge. Halfway across, another interpretive station sums up 12,000 years of local human habitation in 66 words. As you cross the bridge, a corral comes into better view, a remnant of the last days of ranching in the Sandia foothills. Directly behind it, the mountains gain 4,000 feet in less than 3 miles.

The paved walkway ends at a wire fence surrounding a protected wildlife area. To the left, a bridge extends to a shaded wildlife blind overlooking a cattail pond. The Kiwanis Club of Albuquerque installed a plastic lining in 1992 to extend the seasonal life of a spring-fed watering hole for deer, mountain lions, and other creatures you probably won't see here. Note, however, that frogs seem to emerge from the signage. These and other relief designs in the tiles are textural enhancements for visitors with visual limitations.

Cottonwood Spring Trail ends here, but the hike continues. Cross back over the bridge and go straight up the **Nature Trail,** a 0.8-mile loop that begins as a gravel path along the fence. At the top of the hill, a post points the way to Domingo Baca Canyon. That path is part of your return route, so continue straight past it. A slight descent ahead takes you down into the Pino Arroyo. In the monsoon season, you may need to detour upstream for an easier crossing point.

The grounds on the south side of the arroyo are by far the most popular, as evidenced by the increasing number of worn footpaths. You may find yourself at a loss when you reach the point where the trail splits in seven or eight directions. At least three lead to the main parking lot, about 40 yards to your right. It's worth the short detour for commanding views of the city.

The Nature Trail turns east, overlapping **Pino Trail** (140). This segment begins as pebbled asphalt aggregate but soon gives way to crusher fines as it approaches the Philip B. Tollefsrud Memorial, which is often misidentified as the Five Stones of Elena Gallegos. The first of these prominent boulders is inlaid with 38 copper rods, one for each year in the short life of the conservationist Phil Tollefsrud. The remaining four bear symbols to represent the aspects of nature he treasured.

Pino Trail continues through the memorial and gains nearly 2,800 feet in elevation in 4.7 miles before ending at the Crest Trail (130). For this hike, however, it's only another 200 yards or so before you switch to **Trail 342.** You'll find it at the fence posts ahead. Turn left, following a sign indicating the direction of the Nature Trail. This is the only segment of the Nature Trail that permits bicycles and horses, so keep your head up for high-speed riders. Smaller paths appear on either side, but stay on this broad trail as it curves back around to the Pino Arroyo.

Trail 342 connects Pino Trail to the Domingo Baca Route (230). The latter leads into the aforementioned canyon, now better known as TWA Canyon for the airliner that crashed there in 1955. The 7-mile round-trip hike to the crash site is one of the most arduous in the Sandias, and yet visitors enticed by the spectacle of plane wreckage have made it among the most popular.

The trail soon crests at a hilltop, providing one of the most expansive views in the park. Aging signage and more fence posts on the left indicate your next turn. Follow the Nature Trail alongside the protected wildlife area. On hot days, a stand of mature cottonwoods seems to beckon from beyond the fence. Fortunately, the next shade shelter is just around the corner; a right turn at the end of this brief segment leads you back to the wildlife blind.

Follow the paved trail back to your car by taking the right fork ahead—or you can detour straight into the Kiwanis Reservation Area for a quick inspection of its handsome facilities. Exit through the parking lot, and turn right on the road. Cottonwood Springs Trail parking area is right around the corner. Approach quietly and you may likely spot more wildlife here than anywhere on the trail.

Note: A trail map can be acquired from the fee station, or you can download it online. For information on guided hikes, educational programs, and volunteer opportunities offered throughout the year, call Albuquerque's Open Space Division at (505) 452-5210 or visit them at **cabq.gov/openspace/elenagallegos.**

NEARBY ACTIVITIES

The park's information center is tiny but worth a stop for an exhibit that clarifies the many complexities of the Elena Gallegos Land Grant. It keeps the same hours as the park, but it's open only when a park official happens to be there. Your best chance at finding one present is between 9 a.m. and 4:30 p.m.

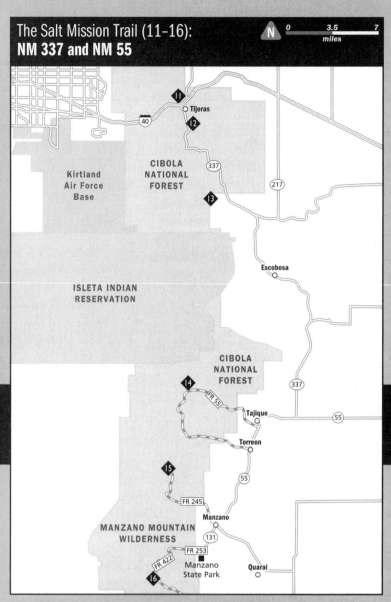

The Salt Mission Trail (11–16): NM 337 and NM 55

N

0   3.5   7
miles

Tijeras

40

CIBOLA NATIONAL FOREST

337

217

Kirtland Air Force Base

Escobosa

ISLETA INDIAN RESERVATION

CIBOLA NATIONAL FOREST

337

55

FR 55

Tajique

Torreon

55

FR 245

Manzano

131

MANZANO MOUNTAIN WILDERNESS

FR 253

FR 422

Manzano State Park

Quarai

THE SALT MISSION TRAIL

11 CANYON ESTATES-FAULTY TRAILS

KEY AT-A-GLANCE INFORMATION

LENGTH: 5.7-mile balloon

DIFFICULTY: Moderate

SCENERY: Travertine grotto, waterfall, seasonal wildflowers, wooded canyons

EXPOSURE: Mostly shaded

TRAIL TRAFFIC: Popular

SHARED USE: Low (closed to equestrians and all vehicles)

TRAIL SURFACE: Packed dirt, rock

HIKING TIME: 2–3 hours

DRIVING DISTANCE: 15 miles (one way) from the I-40 and I-25 exchange

ACCESS: Year-round

LAND STATUS: Cibola National Forest–Sandia Mountain Wilderness

MAPS: Sandia Ranger District; USGS Tijeras

FACILITIES: None

LAST CHANCE FOOD/GAS: All services at Exit 167 (Tramway Boulevard and Central Avenue)

IN BRIEF

Well-marked trails just minutes east of Albuquerque are perfect for casual hikes most of the year. A short stroll up Hondo Canyon leads to a waterfall spilling over a travertine formation. Continue up the Crest Trail to join the Faulty trails for a pennant-shaped loop on gentle terrain through cool pine wilderness.

DESCRIPTION

It's a fact that complicates the organizational scheme of this book: Nearly every hike somehow connects to at least one of the many convoluted routes of old 66. Likewise, the Hondo Canyon's proximity to post-1936 Route 66 is hard to miss. What's more, this hike begins on the Crest Trail (130), which in some ways is similar to the mother road. To riff on Steinbeck: hikers come into 130 from the tributary trails, from the canyon corridors, and the rutted forest roads. They beat paths directly from nearby parking lots and their own backyards in their flight to 130, the mother trail.

In short, hike any Sandia Mountain pathway long enough, and you'll eventually arrive on 130. The Crest Trail runs 26 miles to span the length of the range. It's the connecting leg between Cañoncito Trail and Bart's Trail

GPS Trailhead Coordinates

UTM Zone (WGS 84) 13S

Easting 0373164

Northing 3883867

Latitude 35° 05' 23"

Longitude 106° 23' 29"

Directions ———————→

From I-40 east, take Exit 175 and aim for Tijeras, but turn left *before* you reach the traffic light at the bottom of the ramp. Drive north under the interstate and bear right on Arrowhead Trail ahead. Follow it 0.6 miles to its end at the Canyon Estates trailhead. The hike begins on the west side of the parking circle.

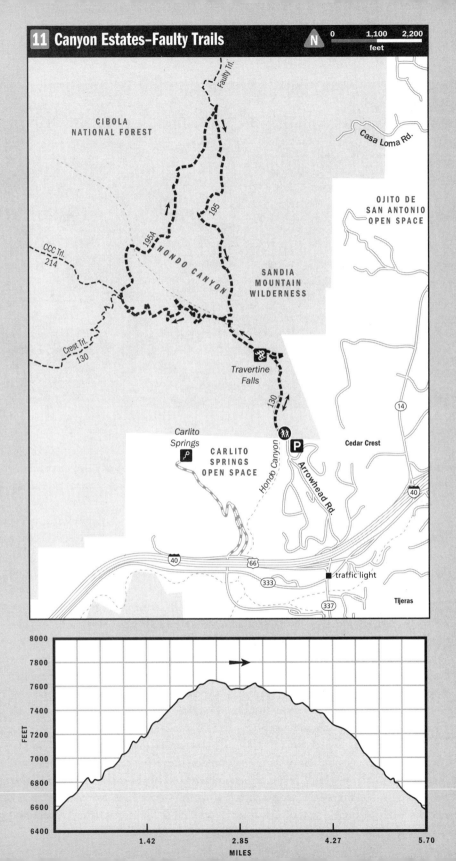

N

0   1,100   2,200
feet

Faulty Trl.

CIBOLA
NATIONAL FOREST

Casa Loma Rd.

OJITO DE
SAN ANTONIO
OPEN SPACE

195

195A

HONDO CANYON

CCC Trl.
214

SANDIA
MOUNTAIN
WILDERNESS

Crest Trl.
130

Travertine
Falls

130

14

Carlito
Springs

CARLITO
SPRINGS
OPEN SPACE

Hondo Canyon

130

Cedar Crest

P

Arrowhead Rd.

40

40

66

333

traffic light

337

Tijeras

8000

7800

7600

7400

7200

FEET

7000

6800

6600

6400

1.42   2.85   4.27   5.70

MILES

Travertine grotto and falls

in hike 17, and it is the extension from Tree Spring Trail to the upper tramway terminal in hike 18; its northernmost end makes up the bulk of the hike from Tunnel Spring in hike 23.

A signboard should illustrate all of that at the Canyon Estates trailhead; but at last check, it had been stripped of several important details, including the map. A sign posted ahead indicates distances to Sandia Spring (5 miles) and Sandia Crest (16 miles). The three trails used on this hike are well marked with wooden posts and blazes at every turn; carefully placed rocks, logs, and limbs help keep you from wandering down countless informal paths and short-cuts between switchbacks. The extra maintenance simplifies navigation. You can help further by sticking to designated trails.

The hike begins alongside a mostly dry creek, which you'll cross a few times throughout the route. The lower trail lacks shade, but tree cover increases intermittently as you gain elevation. It also passes in the shadow of a stone cliff that seems ideal for impromptu climbing practice, provided you don't cause any rocks to fall on hikers below.

Less than 0.4 miles up the trail, a post marks the 100-yard spur to the travertine falls. A popular destination among mini-hikers, the falls are situated in an alcove. By late spring, it becomes a cool green oasis, thanks in large part to box elder and its little twin, poison ivy. The falls are usually just a trickle, but through eons of depositing dissolved limestone, they've created impressive travertine grottos. A cruciform etched at the cave entrance appears to be the handiwork of modern teen Goths, though local lore suggests that it's a centuries-old display of Franciscan devotion.

From the falls, return to the Crest Trail and continue uphill on the designated switchback. A vista opens to the south, across Tijeras Canyon, to reveal the industrial side of the Manzanita Mountains. Although it may not be the view you'd hope for in a national forest, the factory and quarries you see there meet up to 80 percent of Albuquerque's demand for cement. This mountainside blight passes out of view as you approach the top of the waterfall. Farther ahead on the right, several worn paths lead down to the shaded stream that feeds the falls. Stick to the main trail, following rectangular blazes in the trees.

One mile into the hike, you will arrive at the junction with Faulty Trail (195), so named because it roughly follows a fracture in the Earth's crust known as the Flatiron Fault. You'll use this trail on the return route, so stay on 130 for now. The south end of Upper Faulty Trail is another 0.5 miles up, but multiple switchbacks more than double the hiking distance. With an elevation gain of 600 feet, this segment is the most strenuous mile in the hike.

When you reach the clearing at the top, take a breather, and consider this optional detour: as indicated by the marker, the Crest Trail continues to the west. It turns north to meet Embudito Trail (192) at a junction 4.1 miles ahead. Also, although there's no indication of it here at the clearing, the seldom-used CCC Trail (214) starts nearby to the northwest on a more direct 1.8-mile route to the same junction. From there, a short spur leads to South Sandia Peak. Anyone bent on bagging it can set off in either direction, but take a detailed map and be advised of the 1,200-foot elevation gain.

To stick with this more relaxing route, head north past the enormous cairn on Upper Faulty Trail. This 1.3-mile segment gently undulates between 7,540 and 7,650 feet, where ponderosa, oak, and Rocky Mountain juniper flourish. Much of this trail is a quiet walk on a bed of pine needles.

The post marking the junction with Faulty Trail stands 3.5 miles into the hike (not counting the detour to South Sandia Peak). You can pad on a few easy miles by continuing north along the shaded Faulty Trail and returning to this point at your leisure or you can pull a U-turn now to head south on Faulty Trail, back down to the Crest Trail. This segment is not quite as flat as the one above. Turn a rocky corner ahead, and you'll find yourself even with the tops of trees growing from the canyon below. The trail drops to the bottom and quickly climbs out the other side. The mile that follows is a fairly tame descent that ends with a stunning view over Hondo Canyon. If the reason for the name hasn't already become apparent, it should be now—*Hondo* is Spanish for "deep." The remaining bit of Faulty Trail proves to be the most challenging. It's steep, with plenty of loose rock to test your balance. Take it slowly. When you reach the Crest Trail below, turn left, and backtrack 1 mile to the trailhead.

Landscape detail along the Faulty Trail

NEARBY ACTIVITIES

The gated 177-acre site now known as Carlito Springs formerly served as an ancestral Puebloan camp, a stagecoach stop, a Union veteran's homestead, and a tuberculosis sanitarium. It features spring-fed ponds, lush riparian habitats, and ornamental gardens and orchards planted by previous owners. Onsite buildings include a historic house made of travertine, and a stone cabin dating to 1894. To get there, drive back toward Tijeras, and turn right (west) at the traffic light onto NM 333 (Historic Route 66). Drive about 0.5 miles, and turn right (north) onto Carlito Springs Road. Follow the road less than 1 mile to Carlito Springs. Site development is an ongoing project for Bernalillo County Open Space, so check with them before you go by calling (505) 314-0401 or logging on to **www .bernco.gov/live/departments.asp?dept=3946.**

CHAMISOSO CANYON

IN BRIEF

Multiple designated trails, informal paths, and forest roads add up to innumerable hiking routes through this quickly accessible eastern mountain area of Cibola National Forest. The description below spells out three options from one major fork on Chamisoso Trail.

DESCRIPTION

Inadvertently or not, early Spaniards in New Mexico went through a spell of naming mountain ranges after red things—apples, watermelons, the blood of Christ. In "Manzanita," the diminutive suffix (-ita) refers to the size of the mountains, not apples (manzanas). The Manzanita Mountains are smaller versions of the Manzano Mountains to the immediate south, which supposedly took their name from apple orchards cultivated by Franciscan friars in the 1600s. However, it's possible that the smaller range has nothing to do with apples but instead refers to an alternate meaning of *manzanita:* "a lode of gold-bearing quartz." These mountains were once thought to be full of precious minerals, though centuries of mining unearthed few substantial deposits.

The southern tip of the Sandia Ranger District, which extends into the Manzanita Mountains, contains enough designated and informal trails for extensive wandering.

KEY AT-A-GLANCE INFORMATION

LENGTH: Loop options ranging from 5–6.5 miles
DIFFICULTY: Easy to moderate
SCENERY: Canyon trails, elevated forest roads, classic piñon–juniper country with pockets of wavyleaf oak
EXPOSURE: Some canyon and forest shade
TRAIL TRAFFIC: Light to moderate
SHARED USE: Moderate (equestrians, mountain biking; limited motor vehicle access)
TRAIL SURFACE: Dirt roads and trails, rocky arroyos
HIKING TIME: 2–3 hours
DRIVING DISTANCE: 16 miles (one way) from the I-40/I-25 exchange
ACCESS: Year-round
LAND STATUS: Cibola National Forest
MAPS: Sandia Ranger District; USGS Tijeras and Sedillo
FACILITIES: Drinking water at Sandia Ranger Station, located on the east side of NM 337, 0.5 miles south of I-40 (or 0.8 miles north of the trailhead). Consider stopping in for maps and updates on current trail conditions.
LAST CHANCE FOOD/GAS: All services at Exit 167 (Tramway Boulevard and Central Avenue), fast food (Subway) in Tijeras

Directions

From I-40 east, take Exit 175 south to Tijeras. Go south 1.3 miles (or 0.8 miles past the ranger station) on NM 337. Turn left on Chamisoso Canyon Road (Forest Road 462), and park in the dirt lot on the right. The trail starts about 150 yards farther up the road.

GPS Trailhead Coordinates

UTM Zone (WGS 84) 13S
Easting 0374267
Northing 3880834
Latitude 35° 03' 45"
Longitude 106° 22' 44"

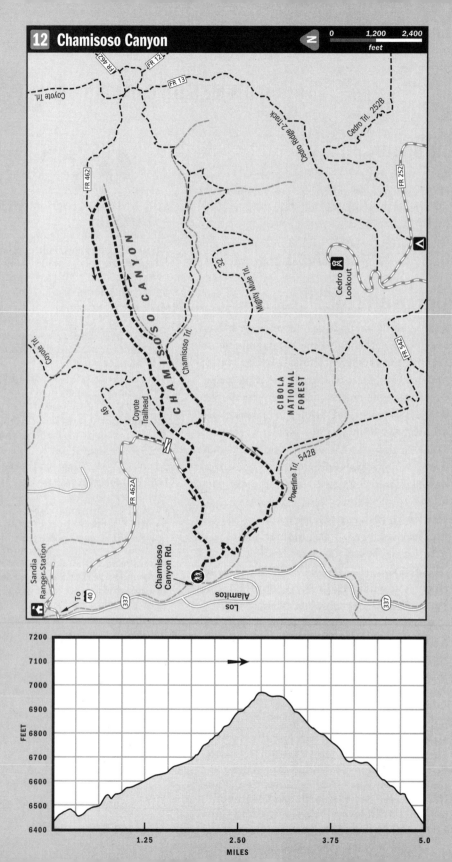

Antler lichen with fruiting bodies

Factoring in a few rugged forest roads, a thorough exploration of the network could take several days, if not weeks. In their rush for the bigger hills on the west side of NM 337, many hikers head straight for trails like Tunnel Canyon. However, most of the Manzanita trails lie within larger public-land tracts on the east side of NM 337, with Cedro Peak standing as the obvious destination. The towers atop this 7,767-foot summit are visible for miles, making it a convenient reference point for hiking in the surrounding areas. A lesser-known area just north of Cedro Peak is Chamisoso Canyon, named for chamiso (saltbush), or chamisa (rabbitbrush). In either case, the suffix (-oso) indicating its abundance throughout the canyon.

Start the hike by walking southeast up Chamisoso Canyon Road (FR 462). Beyond the private driveway on the right, a wooden post marking the Powerline trailhead (542B) stands near the first utility pole on the right. Follow the trail to the south.

Limestone pavements crop up almost immediately on the left. Look closely for marine fossils. Crinoids, animals that are often called sea lilies, are common. Intact stem segments often resemble machine-built objects such as threaded bolts. Fragmented, they look more like puka shells.

After rounding the first bend, the trail splits, with the left branch returning to FR 462. Take the right branch down into the canyon and cross a narrow wash directly beneath the power line. From there, an S-curve leads to a wider arroyo. For the next half mile, the trail aims primarily southeast as it winds in and out of the arroyo. Note the interesting variation in rock features along the way, such as the pocked orange rocks on the left bank and the tilted blocks on the right.

Find the post indicating the Chamisoso trailhead at the point where the power line crosses overhead, and pick up the trail on the left. (Powerline Trail bends around to the right before climbing a steep ridge in a straight line to Sabino Canyon.) Head northeast along Chamisoso Trail, an exposed doubletrack on the right side of the arroyo. About 0.5 miles past the trailhead marker, the trail forks around the point of a small ridge. Stay on Chamisoso Trail by turning right. Note for option 3, below: the left branch climbs north out of the canyon, crossing FR 462 on a 0.4-mile shortcut to Coyote Trail (46).

Chamisoso Trail soon bends back around to the northeast. Stay left on the main doubletrack at the forks within the next 0.1 mile. Within the next 0.5 miles, you'll approach the point of a densely wooded ridge that divides the remainder of the canyon. The trail splits here as well, so get ready to make a decision.

Option 1: On my last hike here, the trails up to this point were a slushy mix of mud and snow. However, the shade of Cedro Peak had preserved most of the snowfall along the right branch ahead, and within moments I found myself sinking to mid-thigh and wishing for snowshoes. Since the right branch is the designated trail, it's usually the easier one to navigate. It snakes along the broad canyon floor, staying close to the main arroyo for about 1 mile before squeezing into an east end of the canyon. From there, multiple paths climb up to FR 13. Mountain bikers often use one of the singletracks coming in from the southeast for kamikaze descents into the canyon.

Although any track or trail running northeast will do, your best exit strategy is via Mighty Mule Trail (32). Near the point where the main arroyo bends southeast, Mighty Mule Trail starts north (to your left) but soon winds east. Within 0.4 miles, it meets FR 13 near the junction of FR 462. Turn left and keep left on forest roads to return to the parking area. Depending on which way you exit the canyon, the right fork will stretch the hike out to a total of 6–6.5 miles.

Option 2: The informal trail along the left branch can be an attractive alternative to the designated trail on the right. I'd avoided it on past hikes because it tends to get choked with brush. Detoured by snow, however, I followed a vague double track to the left, crossed a drainage, and then veered left at the fork just beyond it. It soon narrowed to a path straight up a rocky streambed. Deer paths on higher ground provided a way around downed trees. Uncertain of conditions ahead, I was comforted by the notion that nothing on wheels would likely pass through here (though it appears a Jeep or two made vigorous efforts in the lower section). It's also reassuring to know that access to FR 462 is never more than a five-minute walk up the left side of the canyon, with minimal scrambling on the steeper parts of the slopes.

Less than 0.5 miles up the left branch, the drainage turns left. Continue straight east. The canyon soon widens, exhibiting the spaciousness that characterizes the right branch. From there it's a straight shot across a 0.25-mile clearing to the east end of the canyon. Midway across the clearing, a wide trail runs northwest for less than 0.2 miles to provide the easiest access to FR 462. Turn left on the forest road, and the resulting loop totals 5 miles.

Option 3: All things being equal, hike up one branch and down the other. When you return to the fork, continue back down Chamisoso Trail to the aforementioned shortcut to Coyote Trail. Turn right (north) to climb out of the canyon. Both branches of the Y near the rim lead to FR 462, with the left branch being the shorter of the two. This improvised option, roughly a figure-eight, should come in under 6.5 miles. It's among the first ones I hike as soon as the trails dry out, but your decision may ultimately depend on trail conditions when you visit.

Whichever way you go, head west on FR 462 when you're ready to return to the parking area. It's about 3 miles, mostly downhill, from the junction at FR 13. Vistas along the way are spectacular though occasionally tempered by traffic noise. The upper Salt Mission Trail is popular with bikers, and the thundering flatulence of Harleys with short pipes can resonate to the mountaintops. The relatively soft rumble of semis on I-40 may also detract from an otherwise natural experience. Still, it seems like an even trade-off on days when you need quick access to a national forest. And when you're deep in Chamisoso Canyon, it's easy to forget how close you are to the roads you drove to get there.

NEARBY ACTIVITIES

Visit the Tijeras Pueblo Archaeological Site for self-guided tours of the 14th-century ruins. Excavations from 1948 to 1976 uncovered 200 rooms, though it appears that all but a few have been reburied. The 0.3-mile interpretive trail is nonetheless pleasant and informative. Entered into the National Register of Historic Places in 2005, the site is behind the Sandia Ranger Station in Tijeras. Call (505) 281-3304, or visit **www.fs.fed.us/r3/cibola/districts/sandia.**

13 MARS COURT

 KEY AT-A-GLANCE INFORMATION

LENGTH: 4.7- to 8.2-mile loop options
DIFFICULTY: Easy to moderate, with some short but strenuous climbs
SCENERY: Forested ridges, meadows, abundant birdlife, wildflowers
EXPOSURE: Half shade
TRAIL TRAFFIC: Light to moderate
SHARED USE: Moderate (mountain bikes, equestrians; limited motor-vehicle access)
TRAIL SURFACE: Dirt roads, rocky trails
HIKING TIME: 3–5 hours
DRIVING DISTANCE: 25 miles (one way) from the I-40/I-25 exchange
ACCESS: Year-round
LAND STATUS: Cibola National Forest
MAPS: Sandia Ranger District; USGS Escabosa
FACILITIES: Maps posted on trail
LAST CHANCE FOOD/GAS: Small grocery and café on NM 337, 0.8 miles south of Raven Road; nearest gas station on NM 14 in Cedar Crest, about 4 miles north of Tijeras
SPECIAL COMMENTS: Sandia Ranger Station is located on the left side of NM 337, 0.5 miles south of I-40. Consider stopping in for maps and updates on current trail conditions.

IN BRIEF

Tucked away in a far corner of the Manzanita Mountains, a well-marked network of single-track and former logging roads winds across canyon meadows and forested ridges. Though the trails are easily accessible from a residential area, views from high points give the illusion of deep wilderness surroundings.

DESCRIPTION

For those driving south on the Salt Mission Trail, Mars Court is a final chance to hike in the Sandia Ranger District. Pass it by, and you won't be able to access Cibola National Forest for another 25 miles. Though Manzanita Mountains and the Manzano Mountains appear to be in a continuous north–south trending range, the Manzanitas are a separate subrange. For hiking purposes, the two ranges may as well be 20 miles apart, with Isleta Pueblo accounting for most of the buffer zone between them.

Contiguous military properties further restrict access to most of the Manzanitas. In the not-too-distant past, hikers in nearby Otero Canyon regularly strolled past No Trespassing signs inexplicably posted deep in the woods. In recent years, however, the

GPS Trailhead
Coordinates
UTM Zone (WGS 84) 13S
Easting   0376813
Northing 3872090
Latitude   34° 59' 02"
Longitude 106° 20' 59"

Directions

From I-40 east, take Exit 175 south to Tijeras. Go 8.8 miles south on NM 337. Turn right on Raven Road and follow it 1.6 miles. Turn right on Mars Court. Drive about 200 feet, through the open gateway, and park along the loop before the second gate. The trailhead is next to the first gate.

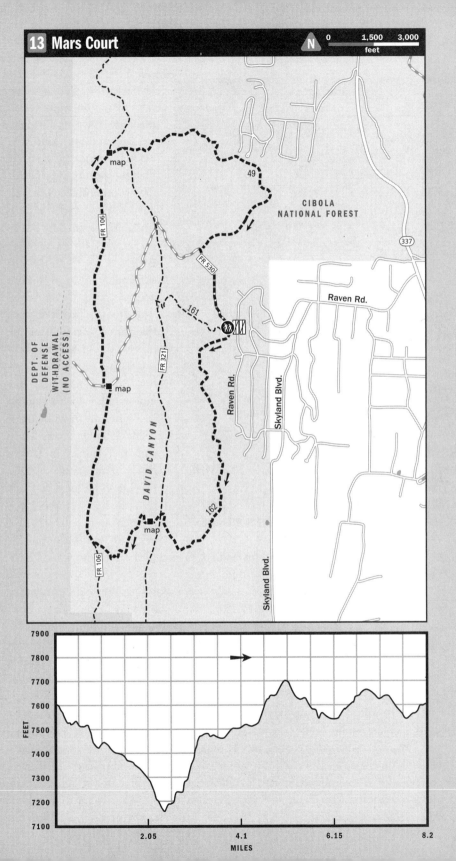

0 1,500 3,000
feet

N

CIBOLA
NATIONAL FOREST

49

337

Raven Rd.

161

FR 530

FR 106

DEPT. OF
DEFENSE
WITHDRAWAL
(NO ACCESS)

FR 321

Raven Rd.

Skyland Blvd.

map

map

DAVID CANYON

162

map

FR 106

Skyland Blvd.

Department of Defense upgraded the signs with unsubtle warnings regarding live ammunition. Hikers who ignored the new postings wound up in court, facing potential six-month jail terms and $5,000 fines. In the ensuing battle for Otero Canyon, the U.S. Air Force seems unlikely to surrender to local hiking activists.

Otero Canyon was the primary destination for hikers and mountain bikers at this end of the Sandia Ranger District, but motorized vehicles tended to dominate the tangle of roads leading from Mars Court. "Drunks in trucks stuck in the mud" is how one longtime local resident described the scenery back then. Recent rehabilitation projects now keep motor-vehicle access to a minimum, and myriad roads blazed through the woods have been reduced to a simplified trail system.

That same local resident describes the scenery now as consisting of "more birds and wildflowers" than she can name. And she could name quite a few, including Mexican squawroot, silvery lupine, the ubiquitous Indian paintbrush, and several types of fern and yucca growing side by side. Gray flycatcher, black-throated gray warbler, and vesper sparrow thrive in the Manzanitas but are rare in the neighboring Sandias. Wild turkey, recently introduced to the Manzanos, now occasionally turn up in the Manzanitas.

The 14-mile Mars Court trail system is basically confined along a stretch of David Canyon about 3 miles long and less than 1 mile wide. Military property flanks the west side, the expanding Tranquillo Pine residential developments encroach on the east, and the reservation cuts off the southern end of the canyon. Yet a hike here approximates the wilderness experience of any backcountry forest—minus the long drive up rugged access roads. More bears than hikers wander the area, judging by tracks along the trail. But the predominant species here seems to be a rare breed of mountain biker, one who contributes to the meticulous maintenance and extensive trail work in the area.

This hike relies primarily on Trail 162, a stretch of FR 106, Trail 49, and a bit of FR 530 for an 8.2-mile loop. As the map indicates, several shorter and longer variations are possible.

Trails 161 and 162 both begin at their respective markers next to the first gate. Trail 161 takes a more direct route into the upper canyon, whereas 162 gradually sinks to the south. Follow 162 as it starts out as a narrow, rocky single-track. It becomes more defined as it enters denser woods. A lush mix of pine and broadleaf shade the path. A break in the trees before the first steep decline offers a glimpse of the forested mountains to the south.

A couple of paths split off at the edge of the cutting-unit boundary, but the main trail is clear. Strategically placed rocks and branches help keep you from straying in the wrong direction, and a post marked "T 162" appears within the first mile. Just ahead, a fading road approaches from the right, and it seems you've reached the canyon floor. Not quite—after a short climb, the trail descends for another mile to the south–southwest, passing a second marker, and then drops for 0.25 miles to the northwest. The canyon floor comes into view as you approach the final switchback. This long, grassy meadow seems more of a narrow valley than a canyon in the traditional Southwestern sense.

A map posted at the crossroads ahead illustrates your route options from here. As you look it over, keep this mind: You're 2.4 miles into the hike, and so far it's been easy. But you've lost more than 450 feet in elevation. So no matter which way you go from here, you've got some climbing ahead of you.

FR 321 (FR 335 on other maps) runs the length of the floor, north to south. A left turn here would take you 1 mile down to the Isleta boundary. It's a pleasant detour along a distinct road that becomes more shaded as the canyon sinks deeper. A fence and signage leave little doubt as to where you must turn around.

To shorten this hike and skip its steepest climbs, turn right on FR 321 and hike north about 1.6 miles to Trail 161. Take another right turn there, and it's a steep 0.7-mile push back to the gate. Or go north 2 miles to FR 530, and then turn right for a more gradual mile-long ascent to the gate. Or go north 2.5 miles to rejoin this hike at the western end of Trail 49.

This hike continues on Trail 162, now named Turkey Trot. It's a 0.8-mile climb to the west rim of David Canyon, about 300 feet above your current elevation. This final segment of 162 is rocky and strenuous but scenic and well shaded. A marker at the top tells you when you've reached FR 106.

The junction of Trail 162 and FR 106 offers limited choices. A detour to the left ends 0.5 miles down at a multitude of signs reading: DANGER UNMARKED UNEXPLODED ORDNANCE AREA and PELIGRO AREA DE BOMBAS INEXPLOTADAS. (It goes on like that.) So unless you need to practice Spanish for military situations, turn right on FR 106 and follow it north. As long as you don't stray down any roads on your left, you won't detect a hint of the U.S. Air Force installation to the immediate west.

The next junction, FR 530, is 1.3 miles ahead. An oversized panel here bears the cryptic message: LEAVING WILDING AREA on one side and ENTERING WILDING AREA on the other. A road barrier and another marker with a trail map also stand nearby. Again, you can turn right for shortcut options. Or to stick to this hike, turn left, and then make a quick right up a steep, rocky road. This ridgeline route is only half the climb of Turkey Trot but somehow takes twice the effort.

The view is your incentive. Aside from a few rooftops poking through the crowns on the east side of David Canyon, it's an uninterrupted vista of forested mountains and canyons on all horizons. Clear across the Isleta Reservation, the twin peaks of Guadalupe and Mosca stand 12 miles to the south–southwest. (You can visit Mosca Peak on the next hike, Fourth of July Canyon–Cerro Blanco.) Just 8 miles to the northwest and covering the next 180 square miles, Albuquerque is nowhere to be seen.

The road tops out at 7,700 feet and then gradually descends 1 mile to the next posted map. From this junction, FR 106 and Trail 236 head north to connect with trails originating from the Otero Canyon trailhead. To stay on this hike, turn right on FR 321. A singletrack soon splits off to the right, only to rejoin 321 near the head of Trail 49 about 0.25 miles downhill.

You could stay on 321 and drop back down into David Canyon and then climb out the other side on 530. Or to stay on this hike, hook around the head of the canyon by starting east on Trail 49. The latter option involves less climbing, but it's about 0.5 miles longer. Dubbed the Cajun Pine, Trail 49 is the least developed in the Mars Court network, so you'll need to pay special attention to the trail. This narrow pathway winds through scrub in a burn zone, where clearings afford final glimpses of the mountains to the south.

The 1.7-mile Cajun Pine ends at FR 530. Turn left on this prominent road, and go uphill 0.4 miles back to the parking area. Or if you need to put in a few more miles, cross the road and start on a new trail, Cajun Turk. Its destination is as much a mystery to me as the rationale that goes into naming these trails.

FOURTH OF JULY CANYON– CERRO BLANCO **14**

IN BRIEF

Crowds turn out each autumn to gawk at leaves, but you can find solitude here throughout most of the year. Meander along established trails from a popular picnic area to the crest of the Manzano Mountains. Clearings on the ridgeline reveal vistas that seem to stretch halfway to the next state.

DESCRIPTION

New Mexico is blessed with two Fourth of July canyons. One is on the border of Colfax and Taos counties, while the more famous one is in Torrance County. Each fall, hikers mob the latter's trails to witness a pyrotechnic display of foliage. This Fourth of July Canyon contains concentrations of bigtooth and Rocky Mountain maples to rival any autumnal clump in New England.

If the crowds are too dense, take heart in the fact that most will turn back within the first mile and won't return for another year because what they don't seem to understand is that the trails are just as colorful in other seasons.

Directions ➤

From I-40, take Exit 175 to Tijeras. Follow NM 337 south 29 miles to the T-junction with NM 55. Turn right, going west 3.2 miles on NM 55 to Tajique. Turn right on FR 55 (also marked as A013) and follow the signs to the Fourth of July Campground, 7 miles up the dirt-and-gravel road. Turn right through the gate, and park in the hiker parking area. Note that the gate is locked November–March. If arriving then, park at the gate and walk up toward the campground. The trailhead is on the left, about 400 feet past the gate.

KEY AT-A-GLANCE INFORMATION

LENGTH: 6.4-mile loop and spur
DIFFICULTY: Moderate
SCENERY: Seasonal wildflowers and foliage, wooded canyons, eastern and western vistas
EXPOSURE: Mostly shaded
TRAIL TRAFFIC: Popular
SHARED USED: Low (livestock; limited equestrian and mountain bike access; no motor vehicles)
TRAIL SURFACE: Gravel forest roads, dirt trails
HIKING TIME: 3–4 hours
DRIVING DISTANCE: 54 miles (one way) from the I-40 and I-25 exchange
ACCESS: Year-round
LAND STATUS: Cibola National Forest
MAPS: Mountainair Ranger District–Manzano Division; Manzano Mountain Wilderness–North Half; USGS Bosque Peak
FACILITIES: Campsites (April–October), picnic area, and restrooms (no water). Facilities are wheelchair-accessible.
LAST CHANCE FOOD/GAS: Ray's One Stop in Tajique
SPECIAL COMMENTS: Information: Mountainair Ranger District, (505) 847-2990; www.fs.fed.us/r3/cibola/districts/mountainair.

GPS Trailhead
Coordinates
UTM Zone (WGS 84) 13S
Easting 0373795
Northing 3850606
Latitude 34° 47' 24"
Longitude 106° 22' 46"

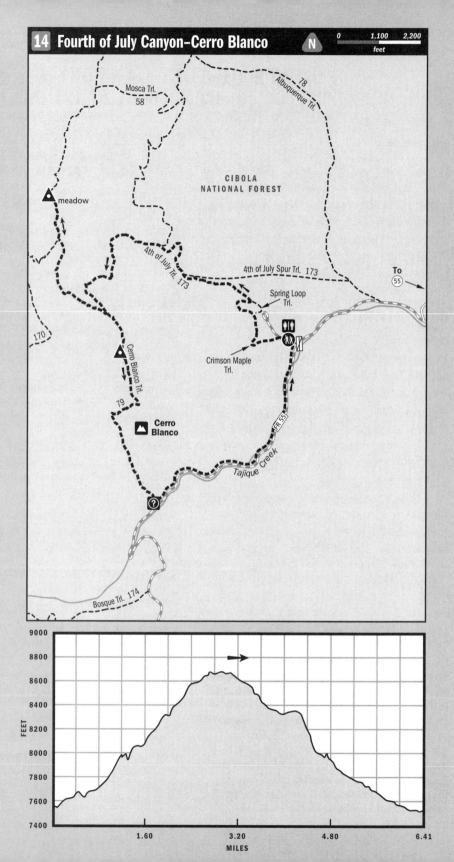

Spring and summer bring neotropical migrants—Central and South American birds of brilliant plumage, such as orange-crowned warblers. Dense clusters of seep-spring monkeyflowers bloom from March to October. Like snapdragons, they can be manipulated to resemble their namesake. A healthy population of Abert's squirrels stays active year-round. Named after the U.S. Army lieutenant who catalogued them during a New Mexico expedition in the 1840s, these tassel-eared arboreal rodents were released into the Manzano Mountains in 1929 and have since thrived here.

Hikers can choose from multiple loop options to explore the area. No two maps agree exactly on where all these trails go. So although the route described below is fairly simple, keep in mind that, like many forest service trails, the designated ways are subject to alteration.

Start your hike with a detour along Crimson Maple Trail. Whether you parked at the gate or in the hiker parking area, the trailhead begins a short way up the gravel road, at the picnic area on the near side of the first restrooms. A prominent sign along the way maps out the trails in the campground area. Just beyond that, another sign indicates where to turn left for Crimson Maple Trail.

A green box at the northwest corner of the picnic area contains brochures with interpretive text corresponding to the 11 numbered stations ahead. Unless you're already well versed in the history and ecology of the Manzano Mountains, this enlightening detour is worth the extra 15 minutes.

Follow numbered signs 1–8 to the end of Crimson Maple Trail, and then turn right on Spring Loop Trail for signs 9–11. Pick up the **Fourth of July Trail (173)** on the other side of the loop and turn left toward a sheltered bulletin board. If this is your first expedition into the Manzanos, take a moment to review the comprehensive display of data, rules, ethics, maps, hazards, and warnings.

After passing through a gate, note the wooden sign pointing ways and distances to nearby trails. Similar signs have been positioned along trails throughout the Manzanos. However, black bears seem bent on destroying them, so don't be surprised if any are missing or defaced beyond legibility.

The next sign indicates the trailhead on the right for the Fourth of July Trail Spur, a 1-mile link to the Albuquerque Trail (78). Continue straight, and cross through a pedestrian gateway ahead.

The trail splits around the Upper Fourth of July Spring within the next 500 feet. A sign seems to be missing here. Some hikers slog straight up the streambed, but a drier trail climbs to the right. Massive alligator junipers tower over the trail as it nears an elevation of 8,000 feet. Yucca and cacti persist on the south-facing slopes, while old-growth maples prefer the damp canyon below.

The trail drops back down just upstream of a round trough. Signage in view ahead marks the eastern edge of the Manzano Mountain Wilderness, as indicated by the icons that forbid bicycles and mopeds beyond this point. (For reference, a sharp right here would put you on a 3.5-mile course back to FR 55 via the Albuquerque Trail.)

Continue straight to the end of the Fourth of July Trail, 0.6 miles ahead. Pine needles soften the path as it climbs up steadily into mixed-conifer forest. Icy patches can linger here for weeks after an early-autumn snow. As the trail seems to level out, crossing through rocky outcroppings, the crest comes into view above. These absorbent limestone bands allow rainwater to sink into the mountain and seep out through the canyons below to support the diverse vegetation.

Signage at the T-junction with **Cerro Blanco Trail (79)** indicates that FR 55 is 1 mile to your left, the Crest Trail is 0.5 miles to your right, and the Fourth of July Campground is 1.5 miles back the way you came. But if you followed this hiking route, including the nature trails, you've done a solid 2-plus miles so far.

Turn right to pick up the **Crest Trail (170)** 0.5 miles ahead, and then turn right and follow it another 0.25 miles. (A new trail segment splits left along the way but soon rejoins the same trail.) Mosca Peak comes into dramatic view before a meadow, where you might find grazing cattle, opens on the right. Incidentally, bovine encounters on this trail commonly end with panicky cows fleeing into the forest. To fully appreciate a heifer stampede in the upper-mountain forest, you must witness the spectacle yourself.

Thickets of Gambel oak start to squeeze in, narrowing the trail. Press through to the clearing on the other side, and then take a moment to rest on the stone bench and enjoy the view. From nearly 8,700 feet, it appears that the closest major towns are mere specks in the vast Rio Grande Valley. It's more than tempting to gaze until the sun sinks behind Arizona, but there's still the matter of getting off this mountain. (For reference, Ojito Trail [171] drops into the canyon of the same name straight ahead, but it is no longer maintained. The Crest Trail goes less than 1 mile to the east side of Mosca Peak before officially ending at the southern boundary of the Isleta Reservation. From there, the 0.8-mile Mosca Trail [58] links to the Albuquerque Trail.)

To continue on this hike, backtrack to the junction of the Fourth of July and Cerro Blanco trails. From there, continue straight along **Cerro Blanco Trail.** The remaining 1.5-mile descent to FR 55 is a cakewalk. The trail is well established and navigable up to the last flicker of dusk, but some worthwhile landmarks crop up about every 0.25 miles, once you are past the junction.

The first is an opening on the left that reveals an outstanding view of the eastern plains. The second is an unremarkable clearing, except that it precedes a sharp turn and descent to the right, followed by another to the left at a particularly rotund pine. The trail then squeezes between rocky outcrops and looming cliffs as it drops down to a stream that's often flowing. Bear left at the signpost/junction ahead, and you'll soon arrive at FR 55. Turn left, and follow this pleasant creekside road 1.4 miles downhill to the gate at the Fourth of July Campground.

Note: Stop by the Sandia Ranger Station on the east side of NM 337 in Tijeras for maps and other information about the Manzano Mountain trails.

Banana yucca (datil) grows on the canyon rim.

Check with the Mountainair Ranger District for prescribed burns and snow clo-sures; (505) 847-2990; **www.fs.fed.us/r3/cibola/districts/mountainair.**

NEARBY ACTIVITIES

Whether it's from the picnic area barbeque grills or the high-altitude heifers, I always get a craving for steak after this hike. The Ponderosa Steakhouse is just your typical local diner/biker bar, but their steak rellenos plate is an authentic feast. To find the restaurant, look for a log-cabin lodge on NM 337, about 7 miles north of Chilili or 12 miles south of Tijeras. Chowtime is Monday–Friday, 4–9 p.m.; call (505) 281-8278.

15 CAPILLA PEAK

IN BRIEF

Though this high-altitude hike is a cool summer retreat and an exhilarating walk year-round, it's best in early fall, when HawkWatch International offers opportunities for an educational, up-close look at various birds of prey. Contact their Albuquerque office for more details about their programs, (505) 255-7622, www.hawkwatch.org.

DESCRIPTION

HawkWatch International maintains two monitoring sites in Cibola National Forest. The more accessible station is at the southern end of the Sandia Mountains. The other is at the end of Gavilan Trail near Capilla Peak, in the heart of the Manzano Mountain Wilderness. Between the two sites, HawkWatch volunteers have managed to band more than

 KEY AT-A-GLANCE INFORMATION

LENGTH: 2-mile out-and-back, with longer options
DIFFICULTY: Easy
SCENERY: Raptors, fire lookout tower, views over the Rio Grande and Estancia valleys
EXPOSURE: Little shade
TRAIL TRAFFIC: Popular in autumn, otherwise low
SHARED USE: None outside banding season
TRAIL SURFACE: Dirt path, gravel road
HIKING TIME: 1 hour
DRIVING DISTANCE: 65 miles (one way) from the I-40 and I-25 exchange
ACCESS: Trails open year-round, but see Special comments below for information on road closures
LAND STATUS: Cibola National Forest
MAPS: Mountainair Ranger District–Manzano Division; Manzano Mountain Wilderness–North Half; USGS Capilla Peak
FACILITIES: Campground, picnic area, fire grates, restrooms (no water)
LAST CHANCE FOOD/GAS: Convenience store (Tiendita) in Manzano, convenience store and gas station (Ray's One Stop) in Tajique

GPS Trailhead
Coordinates
UTM Zone (WGS 84)   13S
Easting   0371324
Northing   3840538
Latitude   35° 41' 56"
Longitude   106° 24' 18"

Directions

From I-40 east, take Exit 175 to Tijeras. Drive south on NM 337 and NM 55 about 41 miles to Manzano, passing through the villages of Escobosa, Chilili, Tajique, and Torreon. At Manzano, turn right on the dirt road marked BO65, directly across from the adobe church. Stay right; the road becomes FR 245. Follow the signs up to the New Canyon Campground, 5 miles from the church. (If arriving between mid-November and late March, the gate will be locked at this point, but you can walk the remaining 3.8 miles, or avail yourself of the option described in Nearby activities, below.) Continue up to Capilla Peak. Park alongside the metal-pipe fence on the left; the trail begins at a gateway near its southern end. There is additional parking at the far end of the fence, near the gated entrance to the fire lookout tower.

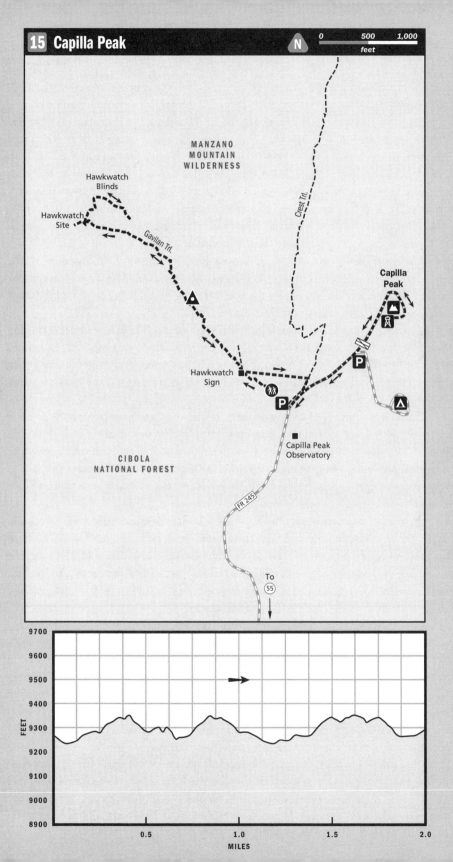

20,000 raptors since 1990. The sites are only 25 miles apart, as the crow flies, but the Capilla Peak site is credited with about 80 percent of the catch and release.

At least 16 species are frequently observed riding the thermals in this strip of the Rocky Mountain Flyway, a migratory route that extends from Veracruz, Mexico, to somewhere up in the Yukon. Sharp-shinned hawks top the list, with nearly 1,500 gliding by each fall. Eagles, falcons, and ospreys also make frequent cameos. Programs run with full-time educators on site each year from February 24 to May 5 at Sandia Spring, and from August 15 to November 5 at Capilla Peak. But even if you miss those windows, a stroll around Capilla Peak is still well worth the harrowing drive up the mountain.

Gavilan Trail begins in an open meadow. Just beyond the opening in the pipe fence is a sign marking the trailhead, but it's about the size of a bumper sticker and difficult to spot from the road. (If you pass a sign the size of a garage door, you're heading north on the Crest Trail.)

Go west into the scrub oak and white fir (though last I looked everything here was painted red, thanks to slightly off-target slurry bombers). Hidden behind the first few stands of trees on your left is a handsome metal sign engraved with raptor images and a statement about the HawkWatch mission. The lookout site is at the end of this 0.6-mile trail.

Standing on the trail with your back to the sign, you'll notice a trail directly in front of you and a fainter one to your left. The former dead-ends around the bend, so climb the rocky slope to your left, and pick up a defined trail at the top. The trail proceeds along a ridge with intermittent views on both sides that are as stunning for their range as for their sheer drop-offs. If you have rambunctious kids in tow, keep them within reach.

A fork to the left along the way soon ends at yet another such overlook, while the trail goes to the right. At the second fork, bear left, and walk out onto an outcrop of the limestone crest. This is the primary lookout, and its vantage is immediately apparent. It's like a grand balcony set 4,000 feet above the valley, cruising altitude for migrating birds of prey, and there's a plastic owl perched upon a 40-foot pole to lure them in even closer.

To reach the next lookout, return to the fork, and turn left. Climb down a rocky passage to a flat area with wildlife blinds. When you're done here, go back the way you came. (A path continuing to the southeast loops back to Gavilan Trail but was closed as of 2007. Do not use it unless it has been reopened.) When you reach the meadow, turn left, and take the shortcut across to the information board. A hop up the berm on the right puts you back on the road.

Capilla Peak (9,368') is about 0.25 miles up the road. The gate is usually locked, but visitors are still welcome to walk up to the fire lookout tower, which is staffed in the summer. Permission to climb the stairs and enter the cab depends on the mood of the fire lookout on duty at the time. If you're lucky, you'll meet Dixie Boyle, who has been spotting fires for the U.S. Forest Service for 25 years. She shares the experience in her history-rich memoir *Between Land & Sky: A Fire Lookout Story* (Outskirt Press, 2007).

A view to the east from Capilla Peak

Whether or not you climb the tower, the views are spectacular in all directions. On the ranchlands 25 miles due east, salt lakes mirror the sky. The big one, Laguna del Perro, is about 12 miles long and 1 mile wide. Pueblo Indians harvested salt from these *salinas* to trade with Plains Indians. Early Spaniards valued salt for its use in extracting silver from its ores. Vying for dominion over the Salinas Province, they established Franciscan missions at three nearby pueblos. Like the plantations that would later come to dominate the American South, these imposing missions fueled fierce discontent. Their ruins at Abó, Quarai, and Gran Quivira now comprise the Salinas Pueblo Missions National Monument. (see Nearby activities below). Incidentally, early Franciscan monks at Quarai are credited for naming this peak *Capilla* ("hood"), possibly for its resemblance to their headwear.

To the southwest, the view stretches beyond the prominent Ladron Peak, clear out to the Bear Mountains, a Cibola National Forest area that is, unfortunately, beyond the scope of this book. And to the immediate southeast is the brilliant pink Capilla Peak Observatory, operated by the Institute for Astrophysics at the University of New Mexico. This research facility is not open to the general public, but you might learn more about its high-tech features if UNM astrophysicists ever discover a way to work the bugs out of their Web site (**www .phys.unm.edu/~cpo/obs.html**).

The Capilla Peak Campground, south of the tower and east of the observatory, is worth a stroll, or at least a drive through before departing the

Capilla Peak Observatory

mountaintop. Originally constructed in the 1930s by the Civilian Conservation Corps, the campground closed in 2003 for major renovations. A reopening ceremony in late 2005 unveiled a stellar eight-unit site that stays true to the CCC's original Adirondack designs. It also remains a popular hangout for black bears.

Note: All trails remain open year-round, but the road closes 3.8 miles short of the trailhead November to April. Also be advised that this last stretch is steep, winding, and narrow. Low clearance and oversized vehicles may have difficulties, particularly in wet weather. Check with the Mountainair Ranger District for conditions, (505) 847-2990, **www.fs.fed.us/r3/cibola/districts/mountainair.**

NEARBY ACTIVITIES

On the return down FR 245, stop at the New Canyon Campground. While it may seem like a ghetto compared to the fancy new shelters above, you might enjoy a shady hike up Cañon de Turrieta, which begins at the north side of the site. New Canyon Trail (101) begins across the road at the green gate and gains 1,000' in 2 miles before linking to the Crest Trail. Forest Service maps rate it as moderate.

The nearest salt mission ruin is at Quarai and is open daily in the summer (Memorial Day to Labor Day) 9 a.m. to 6 p.m. The rest of the year, you can visit 9 a.m. to 5 p.m. Entry is free. To get there from Manzano, drive 5 miles southeast on NM 55. Turn right at Punta de Agua and go west 1 mile. For more information, call (505) 847-2290, or visit **www.nps.gov/sapu.**

KAYSER MILL-PINE SHADOW-COTTONWOOD TRAILS 16

IN BRIEF

Classic wilderness trails wind through forested canyons and mountain meadows. Combined, they create the southernmost loop in the Manzano Mountains and present a variety of options for conquering Manzano Peak, the highest summit in Torrance County.

DESCRIPTION

The hike outlined below runs a counterclockwise loop, starting from the closest access

---

Directions →

From I-40 east, take Exit 175 to Tijeras. Drive south on NM 337 and NM 55 about 41 miles, passing through the villages of Escobosa, Chilili, Tajique, Torreon, and Manzano. On the south side of Manzano, veer right at the fork onto NM 131, following the signs toward Red Canyon. Go 2.4 miles, then turn right before the entrance to Manzano State Park. NM 131 soon becomes Forest Road 253. About 2.5 miles past the Manzano State Park entrance, pass the Red Canyon Picnic Area and continue 3.5 miles straight on FR 422. Just past the junction of FR 275, a sign points the way to the Kayser Mill and Cottonwood trails. You can park on the side of the road to begin the hike here. Or to set up a shuttle at the Pine Shadow trailhead, continue 2.7 miles down the winding FR 422. The parking lot is on the right.

Alternate Route (87 miles): Gates near the Red Canyon Picnic Area and the Cottonwood trailhead are closed November–April. Weather permitting, you can still drive to the Pine Shadow trailhead. From I-25 south, take Exit 175 at Bernardo. Drive 25.6 miles east on US 60. Turn left on FR 422 (Priest Canyon Road) and go north 10 miles. The parking lot at the Pine Shadow trailhead is on the left. The sign for Kayser Mill Trail is another 2.7 miles up the road.

KEY AT-A-GLANCE INFORMATION

LENGTH: 12.3-mile loop or 9.7-mile shuttle

DIFFICULTY: Strenuous

SCENERY: Rockslides, birdwatching, wildlife, wildflowers, forests, meadows, views over the Estancia and Rio Grande valleys

EXPOSURE: Half shade

TRAIL TRAFFIC: Moderate

SHARED USE: Low (trails closed to equestrians, mountain bikes, and all motorized vehicles)

TRAIL SURFACE: Packed dirt, loose rock

HIKING TIME: 7-hour loop or 6-hour shuttle

DRIVING DISTANCE: 65 miles (one way) from the I-40/I-25 exchange

ACCESS: Year-round, weather permitting; note seasonal gate closures in Directions at left

LAND STATUS: Cibola National Forest

MAPS: Mountainair Ranger District–Manzano Division; Manzano Mountain Wilderness–South Half; USGS Manzano Peak

FACILITIES: Restrooms (no water), picnic tables, grills, and corrals at Pine Shadow trailhead.

LAST CHANCE FOOD/GAS: Convenience store in Manzano; convenience store and gas in Tajique.

GPS Trailhead Coordinates

UTM Zone (WGS 84) 13S

Easting   0369660

Northing   3828155

Latitude   34° 35' 13"

Longitude   106° 25' 16"

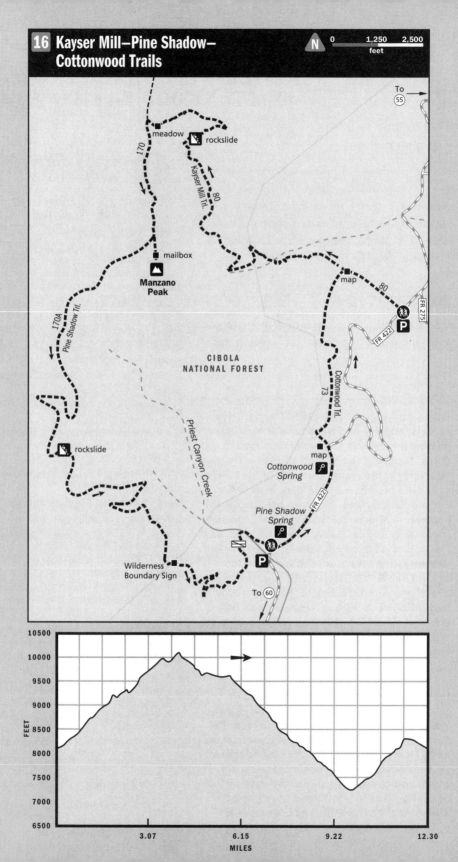

N

0   1,250   2,500
feet

To
55

meadow

rockslide

170

Kayser Mill Trl.

80

mailbox

Manzano Peak

170A

Pine Shadow Trl.

map

80

FR 275

FR 422

CIBOLA NATIONAL FOREST

Cottonwood Trl.

73

P

rockslide

Priest Canyon Creek

map

Cottonwood Spring

Pine Shadow Spring

FR 422

Wilderness Boundary Sign

P

To 60

FEET

10500

10000

9500

9000

8500

8000

7500

7000

6500

3.07   6.15   9.22   12.30

MILES

Rockslide on Kayser Mill Trail

point. However, it is composed of three distinct segments. Read the descriptions for each, and then customize a configuration that best serves your interests. A shuttle hike seems to be the ideal arrangement. Ending your hike at the Pine Shadow trailhead allows for a hard earned après-hike barbeque. The shuttle arrangement also lets you skip the third segment. Though not far from unpleasant, it was unanimously regarded as the least appealing part of the loop.

Lacking two vehicles, however, you'll need to decide whether to embark on an out-and-back or push for the full loop. Seasonal gate closures (November–April) may also limit your choices. But if you still can't make up your mind between a loop and an out-and-back, you can postpone your decision until you reach the peak.

Kayser Mill Trail (80) to Manzano Peak: This 4-mile segment starts from FR 422, at the sign indicating the way to the Kayser Mill and Cottonwood trails. (Some maps show this point as the Kayser Mill trailhead.) Kayser Mill refers to a local lumber operation and the homesteading family who ran it in the 1880s. The trail climbs through the high reaches of spruce and fir. It also tends to vanish under scrub oak. It's not too difficult to stay on track, but it can get prickly for those wearing shorts.

Start by walking 0.4 miles northwest on a rocky road to the northern end of Cottonwood Trail (73). Signs and a trail map stand at this T-junction. Those going for the full loop will be returning here from the south.

The trail soon narrows as it bends west and follows an arroyo up into denser woods. Markers for the wilderness boundary are located on the first switchback ahead. From here the trail aims south about 0.25 miles and then switchbacks north to cross a fork of Kayser Mill Canyon. Along the way you'll catch a glimpse of your goal peaking less than 0.5 miles to the west, and yet you're not quite halfway there.

As you round the corner into the main canyon, views open to the north, revealing a massive rockslide at the head of the canyon. From this perspective it appears as a vertical boulder field, seemingly impassible. Remarkably, the brief passage across is perhaps the easiest part of the hike.

About 0.1 mile past the rockslide, watch for a trail merging on your left. (If you miss it, you'll continue straight into a 0.2-mile loop that is pleasant but completely unnecessary.) Switchback west and stay roughly in that direction until you arrive at an open meadow. Continue another 100 yards or so to the Crest Trail (170). A sign at the junction indicates that Ox Canyon Trail (180) is 1.5 miles to the north. Turn left (south), and follow the Crest Trail about 0.6 miles to the next marker. This small sign indicates that Manzano Peak is 0.25 miles ahead and that the right fork leads 5.5 miles to FR 422; it does not identify the latter segment as Pine Shadow Trail (170A).

Take the left fork for a spur to the peak. A mailbox there contains a notebook where you can document your triumph over the 10,098-foot summit, but don't plan on lingering long in warmer months. Flies, mosquitoes, and other insects occasionally reach plague proportions in the late spring and summer.

Pine Shadow Trail (170A): Begin this 5.7-mile segment by backtracking down the spur to the small sign and turning left (southwest). Pine Shadow Trail, which comprises the southernmost stretch of the Crest Trail, is commonly noted for substantial deficiencies in both pine and shadows; now might be a good time to apply another layer of sunscreen. While it does pass through distinct vegetative zones, its predominantly southern exposure makes this one of the hottest and driest trails in the Manzanos. It is as much desert as forest, with cacti, yucca, and ocotillo growing among juniper, piñon, and ponderosa. Areas of thin vegetation allow for incredible views to the south and east. Plan on taking short but frequent detours to the ridge for equally stunning overlooks to the west.

The trail passes the west side of the peak then seems to vanish at the top end of a small meadow. Look for a cairn ahead, slightly down to the left. The trail resumes just beyond the tree line and levels out on a mile-long curve around the head of Priest Canyon. The namesake priest was a local padre who was murdered by roving banditos centuries ago.

The trail gets sketchy in the scrub of an old burn zone about 1.4 miles from the peak spur. Push straight through the thickets to cross to the west side of the ridgeline. Soon after, it begins to drop noticeably. Scrub thins out to reveal a clear path, but as you proceed downward through a couple of switchbacks, you may get the uneasy feeling that you're going down the wrong side of the mountain. Not to worry—a sharp bend to the left soon takes you around the end of the ridgeline, back to the other side.

The steep descent continues, now with loose rock to test your balance. Cross over another rockslide. It gets easier from here, and it's only 1.7 miles to a sign marking the wilderness boundary. After a couple of switchbacks through a steep meadow, pass through a pedestrian access gate. From there it's just 0.25 miles to Pine Shadow Springs, where you'll likely find a few shallow pools and plenty of shade. There is considerable evidence of bear activity, most notably in the form of mauled wooden signs.

If you planned your day right, you'll have a vehicle waiting nearby in the parking lot. Better yet, you'll have packed a cooler and a bag of charcoal. Reward your sherpas with tasty cold beverages, and fire up a grill in the picnic area. Note that during seasonal gate closures (November–April), your hike will begin and end here.

FR 422 and Cottonwood Trail (73): Those determined to close the loop on foot still have at least 2.6 miles to go, mostly uphill. Exit the parking lot and turn left on FR 422. Stick to the middle of the road in the summer. Your best chance for a rattlesnake encounter is along this stretch, particularly where grassy clumps grow from shallow roadside ditches.

About 0.8 miles up the road, a signboard with a trail map stands at the Cottonwood trailhead. From here you can stay on the road another 2 miles back to the start or make a left to return via Cottonwood Trail. The trail is slightly shorter in distance but considerably steeper. (After 20 minutes on the Cottonwood, my weary hiking crew spotted FR 422 and cut straight east to finish the loop on the road.)

The trail starts in oak and aspen shade as it heads into the canyon behind the signboard. It soon turns north to wind its way up to the east side of a ridge. After a brief respite on a relatively level track, continue climbing across a dry piñon-juniper landscape. Ponderosa joins the mix as you gain elevation, but you won't find much in the way of cottonwood along Cottonwood Trail. After about 1 mile on the trail, begin a mild descent to the signs and map you encountered 11.5 miles ago. Turn right, and follow the rocky road 0.4 miles back to FR 422.

Note: Forest Roads 253 and 422 are usually maintained well enough for regular cars, though they can be difficult after heavy rain. For current conditions, check with the Mountainair Ranger District at (505) 847-2990 or **www .fs.fed.us/r3/cibola/districts/mountainair.**

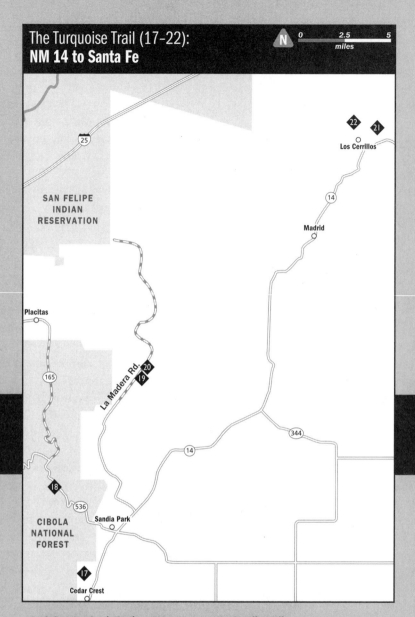

25

22 **21**

Los Cerrillos

SAN FELIPE
INDIAN
RESERVATION

14

Madrid

Placitas

165

La Madera Rd. **20**
19

344

14

18

536

Sandia Park

CIBOLA
NATIONAL
FOREST

17

Cedar Crest

THE TURQUOISE TRAIL

17 CAÑONCITO-BART'S TRAIL

KEY AT-A-GLANCE INFORMATION

LENGTH: 3.5-mile or 7.8-mile balloon options

DIFFICULTY: Easy or strenuous

SCENERY: Travertine falls, seasonal wildflowers, wooded canyons; crest views on 7.8-mile route

EXPOSURE: Mostly shaded

TRAIL TRAFFIC: Moderate

SHARED USE: Low (equestrians; dogs must be leashed for the first mile; no bikes, motor vehicles, or hang gliders)

TRAIL SURFACE: Gravel road, packed dirt, loose rock, pine bedding

HIKING TIME: 2–5 hours

DRIVING DISTANCE: 20 miles (one way) from the I-40 and I-25 exchange

ACCESS: Year-round

LAND STATUS: Cibola National Forest–Sandia Mountain Wilderness

MAPS: Sandia Ranger District; USGSSandia Crest

FACILITIES: Trailhead map and information board

LAST CHANCE FOOD/GAS: All services in Cedar Crest on NM 14

GPS Trailhead Coordinates

UTM Zone (WGS 84) 13S

Easting   0374524

Northing 3888903

Latitude   35° 08' 07"

Longitude 106° 22' 38"

IN BRIEF

A mile-long walk up a quiet road takes you to the east edge of the Sandia Ranger District. From there, two designated trails start from the same point and end less than 1 mile apart on the Crest Trail. Overlooks from 9,200 feet alternate between eastern and western vistas. A shorter loop via Faulty Trail misses the views but visits the waterfalls on the lower Cañoncito Trail.

DESCRIPTION

Most visitors driving the Turquoise Trail National Scenic Byway don't realize that behind the contemporary facade of Cedar Crest lie small but culturally vibrant villages. Many of the families here are the descendants of those who came to settle the Spanish Crown's 90,000-acre Cañon de Carnué land grant.

Cañoncito is an exception. The initial attempt to establish El Cañoncito de Nuanes predates Mexican independence, but its would-be founder, Juan Nuanes, abandoned his efforts in the wake of an Apache attack. His family returned in the 1850s to finish the job, and eventually the modest agrarian community

Directions

From I-40 east, take Exit 175 toward Cedar Crest on NM 14 (Turquoise Trail National Scenic Byway). About 3.5 miles north of the I-40 overpass, turn left on Cañoncito Road and go 0.5 miles west. At the Y, do *not* follow the sign pointing right to Cañoncito. Instead, continue 0.2 miles west on Cole Springs Road, a gravel road. Just past signs reading "Private Land" and "Keep Out" are more signs with instructions for accessing the trailhead. Park on the left side of the road at the gate ahead.

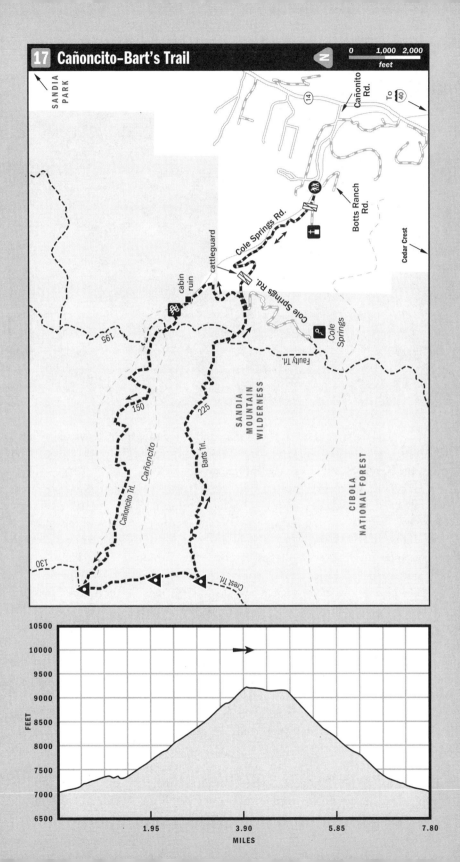

17 **Cañoncito–Bart's Trail**

0   1,000   2,000
feet

SANDIA PARK

Cañonito Rd.

To **14**

To **40**

Botts Ranch Rd.

Cole Springs Rd.

Cedar Crest

cattleguard

cabin ruin

Cole Springs Rd.

Cole Springs

195

Faulty Trl.

150

Cañoncito Trl.

Cañoncito

225

Barts Trl.

SANDIA MOUNTAIN WILDERNESS

CIBOLA NATIONAL FOREST

130

Crest Trl.

10500
10000
9500
9000
8500
8000
7500
7000
6500

FEET

1.95   3.90   5.85   7.80

MILES

boasted a gypsum mine, a quarry, a church, and two dance halls. However, when a 1901 U.S. government survey excluded Cañoncito from the Cañon de Carnué land grant, the Nuanes family lost their entitlement to the land.

Cañoncito Cemetery, located a few steps from the designated parking area, outlines local genealogies with tombstones dating back to the 19th century. Those less keen on visiting the graves of strangers can glean a bit of local history from *Towns of the Sandia Mountains* by Mike Smith. Intimate text and archival photographs detail several villages on the lower Turquoise Trail, and one odd little burg called Albuquerque.

The hike begins at the locked gate on Cole Springs Drive. Before 2001 this gravel road was open to vehicles heading to the Cole Springs Picnic Area, 1.6 miles up. Traffic from the increasingly popular Turquoise Trail overwhelmed local landowners, prompting them to gate what had become a thoroughfare across their property. They now allow visitors to walk from the gate to the national forest boundary. A sign posted at the gate indicates that access privileges will remain in effect for as long as guests respect the posted rules.

The gate seems to deter many visitors from the forest. The Cole Springs Picnic Area has been virtually deserted. Yet walking to the trailhead for Cañoncito and Bart trails really amounts to a pleasant stroll on a quiet road through pine forest. After 0.8 miles, you arrive at the cattle guard that marks the forest boundary. About 200 yards ahead, a sign on the right directs you to Cole Springs and the Cañoncito trailhead. Do *not* climb the steep embankment on the right, as many hikers have done after misinterpreting the directional arrow. Both Cañoncito Trail and Bart's Trail start right around the corner ahead. You can hike the loop in either direction, so choose wisely, grasshopper.

Cañoncito Trail (150) reaches the Crest Trail in 3 miles. Cañoncito starts on a modest climb northeast across piñon- juniper-forested slopes that feature a few trailside yucca and cacti. The path soon turns northwest to enter its namesake "little canyon." After 0.4 miles on the trail, you'll see the stone foundation of an old cabin on the right. A marshy area just ahead indicates the lower reaches of Cañoncito Spring. You'll usually find it flowing stronger as you ascend closer to the source.

Unlike the sudden drop of the travertine falls in Hondo Canyon (hike 11), deposits here create a more gradual decline that resembles a stairway. Water spills down a series of terraces, some of which form pools just deep enough to soak your feet. On hot summer days, there's nothing more refreshing than dousing yourself with hatfuls of cool, crystalline springwater. (An advantage to using Cañoncito Trail as the return route is saving this reward for the last leg of the hike.)

Farther upstream, water gushes down a 20-foot embankment. The trail splits here, with one branch staying close to the stream while another turns wide to avoid the embankment. Both soon pass by a streamside campsite.

A few notable features are within 50 feet of the campsite: a small sign (easy to miss) marks Cañoncito Spring; a limestone outcrop forms a cliff, which kids will find irresistibly climbable; and prominent signs at the junction ahead give the directions and distances for multiple trails and destinations.

For the short loop, take a left on Faulty Trail (195) here, and head south about 0.5 miles to the junction with Bart's Trail.

Those here for the long route should continue up Cañoncito Trail. It soon becomes steeper and rockier. Limestone in this area is rich with marine fossils. About a mile past Faulty Trail junction, tree cover thins and the trail narrows. It can get lost in overgrowth along this stretch. Just when you think you're on the wrong path, square-and-rectangle blazes indicate you're still on course. Shade is still spotty, but now it's coming from spruce and fir, with a hint of aspen. A wooden post ahead marks the T-junction with the Crest Trail.

A 0.8-mile segment of the **Crest Trail (130)** is your connector to Bart's Trail. But before going south for the transfer, turn right for a quick detour. Just a few yards north, the Crest Trail jogs right. Turn left here for a fantastic overlook directly above Bear Canyon. For what it's worth, the canyon crosses the western forest boundary at an elevation of 6,200 feet. Your elevation at the overlook is slightly over 9,200 feet.

Now go south on the Crest Trail, keeping an eye out for numerous overlooks just off the trail. Good views to the east come up on the left about 0.4 miles ahead, and on the uppermost segment of Bart's Trail. If you find yourself walking through a tunnel of bowed oak on the Crest Trail, you've just missed the wooden post that marks the upper terminus of Bart's Trail.

Bart's Trail (225) climbs 1,800 feet in 2 miles. For comparison, the Cañoncito Trail segment from the cabin ruin to the crest gains 1,900 feet in 2.5 miles. Yet Bart's is notorious for being the hard way up to the crest—and worse, for wearing out downhill hikers' knees. Its overblown bad-boy reputation probably stems from its designed purpose. Constructed to provide quick access to the South Peak area, the trail intentionally lacked frou-frou amenities like switchbacks. Credit for its brilliant design and construction goes to Fayette "Bart" Barton and the New Mexico Mountain Club. The trail was completed in 1979, and the Forest Service has since adopted it into their trail system with few modifications.

But what makes Bart's Trail somewhat less challenging is the absence of the vegetation that tends to overwhelm the upper Cañoncito. Bart's holds its shape better, making it easier to follow. And though it lacks Cañoncito's splendid water and rock features, it does have its own *cañoncito*.

Coming from the crest, you cross the head of the little canyon about 1.4 miles down the trail, and you'll stay close to the north rim for the next 0.25 miles or so. About 1.7 miles from the crest, you'll cross Faulty Trail. Those on the short loop should turn left to pick up Bart's Trail at this marked junction.

Bart's then begins its rocky 250-foot descent to the pine bed of the little canyon. Relax your stride as the trail levels out. Take a moment to sniff the ponderosa, which smells like vanilla to some and butterscotch to others. Just 0.3 miles from the Faulty Trail junction, you're back at the trailhead. Turn left on the road to return to the parking area.

NEARBY ACTIVITIES

The 88-acre Ojito de San Antonio Open Space features a meadow, orchard, and piñon–juniper forest on the surrounding slopes. Spend a lazy afternoon in the shade of an ancient willow by the side of a historic acequia. Two natural springs have provided drinking water for wildlife and the nearby community for centuries. To get there from Cañoncito, return to NM 14 and go south 2.4 miles. Turn west on San Antonio Drive. A parking lot and access to the open space are hidden behind the San Antonio de Padua Church. For more information, call Bernalillo Open Space at (505) 314-0401. Or visit **www.bernco.gov**.

TREE SPRING-CREST TRAIL

IN BRIEF

This classic hike combines the 2-mile Tree Spring Trail with a 1.6-mile segment of the Crest Trail to reach the upper terminal of the Sandia Peak Tramway. Aspen shades the upper trail to the subalpine mountaintop, where views encompass 11,000 square miles.

DESCRIPTION

In 1936 the U.S. Forest Service cleared the slopes and established a system of trails at Tree Spring to accommodate the fledgling Albuquerque Ski Club. They called it La Madera Ski Area. A T-bar lift added in 1945 was the longest in the nation, and lift tickets cost $1. You won't see a trace of the original ski area at Tree Spring today, but the trailhead is hard to miss. A large board displays the usual rules and safety info, along with a map of the Sandia Mountains and surrounding environs. The fee station—a red envelope box and a white deposit cylinder—is nearby. Rangers are diligent in this area, so be sure to get that squared away before proceeding.

Tree Spring Trail (147) starts out as a broad path of hard-packed dirt. About 0.75 miles into the hike, it gets rocky and crooks to the left at a faded path that climbs straight up. Just ahead on the left is the marker for Oso Corredor (265), semi-anglicized here as Oso Corridor. This easy, though occasionally

KEY AT-A-GLANCE INFORMATION

LENGTH: 7.2-mile out-and-back

DIFFICULTY: Moderate

SCENERY: Marine fossils, aspen and fir, ski runs, world's longest aerial tramway

EXPOSURE: Mostly shade

TRAIL TRAFFIC: Popular

SHARED USE: Low (skiing; limited mountain bike and equestrian access; no motor vehicles)

TRAIL SURFACE: Dirt, rock

HIKING TIME: 4 hours

DRIVING DISTANCE: 27 miles (one way) from the I-40/I-25 exchange

ACCESS: Year-round; day-use fee $3 per car; free with Sandia Mountain Annual Pass or National Parks and Federal Recreation Lands Annual Pass

LAND STATUS: Cibola National Forest

MAPS: Sandia Ranger District; USGS Sandia Crest

FACILITIES: Restrooms (no water) at trailhead; visitor center, tramway terminus, restaurant, restrooms, and emergency phone at Sandia Peak

SPECIAL COMMENTS: See longer note at end of description.

Directions

From I-40 east, take Exit 175 toward Cedar Crest. From the I-40 overpass, go north 5.9 miles on NM 14. Turn left on NM 536 (Sandia Crest Scenic Byway) and follow it 5.7 miles up to the Tree Spring parking area on the left. The hike begins at the signboards.

GPS Trailhead Coordinates

UTM Zone (WGS 84) 13S

Easting 0372117

Northing 3895438

Latitude 35° 11' 38"

Longitude 106° 24' 17"

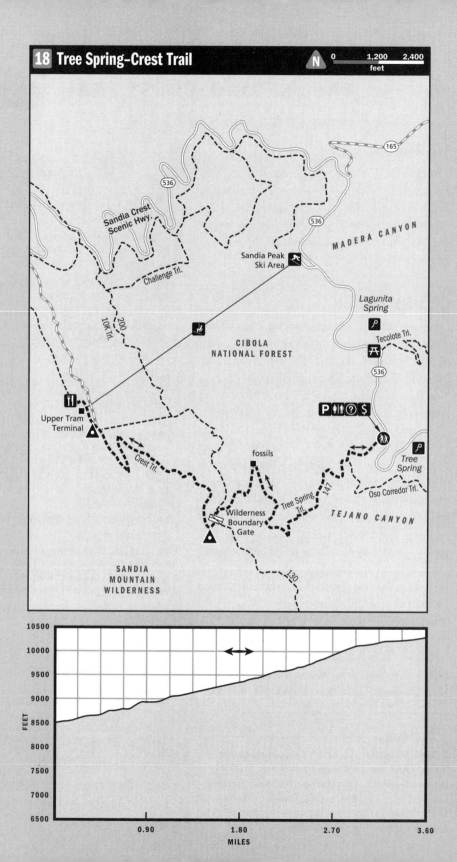

N

0   1,200   2,400
feet

Sandia Crest
Scenic Hwy.

536

MADERA CANYON

Challenge Trl.

536

Sandia Peak
Ski Area

Lagunita
Spring

200
10K Trl.

CIBOLA
NATIONAL FOREST

Tecolote Trl.

536

Upper Tram
Terminal

P ⛹ ⓘ $

Crest Trl.

fossils

Tree
Spring

147

Tree Spring Trl.

Oso Corredor Trl.

Wilderness
Boundary
Gate

TEJANO CANYON

SANDIA
MOUNTAIN
WILDERNESS

130

10500
10000
9500
9000
8500
8000
7500
7000
6500

FEET

0.90   1.80   2.70   3.60
MILES

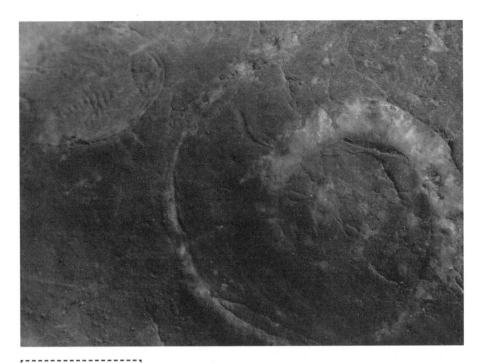

Trilobite and gastropod

soggy, 2.7-mile side trail was named for the numerous black bear sightings in its inaugural season in 1989, a particularly dry summer in the Sandias.

Fine attention to grooming Tree Spring Trail shows on its steeper sections, where erosion might otherwise erase it. Credit the Adopt-a-Trail volunteers who cast aside large stones and terraced the grounds to facilitate your ascent. Just over a mile into the hike, the forest opens to meadows that thrive with wildflowers in warmer seasons. After 1.5 miles, the Sandias' limestone cap pokes through the soil. Look closely at the smooth gray rock for marine fossils. Gastropods (snails) about the size of a quarter are the easiest to spot. Trilobites and crinoids also riddle the rock from here to the peak. Visitors often ask how sea creatures managed to cross the desert and climb these mountains. The answer lies ahead.

For now, a bigger mystery: the limestone is part of the 300-million-year-old Madera group. Beneath it is Precambrian granite that dates back some 1.4 billion years. It seems a few intermediary layers have gone missing. Landscapes often lose bits of their geologic records. Such absentmindedness is called an "unconformity." The Sandias, however, blacked out for more than a billion years in what geologists worldwide refer to as "The Great Unconformity."

Tree Spring Trail nears its end at the boundary of Sandia Mountain Wilderness, marked with a wooden post fence and signs reminding you to check your chainsaws, motorized vehicles, bicycles, and hang gliders at the gate.

Alternate routes: The 10K Trail extends to the right. If you prefer a loop in your route, follow its blue diamonds to the ski slopes. Turn left at the first

Upper terminus of Sandia Peak Tramway

ski run and climb about 0.5 miles uphill to the tram terminal. For the return segment, follow the Crest Trail back to the wilderness-boundary gate. Just be sure not to miss this turn back onto Tree Spring Trail or you'll end up following the Crest Trail down to Canyon Estates, 13 miles to the south—or farther. The Crest Trail is part of the Grand Enchantment Trail, a hiking route between Albuquerque and Phoenix, so you could extend your hike another 700 miles.

The Crest Trail (130) is just beyond the gate. To stay on the planned route, continue straight ahead about 600 yards to the edge of a precipitous drop-off. It's a good spot for a snack break as the next 2 miles are a little strenuous.

Refueled and ready to roll, backtrack halfway to the gate, and turn left to resume north on the Crest Trail. Pass through dense stands of mature fir, intermittent groves of aspen, and sporadic colonies of mushrooms and lichens. The green shaggy growths resembling Spanish moss are an unrelated plant known as "old man's beard."

After a couple of long switchbacks, the trail runs near the ridgeline. Opportunities abound for short detours to secluded overlooks. If the wind dies down for a moment, you'll hear the hum of the tram's pulley system. Follow that sound, and you'll soon emerge from the woods at the top of the ski trails. The red benches and blue poles of the chairlifts are impossible to miss, as is the steep view down the slopes. The skiing here can be the best in the state. Or it can be the worst. Another winter as warm as the 2006 season could cripple the local skiing industry; 2007 saw record snowfall.

The stairs up to the tramway terminal and the restaurant are by the second lift. Once on the wooden deck above, you've reached an altitude nearing 10,400 feet—squarely in subalpine spruce–fir forest archaically known as the Hudsonian Zone. To reach the highest point in the Sandias, you'd have to hike another 1.8 miles north on the Crest Trail. Peaking at a mere 10,678 feet, Sandia Crest doesn't quite crack the list of New Mexico's 100 highest summits. But if you're a dedicated peak bagger, go for it.

Three stations located on the deck identify peaks and landmarks in every direction, some well over 100 miles away. Views cover 11,000 square miles on a clear day. They're also enjoyable from inside the adjacent restaurant. High Finance serves up hearty fare and magnificent microbrews. (Keep in mind, however, that alcohol packs a stronger punch at this altitude). On summer weekends and holidays, an outdoor grill lures hungry hikers from all over the mountain.

The Sandia Peak Tramway is the biggest attraction. At 2.7 miles, it's the world's longest aerial tramway. The longest span between towers is 7,720 feet, and a tramcar at mid-span hangs 900 feet above the ground. "Flights" depart every 20 to 30 minutes, in all seasons, about 10,500 times per year, and have carried more than 8 million passengers since 1966.

At the upper tram terminal, the Four Seasons Visitor Center contains interpretive exhibits on natural history, including an explanation as to how fossilized sea creatures ended up atop these mountains.

Note: If any hikers in your group balk at a trail with a 2,000' gain in elevation, consider dropping them off at the Sandia Peak chairlift and meeting them at the top. The chairlift runs scenic rides on summer weekends and holidays and during Balloon Fiesta. Mountain bikers can also ride up with their bikes to take advantage of 8 miles of downhill singletrack. The chairlift starts from the Sandia Peak Ski Area base lodge, 1.3 miles up the road from the Tree Spring trailhead. Also note that the trails in the ski area tend to stay open when the rest shut down for drought-mandated closures. For more info, call (505) 242-9052 or visit **www.sandiapeak .com**. Check with the Sandia Ranger District for local road and trail conditions in the winter and fire danger updates in the summer: (505) 281-3304 or **www .fs.fed.us/r3/cibola/districts/sandia**.

NEARBY ACTIVITIES

At least a dozen official trails start near the Sandia Crest Scenic Byway. Tecolote Trail (264), a nicely shaded ridgeline route that features a mineshaft, is a relatively flat 1.3-mile out-and-back with a turnaround loop at the end. The trailhead is at the back of the Dry Camp Picnic Ground, 0.5 miles up on the right from the Tree Spring parking area.

On your way back down NM 536, the Tinkertown Museum is on the right. Within the walls of this ramshackle compound lies the labyrinthine *wunderkammer* of Ross J. Ward, the creator and curator of unusual things. Call (505) 281-5233 for more information, or visit them online at **www.tinkertown.com**.

19 GOLDEN OPEN SPACE

KEY AT-A-GLANCE INFORMATION

LENGTH: 3-mile out-and-back

DIFFICULTY: Easy

SCENERY: Views of multiple mountain ranges; mesa-rim overlooks of the Arroyo Seco and San Pedro Creek

EXPOSURE: Little shade

TRAIL TRAFFIC: Low, for now

SHARED USED: Low (mountain biking, equestrians; livestock; pets must be leashed; no motor vehicles)

TRAIL SURFACE: Packed dirt, sand

HIKING TIME: 1–2 hours

DRIVING DISTANCE: 31 miles (one way) from the I-40/I-25 exchange

ACCESS: Daylight hours

LAND STATUS: Albuquerque Open Space

MAPS: USGS Hagan

FACILITIES: None

LAST CHANCE FOOD/GAS: All services in Sandia Park on NM 14

SPECIAL COMMENTS: The trail at the Golden Open Space is slated for completion in late 2008. In the meantime, hiking is permitted, but access requires climbing a locked gate. For updates, contact the Albuquerque Open Space Division at (505) 542-5200 or visit www .cabq.gov/openspace.

GPS Trailhead Coordinates

UTM Zone (WGS 84) 13S

Easting 0379190

Northing 3903968

Latitude 35° 16' 18"

Longitude 106° 19' 42"

IN BRIEF

"Best-kept secret" is the worst cliché, but the City of Albuquerque has been keeping this one hidden in a neighboring county for more than 40 years. Emerging trails now allow you to walk the rim above two deep red cuts in the earth: San Pedro Creek and Arroyo Seco.

DESCRIPTION

The City of Albuquerque acquired this 1,200-acre parcel in Sandoval County in 1964 under the federal Recreation and Public Purposes Act, which required the city to develop it for recreational purposes or return it to the BLM. Early plans for the property had it slated as a campground, one of several that would form a camping ring around the city. The idea never reached fruition. In retrospect, it's probably best it didn't.

Set aside for the preservation of nature, the land has since remained relatively undisturbed. Viewing it from La Madera Road, you might guess it extends for miles as monotonous grazing lands, but a short hike beyond the fence reveals fascinating landforms.

The Golden Open Space does not appear on maps as public land but rather as an anonymous parcel 6 miles west of its namesake

Directions ⟶

From I-40 east, take Exit 175 toward Cedar Crest. From the I-40 overpass, go 6.9 miles north on NM 14. Just past the East Mountain High School, turn left (west) on La Madera Road. As of August 2007, this road was paved 7.4 miles to Faith Drive. From this intersection, cross the cattle guard and continue straight on the dirt road. After 8 miles on La Madera Road, cross a second cattle guard. At 9.4 miles, pull off to the right and park at the gate.

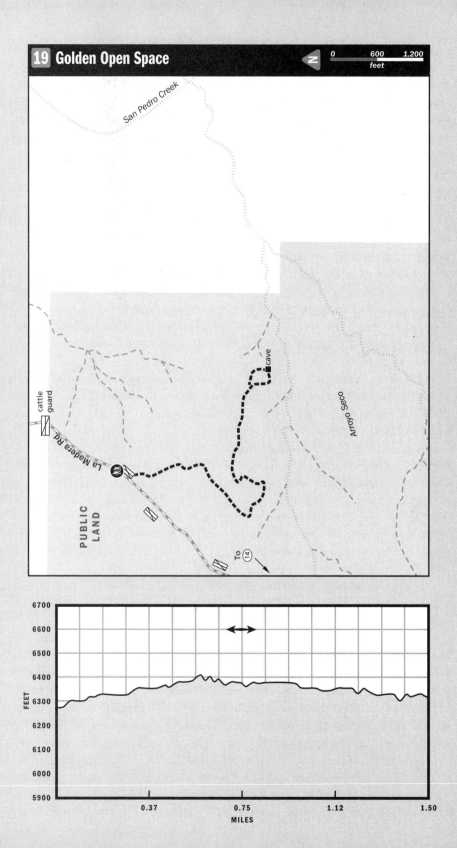

19 **Golden Open Space**

N

0   600   1,200
feet

San Pedro Creek

cave

Arroyo Seco

cattle
guard

La Madera Rd.

PUBLIC
LAND

To (14)

6700
6600
6500
6400
6300
6200
6100
6000
5900

FEET

0.37   0.75   1.12   1.50
MILES

ghost town. I had driven along its barbed-wire fences perhaps a half dozen times in as many years, assuming it was private ranchland. But then small Open Space signs mysteriously appeared on the posts of its padlocked gates. Later, pink and orange survey flags sprouted from the gritty earth, forming a dotted line that wended through juniper savanna. Weeks passed, and the flags were replaced with a freshly scraped path marked with cairns. Unable to locate anyone to take credit for the trail work, I reached the only logical conclusion: the land was beset with *los duendes.*

Some people describe them as industrious elves, others as evil dwarfs. In his 1910 paper "New-Mexican Spanish Folk-Lore," Aurelio Macedonio Espinosa identified *los duendes* as "individuals of small stature who frighten the lazy, the wicked and in particular the filthy." Their origins and motives remain a mystery.

In August 2007, I led a reconnaissance expedition to inspect their progress. Our extensive fieldwork unearthed several pertinent details, the most important of which is this: August really isn't the best time for extensive fieldwork in the Golden Open Space. It's insanely hot. Quite frankly, I don't know how the evil dwarfs can stand it.

The hike begins at a locked gate. The OSD plans to replace it with a pedestrian-access gate once the trail is complete, likely by late 2008. Rules for the Open Space are posted at the trailhead. Climbing over locked gates is not listed among the prohibitions.

A groomed trail runs south up a gently sloping plain. After 0.6 miles of ordinary juniper scenery, the trail arrives at an overlook on the cusp of Arroyo Seco. The main channel of the arroyo heads from the eastern side of Capulin Peak, about 5 miles southwest of the overlook. Once it crosses La Madera Road, numerous tributary washes form and begin to converge, creating the vast drainage network before you. At the point due south of the overlook, it's more than 1 mile wide and nearly 200 feet deep, and it is divided into four or five major channels. At an elevation of 6,400 feet, this overlook is the highest point in the hike.

If you plan to explore the drainages, this overlook will make a useful reference point for navigation. To help you recognize it later, take a moment to study nearby details and try to visualize them as viewed from below.

Continuing with the hike, turn left to follow the trail along the mesa rim. It soon bends north and crosses a shallow wash and then turns east again. About 1.2 miles into the hike, you'll notice a knob rising ahead to your right. Another 0.3 miles on the trail will take you there. This overlook on the southeast corner of the mesa is a good place for a break, with a view even more impressive than the one from the first overlook. But before you take a seat on a rock in the blazing sun, you might be interested in a spot of shade that's closer than you think.

About 20 feet beneath the rim is a shallow cave. It's a little tricky to reach. Follow the rim to the southernmost tip of the overlook, and then turn east and look for an easy way to reach the shelf below. Within a few yards, you should find a point where the descent won't require a scramble. Once on the shelf, turn

Lunch evades a horned lizard.

right (west). If you don't spot it in less than a minute, you probably descended too far. It's no Carlsbad Caverns, but it is big and airy enough for five sweaty hikers to kick back in shaded comfort. Though the ceiling is smudged from past campfires, both camping and fires are prohibited at Golden.

Meanwhile, back on the overlook, the view includes the San Pedro Mountains (8 miles east–southeast), the Ortiz Mountains (10 miles northeast), the south end of the Sangre de Cristo range (35 miles northeast), and the southern Jemez Mountains (35 miles northwest).

San Pedro Creek approaches from the southeast on a course to merge into Arroyo Tuerto, 3 miles north of the overlook. The creek lies just outside the Open Space boundary and inside an area under the protection of a conservation easement managed by the Intermountain Conservation Trust. This natural haven for wildlife also happens to be loaded with archaeological ruins. A better view of it is from the overlook at the easternmost point on the mesa.

As of August 2007, the trail ended at the second overlook. Sources at the OSD say it will be extended along the east rim and then west to return to the trailhead. The resulting loop should total about 3 miles. Although following the rim without the aid of paths and cairns is easy enough, you should avoid wandering off-trail in this area. Vegetation on the mesa is fragile and it doesn't take much foot traffic to create competing paths. Also, cryptobiotic soil is particularly sensitive. This crusty black layer is a balanced community of mosses, algae, microfungi, and bacteria. It binds sandy soil, keeping it from eroding, and it helps seedlings gain footholds in the ground. Watch your step when hiking off-trail in arid lands—a single misstep can wipe out centuries of growth.

In the absence of roads and trails, the least destructive routes follow barren stretches of sand and dirt, bedrock surfaces, and waterways. Exploring the maze of drainages in Arroyo Seco is a great option for a few miles of wandering, but it can be challenging to navigate. Before descending from the second overlook, take a moment to scout possible route options along streambeds and emerging trails.

This segment of the arroyo roughly parallels La Madera Road, so if you're walking upstream, the road is never more than a mile to the northwest. However, you won't always find an easy way out. Some branches end in boxes, where backtracking is the only option. Others take sinuous turns, which eventually disorients. One way to keep your bearings is by prairie dogging. Climb ridges between the channels to pop your head up and have a look around, and repeat as necessary. You should be able to recognize the first overlook. The embankment on the left side of it allows for a fairly easy climb to the rim. You can pick up the trail there, and follow it back to the gate.

If you can't find the trail, take a moment to get your bearings. The most readily identifiable landmark is Sandia Crest, about 8 miles southwest. A colony of broadcast towers graces this peak. Walk with those towers on your left, and you're heading back to La Madera Road.

NEARBY ACTIVITIES

For more hiking trails so brand-spanking new that they don't yet fully exist, hit the Madera access to the Sandia Mountains. To get there, drive back down La Madera Road 2.6 miles from the gate. Turn right on Calle Mañana, and go 0.6 miles northwest to the junction at Stagecoach Road. Jog right through the Forest Service gateway. A pair of pipeline roads continues northwest. They're good for about 0.2 miles and then quickly deteriorate. You may need to park roadside and continue on foot another 0.8 miles northwest. At the point where the pipeline bends west, the road continues straight. A ban on motorized vehicles is slated for roads continuing from this point [N 35° 15" 50' W 106° 22' 15"], and the hills ahead are great for hiking. Don't count on the 2006 Sandia Ranger District map—it shows nothing in the area but Escondido Spring.

LA MADERA ROAD 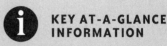 20

IN BRIEF

A long walk on a lonely dirt road takes you to back to early 20th-century mining settlements. A view of the ghost town of Hagan highlights this excursion through scrubby grasslands between the Ortiz and Sandia Mountains.

DESCRIPTION

If you're pressed for time, you could keep driving from this point. In fact, you could drive the entire route. But then there are a few reasons you shouldn't. First, it's rough in spots, as you'll discover just on the other side of the gate. Given a little rain or snow, it becomes impassable. Maybe within the next few years it'll be paved straight through to the San Felipe Casino Hollywood on I-25. For now it's a rambling country road of dust, rock, and sand, and rarely will more than a few pickup trucks attempt the run on any given afternoon.

Also, although the road is great for mountain biking and perfect for a horseback ride, walking is the ideal way to catch the finer details. Stroll this road a dozen times, and you'll find something new every time.

Directions ──────────────→

From I-40 east, take Exit 175 toward Cedar Crest. From the I-40 overpass, go 6.9 miles north on NM 14. Just past the East Mountain High School, turn left (west) on La Madera Road. As of August 2007, this road was paved 7.4 miles to Faith Drive. From this intersection, cross the cattle guard and continue straight on the dirt road. After 8 miles on La Madera Road, cross a second cattle guard. At 9.7 miles, just before the third cattle guard, park off the road in the clearing on the right. The hike begins north of the cattle guard.

KEY AT-A-GLANCE INFORMATION

LENGTH: 14.4-mile out-and-back

DIFFICULTY: Easy

SCENERY: Ghost towns and petroglyphs

EXPOSURE: Little shade

TRAIL TRAFFIC: Low

SHARED USE: Moderate (mountain bikers, equestrians, livestock, pickup trucks)

TRAIL SURFACE: Dirt road, arroyos

HIKING TIME: 5 hours

DRIVING DISTANCE: 32 miles (one way) from the I-40 and I-25 exchange

ACCESS: Year-round

MAPS: USGS Hagan

FACILITIES: None

LAST CHANCE FOOD/GAS: All services in Sandia Park on NM 14

SPECIAL COMMENTS: Bring binoculars. Land on both sides of the road is private property. Although many ruins sit just on the other side of a barbed-wire fence, the primary ghost town is about 300 yards from the roadside.

GPS Trailhead Coordinates

UTM Zone (WGS 84) 13S

Easting   0379505

Northing   3904425

Latitude   35° 16' 33"

Longitude 106° 19' 30

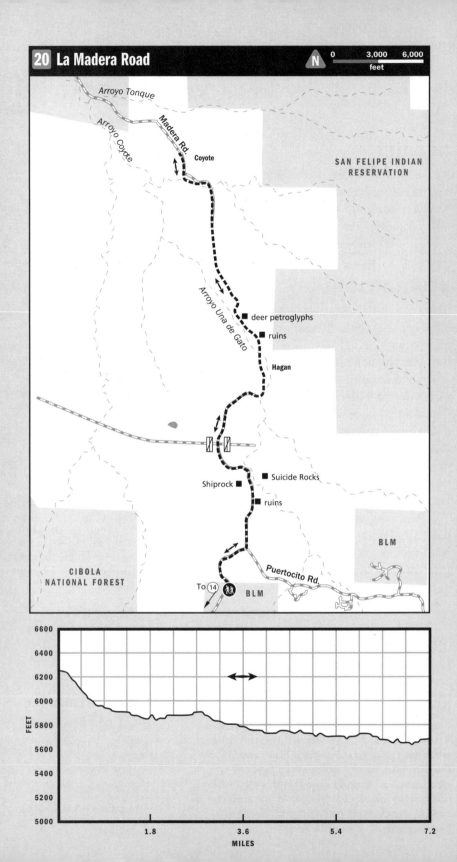

N

0   3,000   6,000
feet

Arroyo Tonque

Madera Rd.

Arroyo Coyote

Coyote

SAN FELIPE INDIAN
RESERVATION

Arroyo Una de Gato

■ deer petroglyphs

■ ruins

Hagan

■ Suicide Rocks

Shiprock ■

■ ruins

CIBOLA
NATIONAL FOREST

Puertocito Rd.

To 14

BLM

BLM

The hike: Cross the cattle guard and head north down the steep, rocky road. It drops 300 feet within the first 0.8 miles. There on the right is Puertocito Road, which leads to its charming old namesake community. At **1.2 miles** into the hike are another fence and a shot-up sign for Diamond Tail Ranch. There's also a bigger note about trespassing, in case you missed the first several warnings. You will see the ruins of Homestead 0.2 miles ahead on the right.

Little remains of this forgotten settlement. Most of its foundations are barely visible in the tall grass, and the few remaining rock walls stand no more than three or four feet. Only resident rodents seem interested in excavating the site—cobalt blue shards of Depression glass glisten in the mounds outside their burrows. Glass with a purple tint indicates manganese, which glassmakers used in the 1890s and early 1900s. The crafting of purple glass ceased during World War I, when manganese supplies went into the production of ammunition.

At **1.8 miles** into the hike, the road squeezes through a pass between two distinct land formations. The one on the left is informally known as Shiprock. A little more originality went into christening the line of cliffs on the right—they're known as Suicide Rocks. The local rancher John Gonzales explained it thusly: "No one ever jumped from there. But you could."

At **2.6 miles** La Madera Road reaches a junction. On the right is the driveway to Diamond Tail Ranch—the real ranch, not the posh subdivision of the same name in nearby Placitas. Watch out for cattle, particularly those with long, sharp horns. They're more likely to retreat than charge, but keep a safe distance just in case. The road on the left leads to Tejon, a ghost town about 3 miles northwest. Proceed north on La Madera Road.

At **3.2 miles** the road bends to the east. Along the right side, erosion has trenched a miniature Grand Canyon, complete with corrugated walls and little chimneys, windows, and arches. It feeds into the Arroyo Uña de Gato, meaning "Claw of the Cat," so named after roundflower catclaw, a mesquite-like desert scrub with thorns that resemble (what else?) cat claws. As the road bends left, heading north again, the wide arroyo will be on your right and the ruins of Hagan come into view on the opposite bank.

At **3.8 miles** into the hike is an imposing steel tower with high-tension power lines crackling overhead. Find a spot of shade on the high arroyo bank and gaze upon the listing remains of central Hagan. Settlements in this area predate Spanish colonialism, but Hagan began in 1902 as a mining town with great aspirations. With a plentiful supply of coal and the backing of the New Mexico Fuel and Iron Company, the town was set to strike it rich. All they lacked was a means of getting their product to market. Unfortunately, a promised railroad didn't materialize within the first two decades. By then, many residents of Hagan and surrounding settlements had lost their investments and so moved on, only to miss the boomtown that would rise in their wake.

In 1924 the Hagan Spur of the Rio Grande Eastern Railroad finally reached the town, and Hagan's heydays commenced. It boasted a grand hotel, a train station, and relatively comfortable adobe homes scattered throughout the hills. A coal-generated power plant supplied electricity to some buildings.

But coal eventually gave way to shale, and residents moved out as the Depression settled in. A few desperate citizens held on, but by 1950 Hagan was officially a ghost town, and its buildings were picked apart for construction projects in La Madera.

Up to 8 miles of abandoned tunnels course beneath the nearby mining area once known as Uña de Gato. Entrances have been sealed, but reports of smoke rising from the nearby ranchlands suggest that residual pockets of coal are smoldering underground.

Half of the platform for the train depot has collapsed into the arroyo. A tomb-sized vault stands above a plot of cement pillars that once supported the wooden floors of the Hagan Mercantile company store. In residential areas, several sturdy walls of adobe and rock still stand, many with window frames intact, but not a rooftop remains.

As you search through the ruins (with binoculars, of course), look for caves in the cliffs in the background. These, too, were once inhabited, or at least camped in, as evidenced by their smudged ceilings. Nearby petroglyphs, however, appear to be the work of a European hand.

After viewing Hagan, continue north another 0.5 miles, crossing the arroyo and a couple of feeder drainages. On the right are the remains of another forgotten settlement, with at least three ruins visible from the road.

At **4.7 miles**, the road squeezes between the arroyo on the left and a short mesa on the right. More petroglyphs—apparently ancient ones this time—can be found in the facing cliff, almost within reach from the road. Look for the shapes of deer or antelope. One of the more curious works features a head with a pair of lollipop-shaped extensions. It's a recurring motif in petroglyphs throughout the Southwest, and its interpretation is open to debate. Some see it as an Indian with a feathered headband. Others regard it as an insect-like character stemming from Anasazi mythology, or as evidence of a prehistoric visitation from antennaed aliens.

At **6.5 miles,** the road crosses a wide arroyo then turns left to roughly follow the streambed for 0.25 miles or so. Check the natural niches in roadside outcrops for folk shrines, but stay alert for vehicles around the blind curves. The road soon turns north again.

At **7.2 miles,** Coyote appears on the right. This little town died out while waiting for the railroad. The train finally arrived, but it was three years too late. A few rock foundations remain, along with pieces of off-white bricks stamped TONQUE.

Coyote is the turnaround point for this hike, but the road continues another 2 miles or so to the San Felipe boundary. The Tonque Brick Factory once stood there, near the site of a pre-colonial pueblo of the same name. Excavated in the 1960s, the Tonque Pueblo continues to hold strong ancestral significance for the San Felipe Pueblo people. Older maps show it on BLM land, but it is now on private property. Up until a few years ago, the area around the factory and pueblo mound was littered with artifacts from past centuries, namely bricks and broken pottery. Souvenir scavengers have since picked it clean.

La Madera Road (also appearing on maps as Madera Road, Hagan Road, Indian Route 844, and County Highway 53) then enters the San Felipe Reservation and continues about 5 miles to the casino on I-25. There seems to be some ongoing uncertainty as to whether or not a right-of-way has been established. So if you intend to push through for a hand of blackjack, check first with the San Felipe Pueblo: (505) 867-3381.

21 CERRILLOS HILLS HISTORIC PARK

KEY AT-A-GLANCE INFORMATION

LENGTH: 4.8-mile loop

DIFFICULTY: Moderate, with two steep inclines

SCENERY: Abandoned mines, grassy hills, rock canyon, "pygmy forest" of piñon and juniper

EXPOSURE: Mostly sunny

TRAIL TRAFFIC: Moderate to popular

SHARED USE: Moderate (mountain biking, equestrians; motorized vehicles restricted to existing roads)

TRAIL SURFACE: Dirt roads, rocky paths

HIKING TIME: 3 hours

DRIVING DISTANCE: 54 miles

ACCESS: Daylight hours

LAND STATUS: Santa Fe County Open Space

MAPS: Brochure map at trailhead; USGS Picture Rock and Madrid

FACILITIES: Trailside benches, interpretive signage, public art, picnic table, restroom; no water. Village View Trail, which starts at the parking area, is a 0.25-mile gravel trail designated for wheelchair use.

LAST CHANCE FOOD/GAS: Convenience stores and gas stations on NM 14, about 26 miles south and 7 miles north of Cerrillos

GPS Trailhead Coordinates

UTM Zone (WGS 84)   13S

Easting   0398153

Northing   3922961

Latitude   35° 26' 42"

Longitude 106° 07' 20"

IN BRIEF

We need more parks like this, with hikes to exercise both body and brain. Interpretive trails here amount to a seminar in New Mexico culture and natural history. Only instead of a sleep-inducing lecture hall, the classroom is rolling terrain with scenic vistas, high-desert wildlife, and historic mines—and that's just a hint of the much bigger things to come.

DESCRIPTION

To understand how Cerrillos Hill Historic Park came to be on the verge of becoming the state's next major attraction, you need to go back, oh, let's say 30 million years. That's about when the Rio Grande Rift yawned, stretched, and ultimately stirred up several deeply embedded laccoliths in what would become Cerrillos Hills. These massive igneous bodies never broke through as volcanoes, but they did fracture the overlying rocks as they rumpled the crust into mountains. Over the ensuing eons, weathering eroded the range down to a chain of cone-shaped hills, while pressured mineral springs flowed into the cracks to form ore veins.

Around AD 900, puebloans began mining veins of blue-green stones. Believed to be an

Directions

From I-40 east, take Exit 175 toward Cedar Crest. From the I-40 overpass, go 32 miles north on NM 14 and turn left onto Main Street toward Cerrillos. Once in the village, turn right at the first stop sign onto First Street. Go over the railroad tracks and drive another 0.25 miles to the Y. Bear left onto CR 59 (Camino Turquesa) and go 0.4 miles, following the signs for Cerrillos Hills Historic Park. The parking lot is on the left. The trailhead is on the right.

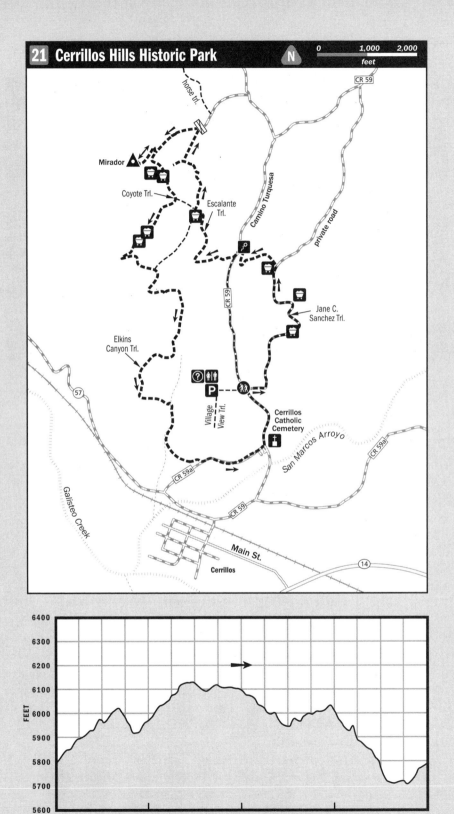

A view from Elkins Canyon Trail

effective evil repellent, worked turquoise was strong currency in the Rio Grande Valley, particularly at the commerce center now known as Chaco Canyon, about 100 miles to the northwest. Galena (lead sulfide) further boosted the mining economy when lead-glazed pottery suddenly became a hot commodity.

Credit for this technological breakthrough in ceramics goes to early 14th-century potters at what is now known as Pueblo San Marcos, 2.5 miles east of Cerrillos Hills. With a stronghold on the turquoise and pottery markets, San Marcos grew, and pueblo developments filled the surrounding Galisteo Basin over the next few centuries.

The mining activity in Cerrillos Hills did not escape the notice of early Spaniards. Priorities in order, they launched the first silver operation in 1581 and established a mission at San Marcos in 1620. Anglo prospectors began moving in on the digs in 1846 and would assume control over the hills in time for the Cerrillos Mining Boom of 1879–1884. The promise of an industrial future earned Cerrillos the nickname "Little Pittsburg," but by 1898 a millennium of mining had exhausted the hills. In the wake of the bust, they abandoned numerous towns and camps, and well over 5,000 holes in the ground.

Few commercial operations survived into the 20th century, with all but a gravel mine closing by the 1960s. In the 1990s the New Mexico Abandoned Mine Land Program sealed the last of the hazardous shafts.

Just when it seemed the hills could finally rest, shockwaves from booms in real estate and tourism rippled down the Turquoise Trail. Development proposals

Cattails grow from algae-rich springs on
Camino Turquesa.

soon threatened to expose what many locals and archaeologists had known for
years: The Galisteo Basin is packed with remnants from multiple cultural occu-
pations, including the largest pueblo ruins in the United States. Just one of 24
known pueblo sites, San Marcos boasts 2,000 rooms, a far higher count than
settlements in Chaco Culture National Historical Park or Mesa Verde National
Park can claim.

The impending invasion of tourists and developers sent preservationists
scrambling to protect the sites. In 2004 the U.S. Congress responded by passing the Galisteo Basin Archaeological Sites Protection Act, which essentially
allows public-land agencies to acquire new lands and bar them from the public.
Accordingly, the Santa Fe County Open Space and Trails Program snatched up
enormous tracts in the Galisteo Basin and the Ortiz Mountains but has yet to
open the spaces and trails.

It all spells good news and bad news for those of us who are itching to run
wild through this remarkable hallway of New Mexico history. The good news:
The sites are currently enjoying unprecedented protection, at least in theory.
Unusual levels of cooperation from local landowners and developers indicate
that the archaeological sites in the Galisteo Basin won't turn into suburban gar-
risons like Piedras Marcadas (hike 5).

The bad news: Thorough archaeological studies, inventories, interpretation, and public-access assessments could take years. A 2007 deadline was

already missed due in part to a congressional failure to provide the $2.5 million required to fully implement the act. Further, a united trail system throughout the Galisteo Basin Complex would require the cooperation of federal, state, and county agencies, and private entities like the Albuquerque-based Archaeological Conservancy, which currently owns 7 of the 24 sites, including Pueblo San Marcos. In short, we need to be patient.

But there's more good news: a number of organizations now offer guided tours to many of the sites. Santa Fe County's management plan should open its Galisteo Basin property, Thornton Ranch, by the end of 2008. The westernmost sites near Cienega (hike 29) are already open for unescorted exploration, as are the spacious lands directly north of the village of Cerrillos.

The 1,100-acre Cerrillos Hills Historic Park opened in 2003. Since then, its developed trail system has grown to exceed 8 miles and continues to expand at a rate that outpaces abilities to keep trail maps updated. The trails are immaculate and stocked with enough interpretive signage for a dissertation on local history and geology. Overall, the CHHP is an exemplary achievement in park management.

The State Parks and Recreation Division has noticed. They have Cerrillos and the historic park pegged in their master plan for New Mexico's 36th state park. With a visitor center on the plaza in Cerrillos and the possible addition of nearly 3,000 acres of adjacent public lands, Cerrillos Hills State Park is slated to open by late 2008 or early 2009. A more ambitious proposal sees the state park as the gateway to 30,000 acres in the Galisteo Basin. As these plans reach fruition, Cerrillos can expect a rush not seen since the boom of 1879.

To get a head start on the crowds, hit the CHHP trails now. They're clearly marked, so you'd hardly need directions from a guidebook. In any case, this route outlines the longest loop in the park as of April 2007.

Start the hike by heading up the steep, wide Jane Calvin Sanchez Trail, formerly Mountain Lion Trail. Within 1 mile, you'll pass three fenced mine shafts then descend to the springs on Camino Turquesa. A sign here details the mineral and organic contents of the small but vibrant springs. (In summary: don't drink the water.)

Turn left, and head down the road about 60 yards to pick up Escalante Trail on the right. After a steep 0.5-mile climb past Cortez Mine Trail, look left for a 60-yard spur to Escalante View, the highest point on this route.

Return to the main trail, and continue 0.1 mile north to a fence that crosses the road. If you want to stretch this hike out a few more miles, find the path on the left about 40 yards past the open gateway. It hooks up with the network of old roads and arroyos between Waldo and Grand Central Mountain (hike 22). Otherwise, take a sharp left before the gate and follow the signs to the Mirador. A sign there identifies the many mountain peaks and ranges in view.

From the Mirador, return to the main trail, and turn right. Within the 0.5-mile descent ahead, four mines dot the trailside. Protective mesh allows you to gape into each one without the risk of falling in. When the trail starts uphill again, you have slightly more than a 0.5-mile climb before the sharp drop into Elkins Canyon.

At the canyon floor, turn right, and follow the streambed trail as it squeezes through a rocky chute. When you emerge from the south end, take the first path on the left and follow a 300-yard easement to Yerba Buena (CR 59A). Turn left on this dirt road and go 0.25 miles to Camino Turquesa. Turn left again to go north past the cemetery and return to the parking area.

Note: For the latest updates on CHHP, check with the Casa Grande Trading Post & Mining Museum. To visit it, follow the directions below, but go straight past First Street and turn left on Third Street. Go south one block and turn right on Waldo Street. Casa Grande is at the end of the block. Call (505) 438-3008 or visit **www.cerrilloshills.org.**

NEARBY ACTIVITIES

The Museum of New Mexico Foundation leads field trips to Galisteo Basin sites that are otherwise closed to the public. Check the MNMF Friends of Archaeology events calendar **www.museumfoundation.org/foa,** or call (505) 982-6366. The Museum of Indian Arts & Culture also leads tours in the area. Check **www.miaclab.org** (click on "events") or call (505) 476-1250. Be aware that these tours are often fully booked weeks in advance.

The Santa Fe Botanical Garden hosts guided hikes and scheduled events April–October at the Ortiz Mountains Educational Preserve, about 8 miles south of Cerrillos. Visit **www.santafebotanicalgarden.org** for the OMEP schedule, or call (505) 428-1684. For more local information, visit **www.galisteoarcheology.org** and **www.turquoisetrail.org.**

22 CERRILLOS HILLS:
Waldo–Grand Central Mountain

GPS Trailhead
Coordinates

UTM Zone (WGS 84) 13S

Easting   0396417

Northing   3923314

Latitude 35° 27' 01"

Longitude 106° 08' 20"

IN BRIEF

On the west side of Cerrillos Hills Historic Park, canyons, closed dirt roads, and horse trails form a rugged transit system between the outskirts of a ghost town and the abandoned mines at the base of Grand Central Mountain. There you can decide whether to scramble the last 500 feet to its 6,976-foot peak or continue exploring its complex foothills.

DESCRIPTION

The hike may turn out up to 0.5 miles longer than expected, given the deteriorating conditions of the road to the cable gate. If you're walking it, you're probably not too impressed with the sights so far. It'll soon get better. Meanwhile, please refrain from asking "Where's Waldo?" That joke got stale in 1987.

Directions ──────────────────────────▶

From I-40 east, take Exit 175 toward Cedar Crest. From the I-40 overpass, go 32 miles north on NM 14 and turn left onto Main Street toward Cerrillos. Once in the village, turn right at the first stop sign onto First Street. Go over the railroad tracks, take an immediate left onto CR 57 (Waldo Canyon Road), and go 1.3 miles. (If you cross a cattle guard after the horseshoe curve, you've gone about 0.15 miles too far.) Turn right onto a rough dirt road and find a place to park. (Don't block the road. It's used for emergency access.) The hike begins at the cable gate ahead, 0.25 miles north of Waldo Canyon Road.

Alternate route (50 miles): From I-25 North take Exit 267 and turn right on CR 57. Drive 6.5 miles south–southeast, then look for a dirt road on the left about 0.15 miles past the cattle guard. Note that most of Waldo Canyon Road is unpaved and can get tricky in wet weather.

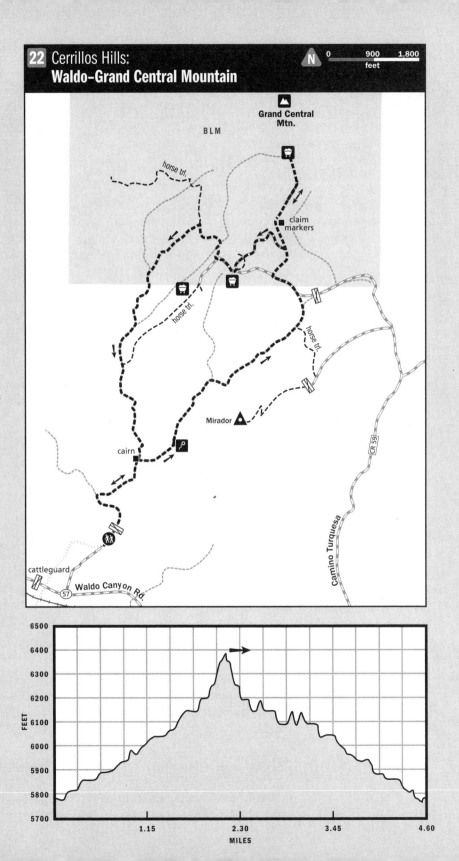

Grand Central
Mtn.

B L M

horse trl.

claim
markers

horse trl.

horse trl.

Mirador

cairn

Camino Turquesa

CR 59

cattleguard

Waldo Canyon Rd.

57

6500
6400
6300
6200
6100
6000
5900
5800
5700

FEET

1.15   2.30   3.45   4.60
MILES

A spectral cloud rises from Cerrillos Hills.

A coal-mining town on the Santa Fe Railroad, Waldo was named for Henry L. Waldo, Grand Master of the New Mexico Masons (1878) and Chief Justice of the New Mexico Territory Supreme Court (1881). The Colorado Fuel and Iron Company built 15 coke ovens in Waldo in the 1890s but closed the mines in 1906. The town persevered by supplying Madrid with well water, hauling up to 150,000 gallons in rail tank cars per day. As Madrid's mining economy began to falter, so did Waldo. A salvage company purchased the town in 1937 and stripped it down by the end of the 1940s. Oddly, the name still appears on maps and road signs. To see what remains, check Nearby Activities.

Getting back to the hike, the road runs up the east side of an alluvial fan that empties into Galisteo Creek to the south. In the northeastern corner, the main channel emerges from the mouth of a canyon. A cable gate has been installed here to prevent unauthorized vehicles from entering. Numerous waterways, old roads, and horse trails multiply the possibilities for navigating the rolling terrain beyond the gate. The choices can get a little overwhelming at times. To help simplify matters, this route breaks down into three relatively simple segments.

Outbound canyon (1.5 miles): The scenery changes dramatically once you step inside the craw of the canyon. Rock shelves and overhangs on the walls are inviting for a shaded respite on hotter days. Deep pockets of sand on the canyon floor can slow the pace, so take advantage of rest stops where you can. After a

0.5-mile walk north from the gate, note a cairn and a prominent wash fanning out from a canyon on the left—that's the return canyon, a branch you'll use to close the loop. For now, bear right to stay in the outbound canyon (so called because the topo maps don't give it a proper name).

About 0.25 miles northeast, the trail passes over a spring. Slog through the mud, or tiptoe around it, and continue northeast. Less than 0.25 miles past the spring, an outcrop resembling a stone wall points downstream and splits the trail. The narrow canyon on the left is worth a quick look, but to continue on this hike, aim to the right.

For the next 0.4 miles, a relatively straight dirt road follows the eastern bank of the winding wash. You can use either the wash or the road. When the two diverge, with the road rising to the northwest and the wash continuing to the northeast, veer left to follow the road. If you come across another cable gate, you've followed the wash about 200 feet too far.

Roads and horse trails (1–3 miles): Once you leave the wash, the landscape opens up to present a tangle of interwoven and overlapping old dirt roads and active horse trails. Head uphill about 0.1 mile along the road and go right at the Y-junction. About the same distance ahead, a horse trail starts on the left. To cut a steep spur from this hike, turn here now; otherwise, continue along the road another 0.1 mile to three wooden posts propped up in rock piles. These are claim markers, and it's apparent that much digging has been done in the vicinity. The road from here fades fast as it climbs the mountain. Less than 0.25 miles past the claim markers, down in the arroyo on the left, is a boarded mine that's losing its battle against the elements.

If you intend to climb Grand Central Mountain, formerly known as Cerro del Oso ("hill of the bear"), the route from here is clear: it's all uphill. Loose rock and maybe an ornery rattler or two can complicate a trip to the summit. Climb if you must, but give it at least 30 minutes, and be careful not to trample the vegetation. The view from the top includes Cerro Bonanza (7,088 feet), about 2 miles north. The escarpment of La Bajada (hike 28) starts about 3.5 miles to the northwest and stretches another 4 miles from there. If you've already done that hike, you might find greater appreciation for it here. No other vantage point reveals the enormity of that obstacle quite like the view from Grand Central Mountain.

Go back down the road, and turn right on the horse trail mentioned earlier. In about 0.25 miles, it intersects another path. Keep going straight down the middle until you pick up the dirt road again, where you'll see a capped mine.

Backtrack option: The route from here gets a little more complicated. If you've had trouble navigating it so far or aren't confident in your route-finding skills, consider turning left here. Follow the main road about 0.4 miles back to the point where you exited the wash in the outbound canyon.

Otherwise turn right, and go past the capped mine. The main road soon takes a sharp left up a steep hill, but avoid that for this hike. Instead, maintain a straight course and cross the wash ahead. From here the horse trail starts north again as though going back up Grand Central Mountain, but it soon hooks west. The next few intersecting washes feed into the return canyon, so take your pick. The trail goes north again about 0.25 miles before its next tack to the west. If you haven't picked a wash by this point, you probably should start heading downstream now—you're running out of defined trail, and I can't vouch for the washes ahead.

Return segment (1.5 miles): Pick a wash, and stick to it, following it downstream. Each one starts out shallow. The walls of the canyon don't rise up and squeeze in until the last 0.5 miles. Then, almost suddenly, you find yourself in a winding chasm that seems to draw the eyes to the rim above. It's oddly mesmerizing, but watch your footing, too. You have a couple of stair-step waterfalls (usually dry) and some flood debris to negotiate. The canyon widens as it approaches the cairn. Turn right, and follow the outbound canyon 0.5 miles downstream to the cable gate.

Note: No trail markers or interpretive signs were in place when I mapped this hike, though it's likely that many will pop up by the end of 2007. For the latest updates, check with the Casa Grande Trading Post & Mining Museum. To get there, follow the Directions, but go straight past First Street, and turn left on Third Street. Go south one block, and turn right on Waldo Street. Casa Grande is at the end of the block. Call (505) 438-3008 or **visit www.cerrilloshills.org.**

NEARBY ACTIVITIES

Venture another 0.5 miles or so up Waldo Canyon Road, and look near the old railroad grade for remnants of Waldo. You'll find structural foundations, the ruins of the coke ovens, and little else. It's worth a stop, if only for a moment of reflection on the vulnerable nature of rural economies. The town site is now private property, so stick to the road. Livelier attractions—galleries, cafes, and a movie ranch are located along NM 14, the Turquoise Trail National Scenic Byway. For more information, call (888) 263-0003 or visit **www.turquoisetrail.org.**

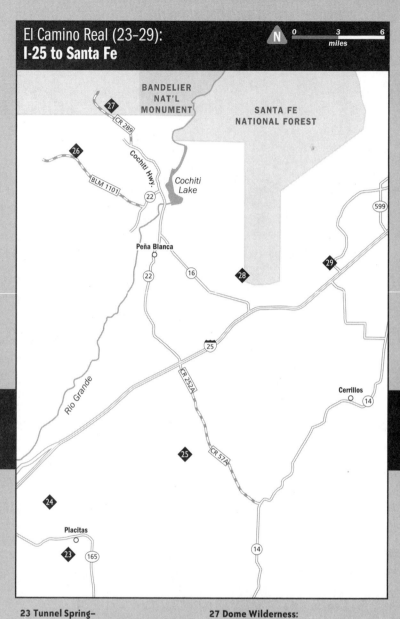

BANDELIER
NAT'L
MONUMENT

SANTA FE
NATIONAL FOREST

CR 289

Cochiti Hwy.

BLM 1101

Cochiti
Lake

599

Peña Blanca

22   16   28   29

Rio Grande

25

CR 252A

Cerrillos   14

CR 57A

25

24

Placitas

23   165

14

EL CAMINO REAL

23 TUNNEL SPRING-AGUA SARCA

KEY AT-A-GLANCE INFORMATION

LENGTH: 9.5-, 6.9- or 4.2-mile loop options

DIFFICULTY: Strenuous

SCENERY: Canyon and valley over-looks, mixed conifer forest, sea-sonal wildflowers, riparian habitat, marine fossils

EXPOSURE: Some forest and canyon shade

TRAIL TRAFFIC: Moderate

SHARED USE: Low (equestrians; closed to all mechanized vehicles)

TRAIL SURFACE: Gravel, packed dirt, loose rock

HIKING TIME: 5–7 hours

DRIVING DISTANCE: 21 miles (one way) from the I-40 and I-25 exchange

ACCESS: Year-round

LAND STATUS: Cibola National Forest–Sandia Mountain Wilderness

MAPS: Sandia Ranger District; USGS Placitas

FACILITIES: Restrooms (no water)

LAST CHANCE FOOD/GAS: All ser-vices available in Bernalillo and Placitas

IN BRIEF

Three trails of varying designations add up to adventurous loop options on the northern end of the Sandia Mountains. Dizzying overlooks and mountain vistas punctuate this scenic journey.

DESCRIPTION

The route described below links two desig-nated trails to form one big loop. Throw in a third trail—an unofficial shortcut known as Ojo del Orno Route—and your loop options multiply. Consider all possibilities to plan a hike that best serves your interests. For exam-ple: To minimize downhill impact on bad knees, follow the hike description in reverse; that is, go up the steep Agua Sarca Trail and return on the gentler Crest Trail.

The Crest Trail (130) begins on the south side of the Tunnel Spring parking area. Start from the gate on the left side of the map and information board. A nearby sign reports the distances to destinations along this majestic trail: Agua Sarca Overlook, 5 miles; Del Agua Overlook, 8 miles; Sandia Crest, 11 miles. In fact, it extends 26 miles to the Canyon Estates trailhead, visited in hike 11 at Hondo Canyon.

GPS Trailhead Coordinates

UTM Zone (WGS 84)   13S

Easting   0369122

Northing   3906327

Latitude   35° 17' 30"

Longitude   106° 26' 22"

Directions ———————→

From I-25 north, take Exit 242 toward Placitas. Follow NM 165 for about 5 miles east, then turn right on Forest Road 231. (Look for a bank of mailboxes and a green street sign for Tun-nel Spring Road on the right. The 5-mile marker is about 50 yards too far.) Follow this steep dirt road 1.4 miles to its end at the Tun-nel Spring trailhead.

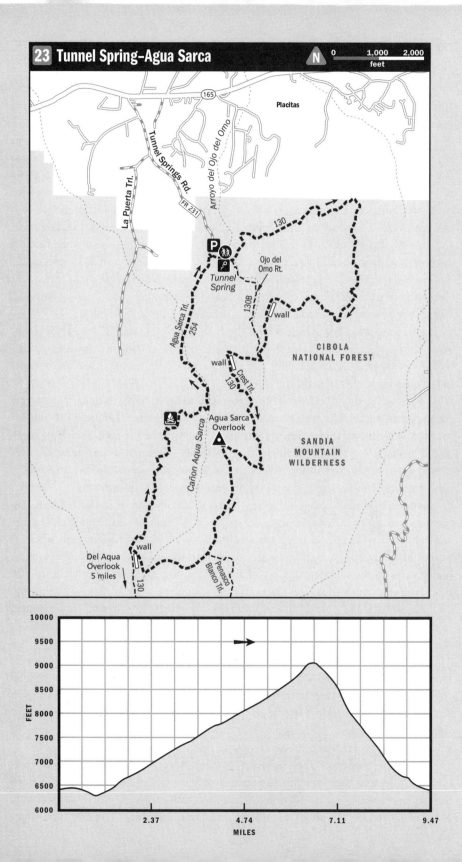

N

0   1,000   2,000
feet

Placitas

165

Tunnel Springs Rd.

La Puerta Trl.

FR 231

Arroyo del Ojo del Omo

130

P

Tunnel Spring

Ojo del Omo Rt.

130B

wall

Agua Sarca Trl.
254

wall

Crest Trl.
130

CIBOLA
NATIONAL FOREST

Cañon Aqua Sarca

Agua Sarca
Overlook

SANDIA
MOUNTAIN
WILDERNESS

Del Aqua
Overlook
5 miles

wall

130

Peñasco
Blanco Trl.

10000

9500

9000

8500

8000

FEET

7500

7000

6500

6000

2.37   4.74   7.11   9.47

MILES

A sign indicating the wilderness boundary stands about 100 yards down the trail. Just past the sign, the Arroyo Ojo del Orno crosses the trail. A right turn here puts you on the shortcut described below.

The shortcut: If you prefer to cut straight to the action, the 0.8-mile Ojo del Orno route will get your heart (and lungs) pounding in the first five minutes. It's a straight shot up a deep drainage, making it the easiest of the three trails to navigate. It'll cut 2.6 miles from the big loop, and it's also the steepest and most strenuous of the three. As an unofficial route, Ojo del Orno receives no maintenance. It appears as an unidentified line of thin red dashes on the map at the Tunnel Spring trailhead but has been omitted from more-recent forest maps. Although it gets enough use to keep the way fairly clear, you may encounter drainage debris and overgrown vegetation. If you take the shortcut, turn left near the top to climb out of the drainage, and then turn right on the trail above. Resume following the directions from Crest Trail (continued) below.

The long way: Some hikers find the first few miles of the Crest Trail somewhat dull. Because it meanders for an hour before getting to the action, this circuitous segment is what I refer to as the French Film Loop. If you enjoy slow-building drama, this is definitely the way to go.

To resume on the Crest Trail, cross the arroyo, and continue past a few more posted signs. The trail roughly follows the wilderness boundary. Look for remnants of mining operations in this area. Ovens used for metal smelting were called *hornos,* for their resemblance to beehives. The name of the aforementioned arroyo, Ojo del Orno, refers to these furnace ovens. Sealed mineshafts and scattered rubble also serve as vague reminders of the mining era.

About 1.3 miles into the hike, the trail rounds the point of a ridge and climbs south. You'll notice a few old Jeep roads running near and crossing the trail ahead. Pay attention to cairns and tree-branch edgings to stay on track. A potentially confusing junction sits 2.4 miles into the hike (about 200 yards past a major bend to the northeast). Continue climbing for another 0.5 miles until you reach the east rim of Ojo del Orno, now decidedly a canyon. A stone retaining wall just around the corner makes a convenient bench. Another 0.3 miles south, or 3.4 miles into the hike, the Crest Trail takes sharp right to cross the head of the canyon.

Crest Trail (continued): Just 0.3 miles east of the upper Ojo del Orno, a second stone bench overlooks Agua Sarca Canyon. Though this is not the official overlook, the view is breathtaking. Nearing 7,600 feet, you may notice a drop in temperature, particularly if strong winds greet you at the canyon rim. Say goodbye to the piñon–juniper zone as you prepare to wade through a waist-high canopy of scrub oak. Long pants are a wise choice on this hike, even in the summer.

The trail angles south–southeast, veering away from the ridgeline for just under a mile, and then switchbacks sharply to your right (northwest) to return to the rim at the Agua Sarca Overlook. It's a good 500 feet higher than the last one. Marine fossils are abundant in nearby limestone outcrops. The trail continues

roughly south for about 0.8 miles before reaching the northern end of Peñasco Blanco Trail, which dives through thickets of oak on your left. The namesake "white bluff" (more of a gray limestone formation) is visible to the east.

From here the trees thin out, allowing for profusions of wildflowers in the spring and summer. Orange and red versions of the Western wallflower stand out against white blooms of fendlerbush. Near the head of Agua Sarca Canyon, a distinctive boulder is a good place to sit and enjoy the view. About 100 yards or so later, cross the shallow Agua Sarca streambed. Older maps show a path following the west side of the drainage almost all the way back to the Agua Sarca trailhead. If such a route still exists, it would be easier to navigate than the designated trail ahead, but then it probably wouldn't be quite as scenic. Go another 0.2 miles northwest to the next switchback. Those who went the long way are now 6.5 miles into the hike.

Agua Sarca Trail (254): This 3-mile route meets the Crest Trail at the bend in the switchback. There's no marker here, but the low end of a long retaining wall points directly at the trailhead. Turn right and prepare to follow a sporadic path. Give yourself a minimum of 2 hours to complete this section.

Study four different maps of Sandia Mountain trails, and you will find as many incarnations of Agua Sarca Trail. Adding to the confusion are scores of small cairns placed by well-intentioned hikers who thought they knew the best way but then gave up at obvious points of uncertainty. On the plus side, all this really means is there's more than one way to get through the canyon.

For the upper portion of the Agua Sarca route, your best bet is to stick to paths closest to the ridgeline. The drop on the other side is a sheer 300 feet or

Horned lizard on the lower Crest Trail

more, and views to the west are spectacular. The path often ducks down to the right (east) to avoid outcrops and dense vegetation, only to vanish momentarily in scrub, exposed limestone, and scree. You should find several opportunities to return to the edge for more views over the Rio Grande Valley. The parting glance comes about 0.8 miles down the line, where a more clearly defined but particularly steep section of trail angles northeastward, deeper into the canyon.

The grade lessens slightly on a brief stretch heading north. (According to a 2006 forest map, a more recent version of Trail 254 crosses through here, with a right turn leading down to the canyon floor. I didn't notice it and so stayed north on the old trail.) A fork soon gives you a choice between a steep path (left) and a steeper one (straight ahead). Both lead to a prominent landmark that's either an elaborate fire pit or a crude stone hearth. A lean-to and other Boy Scout projects are nearby. Exit the east side of the site, and turn left to begin the descent toward the stream below. On this 0.5-mile final approach to the canyon floor, dense vegetation occasionally simulates jungle conditions, and musky aromas heighten your awareness of local wildlife.

Once you spot the stream, you're in the clear. Just turn left (north), and follow it down for the next 0.7 miles, crossing it a few times along the way as the path widens into an old Jeep road. (Intersecting roads and trails are easy to ignore on the way down but can be confusing on the way up.) After the third crossing, the road leaves the sandy streambed to climb over a saddle to the northeast. From there it's all downhill to FR 231, where you'll turn right to return to the parking area.

PLACITAS: Las Huertas Creek 24

IN BRIEF

Near the village of Placitas, this hike relies on natural waterways cut through low rolling foothills in the Las Huertas Basin. The 560-acre Placitas Open Space and 4,000 acres of adjacent BLM land add up to a roomy place to roam in the footsteps of ancient Puebloans, conquistadors, homesteaders, miners, and others.

DESCRIPTION

The village of Placitas has a certain charm that belies its turbulent past. Troubles in the area escalated in the early 1820s with a series of Apache raids on Las Huertas. The walled town was evacuated in 1823, and most families retreated to Algodones, 6 miles northwest. Many returned 17 years later to start over. Struggling to reestablish their community, they called their scattered collection of small farms Las Placitas ("the villages"). But the problems didn't end there.

The 1850s brought a rush of Anglo miners. By the century's end, a violent grudge had

- -

Directions ———————————————➤

From I-25 north, take Exit 242 toward Placitas. Turn right (east) on NM 165 and go 6.9 miles. Turn left on Camino de Las Huertas and go 2.9 miles. Turn left on Llano del Norte. Go 0.4 miles, then follow the road as it bends left. (Toad Road will be on the right.) Continue west another 0.9 miles on Llano del Norte to two gates. Go through the first gateway (but not the second one) and turn left. Drive 100 yards southwest to a drop gate. Drive through and fasten the gate behind you. Continue another 250 yards and park at the signpost at the end of the road. The trail starts between a pair of juniper trees straight ahead at the mesa rim.

KEY AT-A-GLANCE INFORMATION

LENGTH: 4-mile loop

DIFFICULTY: Easy

SCENERY: Juniper grassland, mountain and mesa views, lizards, rabbits, and maybe wild horses

EXPOSURE: Little shade

TRAIL TRAFFIC: Moderate

SHARED USE: Low (off-road vehicles on BLM segments)

TRAIL SURFACE: Sand, river rock

HIKING TIME: 2 hours

DRIVING DISTANCE: 27 miles (one way) from the I-40 and I-25 exchange

ACCESS: Daylight hours

LAND STATUS: Albuquerque Open Space; BLM–Rio Puerco Field Office

MAPS: USGS Placitas

FACILITIES: None

LAST CHANCE FOOD/GAS: All services on NM 165 in Placitas

SPECIAL COMMENTS: For information on events involving Placitas Open Space and Las Huertas Creek Watershed Project, contact Las Placitas Association at (505) 867-6330, or online at www.lasplacitas.org. You can download the Placitas Open Space Bird Checklist and the List of Flowering Plants from their site.

- -

GPS Trailhead
Coordinates

UTM Zone (WGS 84)   13S

Easting   0367280

Northing   3911796

Latitude   35° 20' 23"

Longitude   106° 27' 38"

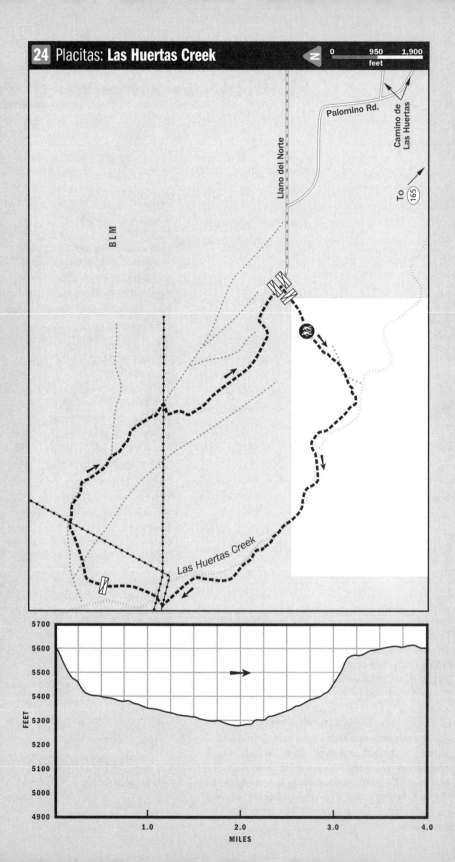

0   950   1,900
feet

Palomino Rd.

Llano del Norte

Camino de
Las Huertas

To
165

B L M

Las Huertas Creek

5700
5600
5500
5400
5300
5200
5100
5000
4900

FEET

1.0   2.0   3.0   4.0
MILES

developed between Catholics and Presbyterians. But perhaps the most unsettling period started in the 1960s with the arrival of the counterculture movement. What began as experiments in communal living ultimately devolved into enough drug-addled mayhem to rival that of the Manson family.

Today the seemingly endless construction of millionaire homes suggests that the curse of Placitas has finally lifted, though some longtime residents would argue that this marks only the beginning of another one. Either way, the ruins of the old and ancient settlements hidden throughout the hills have not been forgotten. Recent area surveys recorded at least 72 archeological sites, not counting hippie ruins. So far, 16 are eligible for the National Register of Historic Places, some dating back 11,000 years. Site locations are not made public, but here's a hint: you'll pass within a whisper of at least three of them and probably won't notice anything more than grass and rock.

The City of Albuquerque acquired these 560 acres near Placitas in 1966 under the federal Recreation and Public Purposes Act, which required the city to develop it for recreational purposes or return it to the BLM. Lacking a hard deadline, they left the property undisturbed for 29 years. In 1995 an Albuquerque resident proposed a shooting range for Placitas Open Space. The proposal was denied, and local community organizations have since assumed a more proactive approach to minding the open space and other public lands along the lower Las Huertas watershed.

Las Placitas Association completed their Open Space Master Plan in 2002, proposing a designated trail system, interpretive signage, picnic shelters, restroom facilities, native revegetation projects, fence removals, and gates affording easier access. By 2007 they managed to untangle enough red tape to successfully post a list of regulations in the parking area and remove a barbed-wire fence. The remaining improvements may soon follow. At last check, a few pathways have been staked out, but the signpost has been relieved of its regulatory signage.

The land north of Placitas Open Space is one of the most desired properties in the BLM's Rio Puerco inventory. At least three Indian pueblos have aboriginal land claims relating to this land. The Wild Horse Association wants to turn it into a horse preserve. Ranchers want to use it for cattle grazing. Oil companies want to drill it. Mining companies want to dig gravel quarries. The Placitas Board of Realtors has asked BLM to dispose of lands for real-estate development. And the Village Academy Charter School wants to build a school there. The BLM says its plan for the land will take about two years to develop. Hikers, enjoy it while you can.

At the trailhead, views are wide open in all directions. Forty miles northwest, Cabezon resembles a cork in an anthill. Five miles south, the dramatic tilt of the Sandia range is revealed in profile. Las Huertas Creek starts just below Capulin Peak, about 8,600 feet up in the Sandias. The creek runs 15 miles as though aiming toward Cabezon but empties into the Rio Grande near Algodones.

In past centuries, it was a reliable stream that supported populations of elk, pronghorn antelope, gray wolf, and bighorn sheep. Human activity since the mid-1800s has devastated the habitat. In 1906 just 5 miles south of Placitas, local rancher Augie Ellis shot the Sandia's last grizzly bear. The last trout was fished from the pools of Las Huertas Creek sometime in the 1930s.

At least 20 horses have been known to frequent the Placitas environs in the early-morning hours. Their origins are unclear. Some local residents believe them to be descendants of Spanish mustangs. Others regard them as feral nuisances and hope to have them removed by the end of 2007. Unclaimed horses in New Mexico are often placed into adoption programs or slaughtered for bear bait.

Animal life today still includes coyote and gray fox. Bald eagle, peregrine falcon, and the rare willow flycatcher have been spotted along the creek. Jackrabbit and cottontail are far more common, and several lizard species run riot in warm months.

The segment of the creek on this hike is about 80 yards wide, on average. While you probably won't find much evidence of water in its sand and cobblestone streambed, it can overrun its banks in a good monsoon season.

The hike begins on the rim 200 feet above the creek. To find the trailhead, locate the Albuquerque Volcanoes on the southwest horizon, and walk straight toward them. The trail starts with a steep, rocky descent. Along this 0.3-mile segment, the path intersects a wash. Like many trails and waterways in the area, the two merge and diverge as though loosely braided. You can follow either.

Plans call for a trail along the near bank. For now there's a fading doubletrack. In any case, the creek itself makes a more interesting route, so drop down, and turn right to explore the wide, cobbled streambed. About 0.5 miles downstream, you'll reach the north Open Space boundary, indicated by a washed-out fence line that crosses the creek.

About 1.7 miles into the hike, directly beneath the power lines, you'll see a pronounced doubletrack splitting off to the right. Follow the road out of the creek to a drop gate 0.25 miles north. Go through, and latch it behind you. Stay on the road as it curves around the northwest end of the ridge. Continue east, past a wide draw opening on your right. Go around the end of the next ridge. Directly beneath the utility lines, turn right into a second draw.

Walk up the wide, sand-and-gravel streambed southeast 0.7 miles. Once again, directly beneath the crackling power lines, you'll find a doubletrack splitting off to the right. Exit the wash and follow the road straight up the ridgeline. You'll soon climb high enough to look down into both draws. Take a moment to look behind you for a view of the mesas to the northwest.

After 0.25 miles, the terrain on the ridgeline road starts to level out. Soon you should be able to spot your car through the juniper ahead on your right. Stay on the main road as it turns left. Once past the head of the second draw, it turns right and leads you straight back to the two gates. Go through the first one (but not the second one), and turn right. Return to the parking area the same way you drove in. Don't forget to latch the gate behind you before driving off.

The Sandia Mountains, as seen from Placitas

NEARBY ACTIVITIES

Built in the old hacienda style and surrounded by spring-fed orchards, Anasazi Fields Winery provides a relaxing oasis for wine tasting and tours. The winery is open Wednesday to Sunday, 12–5 p.m. Special events are held seasonally. To get there from Placitas Open Space, return to NM 165, and go 0.8 miles west to Camino de los Pueblitos. Turn right, and go northeast 0.2 miles to the winery. For more information, call (505) 867-3062, or visit **www.anasazifieldswinery .com.**

25 BALL RANCH

KEY AT-A-GLANCE INFORMATION

LENGTH: 4.5-mile loop, 9.6-mile balloon without gate key
DIFFICULTY: Moderate
SCENERY: Winding canyon, petrified wood, red mesas, hilltop overlook
EXPOSURE: Some canyon shade
TRAIL TRAFFIC: Low
SHARED USE: Low (equestrians, mountain bikers; livestock; limited motor-vehicle access)
TRAIL SURFACE: Sand, dirt
HIKING TIME: 2 hours, 4.5 hours without gate key
DRIVING DISTANCE: 41 miles (one-way) from the I-40/I-25 exchange
ACCESS: Year-round (see below)
LAND STATUS: BLM—Rio Puerco Field Office (ACEC)
MAPS: Map available from BLM office; USGS San Felipe Pueblo NE
FACILITIES: None
LAST CHANCE FOOD/GAS: Convenience store, food, gas at Exit 259
SPECIAL COMMENTS: For roads beyond the gate, a high-clearance vehicle is helpful. 4WD recommended after wet weather. (Or, cover the Ball Ranch roads on a mountain bike.) Pick up a gate key from the BLM office at 435 Montano Road NE in Albuquerque. Though it's not usually necessary, you can also call ahead to reserve a key: (505) 761-8600.

GPS Trailhead Coordinates

UTM Zone (WGS 84)   13S
Easting   0381722
Northing   3916637
Latitude   35° 23' 10"
Longitude   106° 18' 08"

IN BRIEF

Surrounded by tribal lands and accessed by rough easement roads behind locked gates, the trailhead can be a challenge to reach—but it's worth the extra effort. This hike follows arroyos and old ranch roads from the lowest canyon to the highest ridge to give you the full flavor of this seldom-visited public land.

DESCRIPTION

Try using the BLM map to navigate the BLM easement road and you may soon realize the lines don't fully articulate the twisted reality of the roads. Fortunately, signs installed in 2006 effectively spell out where you can and cannot go. Unfortunately, signs in remote areas often disappear or get shot beyond recognition.

If that happens to be the case, use these **road directions** to get from the locked gate to the drop gate: About 0.8 miles past the locked gate, the road bends south and arrives at a fork. Bear right, and cross the arroyo. This is the roughest bit of road; consider going ahead

Directions

From I-25 north, take Exit 259 and turn right on County Road 252A (formerly NM 22). Measuring from the top of the northbound exit ramp, go south 5.9 miles to the second gate on the right, marked Ball Ranch. (GPS coordinates for the gate are N 35° 23' 30", W 106° 16' 12") If you have the key, unlock the gate. *Inspect the gateway area for objects that could puncture tires.* Drive through and lock the gate behind you. Follow the BLM signs 2.2 miles to the drop gate. (See Description for more details.) Unlatch the gate, drive through, and close it behind you. Continue straight (west) 0.1 mile and turn left (south) at the first junction. Go 0.3 miles and park near the windmill.

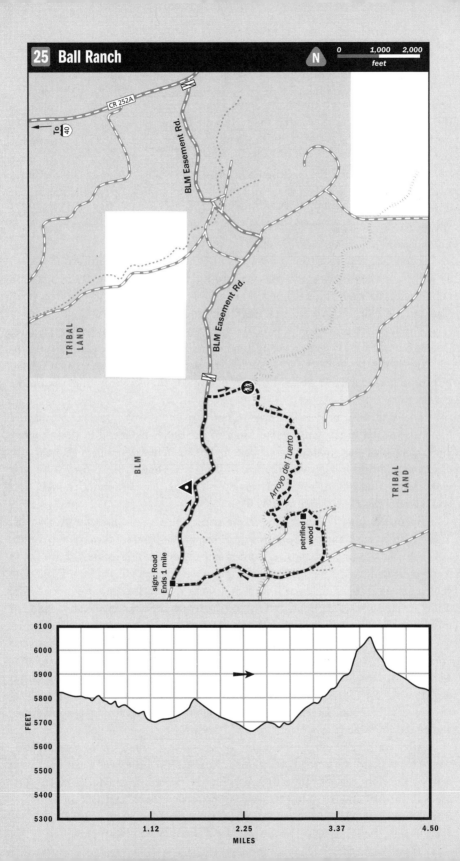

on foot to scout out the best way to cross the arroyo. Go straight through the junction on the other side of the arroyo, and continue southwest 0.3 miles to the next junction. Take a sharp right, and go 1 mile west–northwest [0.6 miles northwest and 0.4 miles west] to the drop gate. The windmill is just around the corner to the left.

When you reach the parking area, take a moment to get oriented. Check your tires for flats (I've had three in as many visits to Ball Ranch). Listen to the windmill as it groans ominously in the breeze. Note that the last stretch of road you drove down is part of the return loop, as is the road that extends west from the junction and climbs over the hill.

There are a hundred different ways to explore this little BLM venue known as Ball Ranch, and twice as many ways to get lost or inadvertently trespass on tribal land. To keep things simple, this hike is confined to one of three small tracts in the Ball Ranch Area of Critical Environmental Concern (ACEC).

The ACEC status was set in part to protect five rare plants found here, including the Santa Fe milkvetch, a purplish perennial that went missing for a full century (from the 1840s to the 1940s), and the paper-spined cactus, which turned out to be not so much rare as difficult to spot for the way it mimics clumps of grama grass.

The ACEC also protects Stearns' Quarry, a deposit of fossilized wood and bone discovered in the late 1940s. Most of the bones belonged to titanotheres, an extinct group of mammals related to horses. They resembled rhinos with exaggerated horns but grew to the size of Indian elephants. Big as they were, you won't likely find any of their remains on this hike. Pay attention, though, and you'll find loads of petrified wood.

Begin the hike by heading past the windmill, straight into the Arroyo del Tuerto, which runs along the south side of the parking area. Like so many routes in this book, this one depends on both roads and waterways—rarely, however, is it more difficult to distinguish between the two. Despite a nearby sign forbidding vehicles beyond this point, you'll find tire tracks running up and down the wide, sandy wash. Turn to the right, and follow them into the canyon ahead, keeping in mind the usual precaution about traveling in arroyos: beware of flash flooding.

The canyon soon narrows, running deep and sinuous as it squeezes between two hills. Look for birds' nests in the pocked walls. Keep an eye on the ground as well. On my first hike through here, I encountered a tarantula the size of a fried egg. It was recently deceased, regrettably, but still quite a surprise on a chilly December afternoon. I returned nine days later, a full week after a good snow, and found only the tracks of rabbits and bobcats.

After walking about 1 mile down the streambed, you'll notice that the canyon shallows and the arroyo straightens. At the top of the last sharp bend, the wall on the right reveals tan, pink, and green striations. Meanwhile, on the left, the wall shrinks down to a low bank. Exit the arroyo there, and pick up a double-track running south.

Cholla cactus

About 0.2 miles from the arroyo exit, the road crosses a wash. Do *not* follow the road around the bend to the west. Instead, take a sharp left, and follow the road/wash as it crooks southward. The road soon diverges from the wash. Continue south, keeping the wash on your right.

About 0.2 miles from the left turn, the wash shallows down to a sandy bed. You'll see it in a distinct clearing through the juniper on your right. This is where you'll exit the path for a short detour.

Turn right, and cross straight over the wash. Continue west about 200 feet, until you see a hillside littered with strange dark rocks, some with a brilliant patchwork of lichen. Closer inspection reveals a woody grain in the stone surface. It doesn't take an expert eye to see they were once trees, albeit several million years ago. (The GPS coordinates for the petrified wood area are N 35° 22' 52", W 106° 18' 58".)

Return to the trail, and turn right to continue south. Follow the trail another 0.2 miles as it bends southwest and climbs to the top of a low pass on the ridge ahead. Sandia Peak emerges in full view 13 miles to the southwest as you ascend to the grassy plateau. The trail, however, pretty much fades out.

Just continue down the other side of the ridge, cutting around some deep ruts on the left, and within 100 yards you'll intercept another prominent wash/road. Follow it west. Within 0.25 miles it'll turn the color of cinnamon and bend north. Stay on the red road another 0.4 miles, and you'll end up in the middle of the Arroyo del Tuerto. You're now less than 0.5 miles downstream from the

Petrified wood with a patchwork of lichen

point where you exited the arroyo. If you're low on energy, here's a shortcut: turn right here to follow the arroyo 1.5 miles back to the windmill.

Otherwise, you're slightly more than halfway through the loop, mileage-wise, with another 2.2 miles and a 500-foot gain in elevation ahead. Those determined to complete the loop properly should continue straight on the main northbound road another 0.6 miles to the BLM easement road. Don't bother looking for more-direct routes via waterways to the hilltop unless you're in the mood for tricky climbs up steep drop-offs.

When you arrive at the easement road, you'll see the backside of a sign that states: "Road Ends 1 Mile" (referring, of course, to the road you just traveled). Turn right, and follow the easement road about 0.8 miles to the top of the hill. The views are gorgeous in all directions. It's even better at night when Santa Fe glimmers to the northeast, while the Sandias shield the glow of Albuquerque in the southwest.

To finish the loop, go straight down the east side of the hill, and turn right at the bottom to get back to the windmill. (Or, if you parked outside the locked gate, continue straight ahead.)

As you drive out of Ball Ranch, secure both gates behind you. Also, check your tires again before getting back on the interstate.

KASHA-KATUWE TENT ROCKS NATIONAL MONUMENT

IN BRIEF

Tapering hoodoos up to 90 feet tall are the primary attractions at Tent Rocks. Enter a sinuous slot canyon to admire them from below, and then climb high upon a ridge to gaze down upon them. In warm seasons, wildlife comes in furred, feathered, and spiked varieties, and wildflower identification can turn into a full-day affair.

DESCRIPTION

Since it was designated a national monument in 2001, Tent Rocks has seen crowds in the lower Peralta Canyon increase steadily. Although you could arrive to find it virtually deserted, particularly in winter or on a midweek morning, you're likely to find a camera safari or a busload of schoolchildren around every corner.

For now, hiking in the 4,148-acre monument is restricted to a total of 2.2 miles of developed trails. The BLM, in partnership with the Pueblo de Cochiti, is currently working on opportunities for visitors to enjoy other areas of the monument. Recent proposals indicate that an old pumice-mine road and nearby laterals will be converted into foot trails.

KEY AT-A-GLANCE INFORMATION

LENGTH: 3.3-mile loop and spur
DIFFICULTY: Moderate
SCENERY: Birds and wildlife, seasonal wildflowers, premium hoodoos
EXPOSURE: Some canyon shade
TRAIL TRAFFIC: Popular
SHARED USE: Low (dogs must be leashed; no horses or vehicles)
TRAIL SURFACE: Packed sand and gravel, bedrock
HIKING TIME: 2 hours
DRIVING DISTANCE: 55 miles (one way) from the I-40 and I-25 exchange
ACCESS: November 1–March 10, 8 a.m.–5 p.m.; March 11–October 31, 7 a.m.–7 p.m. Visitors must be out by closing time. On-site fee is $5 per noncommercial vehicle. Federal Land Recreation Passes are accepted.
LAND STATUS: BLM–Rio Puerco; Cochiti Pueblo
MAPS: Brochure map available at park entrance station; USGS Canada
FACILITIES: Picnic area, the facilities, Cave Loop Trail, and Veterans' Memorial Overlook are wheelchair-accessible.
(SEE additional information at end of Description.)

Directions

From I-25 north, take Exit 259 toward Peña Blanca. Turn left on NM 22 and go 12.2 miles north to the junction with Cochiti Highway. Turn left to stay on NM 22 another 1.8 miles. Turn right on Tribal Road 92, which connects to Forest Road 266 and BLM Road 1011. Go 0.5 miles west to the fee station. Continue 4.7 miles on a gravel road to the designated parking area on the right.

GPS Trailhead Coordinates

UTM Zone (WGS 84) 13S
Easting 0372233
Northing 3946864
Latitude 35° 39' 27"
Longitude 106° 26' 41"

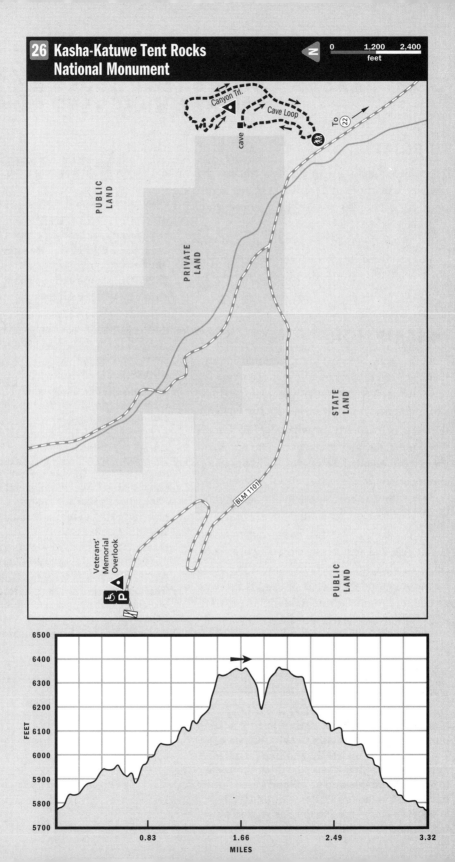

0   1,200   2,400
         feet

N

PUBLIC LAND

PRIVATE LAND

STATE LAND

PUBLIC LAND

Canyon Trl.

Cave Loop

cave

To 22

BLM 1101

Veterans'
Memorial
Overlook

P

FEET

6500
6400
6300
6200
6100
6000
5900
5800
5700

0.83   1.66   2.49   3.32

MILES

An invitational preview of the anticipated routes revealed a typical Parajito Plateau landscape of juniper and ponderosa. Those who have hiked the main area a dozen times already might appreciate the upper canyon trails when they open. Or if nothing else, the extra space should help disperse the crowds. But if you haven't yet seen the jaw-dropping spectacle in the lower canyon, make it your top priority.

The National Recreation Trail is composed of two segments: Cave Loop Trail and its spur, Canyon Trail. Both segments are well groomed and clearly marked. An information kiosk at the trailhead will further help keep you on the right track.

The big attraction here is Kasha-Kutuwe, but there's more to it than the words imply. Meaning "white cliffs" in the traditional language of the Cochiti people, Kasha-Katuwe is packed with fascinating formations. To summarize the complex geologic processes at work: When the Jemez volcanic field erupted 6 to 7 million years ago, it piled 1,000 feet of pumice, ash, and tuff upon the Parajito Plateau. Over the ensuing millennia, wind and rain cut into the soft rock layers, eventually carving deep canyons. But in places where durable caprock withstood erosion, it protected the soft rock directly beneath it. The result: hundreds of towering conical spires known as tent rocks, each donning a boulder for a hat. Their shapes resemble tipis and castle towers. When covered in snow, they evoke the soft-serve creations of Tastee-Freez. It's a bizarre landscape, to say the least. To see another one like it, you'd need to travel to Cappadocia in central Turkey.

Cave Loop Trail begins at the kiosk north of the parking area and soon splits in two. Take the left path for the long way to Canyon Trail—it leads you through a small party of tent rocks, with the tallest among them standing no higher than a streetlight. These hoodoos have lost their caps and are gradually melting.

As the lesser-traveled of the two trails, Cave Loop is where you're more likely to spot animal life. Ground squirrels, chipmunks, coyotes, and rabbits are prevalent. Also keep an eye out for horned lizards, or "horny toads," in the traditional language of Texans. A member of the iguana family, short-horned lizards are common throughout much of New Mexico, from desert grasslands to mixed conifer forests and mountain meadows. Colored and patterned to match their environment, these spiked reptiles are difficult to spot unless they're moving, and they often stay perfectly still until they're a step away from getting trampled. In addition to using camouflage and their spiny heads, they can defend themselves by squirting a noxious dose of blood into a predator's eyes and mouth. You'll sometimes find these charming creatures plunging their sticky tongues into anthills.

Located at the top of the loop, the cave is a scooped-out hole in the wall. The trail follows the wall down to a drainage. After 0.7 miles on the loop, you arrive at a T-junction. Turn left into the canyon.

Canyon Trail is easily one of the best short hikes in New Mexico. This

1.1-mile spur features tent rocks up to 90 feet tall, and a slot canyon more than 1,000 feet long. Mind your step in winter—a little snow and ice can turn the narrow, winding segments into a bobsled run. In wide sections, scan the base of the wall for petroglyphs and handprints. It takes a sharp eye to find them. (*Hint:* pay special attention to the left wall near a stray tent rock paired with a ponderosa.)

In spring and summer, white-throated swifts spend their days careening through the canyon. Unlike swallows, they won't stop to rest until the sun goes down. At night they roost in cantaloupe-sized niches high in the rock walls.

At the head of the canyon, the trail turns steep, climbing 200 feet in 0.3 miles. A couple of steps require some upper-body effort, but if you can climb up on a kitchen counter, you'll manage. When you reach the top, refrain from exploring informal paths. They enter private property to the immediate west. The designated trail descends southeast on a vertigo-inducing ridge traverse and ends at a 360-degree overlook. There are gorgeous views in every direction, and the most frequently overheard comment here seems to be, "Oh look, I can see my car!" Yup, that's it all right, a little more than 0.5 miles southwest and 500 feet lower than the vista point.

Backtrack to the mouth of the canyon. From there, continue straight on Cave Loop Trail 0.4 miles to the parking lot.

The Veterans' Memorial Scenic Overlook was dedicated in 2004 to American veterans, with special recognition to those from the Pueblo de Cochiti. This stately terrace perched on the ridge overlooks Cañada Camada ("similar canyon") near its confluence with Peralta Canyon. Views include the Dome Wilderness and Jemez Mountains, and tent rock assemblies in the upper canyon. These ghostly regiments of ashen spires stand on the far side of an unseen river below.

Dead piñon trees surround the overlook. As elsewhere on the plateau, pine bark beetles (also called *Ips*) have proven themselves merciless throughout the monument. But the manzanita still thrives on cliffs and ridges. This evergreen shrub can be identified from its emerald leaves, red-orange bark, and pinkish-white flowers in warm seasons. Banana yucca, golden pea, and redwhisker clammyweed provide additional color.

Relatively few visitors go to the Veterans' Memorial Scenic Overlook. The road is probably the primary deterrent, though most cars should be fine in dry conditions. From the National Recreation Trail parking area, turn right and drive 3.8 miles up the washboarded road. En route, you'll ford a shallow stream then bear left at a fork. About 0.6 miles past the second hairpin turn, pull over into the parking area on the right.

NEARBY ACTIVITIES

No doubt you saw Cochiti Dam on the east side of NM 22. It's the world's 11th-largest earth-filled dam. Behind it lies Cochiti Lake, a popular area for camping, bird-watching, fishing, swimming, and no-wake boating. Basic food and gas services are available in the nearby town of Cochiti Lake. To get there, return to the junction of NM 22 and Cochiti Highway, where you'll turn left. Access to the lake is 1 mile north on the right. A plaza with a convenience store–gas station is 0.4 miles farther north. For more information, visit **www.cochitipueblo.org.**

MORE KEY AT-A-GLANCE INFORMATION

LAST CHANCE FOOD/GAS: Convenience store–gas station in the town of Cochiti Lake (see Nearby Activities above).

SPECIAL COMMENTS: The monument is subject to closures due to inclement weather and by order of the Pueblo de Cochiti Governor. Check with the Pueblo main office for current conditions or closures: (505) 465-2244. For other information, contact the BLM office in Albuquerque at (505) 761-8768, or online at **www .nm.blm.gov/recreation/albuquerque/kasha_katuwe.htm.**

27 DOME WILDERNESS:
Eagle Canyon–Turkey Springs

KEY AT-A-GLANCE INFORMATION

LENGTH: 8.4-mile out-and-back

DIFFICULTY: Moderate to difficult

SCENERY: Wooded canyons, volcanic cliff formations

EXPOSURE: Some canyon shade

TRAIL TRAFFIC: Low to moderate

SHARED USE: Low (equestrians; closed to all mechanized vehicles)

TRAIL SURFACE: Fine gravel, dirt, sand

HIKING TIME: 4–5 hours

DRIVING DISTANCE: 53 miles (one way) from the I-40/I-25 exchange

ACCESS: Year-round, but note Special comments on possible gate closures. Permits required for backpacking in Bandelier National Monument.

LAND STATUS: Jemez Ranger District; Bandelier National Monument

MAPS: Santa Fe National Forest–West Half; USGS Canada, Cochiti Dam

FACILITIES: None

LAST CHANCE FOOD/GAS: Convenience store and gas station on Cochiti Highway, 2.8 miles south of the turnoff for FR 289

SPECIAL COMMENTS: See longer note at end of description.

GPS Trailhead Coordinates

UTM Zone (WGS 84) 13S

Easting 0374791

Northing 3952863

Latitude 35° 42' 42"

Longitude 106° 23' 03"

IN BRIEF

The west half of the Cañada–Capulin Trail is a rugged route between Eagle Canyon and Turkey Springs. This wilderness trail crosses three canyons and drops into a fourth, visiting massive volcanic formations along the way. You can hit this route's scenic highlights with a considerably easier 5.6-mile out-and-back. But if your goal is to sneak through the back door of Bandelier National Monument, be prepared for 8 miles minimum on roller-coaster terrain.

DESCRIPTION

On April 26, 1996, a fire raged 25 miles west of Santa Fe, blackening the skies and casting an eerie Halloween glow over the City Different. The culprit: a camper who had failed to heed New Mexico's most celebrated native son, Smokey Bear. The damage: more than 16,500 acres burned, including most of Dome Wilderness and the neighboring wilderness area in Bandelier National Monument. More than a decade later, charred and desolate slopes on St. Peter's Dome still remind us of the notorious Dome Fire.

The 8,464-foot St. Peter's Dome, which supposedly resembles the dome on its namesake

Directions

From I-25 north, take Exit 259. Turn left, and go north 12.2 miles on NM 22 to the junction at Cochiti Dam. Continue straight 4.5 miles on Cochiti Highway, then turn right on FR 289. (If you reach the gate for Rancho de la Cañada, you've gone about 0.3 miles too far.) Follow the dirt road about 3.5 miles to a hairpin turn. Park on the side of the road just before the turn. Walk up the road a few yards and look to the right for the Dome Wilderness sign, which points the way to the trailhead.

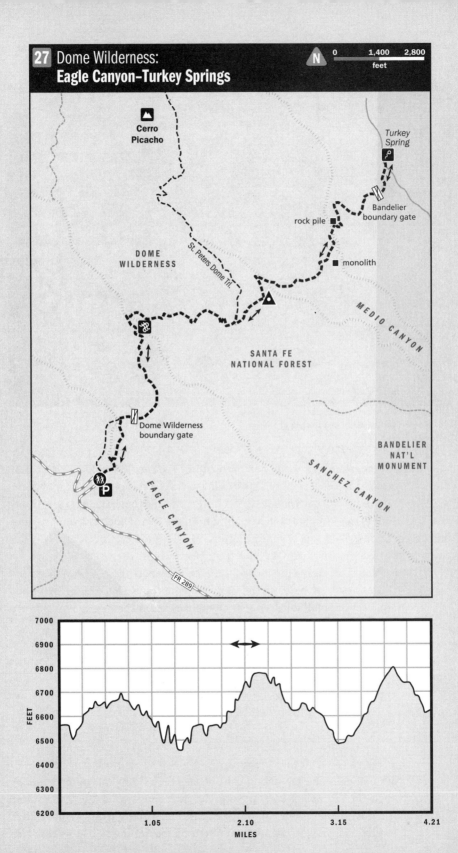

N

0   1,400   2,800
feet

**Cerro
Picacho**

*Turkey
Spring*

**DOME
WILDERNESS**

St. Peters Dome Trl.

rock pile

*Bandelier
boundary gate*

monolith

**SANTA FE
NATIONAL FOREST**

MEDIO CANYON

Dome Wilderness
boundary gate

**BANDELIER
NAT'L
MONUMENT**

SANCHEZ CANYON

P

EAGLE CANYON

FR 289

FEET

7000
6900
6800
6700
6600
6500
6400
6300
6200

1.05   2.10   3.15   4.21

MILES

View at the southern rim of a branch of Medio Canyon

basilica in Rome, stands near the northern end of the smallest wilderness area in the Southwest. At 5,200 acres, the Dome Wilderness is a complex landscape where the Sanchez and Medio canyons reach up into the San Miguel Mountains. Combined, these features amount to challenging hiking terrain. Each canyon crossing on the route described below might not seem like much on fresh legs, but the cumulative effect approximates a 1,700-foot gain and loss in elevation.

To ease the hike, this route avoids the area's steepest trails by roughly conforming to the southern base of the San Miguels. However, piñon downfall poses a unique set of small but frequent challenges. As if the Dome Fire weren't devastating enough, bark beetles have been particularly vicious in this backcountry region. Trail maintenance is occasionally left to volunteer units, such as the Middle Rio Grande chapter of the Back Country Horsemen of America. Natural processes often outpace their hard efforts to clear the trails.

Where the trail gets sketchy, keep a sharp eye out for ducks (small versions of cairns, often assembled from two or three rocks). Watch for arrangements of rocks or sticks laid across side paths. These are subtle but important signs meant to deter you from straying off in the wrong direction. Also, take a moment to look back every so often so that the return route will seem more familiar.

The hike starts out easy enough, heading north from the outer bend of a hairpin turn on FR 289. Maps and signage rarely agree on the names and numbers of trails in the Dome Wilderness, but "St. Peter's Dome Trail (118)" is posted at this end of the trail. Another sign at the trailhead claims that the

Bandelier National Monument boundary is 3.5 miles ahead, a measurement apparently taken from the gate 0.5 miles up.

The fine gravel trail leads into the conifer shade of Eagle Canyon, so named for Joseph Eagle, a key developer of the Cochiti Gold Mining District in the late 19th and early 20th centuries. A wooden marker posted at the canyon floor directs you out via a natural staircase in the rock wall. Less than 0.5 miles into the hike, an arrow on a post points you right. A gateway just ahead marks the southwestern boundary of the Dome Wilderness.

The trail soon curves north to gradually descend into Sanchez Canyon. About 1.4 miles into the hike, you arrive at a stream that has been described elsewhere as "reliable" and "permanent." In the summer of 2007, with monsoon season already under way, it was better described as "slightly moist." If, however, you do find it flowing steadily, check it carefully before crossing. A short distance downstream, it plunges 80 feet deeper into Sanchez Canyon.

From the stream crossing, the trail climbs east 0.8 miles. You'll find an overlook of the falls within the first 100 yards or so. Farther up on your left are good views of cliff formations that comprise a south-facing wall of Sanchez Canyon. Details in this volcanic mass evoke ancient temples, castle towers, and cathedral facades with lancet windows. After a couple of switchbacks to the ridge, the trail fades as it crosses bedrock. Turn to your right for a view of Cochiti Lake, about 7 miles to the southeast. Resume your east–northeastward trajectory, and after about 100 feet, you'll reach a T-junction. Here, at 2.2 miles into the hike, a sign indicates that the Dome Trail (118) climbs north, while Turkey Springs Trail (119) commences to run northeast to Bandelier National Monument. Continue straight toward Turkey Springs.

About 0.3 miles past the junction, you arrive at the southern rim of a branch of Medio Canyon. Before turning left for the descent, go straight to reach the prominent outcrop ahead for a preview of the cliffs on the other side. Unlike the formal architectural details found in Sanchez Canyon, the wind-sculpted tuff formations here evoke quirkier moods. (The caricatured expressions of Tiki gods come to mind.)

For a closer look, follow the trail across the pine-shaded canyon. Amusing hoodoos stand near the base of the cliff. Cacti grow thick around here, so watch your step. The trail continues southeast and squeezes between a pair of rock shelters at 2.8 miles into the hike. This is a good point to pause and reconsider your hiking objectives. The trail ahead becomes more strenuous, with diminishing returns in terms of scenic value. Maintenance also seems to taper off, making it increasingly difficult to follow. In short, the novice hiker might be better off turning back here.

Those determined to visit the monument wilderness can continue onward as the trail curves northeast. Ahead on the right, a monolith towers on the edge of an arroyo in a deeper branch of Medio Canyon. About 0.25 miles past the streambed crossing at the monolith, you cross another drainage. An unusual rock pile comes into view on your left. The trail does *not* continue north past the rock pile. Instead

it hooks right in the first of a 0.4-mile series of switchbacks to the ridge above.

From the ridge top, the boundary gate is a mere 300 yards away, but a disaster area of downfall swallows the trail. For those with GPS units, these are the coordinates for the boundary gate: N 35° 44' 05", W 106° 21' 25".

Aim downhill to the north–northeast until you intercept a shallow gulley. (If you walk by a stout pair of old alligator junipers with whitish trunks, you're on the right track.) Follow it as it curves east to the boundary gate. Prominent signage here clearly identifies the monument boundary and its rules. Read the fine print for an interesting footnote about this backcountry wilderness: "Electronic sensors and remote video surveillance systems may be in use."

The trail improves as it curves north down a red slope to an outflow of Turkey Spring. It's little more than a trickle, barely audible from more than 50 feet away, but you should find more than enough running water to cool your feet for the return hike. (As with any wilderness stream, it must be treated before drinking.)

A nearby sign indicates that Capulin Canyon is 4 miles to the north and Cañada Ranch is 6.5 miles back the way you came. Retrace your steps 4.2 miles to return to the trailhead.

Note: FR 289 gets rough and rocky in spots, and it is treacherous when wet. Most cars with normal clearance should be OK in dry conditions but the road is subject to weather-related closures. Contact the Jemez Ranger Station for current conditions by calling (505) 829-3535 or visiting **www.fs.fed.us/r3/ sfe/districts/jemez.**

LA BAJADA 28

IN BRIEF

A hike in the nearest corner of the Santa Fe National Forest takes a legendary route to a mesa top, skirts the rim of an expansive canyon, then drops down to follow the Santa Fe River back to the start.

DESCRIPTION

A bit of local history will help you prepare for a few obstacles you'll face on this hike. In the Spanish colonial era, New Mexico was divided into two major governmental and economic regions: the Rio Arriba and the Rio Abajo, the upper river and lower river, respectively. The physical boundary between them was a steep slope on the edge of La Bajada Mesa.

From 1598 to the mid-19th century, La Bajada, or "the descent," was a traffic nightmare for oxcart travelers along the Camino Real. An ostensibly gentler route ran through the Santa Fe River Canyon, but it was vulnerable to rain and snowmelt. Accordingly, the community at the eastern end of the canyon is La Cienega, which translates from Extremaduran as "marsh" or "swampy land." Indeed, with snowmelt or summer monsoons, the canyon floor is *muy cienegoso*.

Directions ———————→

From I-25 north, take Exit 264 and drive 3.8 miles north–northwest on NM 16. Turn right for La Bajada and the Tetilla Peak Recreation Area, and go 1 mile. Turn right again and follow the road 1.5 miles. (As you approach the bridge, note that the road coming in from your right is a potential return route on your hike.) Cross the bridge and turn right at the T-junction ahead. Park in the dirt lot on your immediate right.

KEY AT-A-GLANCE INFORMATION

LENGTH: 6.8-mile loop

DIFFICULTY: Moderate, with one difficult descent

SCENERY: Views from atop 500-foot cliffs; petroglyphs and pueblo ruins; river canyon

EXPOSURE: Minimal shade

TRAIL TRAFFIC: Low to moderate

SHARED USE: Moderate (mountain biking, equestrians, camping; livestock; limited motor-vehicle access)

TRAIL SURFACE: Dirt, rock

HIKING TIME: 4 hours

DRIVING DISTANCE: 45 miles (one way) from the I-40 and I-25 exchange

ACCESS: Year-round

LAND STATUS: Cochiti Indian Reservation; Española Ranger District

MAPS: Santa Fe National Forest (West Half); USGS Tetilla Peak

FACILITIES: None

LAST CHANCE FOOD/GAS: Convenience store, food services, gas station at Exit 259

SPECIAL COMMENTS: This hike begins and ends on Cochiti land. Respect the privacy of local residents and the authority of pueblo officials, who have been gracious in allowing access to the river and the mesa.

GPS Trailhead Coordinates

UTM Zone (WGS 84) 13S

Easting 0387952

Northing 3934887

Latitude 35° 33' 05"

Longitude 106° 14' 10"

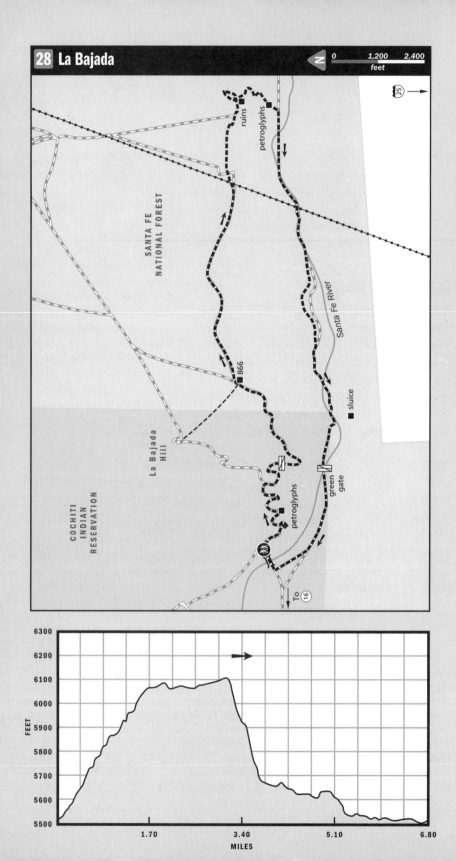

N

| 0 | 1,200 | 2,400 |

feet

25 →

ruins

petroglyphs

SANTA FE
NATIONAL FOREST

Santa Fe River

866

sluice

La Bajada
Hill

petroglyphs

green
gate

COCHITI
INDIAN
RESERVATION

To 16

6300

6200

6100

6000

5900

5800

5700

5600

5500

FEET

1.70   3.40   5.10   6.80

MILES

Around 1860 the U.S. Army opened the first known wagon road to climb the mesa. In the winter of 1923–24, prison labor equipped with pickaxes and dynamite modified the wagon road, reducing its grade by 2 percent and eliminating 7 of its 23 hairpin turns. From 1926 to 1932, La Bajada Hill was regarded as the most harrowing segment of Route 66. In 1932 the alignment that would become Interstate 25 was laid out 5 miles to the east. From then on, the redundantly named Bajada Hill would be neglected by all but the most adventurous travelers. No doubt you noticed the twisted trail carved into the escarpment as you approached the village of La Bajada.

The hike begins on the road heading south from the parking area. Before turning left for the ascent, note the irrigation ditch on the right side of the road. You may want to use it in the last leg of your return route. (Another option is noted in Directions above.)

As you ascend La Bajada, scan the basalt boulders for petroglyphs. Ancient designs appear alongside more-recent scribbles, initials, and dates. A gallery of these pecked rocks is located on the right side of the bend in the third switchback. The terrain is ideal for rattlesnakes, so watch out for those as you're poking around the rocks.

After rounding the sixth switchback, you'll hit a Y-junction. Unless you want to add a couple of miles to the hike via an older alignment, keep right. (See Optional routes below.) At this point, you're nearly halfway up the 1.8-mile segment to the top of the 500-foot escarpment.

After two more switchbacks, or 1 mile into the hike, you'll pass through an open gate. It should be closed, but at last check, it looked as though a truck had run over it. The north–south fence approximates the boundary between Cochiti land and the national forest. (For the remainder of the hike, you may wonder how this treeless land ever came to be regarded as any kind of forest.) After one more switchback and another 200-foot elevation gain, the road tops out at the rim of the mesa. Congratulations, you've just conquered La Bajada Hill.

Actually, it's not so much a hill as a volcanic escarpment. Note the volcano, Tetilla ("breast" or "nipple") Peak, rising 3.5 miles to the north. Its pointed appearance on the Caja del Rio Plateau makes it easy to identify. Now that you've got your bearings, the next stop on this route is 1.4 miles due east. You can make a beeline for it—your best choice when the roads are buried under snow. Or locate a solitary post inexplicably numbered 866, with lost car parts piled nearby. A line of whitish rocks extends about 100 yards north of the post. Turn right at the break in the rocks, and follow the road northeast. About 0.25 miles ahead, it'll bend slightly southeastward.

After crossing under two sets of power lines, the road turns sharply northeast, parallel to the lines. At this point, leave the road, and continue 0.3 miles straight east along a faded path to a notch in the rim of a wide alcove. About 450 feet below to the right, the Santa Fe River winds along the canyon floor. Straight ahead, the descent to a shelf in the alcove is only about 150 feet. Giant mounds of basalt boulders in the alcove resemble crumbled castles. Look carefully and you may be able to distinguish natural rock piles from the ruins of an ancient pueblo. Rock-lined paths between the mounds hint at where the more popular structures once stood.

Options for a safe descent are limited, so pick your way down carefully. From the notch, the path drops down a steep rut and splits in several directions. Follow whichever one looks easiest. The hilly shelf below is about the size of a baseball field, with winding paths that can take hours to explore. The eastern edge drops off into a feeder canyon. The more readily identifiable ruins are near the southern edge.

When you're ready to continue on the hike, descend the rocky trail south to the river. Dozens of petroglyphs are scattered throughout the rocks near the lower part of the trail. They're easier to spot when you look uphill because most face south. Locate the dirt road on the near side of the river, and turn right to follow it west. From here on out, the terrain remains relatively flat but is not necessarily any easier. Under normal conditions, you simply stroll downstream 2.8 miles until you're out of the canyon, and you might wonder how anyone could regard the trickle of water as a river.

However, as mentioned earlier, recent snowmelt or summer monsoons can cause problems, particularly in those places where the road crosses the river without the benefit of a bridge. You can avoid crossing by following alternate paths; but when the stream runs up against the base of the canyon wall, you may need to backtrack for an easier place to ford the river. This otherwise simple task calls for creative solutions in wetter seasons. Some observations made on previous hikes may prove helpful: First, washed-out footbridges usually turn up on the opposite bank. Second, dead tree limbs make unreliable vaulting poles. Finally, wet feet aren't such a bad thing after all.

If you follow the road diligently for about 2 miles, you'll arrive at a green gate. Beyond it lies Cochiti land. Once through the gate, you have two options for returning to the parking area, both based on local advice. The first option: Locate the east end of the ditch mentioned earlier. It's on the north bank, about ten feet above the river. Although this way is evidently wide enough for cows, it can get overgrown and take a bit of bushwhacking. It also involves a tight squeeze through a hole in a barbed-wire fence. On the plus side, it's shorter and you won't need to cross the river again. The second option: Follow the road across the river and continue to the road you drove earlier. Then turn right, and cross the bridge back to the parking area.

If you didn't stick to the main road, chances are you'll get wedged in on the south side of the river. Shortly before realizing this minor predicament, you'll spot a wooden sluice bridging a crevice in the south wall of the canyon. At this point, your best bet is to continue down to the next crevice and scramble out of the canyon there. Drop back into the canyon when you see the road below. You'll have bypassed the green gate, so just head east until you reach the road to the bridge. Turn right to return to the parking area.

Optional routes: In wet seasons, you may want to avoid the canyon floor. For a shorter, simpler hike, try the Bajada loop. Start by following the hike, as described, to the mesa top. Instead of turning right after post 866, continue straight toward Tetilla Peak just over 0.5 miles. Take a sharp left at the junction, and then walk the road southwest about 0.5 miles to the western rim of the mesa. The road turns north for a tight M-shaped series of switchbacks. Once through those, stay on the main track south for about 0.75 miles back to the Y. Or, to extend this route, explore the various road alignments above and below the rim; some appear as linear depressions through the mesa-top grasslands, whereas others are hardscrabble tracks in the escarpment below.

29   LA CIENEGA AND LA CIENEGUILLA

IN BRIEF

A pair of hikes explores the only two sites currently open in the Galisteo Basin. La Cienega focuses on the natural scenery high above and deep below the rim of the Cañon Santa Fe, while La Cieneguilla is all about the petroglyphs.

DESCRIPTION

Just a mile off the interstate, the southern Santa Fe suburb of La Cienega is oddly reminiscent of New Mexico's more northern villas. Milagro, the fictional hamlet of John Nichols's *Beanfield* trilogy, comes to mind. And at times the narrow winding streets of La Cienega have the feel of an older, quieter country. Yet there's so much to see and do that you might not know where to begin. Then again, with its main attractions closed for most of the year, your best bet is to start on open land.

La Cienega Area of Critical Environmental Concern, designated in 1992, refers to 3,556 acres along the Santa Fe River Canyon. It contains riparian wildlife such as garter snakes, tree lizards, weasels, and several species of bats.

It also abounds in cultural resources associated with the Galisteo Basin. (For more details, see hike 21: Cerrillos Hills Historic

GPS Trailhead Coordinates

UTM Zone (WGS 84)   13S

Easting   0397400

Northing   3936050

Latitude   35° 33' 46"

Longitude   106° 07' 56"

Directions

From I-25 north, take Exit 271. Turn left on NM 587 (Entrada La Cienega) and go north 1 mile. Turn left on County Road 54 (Camino Capilla Vieja) and go 0.4 miles. Pull over and park on the right shoulder, across the street from a small sign for the Rael Ranch. The hike begins on the red dirt road going north into the hills.

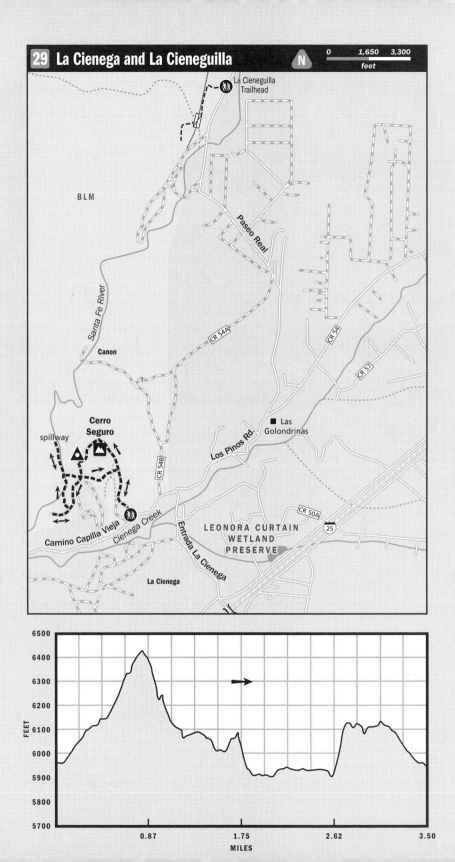

N

0   1,650   3,300
feet

La Cieneguilla
Trailhead

BLM

Paseo Real

Santa Fe River

Canon

CR 54A

CR 54

CR 57

Cerro
Seguro

spillway

Las
Golondrinas

Los Pinos Rd

CR 54B

Camino Capilla Vieja

Cienega Creek

Entrada La Cienega

CR 50A

25

LEONORA CURTAIN
WETLAND
PRESERVE

La Cienega

FEET

6500
6400
6300
6200
6100
6000
5900
5800
5700

0.87   1.75   2.62   3.50
MILES

Park.) Evidence of prehistoric and early historic pueblos is scattered along the Santa Fe River. Determining which ones constitute the pueblos of Cienega and Cieneguilla has been a matter of debate for centuries. The self-trained anthropologist Adolph Bandelier remarked on the considerable size of a pueblo he'd referenced earlier as "Cienega or Cieneguilla." However, later surveys failed to locate any major ruins in the area, suggesting that whatever he observed in 1892 had mostly vanished by 1915. Still, visitors today can easily spot pueblo mounds and petroglyphs along these hikes. Whatever you happen to stumble upon, leave it the way you found it.

The hike at La Cienega begins on a dirt road that's closed to motorized vehicles. It starts through a valley and climbs steadily for about 0.7 miles to a ridge on the northeastern flank of Cerro Seguro. Here you'll catch the first glimpse of the Santa Fe River Canyon. About 0.75 miles to the north, white stones form a cross on the sloping western wall of the canyon. Hidden beneath it on the canyon floor is the tiny community of Cañon.

Turn left on the ridge and follow a steep, rocky footpath to the summit. By this point you've gained 500 feet in elevation in 0.8 miles. What you find up here depends on the mood of local pilgrims. White picket crosses once stood here, later to be replaced with a curious assortment of offerings: a gold lamé flag, river cobbles soaked in scented oils, and sprinklings of corn and salt.

Take a moment to get oriented. The Santa Fe River begins about 25 miles to the northeast, near Santa Fe Baldy in the Santa Fe Mountains and the Santa Fe National Forest. It crosses the Santa Fe Trail in the town of Santa Fe, passes north of the Santa Fe Municipal Airport, and then traverses the Santa Fe River

Canyon directly in front of you. The river exits the canyon before crossing the western boundary of Santa Fe County and then bends to the north to join the Rio Grande near Cochiti Pueblo, about 12 miles to the northwest.

Other visible landmarks from Cerro Seguro include Las Tetillas, hills of slightly lesser stature rising a mile to the west, and the somewhat larger Cerro Bonanza, 4.5 miles due south. At the same distance, to the east, is the former New Mexico State Penitentiary, the site of the bloodiest prison riot in American history (1980) and the filming location for the farcical prison romp *The Longest Yard* (2005).

Continue walking south, heading downhill along the ridge. There's no obvious trail so choose your steps carefully along the path of least impact; that is, try not to trample the vegetation. About halfway down, angle right toward an outcrop that overlooks the canyon. The view from here gives you a better idea about what lies ahead on the lower portion of the route. Proceed down to the northern corner of the mesa. Once on flat ground, note a massive rock formation protruding from the slope below. The gulley on its southern side is the way out of the canyon on the return part of this route. It's not as long of a climb as the hill, but it is steeper.

Follow the mesa rim to the south. About 0.25 miles past the gully you will come to a downed barbed-wire fence. Another 60 feet ahead, a cleft in the rim forms a natural staircase through the basalt cap rock. Before stepping down, consider strolling along the rim another 0.25 miles or so to enjoy the views and look for petroglyphs in the caprock below. Collared lizards also lurk nearby, but they're shier than their Albuquerque brethren.

Return to the cleft, and head down toward the river. Once on the canyon floor, turn right at the acequia (irrigation canal), and follow it north. The wreckage of a white Subaru is about 0.25 miles upstream. Another 60 yards ahead is the low end of the gully mentioned earlier. The thin vegetation at the low end and the absence of caprock at the rim make this spot one of the few viable passages out of the canyon.

Continue upstream for now. How far you go may depend on the river. You'll have to cross it at least once to get to the spillway 0.3 miles ahead. At uncertain times of the year, a broad jump or stepping-stones will suffice. At other times, your best strategy is to just resign yourself to wet boots. The canyon floor is the highlight of the hike, particularly when the river actually flows like a river, or at least a decent creek.

The spillway is the turnaround point on this route. (An impressive pair of horseshoe canyons starts another 0.5 miles upstream, but I've never slogged up that far.) Return to the gully, and climb up to the rim.

Once back on the mesa, head downhill. Do *not* take the obvious dirt road—it becomes a private drive. Instead, locate a faint doubletrack to the left of the dirt road; it runs between a drainage and the base of the hill. If you can't pick it out, just hook around the base of the hill for a little more than 0.25 miles, until you cross an arroyo. (Head downhill too soon and you'll cross it twice in deeper sections.) The road you came up on is about 50 yards past the

The spillway marks the turnaround point on the hike at La Cienega.

arroyo. Turn right, and follow it 0.5 miles downhill to the car.

The hike at La Cieneguilla is an easy 1.4-mile round-trip out-and-back featuring a high concentration of fantastic petroglyphs. It's also much drier. To get there from the Cienega trailhead, drive back to the junction of Camino Capilla Vieja and Entrada La Cienega. Go 1 mile straight northeast on Los Pinos Road, where it bears north to become CR 56 (Paseo Real). Continue north another 2.8 miles. Turn left, and park in a fenced parking area.

From the parking lot, walk 0.1 mile west along the well-defined trail to a wire fence. Turn left, and follow the trail south about 0.4 miles along the fence. Shortly after crossing a shallow arroyo, veer right on a path that stays closer to the fence. Go through the first gateway, and take the path straight up the escarpment. Look for petroglyphs as you approach the rim. A few panels have gone missing in recent years, but several dozen works remain. Turn left, and stay on the path below the rim. Images you will see in the next 0.25 miles include stars, spirals, hands, elks, mustangs, a snake-headed eagle, and numerous versions of kokopelli, the hunchback flutist.

NEARBY ACTIVITIES

El Rancho de las Golondrinas is a living-history museum in a 200-acre farming valley. Villagers in period clothing inhabit the original buildings, which date from the early 18th century. (Imagine a northern New Mexico version of Colonial Williamsburg, and you'll get the idea.) Admission fees range from $1 to $12. Open for self-guided

Petroglyph panel at La Cieneguilla

walking tours Wednesday to Sunday, 10 a.m. to 4 p.m. (June to September). There are special events throughout the year. Call (505) 473-4169 or visit **golondrinas.org**. The entrance is on Los Pinos Road, 1 mile northeast of Entrada La Cienega.

Leonora Curtin Wetland Preserve is a 35-acre preserve featuring a nature trail that winds through an open meadow to a natural *ciénega* or marsh. A second trail covers an arid upland area. Open Saturdays from 9 a.m. to noon and Sundays 1 to 4 p.m. (May to October). For more information, call Santa Fe Botanical Gardens at (505) 428-1684 or visit **santafebotanicalgarden.org**. To get there, head back to I-25, and turn left onto West Frontage Road immediately before the exit ramps. The entrance to the preserve is 1.4 miles ahead on the left.

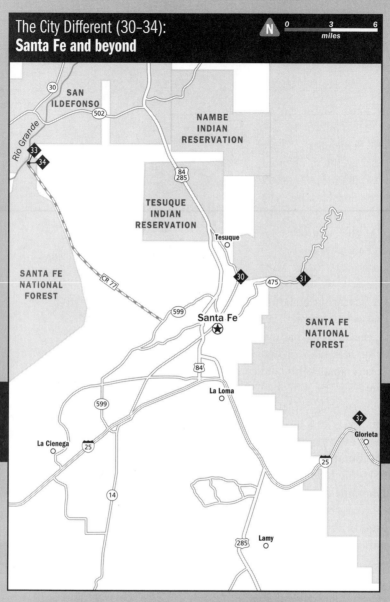

SAN
ILDEFONSO

Rio Grande

NAMBE
INDIAN
RESERVATION

84
285

TESUQUE
INDIAN
RESERVATION

Tesuque

SANTA FE
NATIONAL
FOREST

CR 77

30   475

599

Santa Fe

SANTA FE
NATIONAL
FOREST

84

La Loma

599

Glorieta

La Cienega

25

25

14

Lamy

285

THE CITY DIFFERENT

30 BISHOP'S LODGE– BIG TESUQUE CREEK

KEY AT-A-GLANCE INFORMATION

LENGTH: 5-mile loop

DIFFICULTY: Moderately strenuous

SCENERY: Piñon–juniper foothills in the Sangre de Cristo Mountains, riparian woodland, historic buildings, and gardens

EXPOSURE: Mostly sunny on the Green and Blue trails, more shade on trails 399 and 354

TRAIL TRAFFIC: High

SHARED USE: High (Forest service trails popular with dog owners and mountain bikers. All trails popular with equestrians until the first snow. Closed to all motorized vehicles.)

TRAIL SURFACE: Dirt, sand, loose rock

HIKING TIME: 3–4 hours

DRIVING DISTANCE: 65 miles (one way) from the I-40 and I-25 exchange

ACCESS: Year-round, daylight hours. Some trails may be impassible in the winter.

LAND STATUS: Private; Santa Fe National Forest–Española Ranger District

MAPS: Santa Fe National Forest–East Half; USGS Santa Fe

FACILITIES: Resort and spa (See Nearby activities)

LAST CHANCE FOOD/GAS: All services in Santa Fe

GPS Trailhead Coordinates

UTM Zone (WGS 84) 13S

Easting   0417660

Northing   3954639

Latitude   35° 43' 56"

Longitude   105° 54' 38"

IN BRIEF

The Bishop's Lodge stands on the near corner of 1,500 contiguous square miles of national forest. Link its marked trails over hilly terrain with gentler designated trails in the Santa Fe National Forest for a hike that culminates with the cottonwood-shaded promenade along Big Tesuque Creek.

DESCRIPTION

Long before it became a premium resort, the Bishop's Lodge was the site of a small ranch, a private chapel, and splendid gardens. The bishop who first lodged here in the 1850s was Jean Baptiste Lamy, perhaps better known as Father Latour from Willa Cather's biographical novel, *Death Comes for the Archbishop*.

Christened the Villa Pintoresca, the bishop's ranch stood in the Little Tesuque Valley, about 4 miles north of St. Francis Cathedral. In reverence to the sanctity of a good long stroll, he often made the journey on foot and required his visitors to do the same.

Visitors today can put in a sufficient walk on the trails at the 450-acre resort. With a policy that no doubt appeals to the bishop's generous spirit, all are welcome to hike here. You might expect little more than

Directions

From I-25 north, take Exit 282 and follow Saint Francis Drive (US 84) north 3.6 miles. Turn right on the *second* Paseo de Peralta. (It's a loop.) Head east 1 mile, then turn left on Washington Avenue, also known as Bishop's Lodge Road. Go north 3 miles, following the signs to he Bishop's Lodge Resort. Turn right and follow the driveway to the parking area. See Description for directions to the trailhead.

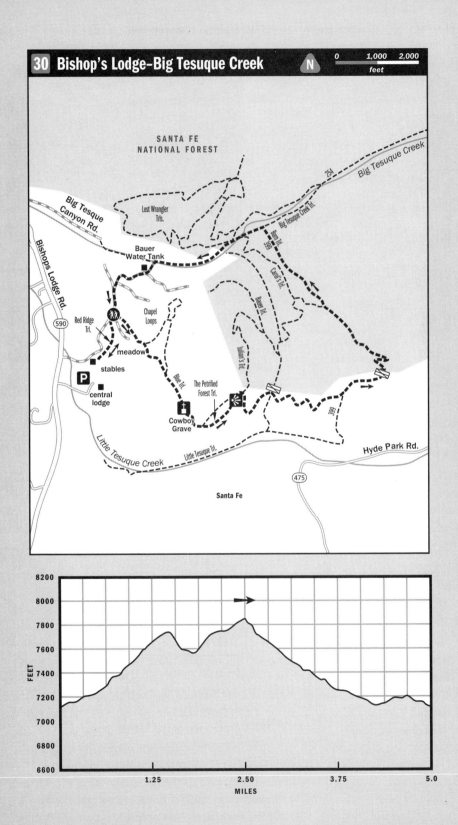

N

0   1,000   2,000
feet

SANTA FE
NATIONAL FOREST

Big Tesuque Creek

254

Big Tesque
Canyon Rd.

Lost Wrangler
Trls.

Big Tesuque Creek Trl.

Bishops Lodge Rd.

Bauer
Water Tank

Burn Trl.
399

Carol's Trl.

590

Bauer Trl.

Red Ridge
Trl.

Chapel
Loops

meadow

Julian's Trl.

stables

P

central
lodge

Blue Trl.

The Petrified
Forest Trl.

Cowboy
Grave

399

Little Tesuque Creek

Little Tesuque Trl.

Hyde Park Rd.

475

Santa Fe

8200

8000

7800

7600

7400

FEET

7200

7000

6800

6600

1.25   2.50   3.75   5.0

MILES

Big Tesuque Creek Trail is twice the fun on four legs.

sissified pathways for wine-and-cheese picnickers at such a swanky establishment, but you would be sorely mistaken. A few segments are tough enough to count as penance. Factor in connections with the forest service system, and you get enough trails for an epic pilgrimage.

Before you hike, stop by the reception hall in the Central Lodge. The concierge can provide you with a detailed map, directions for reaching the trails, and other pertinent instructions. In addition to standard disclaimers about hiking at your own risk, heed any advisories regarding wildlife, such as bears and mountain lions known to frequent the area, and potential conflicts with the skeet range, near the Yellow Trail. Stay on the easements when crossing private property. Avid birders should also ask for the Bishop's Lodge bird list. Finally, for a less demanding walk, request an art-tour brochure map, featuring outdoor sculptures from a local bronze foundry, or take the short nature walk, which starts in the garden by the chapel.

This hike begins at the horse stables, located about 200 yards north of the Central Lodge. The wranglers there can field any questions about the trails that the concierge couldn't answer. Follow the dirt road north about 0.25 miles. Just past a private drive on the right, a small white sign marks the start of the Green Trail. Follow this wide path about 0.25 miles southeast to the edge of a long meadow. A signed fork indicates the trail to the left commences the **Chapel Loops.** The more direct route skirts the east side of the meadow and then ducks left behind the tree line, near the far end. Continue uphill less than 0.25 miles to the junction of the Chapel Loops and the Blue Trail.

By now you'll have surmised that an extensive web of informal trails, game paths, and drainages span these piñon–juniper foothills. Disorientation comes easy without the aid of the subtle white signs so it's important to keep an eye out for them and stay on the beaten tracks, which over centuries of use have been worn down to a trench in places. If you happen to wander off, fences and signage in the area should steer you back in the right direction, but you still run the risk of bumbling down a lost trail.

The Blue Trail keeps you climbing to the southeast. About 1 mile into the hike, a rustic cross stands over a pile of stones on the right. This "cowboy grave" makes a useful prop for regaling kids with tall tales about the Old West. The path gets steeper as it climbs the next 0.25 miles to a fork. It's a loop so take your pick. Chunks of petrified wood scattered on the northwest slopes give this trail its other name, the **Petrified Forest Trail.**

Signs indicate the way to the viewpoint at the top end of the loop, about 1.5 miles into the hike. The 7,743-foot summit is the highest point on the Bishop's Lodge property. Peaks exceeding 12,000 feet are lined up behind the ski basin, 8 miles to the northeast. About 45 miles in the opposite direction, the Sandias rise to flank Albuquerque's east side.

From the viewpoint, leave the lodge's color-coded system for the **community trails.** These connecting routes to the national forest are also marked with white signs, although the signs are fewer. The trail turns southeast for a short but steep drop into a canyon. About halfway down, it switchbacks northeast for a more gradual descent to the floor. If your energy is flagging at this point, consider taking the trail through the open gateway on your left. Stay along the main drainage north to Big Tesuque Creek. This shortcut through the canyon can subtract a mile and a steep climb from the overall hike.

Otherwise, continue straight up the west-facing slope ahead. At least two distinct trails cross this steep terrain, with both reaching the ridge ahead in about 0.25 miles. Once at the crest, angle to the northeast (your left) for an easier 0.25 miles. The trail soon runs along the left side of an arroyo. Climb a little farther to top out near 7,850 feet, and then cross into the national forest by going through the drop gate. Latch it behind you, and begin the descent into the Burn.

You're now halfway through the loop, distance-wise, with the hardest parts behind you. From here, switchbacks on the **Burn Trail (399)** lead you through a steep, grassy meadow—the result of a forest fire more than 50 years ago. Once you reach the floor, it's a fairly straight mile northwest to Big Tesuque Creek. Also called the Juan Trail, 399 follows an intermittent stream through bear-clawed ponderosa. Along the way, it crosses rock dams installed by the Civilian Conservation Corps in the 1930s.

A wooden sign at the junction with the **Big Tesuque Creek Trail (254)** gives the distances to the ski basin and to the next hike in this book, Hyde Memorial State Park. It also indicates that Bishop's Lodge is 1 mile to the left. You'll

Bishop Lamy Chapel

have to walk a little farther than that, but the gorgeous streamside trail makes it seem too short. Overlapping Winsor Trail, Big Tesuque Creek Trail is a local favorite. Though log crossings can get tricky with winter ice or spring runoff, few places are as cool as this in the heat of summer. To extend your walk along this trail, turn right at the sign and follow the gurgling brook upstream. A popular turnaround point is the river crossing at the "big pine," about 0.25 miles upstream.

Otherwise, turn left and head downstream for just under 1 mile. A left turn at the end of a coyote fence puts you on the road back to Bishop's Lodge. About 0.3 miles past the water tank, you'll see the sign for the Green Trail on your left. Continue down the road another 0.4 miles to return to the stables.

NEARBY ACTIVITIES

The best part about hiking from the Bishop's Lodge Resort is the opportunity to reward yourself for the effort. The Sunday brunch at Las Fuentes Restaurant is a Santa Fe favorite, and its dessert menu is sinful. For more casual fare, try the Sunflower Poolside Bar & Grill. The award-winning ShàNah Spa offers treatments inspired by Native American healing traditions. Other activities available include guided horseback riding and skeet and trap shooting. Call ahead, (505) 983-6377 or (800) 732-2240. For more information, visit **bishopslodge.com.** For spa information and reservations, call (505) 819-4000 or (800) 974-2624, or visit **shanahspa.com.**

HYDE MEMORIAL STATE PARK 31

IN BRIEF

An old favorite at the southernmost tip of the Rockies is a short drive from the Santa Fe Plaza. The nostalgic campgrounds in Hyde Memorial State Park attract wildflower enthusiasts in the summer and aspen lovers in the fall, whereas winter crowds come for the sledding, snowshoeing, and cross-country skiing.

DESCRIPTION

The trail starts out deceptively quaint, with a wooden fence by the roadside, a rock border, and a stone bridge over Little Tesuque Creek. On the far side of the bridge is a black mailbox with trail guides, and a new sign with additional details about Hyde Park Circle Trail. The park plans to install more interpretive signage like this throughout Circle Trail in 2007.

Take a moment here to limber up, giving the calves and hamstrings an extra stretch. The first mile is like a good workout on a Stairmaster, only far more scenic. You ascend from a lush creek-side forest to thinner stands of fir and pine as the trail climbs steadily from an elevation of 8,400 to just over 9,400 feet. It seems longer than a mile, and maybe

KEY AT-A-GLANCE INFORMATION

LENGTH: 3.3-mile loop, optional spur

DIFFICULTY: Moderate

SCENERY: Campgrounds, views of Santa Fe from 9,400', evergreen, alder, aspen

EXPOSURE: Mostly shade

TRAIL TRAFFIC: Popular

SHARED USE: Low (no horses, bikes, or motor vehicles)

TRAIL SURFACE: Fine gravel, rock

HIKING TIME: 2 hours

DRIVING DISTANCE: 68 miles (one way) from the I-40 and I-25 exchange

ACCESS: Day-use activities 6 a.m.–9 p.m.; gate hours 7 a.m.–11:00 p.m.; $5 per vehicle or New Mexico State Parks Annual Pass

LAND STATUS: State park

MAPS: Trail maps available at visitor center and trailhead; USGS McClure Reservoir

FACILITIES: Water, restrooms, campsites, RV hookups, picnic shelters, wheelchair-accessible tables, grills, and restrooms

SPECIAL COMMENTS: See longer note at end of description.

Directions

From I-25 north, take Exit 282 and go 3.6 miles north on Saint Francis Drive (US 84). Turn right on the *second* Paseo de Peralta. (It's a loop.) Go east 1 mile, then turn left on Washington Avenue, also known as Bishop's Lodge Road. Go north 0.18 miles and turn right on Artists Road, which becomes Hyde Park Road (NM 475). Continue 7.4 miles and turn right at the Hyde Memorial State Park Visitors Center and Lodge. Park near the lodge and pay at the station next to the visitor center. The trailhead is directly across Hyde Park Road.

GPS Trailhead Coordinates

UTM Zone (WGS 84) 13S

Easting   0424269

Northing   3954400

Latitude   35° 43' 50"

Longitude 105° 50' 15"

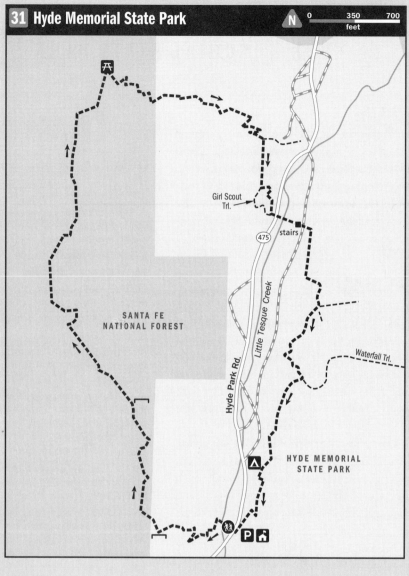

N

0   350   700
feet

Santa Fe
National Forest

Girl Scout
Trl.

475   stairs

Little Tesque Creek

Hyde Park Rd.

Waterfall Trl.

HYDE MEMORIAL
STATE PARK

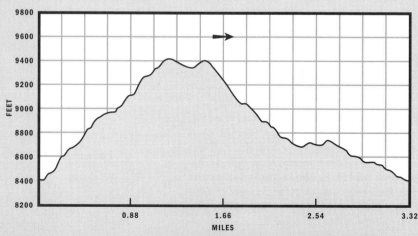

9800
9600
9400
9200
9000
8800
8600
8400
8200

FEET

0.88   1.66   2.54   3.32
MILES

it is if you count backsliding on loose gravel. Multiple switchbacks contribute to the illusion that the top is just around the bend. Park benches near the 0.25- and 0.75-mile marks provide brief respites from exertion.

Keep an eye out for garter snakes and horned lizards prowling through the pine needles. Black bear, mule deer, and porcupine also inhabit the area but are rarely sighted. A favorite among the summer wildflowers is scarlet gilia, or sky-rocket. Oregon grape blooms in the spring and resembles holly with blueberry clusters when it ripens in the late summer. The plant is better known for its medicinal uses than for its snacking value. The berries are edible, though bitter, and children have been known to feel queasy after eating a few. You'd be better off foraging for wild strawberries.

You know you're near the top when the rocks begin to sparkle with mica. When the trail finally does level off, push on just another 0.25 miles. Past an area of storm-felled trees you will find two picnic tables and the best views in the park. Santa Fe sits near to the west, while the Jemez Mountains comprise the bulk of the shadowy heaps in the distance.

The trail extending north from the tables was closed in recent years for revegetation, and there are no plans to reopen it. Now, subtle black signs direct hikers to the right, back down the mountain through another course of switch-backs. Some impatient hikers have trampled shortcuts straight down—refrain from following in their footsteps.

An unmarked fork turns up about 2 miles into the hike. This is *not* the small loop seen on park maps. Instead, the left fork leads to the RV area. Unless you need the shortest route to the restrooms, avoid the detour to this shabby corner of the park.

The trail turns south from the right fork and leads you to Girl Scout Interpretive Trail. The history of the Scouts in this area predates the founding of Hyde Park. Benjamin Hyde, affectionately known as "Uncle Bennie," became Santa Fe's scoutmaster shortly after moving to town in 1927. His wife, Helen, bequeathed the land to the state in the year following his untimely death in 1933.

Girl Scout Trail, with rock borders and labeled trees, is the small loop, so either side will get you to its trailhead. From there, cross back over the road. (If you find a metal gate with a tire shredder, you've completely missed Girl Scout Trail. In that case, just follow the dirt road down to trailhead sign mentioned below.)

Now begins the part of Circle Trail where many hikers lose their way. Park maps show a skating pond in this vicinity, but warm winters in recent years may see it soon replaced with an amphitheater. In any case, look for a nearby bridge, followed by a staircase in the embankment. At the top of the stairs is an Adirondack shelter and beyond that a dirt road. Straight across the road is a trail sign showing two hiker icons. If you don't find it, you can follow the dirt road south, passing campsites en route back to the lodge. The upper trail offers a bit more seclusion, though you may still be able to spot campsites through the trees, hear campers' songs, and smell what's cooking on the grills. The area is far more peaceful when the main camping loop closes for the winter (November 1 through Easter).

About 0.25 miles into the upper trail, or 2.7 miles into the hike, you'll reach the intersection with the old Waterfall Trail. At last check, it was unmarked, but that should change soon. Turn right here and go downhill to the Group Shelter #2 area. A small black sign behind the group shelter indicates where Circle Trail resumes, and another sign shows where the new Waterfall Trail begins. This short spur is a cool side trip up a shady little canyon. Recently rerouted to follow a rocky stream, the riparian path seems a world away from the rest of the park. Though it flows only after heavy rains or snowmelt, it's well worth a 30-minute detour, even when it lacks a waterfall.

To continue on Circle Trail, return to the Waterfall trailhead, and cross the bridge. At 0.25 miles or so past the bridge, a steep clearing will begin to show through the trees. That's the sledding area. In the 1940s and 1950s, it was Santa Fe's first and only ski basin, complete with a towrope powered by a Cadillac engine. The structure at the base was built by the Civilian Conservation Corps in 1938 and allegedly used then as a cooking school. You'll recognize it now as the Hyde Park Lodge. A couple of switchbacks take you back down to the parking area.

Note: The segment on the west side of road boasts the better views, but it's a steep mile up, followed by a steep mile down. For a more relaxing hike, stick to the lower, shadier trails on the east side of the road. Check for maintenance or snow closures by calling (505) 983-7175 or visiting **www.nmparks.com.**

NEARBY ACTIVITIES

Hyde Park is the gateway to endless opportunities for outdoor recreation. Start by driving north 8.4 miles on Hyde Park Road, also known as the Santa Fe National Forest Scenic Byway. It ends at the Santa Fe Ski Area, near the southwest corner of the vast Pecos Wilderness. The Hyde Park Visitors Center has all the information you need for exploring this part of the Santa Fe National Forest. Or you can plan ahead by contacting the Española Ranger District at (505) 438-7840, or **www .fs.fed.us/r3/sfe/districts/espanola.**

32 | GLORIETA CANYON

 KEY AT-A-GLANCE INFORMATION

LENGTH: 7.2-mile out-and-back

DIFFICULTY: Moderate

SCENERY: Aspen, mixed conifer, early 20th-century ruins

EXPOSURE: Mostly shade

TRAIL TRAFFIC: Heavy

SHARED USE: Heavy (mountain biking, equestrians; popular with dog owners; restricted motor vehicle access)

TRAIL SURFACE: Dirt, loose rock

HIKING TIME: 3–4 hours

DRIVING DISTANCE: 74 miles

ACCESS: Year-round

LAND STATUS: Private trailhead area; Santa Fe National Forest–Pecos/Las Vegas Ranger District

MAPS: Trail maps available at conference center; Santa Fe National Forest–East Half; USGS Glorieta, McClure Reservoir

FACILITIES: Signed trails, vending machine at parking area, food services and restrooms at New Mexico Hall; most facilities at conference center are ADA compliant

LAST CHANCE FOOD/GAS: Gas stations in the town of Glorieta

SPECIAL COMMENTS: This hike starts on private land. See longer note at end of description.

GPS Trailhead
Coordinates

UTM Zone (WGS 84) 13S

Easting   0430294

Northing   3940181

Latitude   35° 36' 10"

Longitude 105° 46' 10"

IN BRIEF

Take a break from yucca and cacti for a cool hike through aspen and spruce. The shaded canyon route visits relics from the last century, while short side paths lead to abandoned mines. Vintage cars stuck along the trail suggest it was once a horrible road. The traffic now is an intermittent stream of mountain bikers, equestrians, and hikers with pack-mule dogs.

DESCRIPTION

Will Rogers once observed: "Whoever designed the streets in Santa Fe must have been drunk and riding backwards on a mule." Apparently, the same engineering process was applied to a nearby segment of interstate highway. Northbound lanes on I-25 from Santa Fe go directly southeast to the Glorieta Unit of Pecos National Historical Park. This misdirection is temporarily corrected between Cañoncito and Glorieta Pass, but from there it turns southeast

---

Directions →

From I-25 north, take Exit 299 at Glorieta. Turn left to cross the bridge over the interstate, then turn left again, following the signs to the Glorieta Conference Center. The main entrance is less than a mile from the exit. Stop at the security gate for a map and directions to the hiker parking lot. If the gate is not manned, turn right and follow the signs 0.5 miles to guest registration at New Mexico Hall. Trail maps and advice are also available at the reception desk. From there, drive about 0.25 miles north on Oak Road to the hiker parking lot. Walk across the bridge then up to the right, past the service area and into the RV park. A wooden box with a hikers logbook is located on the right side of the road. Continue north along the road to the end of the RV park. Turn left to go through a locked gate. The trail begins here.

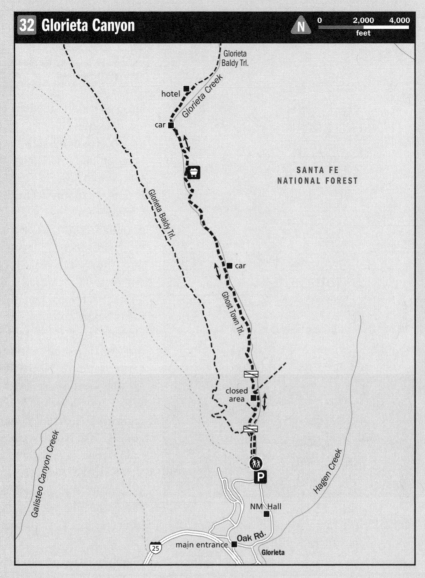

N

| 0 | 2,000 | 4,000 |

feet

Glorieta
Baldy Trl.

hotel

Glorieta Creek

car

SANTA FE
NATIONAL FOREST

Glorieta Baldy Trl.

car

Ghost Town Trl.

closed
area

Galisteo Canyon Creek

Hagen Creek

P

NM Hall

Oak Rd.

25 main entrance

Glorieta

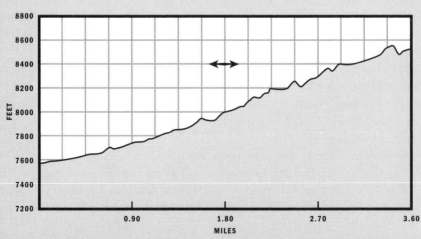

8800			
8600			
8400			
8200			
8000			
7800			
7600			
7400			
7200			

FEET

0.90   1.80   2.70   3.60

MILES

> **Always be prepared for sudden changes in weather.**

again as it skirts the base of Glorieta Mesa.

North and South have been at odds here before. On March 28, 1862, the Union captain Gurdin Chapin (my great-great-grandfather-in-law) led a reconnaissance mission into the woods at Glorieta Pass. His cavalry unit advanced fewer than 800 yards before spotting Confederate troops in attack position. In the ensuing battle, later to be known as "the Gettysburg of the West," the South's Texan regiments ultimately outgunned the North's Colorado units. Meanwhile, however, the New Mexico Volunteers had scrambled and rappelled down the cliffs of Glorieta Mesa to torch a supply train behind enemy lines. With their provisions incinerated, the Rebs had no choice but to fall back.

Two weeks later, Colonel Gabriel René Paul (Chapin's father-in-law) led attacks on retreating Confederate troops near Peralta, about 10 miles south of Albuquerque. This battle was immortalized (and greatly exaggerated) a century later in Sergio Leone's cinematic masterpiece *The Good, the Bad and the Ugly.* In terms of ending the South's advancements into northern New Mexico and ultimately defeating the Confederate campaign to win the West, the more significant showdown was the Battle of Glorieta Pass.

But the South would rise again. In 1949 the Southern Baptist Convention settled on Glorieta for the site of their western assembly. Construction of the Baptist Conference Center began in 1952, and the venue has since grown into the resort-like complex that dominates the town today. Now operating as the LifeWay Glorieta Conference Center, this 2,200-acre facility is an open gateway to a few of the finest trails in the southern Sangre de Cristo Mountains. Detailed trail maps and a designated parking area are provided as an additional courtesy to those who come here just to hike.

The hike begins at the north end of the RV park, about a 0.4-mile walk from the hikers parking area. Signs posted just past the gate indicate that the Glorieta Baldy and Broken Arrow trailheads are nearby to the left. The arrow pointing right shows the way to the ghost town, misspelled here with spooky letters for the campy fun of it.

What remains of the neglected settlement near the end of the trail doesn't quite amount to the makings of a very Brady adventure, but natural scenery throughout the canyon is reason enough to hike this route more than once. In May and June, wild iris blooms in watercolor pastels, while scarlet columbine glows as though electric. Look closely at the latter and you'll see how it got its name. (*Hint:* Columbine means "dovelike.") Stands of aspen create pockets of gold in autumn.

Start north along the road and bear left at the first fork ahead, then veer right at the second fork. The third fork is the important one: go left and keep the creek on your right or you'll end up in the wrong canyon. Just 0.5 miles from the trailhead, you'll arrive at a second gate that's identical to the first one. Go through the pedestrian access, and continue north.

The trail from here is easy to follow. It slims down as it exits the meadow and enters the narrow, wooded canyon. Another sign reminds you of the directions to the trailhead and to the ghost town but says nothing of the steep footpath on the left. (It seems to be a discontinued segment of Glorieta Baldy Trail.) Just past the sign is another fork. Take your pick: low and damp or high and dry. The branches rejoin about 500 feet upstream.

The creek fades in and out along the way, sometimes spilling over the trail. It can get muddy in spots, particularly after a heavy summer rain, or slick with ice in the winter. On the plus side, the predominantly south-facing slope and relatively low altitude help thaw out this trail sooner than most others in northern New Mexico. Bamboo shoots adorn the creek side, as does the body of a Chevy Humpback, or maybe a Packard, judging by the X-member frame. Apparently a mid-1930s model, the unfortunate vehicle has been stranded 1.5 miles up the trail for at least half a century.

Another fork appears 0.8 miles past the car. Again, the diversion is temporary, but cliffs flanking the left branch make it the more scenic way to go. Just past the merge, look for a clearing on the right. A new shelter stands close by on the west side. On the north side, an old miner's cabin is about a breath away from a complete collapse. Footpaths lead off to the south and east to weave through clusters of abandoned mines. It's worth a quick detour, but heed the posted warnings.

A half mile past the clearing, you arrive at a wooden bridge that probably wouldn't survive another crossing. Go around it. Another car is parked ahead on the left side of a meadow. It's in slightly better shape than the last one but still doesn't leave much to identify. A '39 Plymouth sedan might be a good guess based on its outside door hinges and square headlights. Beyond it on the right, you will come to the site of an old sawmill, as evidenced by a heap of lumber and the scar of a skid trail on the sloping canyon wall. Everything else in the meadow is broken boards and rusty nails—watch your step.

This site is generally referred to as the "Glorieta Ghost Town," which seems a bit off when you consider that the town of Glorieta is a few miles south and still somewhat alive. A relatively flat 0.25 miles past the sawmill, a two-story hotel once faced the craggy cliffs towering to the east. Little more remains of it than a stone foundation no bigger than an economy-motel suite. Behind it, a makeshift wooden cross stands at the head of a stony grave. Hidden farther back to the right, a narrow shaft tunnels into solid rock. Its depth exceeds the range of pocket flashlights.

The route ends here, but the trail continues northeast. Seasoned hikers can proceed uphill if they wish. At about the point where the creek bends up to the west, the trail turns north. From there it's a steep half mile up to La Cueva Ridge. Glorieta Baldy is 1.5 miles west. Taking into account the walk between the parking area and the trailhead, the full loop runs about 12 miles, with an elevation gain and loss of 2,700 feet.

Note: Please observe the policies established by the Glorieta Conference Center for access to trails in the adjacent national forest. Inquire at the GCC for further directions before hiking beyond the route described here.

NEARBY ACTIVITIES

The Glorieta Conference Center lists a climbing wall, rappelling tower, and paintball battlefield among the recreational amenities available to both guest and nonguest groups. Rates are around $15 per person, per hour, with a minimum of ten persons per group. Reservations are required and generally must be made two weeks in advance. For more details, call the GCC at (800) 797-4222 or visit **www .lifeway.com/glorieta**.

For further enlightenment, reflect upon the world-renowned iconography at the Pecos Benedictine Monastery. The chapel on the 11,000-acre monastic property was originally built as part of a dude ranch for vacationing city slickers more than 50 years ago, and the adobe building that houses the Abbey Gift Shop previously served as a stop on the Pony Express. To get there from the GCC, drive straight from the main entrance to Pecos, about 6.5 miles east on NM 50. Turn left at the junction with NM 63, and go north about 1.5 miles. The monastery entrance is on the left. For more information, call (505) 757-6415 or visit **www.pecosmonastery.org**.

BUCKMAN: Otowi Peak 33

IN BRIEF

Otowi Peak sits on the San Ildefonso reservation boundary, 1,100 feet above the Rio Grande. A rough, unmarked trail up the south side of Buckman Mesa is the best way to make your approach. Views from the top and geologic features along the way are astounding.

DESCRIPTION

Founded in the 1880s, Buckman was a stop on the Chili Line, a narrow gauge out of Santa Fe that followed the east bank of the Rio Grande up to Española and on to Antonito, Colorado. At the core of the town was a sawmill established by the Oregon lumberman Harry Buckman, who also lent his name to the mesa and the road. A nearby wagon ford across the Rio Grande is known as (what else?) Buckman Crossing.

The Chili Line rolled up its tracks in 1941, and nothing remains of the town today except the name. Since 1984 the mesa has appeared on maps as "La Mesita" but is still better known as Buckman Mesa. The surrounding area is now mined for Santa Fe's

KEY AT-A-GLANCE INFORMATION

LENGTH: 4.6-mile out-and-back

DIFFICULTY: Moderate

SCENERY: Panoramic mountain views, river gorge, volcanic mesas

EXPOSURE: No shade

TRAIL TRAFFIC: Moderate

SHARED USE: Low

TRAIL SURFACE: Dirt, sand, rock, cinder

HIKING TIME: 3 hours

DRIVING DISTANCE: 76 miles

ACCESS: Year-round

LAND STATUS: Santa Fe National Forest–Española District; Santa Fe County

MAPS: Santa Fe National Forest–West Half; USGS White Rock

FACILITIES: None

LAST CHANCE FOOD/GAS: Convenience store gas–station on Airport Road, 0.25 miles east of NM 599 (20 miles from trailhead)

SPECIAL COMMENTS: In dry conditions, most cars can handle the last 9 miles of the drive, but be advised that it is a bumpy ride. Pack river sandals for a cool wade on hotter days.

Directions ⟶

From I-25 north, take Exit 276B, and go 9.8 miles northeast on Veterans Memorial Highway (NM 599). Exit at Camino La Tierra and turn left (north). As of July 2007, only the 5.8-mile portion of CR 77 known as Camino La Tierra has been paved. The remaining 9 miles of CR 77, known as Buckman Road, is a heavily corrugated dirt road. Improvements and realignments are slated for the near future. In any case, follow Camino La Tierra/Buckman Road 15 miles northwest to its end at the Rio Grande. Park in the clearing on the right. The hike begins here.

GPS Trailhead Coordinates

UTM Zone (WGS 84)   13S

Easting   0395167

Northing   3966395

Latitude   35° 50' 10"

Longitude   106° 09' 39"

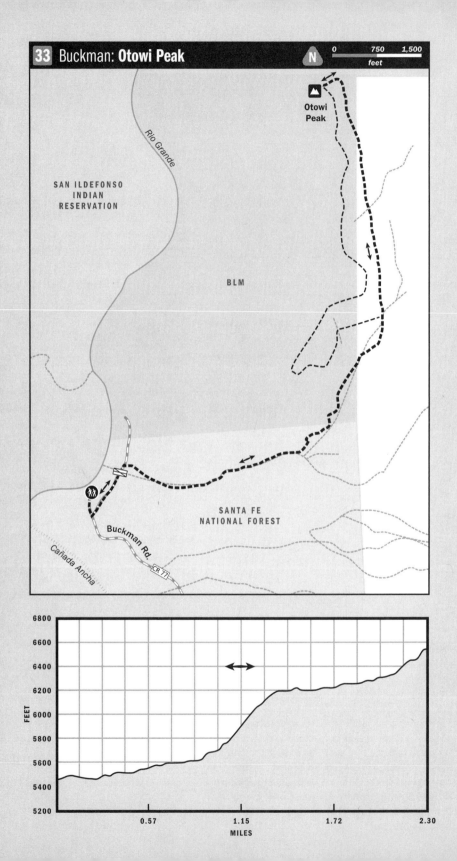

0   750   1,500
feet

Otowi Peak

Rio Grande

SAN ILDEFONSO
INDIAN
RESERVATION

BLM

Buckman Rd

Cañada Ancha

CR 77

SANTA FE
NATIONAL FOREST

FEET

6800
6600
6400
6200
6000
5800
5600
5400
5200

0.57   1.15   1.72   2.30

MILES

most precious commodity. The Buckman well field draws water from 1,400 feet below the land surface and pumps it 15 miles to the City Different. It seems an arduous process, given the substantial flow in the adjacent river. However, under the Rio Grande Compact of 1939, New Mexico must allow a percentage of that water to reach Texas. The amount is based on measurements taken at Otowi Bridge, located about 1.5 miles upstream from Buckman Crossing. In particularly wet years, Texas is entitled to as much as 87 percent of the volume that passes beneath Otowi Bridge. (*Otowi* is the Tewa word for "gap where water sinks," referring to a place where Pueblo Creek often disappeared into the sand.)

The highly eroded west face of Buckman Mesa is evidence of the river's vigorous flow in the distant past. It has undermined nearly half of Otowi Peak, causing large landslides. Enough basalt from the mesa rim tumbled down to dam the river, creating lakes that backed up 12 miles to Española. The rock dam has long since washed away, and the river now flows at a gentler pace. During high snowmelt, you may see kayakers and rafters putting in or taking out at the end of Buckman Road.

The hike to the top of Buckman Mesa is not as difficult as it seems from below. Two fingerlike extensions poke southwest from the corner of the mesa, with the longer one pointing directly at the parking lot. The easiest way to the mesa top is up the ravine between the fingers.

From the parking area, walk about 100 yards back up Old Buckman Road, then turn left on a smaller road heading northeast through stands of tamarisk. Less than 0.2 miles ahead, go through a gateway at a cattle guard. You will soon arrive at the edge of a wide, sandy wash. Turn right at the wash, and follow it upstream into the narrow canyon ahead.

About 0.6 miles up the wash, the streambed turns to the southeast. Just past the uppermost bend, look for a rock cairn and an eroded path on your left. Exit the wash here, and begin climbing a ravine to the northeast. The path gets sketchy in places so keep watch for more cairns and footprints. The path follows a drainage. Most hikers seem to prefer keeping it on their right throughout most of the ascent.

The distance from the wash to the mesa top is about 0.6 miles. As you approach the mesa rim, the path briefly merges with the drainage and then exits on the right side. As the terrain levels out, the path curves around to the left, heading north–northwest toward Otowi Peak.

From here, the base of the cone is just a 0.5-mile walk, with a few deep cuts to cross along the way. An alternate approach bows to the east, around the cuts. Either way, your destination peak rises 300 feet above the surrounding mesa top, making it an obvious target.

From the base of Otowi Peak, a few paths cross the cindered slopes to the 6,547-foot summit. Its eastern side is the easiest to climb. Be advised, however, that compasses are unreliable near the cone. Another path goes to a vent about

100 feet south–southeast of the summit. The vent, often referred to as the "blow hole," is hidden behind rocks and difficult to spot from more than a few yards away. Explore it only with the utmost caution—the opening starts out steep and quickly approaches verticality.

The 360-degree overlook from the peak includes views of the Sangre de Cristo Mountains to the east and northeast. The canyons and potreros of the Parajito Plateau are to the west. The Rio Grande is just 0.5 miles west and 1,100 feet below, flowing south into White Rock Canyon, which, aside from a few caliche stains, isn't really all that white. The popular White Rock Overlook is fewer than 3 miles to the southwest, but you'd have to drive about 50 miles to get there.

Black Mesa stands about 6 miles north. Emblematic of San Ildefonso Pueblo, the little mesa is historically noted as the site of successful resistance against the Spanish reconquest in 1694. The east–west reservation boundary, about 100 yards north of the peak, is off-limits. Avoid any paths heading in that direction. (For information about visiting San Ildefonso Pueblo, see Nearby Activities below.)

To vary the return segment to the ravine, consider a breathtaking walk along the crescent-shaped west rim. You can follow it south to the fingertip. From this amazing precipice, continue following the rim northeast 0.4 miles to intercept the path that brought you up here. You'll find it in the second drainage. Turn right to descend into the ravine, back to the wash below.

NEARBY ACTIVITIES

San Ildefonso is likely the best of the "living pueblos" for a self-guided tour. Settled in the 1300s, this Tewa village contains adobe buildings, ceremonial kivas, a central plaza, and a 1905 church built upon the ruins of a 17th-century mission, with fishing pond and picnic areas nearby along the Rio Grande. Best known for its black-on-black pottery, the pueblo receives an average of 20,000 visitors annually. The visitor center sells maps and permits for noncommercial photography, sketching, and recording, permitted except during ceremonials. Open daily from 8 a.m. to 5 p.m. Admission is $5 per vehicle. For more information, call (505) 455-3549.

To get there, return to NM 599, and go northeast 3.5 miles to its end. Take US 84 north 14 miles to Pojoaque. Turn left on NM 502, and go about 5 miles west to the pueblo.

BUCKMAN: Soda Springs–Caja del Rio Canyon

IN BRIEF

The first leg is a 3.2-mile hike down White Rock Canyon from the lost town of Buckman to a secluded meadow on the bank of the Rio Grande. From there you can embark on a challenging route over the northernmost tip of the Caja del Rio Plateau to the mouth of Diablo Canyon or just stroll back the way you came.

DESCRIPTION

The area around the northern tip of the Caja del Rio Plateau contains too many sights to see in one day. Make a sincere effort to run by as much as you can because the road to Buckman is not one you'll want to drive again soon. This loop covers a lot of ground, both high and low, so it helps to break it down into several segments.

To Soda Springs: Trail 306 from the parking area to Soda Springs is 3.2 miles of old doubletrack over gently rolling terrain above the east bank of the Rio Grande. Across the road from the parking area is a tangle of roads and washes. Walking from the Rio Grande, take the first right, and stick to

---

i KEY AT-A-GLANCE INFORMATION

ENGTH: 6.4-miles out-and-back, 8.2-mile loop, or 10-mile loop and spur

DIFFICULTY: Moderate out-and-back, difficult loop

SCENERY: High desert chaparral, seasonal wildflowers, river gorge, volcanic mesas

EXPOSURE: Mostly sunny

TRAIL TRAFFIC: Moderate

SHARED USE: Moderate (mountain biking, equestrians, rock climbing, limited motor vehicle access)

TRAIL SURFACE: Dirt, sand, rock

HIKING TIME: 4–6 hours

DRIVING DISTANCE: 76 miles

ACCESS: Year-round

LAND STATUS: Santa Fe National Forest–Española District

MAPS: Santa Fe National Forest–West Half; USGS White Rock

FACILITIES: None

LAST CHANCE FOOD/GAS: Convenience store–gas station on Airport Road, 0.25 miles east of NM 599 (20 miles from trailhead)

SPECIAL COMMENTS: In dry conditions, most cars can handle the last 9 miles of the drive, but be advised that it is a bumpy ride. Pack river sandals for a cool wade on hot days.

Directions →

From I-25 north, take Exit 276B, and go 9.8 miles northeast on Veterans Memorial Highway (NM 599). Exit at Camino La Tierra, and turn left (north). As of July 2007 only the 5.8-mile portion of CR 77 known as Camino La Tierra has been paved. The remaining 9 miles of CR 77, known as Buckman Road, is a heavily corrugated dirt road. Improvements and realignments are slated for the near future. In any case, follow Camino La Tierra/Buckman Road 15 miles northwest to its end at the Rio Grande. Park in the clearing on the right. The hike begins here.

GPS Trailhead Coordinates

UTM Zone (WGS 84)   13S

Easting   0395167

Northing   3966395

Latitude   35° 50' 10"

Longitude   106° 09' 39"

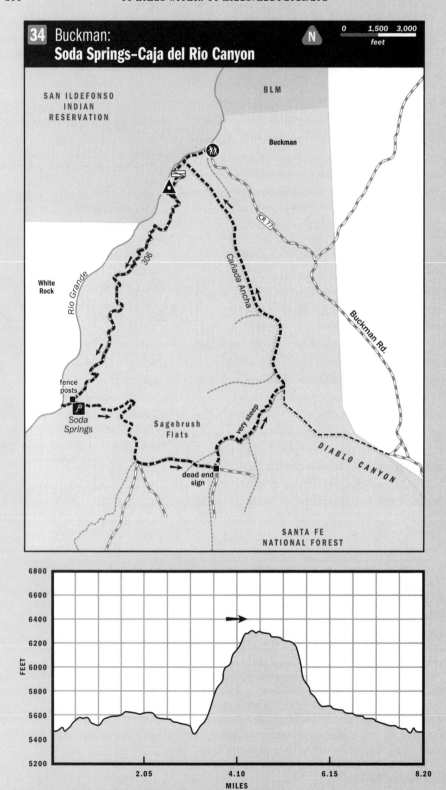

34 Buckman:
Soda Springs–Caja del Rio Canyon

N

0   1,500   3,000
feet

SAN ILDEFONSO
INDIAN
RESERVATION

BLM

Buckman

CR 77

Cañada Ancha

306

Rio Grande

White
Rock

fence
posts

Soda
Springs

Sagebrush
Flats

very steep

dead end
sign

DIABLO CANYON

Buckman Rd.

SANTA FE
NATIONAL FOREST

FEET

6800
6600
6400
6200
6000
5800
5600
5400
5200

2.05   4.10   6.15   8.20
MILES

Spires along Trail 306 to Sagebrush Flats

the track that best parallels the river. In about 0.25 miles, you arrive at Cañada Ancha—a sandy arroyo that's as wide as the river it feeds. Those going on the loop will be following it downstream 2 miles to return to this point. About 200 feet to the right are popular picnic beaches, as evidenced by the littered shore.

Cross the arroyo, and continue on the road. It soon bends left and then makes a sharp turn right. A gate around the corner indicates how far motorized vehicles are permitted to drive in this part of the national forest. The loud hum past the gate is Buckman Well #8. Go around it, uphill to the right. Admittedly, the scenery can be unappealing for the first 0.5 miles, but once you get past the power lines ahead, it returns to relatively natural splendor.

At the crest of the hill past the power lines, look on the left for an old fence. Turn right for a two-minute detour to the point at the end of the fence. The overlook there is about 100 feet above the river. Take a good look—though you may hear rafters or kayakers hooting below during the snowmelt season, you won't see much of the river again until you're near the end of the road.

Back on the road, about 0.25 miles past the detour, the trail splits. Bear left (the right branch seems to go down to the river). About 0.1 mile past that, the trail forks again; this time turn right (the left branch drops into an arroyo). From this point on, the way is clear. Just stick to the main road, put the book away, and enjoy the scenery. About 2.3 miles ahead, the road dies out as it drops into a wooded arroyo. Turn right before the arroyo, and follow a path down to a quiet, shaded spot on the edge of the Rio Grande.

Soda Springs to Sagebrush Flats: You can return to the parking area the way you came or take a challenging loop over the mesa. The segment to the rim of Sagebrush Flats gains more than 800 feet in elevation in 1.2 miles, most of it along a narrow, winding path best described as *jackassable* (fit for mules but not horses). Keep in mind that the climb up is easy compared to the climb down the other side. Read ahead so you know what you're in for before going up there.

As you're leaving the river, about 100 yards up the road, old metal and wooden fence posts stand at the roadside. The path beginning there on the right is the segment of Trail 306 to Sagebrush Flats. This end of it can nearly disappear under tall grass in a good monsoon season, but head straight east for 200 yards or so, and you'll pick up a trail of red lava rock winding up the steep cliffs. The trail isn't marked, but it shows signs of occasional use and light maintenance so it's easy enough to follow. Any forks you encounter on the lower part are just shortcuts across switchbacks.

Rockslides occasionally erase crucial bits of the trail—proceed with caution. At 0.9 miles into the climb, the trail bends left, and a red lava canyon with pointed spires opens on the right. From here the trail begins to break apart as it heads up from the confluence of two gullies. Go up the path between them, then bear south (to your right). Be aware that iron-rich lava can affect compass readings. If you lose the path, just aim toward the back end of the gulley on the right. The trail picks up there and develops into a primitive doubletrack as it levels out near the rim. It soon intersects a Jeep road. A sign for Trail 306 once stood at the junction here but more recently appeared to be the victim of a hit-and-run; look for pieces of it on the ground.

Sagebrush Flats to Cañada Ancha: The stretch across the aptly named Sagebrush Flats is 0.9 miles, rim to rim. Maybe you expected to find scoria cones and viscous flow-domes up here, but that volcanic field begins about 1.5 miles farther south. It's well worth exploring on another hike. For now, turn left on the Jeep road and follow it just under half a mile. Make it quick—the Caja del Rio Plateau can get pretty toasty, even when you can see that the peaks just 20-odd miles due east are still covered in snow.

Cross a pronounced wash to find a signpost on the right side of the road. A board bolted to the post bears the hastily scratched message: DEAD END ROAD. That's your cue to turn north, and follow the wash downstream.

The descent to Cañada Ancha drops nearly 600 feet in 0.8 miles, starting with a deceptively simple stroll down the wash. The first drop curves down like a grand staircase, but the second one plummets like an elevator shaft. Locate footholds in the right-hand corner, below the edge. Once you find those, it's as easy as climbing down a kiva ladder. Just use care and common sense. Do not try it in wet or icy conditions.

None of the remaining drops is quite so drastic. However, they add up to a strenuous descent. Give this segment at least an hour, during which time you might wonder if there are easier ways off this mesa. I'm sure there must be a few, probably at the end of the dead-end road, but it seems unlikely that any could be

An important landmark for following the loop route

more interesting than this one.

The drainage cuts through several distinct layers of basalt, ash, and cinders from multiple eruptions of both the local volcanic field and the Valles Caldera, which is about 20 miles west. At the low end of the drainage, an oasis of shade trees and maybe a few lingering pools offer cool respite. Take advantage of it before continuing out to Cañada Ancha at the mouth of the Caja del Rio Canyon. Assess your energy level, water supply, and remaining hours of daylight. If any of the preceding is almost out, turn left, and follow the wash downstream for a flat 2 miles to close the loop.

Diablo Canyon spur: On the other hand, if you're reinvigorated, turn right for a detour through the Caja del Rio Canyon, known locally as Diablo Canyon. An outstanding hike in its own right, this mile-long passage boasts an assortment of columns, slots, caves, cracks, crags, and cliffs. And with more than 100 routes to conquer, it's a popular spot with rock climbers. The area was closed in October 2006 for the filming of *3:10 to Yuma*. A tragic accident on the set may discourage studios from using Diablo Canyon (or from casting Russell Crowe as a cowboy) in future projects.

The canyon detour is 1.7 miles out and back, pushing the overall hike into the 10-mile range. Alternatively, you can drive around to the west end and hike in from there. Look for a turnoff on the right 2.8 miles from the parking area. Do not drive into the wash unless your vehicle is reliable in deep sand. Also be aware that flash flooding in the canyon has been known to carry away a vehicle or two.

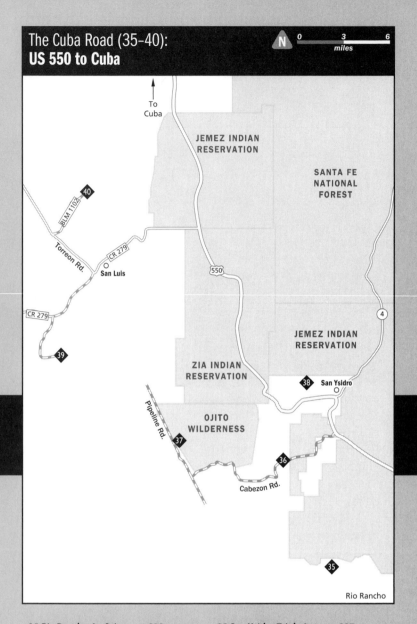

To
Cuba

JEMEZ INDIAN
RESERVATION

SANTA FE
NATIONAL
FOREST

40

BLM 1102

Torreon Rd.

CR 279

San Luis

550

CR 279

4

39

ZIA INDIAN
RESERVATION

JEMEZ INDIAN
RESERVATION

38   San Ysidro

Pipeline Rd.

OJITO
WILDERNESS

37

36

Cabezon Rd.

35

Rio Rancho

THE CUBA ROAD

35 RIO RANCHO: La Ceja

KEY AT-A-GLANCE INFORMATION

LENGTH: 1.1-mile balloon, longer out-and-back options

DIFFICULTY: Easy

SCENERY: Barrancas (eroded cliffs), diverse wildflowers and cacti

EXPOSURE: Shade along the streambeds

TRAIL TRAFFIC: Low

SHARED USE: Moderate (livestock, motor vehicles)

TRAIL SURFACE: Dirt road, sandy ridges and draws

HIKING TIME: 1 hour (or more)

DRIVING DISTANCE: 37 miles (one way) from the I-40 and I-25 exchange

ACCESS: Daylight hours; State Trust Land Recreational Permit required

LAND STATUS: State trust land

MAPS: USGS Sky Village NE (Cerro Conejo)

FACILITIES: None

LAST CHANCE FOOD/GAS: All services on US 550 in Bernalillo

SPECIAL COMMENTS: A more direct driving route will emerge as more roads are paved, which seems to occur daily in Rio Rancho. The last 6.5 miles of Rainbow Boulevard may remain unpaved. The last 0.4 miles get a little rough, but most cars should be OK in dry conditions.

GPS Trailhead Coordinates

UTM Zone (WGS 84) 13S

Easting   0338046

Northing 3918864

Latitude 35° 24' 00"

Longitude 106° 47' 00"

IN BRIEF

From the far corner of the West Mesa, the view plunges to a sculpted landscape below. Admire it from above with a hike along the rim or descend into the labyrinth of ridges and ravines to explore it up close.

DESCRIPTION

The Albuquerque Basin spans west to the Rio Puerco and east to the Sandia foothills, a distance of 20 to 30 miles. It's one of the largest and deepest basins of that fracture in the Earth's crust known as the Rio Grande Rift. The original basin is more than 5 miles deep but has since filled in with sediments eroding from the surrounding mountains.

The Llano de Albuquerque, better known as the West Mesa and less well known as Ceja Mesa, is a remnant of the broad floor of western basin between the Rio Grande and the Rio Puerco. It now stands more than 400 feet above the present floodplain of the Rio Grande and more than 500 feet above the Rio Puerco Valley. How it achieved this impressive stature is not entirely clear. Whether the *llano* (pronounced YAH-no, and meaning "plain") uplifted or the surrounding valley sank, it

Directions

From I-25 north, take Exit 242 at Bernalillo. Turn left on US 550 and go 2.5 miles to NM 528 (Rio Rancho Boulevard). Then turn left and go 1.8 miles to Idalia Road. Make a right and go 2.4 miles to Iris Road. Make another right, and drive 0.6 miles to Paseo del Vulcan. Turn left, go 5 miles to 10th Street NE, then turn right and go 0.3 miles to King Boulevard. Turn left again, and go 2 miles to Rainbow Boulevard. Turn right onto this dirt road and follow it 6.5 miles to its end.

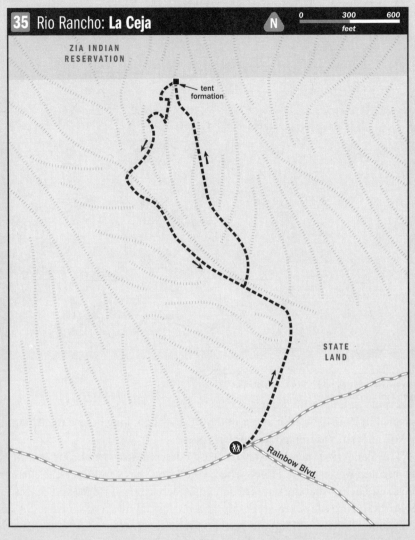

ZIA INDIAN
RESERVATION

tent
formation

STATE
LAND

Rainbow Blvd.

N

0   300   600
feet

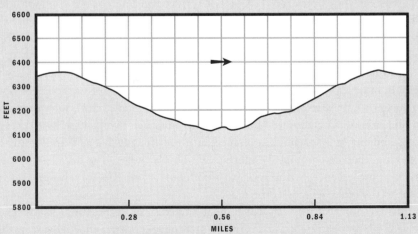

To avoid trespassing on Zia land, do not hike beyond this formation.

happened in a geologic rush about 600,000 years ago, long before the Albuquerque Volcanoes first pimpled its eastern edge.

The llano rises gently from the east but comes to an abrupt end at the northern and western rim. Here's where you'll find the barrancas—the cliffs and steep slopes below that are cut into an endless labyrinth of ridges and drains. On the northern rim, the scarp arches up to a precipice known as La Ceja (SAY-ha, and meaning "eyebrow"). Similarly, the 70-mile-long west-facing escarpment of Ceja Mesa is sometimes referred to as Ceja del Rio Puerco. (In common local usage, I've never heard anyone outside my circle of map-freak associates use the word *ceja* to refer to anything but eyebrows. Hence, if you stop to ask for directions to La Ceja, you'll likely get an arched eyebrow in reply.)

Rio Rancho occupies the northern part of the Llano de Albuquerque, with the bulk of development concentrated well to the southeast of La Ceja. For now, the western half is relatively empty. Various local peoples have long used this outland to conduct elaborate funeral rites for their elderly possessions. Old cars, sofas, and major household appliances are sacrificially burned and/or tossed from cliffs then ceremoniously adorned with bullet holes. The decades-old rituals face obsolescence as the modern developments of Rio Rancho creep ever closer to the outer fringes of the mesa.

To the north of western Rio Rancho lies the Zia Reservation. Sandwiched between the impending crunch of residential developments and the vast pueblo

land are seven contiguous sections of state land. Sections are generally designated as 1-square-mile parcels. At La Ceja, however, the rim of the llano defines
the southern Zia boundary, effectively shaping six of the state-land sections into
a row of broken teeth.

The hike at La Ceja isn't so much about following a certain route but rather
knowing where you should and should not go. Problem is, if boundary notices
ever *were* posted, they're gone now. To stay in fair play, you need to be aware of
a few landmarks.

For the most part, the barrancas are on Zia land, meaning that hikers keen
on thoroughly exploring them first need to obtain permission from the Pueblo
administration. However, Section 36 is an unbroken tooth; that is, it extends
beyond the rim, creating a more convenient opportunity for impromptu exploration. At about 200 acres, the state's portion of barrancas may seem a mere
puddle in the ocean. Rest assured: it's enough to get in over your head if you're
not careful.

Rainbow Boulevard ends at a crossroads near the center of Section 36. The
barrancas are not visible from here—sand dunes and juniper block the view. The
rim is just a few yards ahead. Follow the trail of shotgun shells to a point where
cars and appliances spill down into a heap reminiscent of bone piles at the bottom of a buffalo jump. It's a tragic sight, but it's generally confined to the area
around this dirt-road junction.

Before deciding whether to embark on a rim hike (outlined below) or to
venture down into the barrancas, assess the landscape. The steep slopes and
serpentine draws don't seem traversable, but they are easier to negotiate than
they initially appear. The rumpled terrain fills in the valley from the West Mesa
to the gypsum slope of White Mesa, which shines like a glacier, about 9 miles
to the north–northeast.

The barrancas are shaped from malleable sediments, mainly silt and coarse-
grained sand, with bits of red granite, obsidian, quartz, sandstone, and petrified
wood in the mix. Exposed pockets of smooth pebbles and cobbles resemble
colorful abstract mosaics throughout the gullies below.

For a hike in the barrancas, turn right at the rim, and follow it about 300
yards to the northeast. There a ridge branches out and gradually descends to the
northwest. Follow it out about 100 yards to a fork. Stay to the right and continue
another 0.25 miles to a formation that resembles a pitched roof or a large pup
tent. (See photo on the previous page.) Getting around it on this narrow ridge
may prove difficult, which is just as well because it approximates a point on the
otherwise invisible state land–Zia boundary. (In other words, stay south of the
tent formation.)

From here, turn left, and negotiate your way down to the streambed. Use a
diagonal approach on the steep slopes for more secure footing, and use a feeder
wash to avoid the otherwise vertical bank at the bottom. Turn left, and follow
the sinuous main channel upstream about 200 yards to a dead end. Climb up the

embankment, and then turn left at the crest of the ridge. Follow the ridge uphill, and in less than 0.25 miles you should be back on the rim. Now that you know how easy it is to get in and out of the barrancas, you can explore them further at your leisure.

Of course a descent into these twisted gullies is not a requirement for a fine hike at La Ceja—you can just as well enjoy a **hike along the rim.** Starting your walk from the end of Rainbow Boulevard, you have miles to wander in either direction before you run out of state land. You can also wander down a single-lane dirt road that's set back 10 to 100 feet from the rim. It often forks, so when in doubt, follow the branch that stays closest to the rim. It also gets too sandy and steep around La Ceja for most cars, but you might encounter an off-highway vehicle or two.

If you're facing the barrancas, the road to the right curves to the northeast as it drops from La Ceja. After about 2.5 miles, it takes a sharp turn to the southeast at a mesa corner. From here, a 1.4-mile stretch of east-facing scarp marks the eastern boundary of state land.

The road to the left undulates upward to Cerro Conejo (SAIR-oh koh-NAY-ho, "Rabbit Hill"), about 3 road-miles west. Peaking at 6,615 feet, it approximates the point where the southwest corner of the Zia Reservation meets the northwest corner of state land. Bones found near Cerro Conejo belonged to land mammals that inhabited the area 9 to 16 million years ago.

On my most recent walk along the rim, I crossed fresh cat tracks but couldn't be sure whether they were from a mountain lion or just a really big bobcat. Fuchsia petals emerged from hedgehog cacti. Piñon seemed to flourish despite devastating bark-beetle outbreaks elsewhere in the state. Glittering sands whipped off the mesa as winds gusted up to 40 mph, and in a sure sign of spring-time at La Ceja, semiautomatic weaponry crackled behind a not-too-distant hill while a pair of quail scrambled for cover.

WHITE MESA BIKE TRAILS AREA

IN BRIEF

Fifteen miles of well-marked trails—open to both biking and hiking—explore a land packed with geological curiosities. Though this hike hits most of the major features, it covers just a fraction of all possible routes on this endlessly fascinating terrain.

DESCRIPTION

A large trail map stands at the trailhead just beyond the green gate. Numbers on the map correspond with trail junctions, where smaller versions of the same map are located. This route follows the numbers in this order: Outbound: 1–3, 21, 22, 12, 11, 10. Return: 10–17, 23, 1. The connecting segment between 17 and 23 is a well-defined dirt road that does not appear on the maps.

Now that you've got the instant overview, follow the doubletrack to Junction 1. Keep to the left along a path on a low ridge. More roads meet at Junction 2 than the maps show, but continue straight.

The first 0.3 miles are on the dull side, but the scenery changes abruptly at Junction 3. Here, on the cusp of a scooped valley, it

Directions

From I-25 north, take Exit 242 at Bernalillo. Turn left on US 550 and go northwest 21.2 miles. (San Ysidro is about 2 miles too far.) Turn left on Cabezon Road. (Look for the brown sign for Ojito Wilderness and White Mesa Bike Trails on the right, followed by a green street sign for Cabezon Road on the left.) Go left at the first fork ahead. After 4.4 miles on Cabezon Road, turn right, into a fenced parking lot for the White Mesa Bike Trails Area. The trailhead is at the gate in the northeastern corner of the parking lot.

---

i KEY AT-A-GLANCE INFORMATION

LENGTH: 5.1-mile loop and spur

DIFFICULTY: Moderate

SCENERY: Gypsum ridges, painted desert, classic anticline, wildlife

EXPOSURE: Minimal shade

TRAIL TRAFFIC: Moderate

SHARED USE: Moderately popular (mountain biking, separate horse trail; no motorized vehicles)

TRAIL SURFACE: Sand, dirt, loose rock, gypsum

TRAIL SURFACE: Dirt, rock

HIKING TIME: 3 hours

DRIVING DISTANCE: 42 miles (one way) from the I-40 and I-25 exchange

ACCESS: Year-round

LAND STATUS: BLM–Rio Puerco Field Office

MAPS: USGS SKy Village NE (Cerro Conejo), San Ysidro

FACILITIES: Detailed maps at trailhead and trail junctions

LAST CHANCE FOOD/GAS: Convenience store gas station in San Ysidro (See Directions below)

SPECIAL COMMENTS: For a more detailed explanation of the complex geological features here, visit geoinfo.nmt.edu/tour/landmarks/san_ysidro.

GPS Trailhead Coordinates

UTM Zone (WGS 84) 13S

Easting   0332955

Northing   3929878

Latitude   35° 29' 54"

Longitude   106° 50' 30"

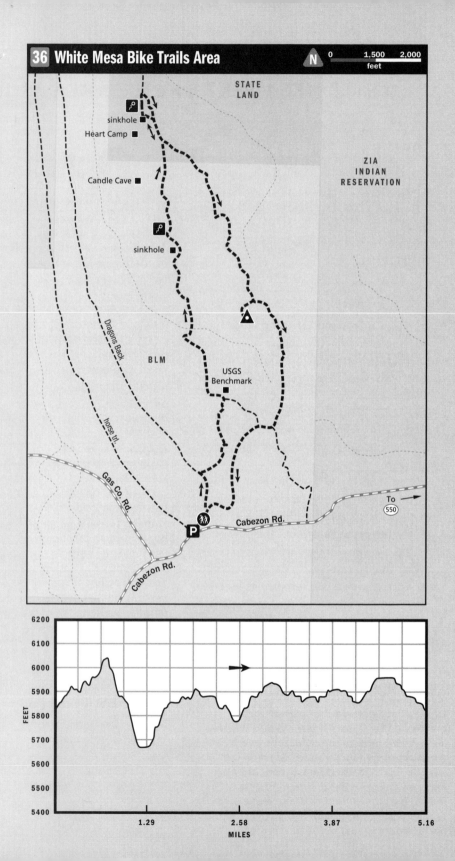

36 White Mesa Bike Trails Area

N   0   1,500   2,000
feet

STATE
LAND

sinkhole

Heart Camp

Candle Cave

ZIA
INDIAN
RESERVATION

sinkhole

Dragons Back

BLM

horse trl.

USGS
Benchmark

Gas Co. Rd.

To
550

Cabezon Rd.

P

Cabezon Rd.

FEET

6200
6100
6000
5900
5800
5700
5600
5500
5400

1.29   2.58   3.87   5.16

MILES

appears a leviathan took a bite out of the Earth's crust. If such an enormous creature did exist, it might resemble the ridge to the left, aptly named Dragon's Back. The harrowing 3.25-mile bike path along its spine leaves little room for error. It's a ride best left to circus performers.

At least two paths run off to the right at Junction 3. The more popular one sticks close to the rim, while the official trail takes the higher ground. Either way, keep the rim on your left until you hit Junction 21.

Straight ahead of 21, the rim rises nearly 100 feet to an overlook. The dark stump-like cylinder at the peak is a USGS benchmark. There, you'll find the best views on the trail system, but watch the kids—the drop on the other side is a sheer 200 feet or more. Many casual hikers are content in making this their destination for an out-and-back that totals up to 1.6 miles, but we're just getting started.

Take a moment to scope out the terrain ahead. The next leg of the hike is the narrow gypsum ridge reaching out on the left like Dragon's Back in miniature. It points toward an elongated dome informally known as Travertine Ridge, which stretches along the floor of the valley. The turnaround point for this hike is on the far side of its central apex. With binoculars or a sharp eye, you can make out the trail curving around it to the right. Now note the yellowish sandstone ridge at the far end of the valley. It extends south for the entire length of the east rim—that's your return route.

Dragon's Back and the sandstone ridge mark the flanks of the Tierra Amarilla Anticline, sometimes called the San Ysidro Anticline. Don't be surprised to find

a geology class on a field trip here. This fold in the surface exposes a chronological sequence of rock layers. The oldest rock, at the core of the anticline, is composed of red to green siltstones and mudstones deposited on the floodplain of a river system about 210 million years ago. Dinosaur bones and gizzard stones from more recent times occasionally turn up in nearby washes. (Fossil collecting is strictly prohibited here so leave them where you found them.)

Another landmark worth noting, though it's not on public land, is White Mesa, peeking up about 2 miles to the northeast. B-movie trivia buffs take note: much of the sci-fi thriller *Ghosts of Mars* was shot there in 2000. The gypsum mesa required thousands of gallons of food dye before it could pass for the red planet. It took several reapplications because frequent monsoon rains kept washing it back to its natural albino state.

To continue the hike, follow the white ridge down into the valley. The red valley floor can get sloppy after rain or snow, but you'll soon climb out of it as you ascend Travertine Ridge. Once on the ridge, the trail skirts around the right side of a series of domed hills. Sinkholes at the top of any one of them reveal cavernous interiors. These travertine hills sound hollow under a pair of hiking boots, and walking on them may give you the sensation of treading on thin ice. So, are any too fragile to support the weight of, say, a hiker? According to one geology expert, that's a good question.

Mineral springs—not fit for drinking—leak out near the trail. A more active one bubbling up on the left is about the diameter of a rain barrel but probably deeper. You may notice the greenery and sulfuric smell before finding the water. Enjoy this unusual little ecosystem from a distance because the surrounding mud is also deeper than you think.

Past the spring, the path curves around the right side of two more mounds. As you reach the far side of the larger one, consider this off-trail detour: Continue around the north base of the mound about 500 feet until you reach the edge of a cliff. To the immediate left, two deep fissures split the west side of the hill wide open. Climb down the cliff to explore them. Poke around enough and you'll find a cave stocked with votive candles.

When you're ready to move on, return to the point where you climbed down, and then follow the base of the cliff north about 500 feet to a low point where it's easier to climb back up. Then follow the dry wash east, back to the main trail. Turn left, and you'll soon reach Junction 12. Another sizable hump rises up on the left, and another valley opens up ahead on the right. In view beyond the valley, the oft-dry Rio Salado and US 550 skirt the southern end of Red Mesa.

At Junction 11, turn left and follow a footpath uphill. It soon crosses a fissure that widens to the left. Follow it south to another sinkhole. An opportunity for another off-trail detour begins here. About 400 feet southwest of the sinkhole is a rectangular landscape feature resembling a small corral; perhaps it was used as one long ago. Its sheltering walls make it an ideal spot to break for lunch on hot days or to pitch a tent on windy nights. Some refer to this place as Heart Camp because a curious collection of heart-shaped stones has been placed on the walls. As with Candle Cave, no one seems to know when or why the tradition began.

Return to the crack on the ridge, and follow it north. Springs seep out and wash over rippled mineral residue. Junction 10 stands at the base below. You could continue south on the trail another 2 miles. Or, to follow this route, turn around here, and walk along the east side of the mound, back to Junction 12. Bear left to Junction 13.

From Junction 13, the smaller path on the right is more scenic and less confusing than the road on the left. It also runs closer to the rim, which you'll keep on your right for the next 0.8 miles to Junction 16. There, on the right, you'll find a 0.25-mile (round-trip) detour down a dead-end ridge with breathtaking drop-offs on both sides. It leads to a scenic overlook.

Just under 0.7 miles past Junction 16, the trail splits in at least four directions in a kind of roundabout at Junction 17. From here you have three options for returning to the parking lot. The navigationally challenged might find it easiest to return to the anticline overlook, about 0.25 miles to the northwest via Junction 20, and then backtrack to the parking lot from there. More-energetic hikers might enjoy the 0.55-mile trail south to Cabezon Road; turn right, and follow the road about 0.5 miles from there back to the parking lot.

This route follows a marginally shorter way along a dirt road not indicated on the maps. From Junction 17, it heads west about 0.1 mile before bending southwest for another 0.1 mile. There it joins the doubletrack running straight south from Junction 20. After going 0.3 miles south, turn right at the fork to reach Junction 23. Turn left there to reach Junction 1 and the parking lot.

37 OJITO WILDERNESS: The Far Side

KEY AT-A-GLANCE INFORMATION

LENGTH: 5.4-mile double loop

DIFFICULTY: Moderate

SCENERY: Hoodoos, banded mesas; wildlife

EXPOSURE: Minimal shade

TRAIL TRAFFIC: Low

SHARED USE: Low (equestrians; livestock; no vehicles off designated roads)

TRAIL SURFACE: Dirt, rock

HIKING TIME: 2–3 hours

DRIVING DISTANCE: 52 miles (one way) from the I-40 and I-25 exchange

ACCESS: Year-round

LAND STATUS: BLM–Rio Puerco Field Office; Wilderness Area

MAPS: USGS Ojito Spring; brochure maps available from the BLM office in Albuquerque and www.nm.blm .gov/recreation/albuquerque/ ojito_wsa.htm

FACILITIES: None

LAST CHANCE FOOD/GAS: Convenience store–gas station in San Ysidro (see Directions below)

SPECIAL COMMENTS: See longer note at end of Description.

GPS Trailhead Coordinates

UTM Zone (WGS 84)   13S

Easting   0322063

Northing   3932004

Latitude 35° 30' 56"

Longitude 106° 57' 44"

IN BRIEF

Lacking formal trails, the newly designated Ojito Wilderness can be difficult to navigate. This improvised route on the far side of the wilderness takes you to hoodoo colonies and the highest point in the Ojito.

DESCRIPTION

Since the original Wilderness Act passed in 1964, the National Wilderness Preservation System has grown to include 680 areas nationwide. The first was New Mexico's own Gila Primitive Area, as it was then called. Another 22 followed in about as many years. With nearly 1 percent of New Mexico's public lands designated as wilderness, the state would let it rest at that for the next 18 years. The hiatus finally ended with the Ojito Wilderness Act of 2005, which permanently protects more than 11,000 acres of insanely beautiful land next to the Zia Reservation. (Credit the New Mexico Wilderness Alliance, a nonprofit conservation group, for boosting the Ojito campaign and for guiding the hike described below.)

There are no formal trails in the Ojito, but the navigationally challenged can enjoy a

Directions

From I-25 north, take Exit 242 at Bernalillo. Turn left on US 550 and go northwest 21.2 miles. (San Ysidro is 2 miles too far.) Turn left on Cabezon Road. (Look for the brown sign for Ojito Wilderness on the right, followed by a green street sign for Cabezon Road on the left.) Once you make the turn onto this dirt road, reset your odometer. The next 15 miles can get a bit tricky. Refer to the detailed mileage guide at the end of the Description.

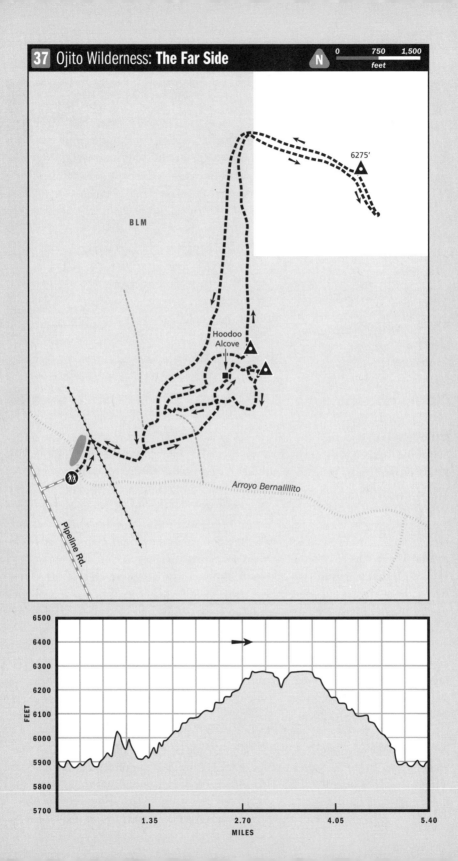

N

0   750   1,500

feet

BLM

6275'

Hoodoo
Alcove

Arroyo Bernalillito

Pipeline Rd.

6500
6400
6300
6200
6100
6000
5900
5800
5700

FEET

1.35   2.70   4.05   5.40

MILES

stroll into the wilderness by sticking to major arroyos and washes, or any number of old dirt roads that crisscross the rugged terrain. Just make sure your chosen route doesn't fade beneath your feet. Mechanical forms of transportation—including mountain bikes—are banned from wilderness areas, leaving roads to the reclamation of nature. The Ojito is also a wonderful place to simply wander, provided you leave a reliable trail of breadcrumbs. Venture too far off any beaten track, and even an expert with a compass and a topo map may struggle to find a way out. It's true—I've seen it happen.

With that in mind, this hike will lead you into a remote area of the Ojito, where there are neither roads nor arroyos to follow. Think of it as a way of getting acquainted with freeform hiking in these wilds, and be prepared for spontaneous diversions from the route described below.

The hike begins in the parking area on the south side of a pond. It might be hidden behind scrub or dried up from drought, but it'll be evident from the raised embankment curving around its east side. Walk upon the bank, heading north toward the power lines. While up there, take a moment to survey the layout to the east. From this angle, it appears as a long, narrow valley. On the right is a stocky little mesa, backed by the considerably larger Bernalillito Mesa. An arroyo of the same name runs on the near side of the smaller mesa. It seems a viable passage into the valley except that it's stuffed with tamarisk and a barbed-wire fence, so ignore all that. This hike is more concerned with exploring the unnamed mesa on the left.

Once directly beneath the lines, you'll see two paths. (More may wear in as the popularity of this hidden area escalates.) One path climbs up the ridge to the left; the other dips down to the right to hook past it. Follow the latter. As you round the point of the ridge, you'll see another one ahead and a gulch lying between them. Make a note of the gulch; you'll be coming out of its mouth on your return route.

The second ridge point doesn't extend out as far as the first does—it just rises straight up 100 feet like a castle turret. A third point, similar to the second, stands about 0.25 miles beyond it. Between them is a recess containing a fantastic gallery of hoodoos. You may encounter a deep cut on your way to the alcove, in which case, detour to the right to get around it.

For the uninitiated, hoodoos are erosion's more fanciful work. Trademarks of the Colorado Plateau, which ends a few miles to the west, these phantasmal formations usually stand in tall columns of sedimentary rock with protective caps. Most of the specimens here are on the small side, some hardly qualifying as mere goblins, but they're as spirited as any, and the colorful assembly is worth a close inspection.

Make your way to the far right corner of the alcove. Tucked behind the tallest hoodoo in the bunch is a gradual slope. Use it to walk up to the first tier of the mesa wall. Pick your way carefully, and you shouldn't need to use your hands to climb or descend any part of this hike. (Or if you enjoy scrambling, do so accordingly.)

At last check, a collapsed fence lay where the ground levels out. Proceed past it and out to the rim for wide-open views to the east. When you're ready to move on, turn around, and climb down into a smaller alcove, where more hoodoos and goblins await. The easiest way down begins at a point near the downed fence.

Once back on terra firma, explore the hoodoos as you head south to exit the alcove. Turn right when the ridge on your right is low enough to cross. Go straight past the first alcove, and follow the base of the mesa west to an inside corner formed by the mesa wall on your right and the ridge straight ahead. En route you may encounter the cut again; this end of it roughly points to the best place to climb up the mesa.

Once above the rim, the volcanic plug known as Cabezon Peak (hike 39) comes into view about 10 miles to the northwest. Turn right, and follow the mesa rim half a mile to a higher overlook. Be careful near the edges. Some parts are mere overhangs cracked straight through, and large rockslides 200 feet below suggest they're prone to give way.

The view from the overlook is astonishing, but you haven't reached the top yet. The highest point in the Ojito Wilderness stands 0.7 miles to the north. If you have your recreation permit from the State Land Office, turn left, and follow the rim toward the summit. As the rim curves out to your right, start veering to the left. The west side is a more gradual incline to the top tier.

When you're ready to return to the parking area, aim south toward the corner where you climbed up. (If uncertain, just follow the rim again.) About 200 feet or so west of the upper corner is the east side of the gulch noted early in the hike. You should be able to see the parking area from here. Find a reasonable place to descend to the streambed. Turn left to reach the mouth, then turn right to pick up the path you started out on.

Note: The highest point in the Ojito currently falls on State Trust Land, meaning a recreation permit from the State Land Office is technically required to hike there. Also, while not required for this hike, a GPS unit with tracking features is always recommended in the Ojito.

DRIVING DIRECTIONS — MILEAGE GUIDE

In dry conditions, most cars can handle the 15 miles of back roads leading to the trailhead, though it can get rough at arroyo crossings.

0.0 Arrive at the junction of Cabezon Road and US 550.

<0.1 Go left at the Y.

3.9 Enter public lands. Note the trailhead on the right. Sometimes referred to as Colored Bluffs Trail, this is an easy hike with a few moderately steep slopes. It follows a faded doubletrack north just over 0.5 miles to Junction 17 of White Mesa Bike Trails (see hike 37) then continues another 0.5 miles north to an area of multicolored rocks.

4.4 Arrive at the parking area for WMBT.

4.6 GasCo Road, on the right, leads to the horse trail. Continue on the main road as it curves left (south).

5.8 Turn right (west) at the Y.

8.1 The main road turns right (northwest).

9.3 The road bends left (west) at the wilderness sign.

9.9 A parking area on the left and fence on the right mark Puñi View. A popular full-moon hike in warmer seasons, this easy 2-mile out-and-back starts at the fence. A doubletrack runs north about 1 mile to the edge of a small mesa, where the trail fades. Nearby, though unmarked, is the site where two hikers found unusual bones in 1979. Excavations later revealed the 110-foot skeleton of a seismosaurus. A replica is on display at the New Mexico Museum of Natural History in Albuquerque.

11.0 Shortly after crossing Arroyo la Jara, note a faded doubletrack on the right. Informally known as Hoodoo Pines, this easy out-and-back runs just over 2 miles, leading to everything its names suggests—and more.

12.4 Turn right (northwest) at Pipeline station and the junction with Pipeline Road.

14.0 Cross the Marquez Wash

14.9 Turn right, and park in the clearing ahead.

SAN YSIDRO TRIALS AREA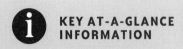

IN BRIEF

A unique slot canyon area at the southern tip of the Sierra Nacimiento offers a comprehensive lesson in geology—or, for the layperson, just a lot of strange rocks to gawk at.

DESCRIPTION

The Sierra Nacimiento is by far the elder of the two Rocky Mountain ranges that stretch down into the Jemez Pueblo. And since it also has the longer reach, the Sierra Nacimiento has been proclaimed "the southernmost tip of the Rockies." However, they share this distinction with the Sangre de Cristo Mountains, located about 60 miles due east.

The gray and pink granite that forms the bulk of the Sierra Nacimiento is getting on in years—around a billion in all. About 220 million years ago it sat at the bottom of an inland sea and later under deltas and rivers as the sea retreated.

The receding waters left deposits that would later become thick layers of shale and sandstone—the cross bedding seen in the mesa cliffs today from eastern Nevada to the Texas Panhandle. Known as the Chinle

Directions

From I-25 north take Exit 242 at Bernalillo. Turn left on US 550, and go 25 miles to a weigh station on the right (1.5 miles past the town of San Ysidro). The paved turnoff for the San Ysidro Trials Area is at the far end of the weigh station. Drive up to the locked gate on the left side of the parking area. (If you don't have the key, park here and walk through the pedestrian gate.) Follow the dirt road 1.2 miles to the parking area, and park near the signboard. The trailhead for this hike is directly behind the signboard.

KEY AT-A-GLANCE INFORMATION

LENGTH: 2.7-mile loop (3.9-mile balloon without gate key)

DIFFICULTY: Easy to moderate

SCENERY: Sinuous canyons, hardrock desert, sandstone and gypsum mesas

EXPOSURE: Some canyon shade

TRAIL TRAFFIC: Low

SHARED USE: Low to moderate (mountain bikes, equestrians; livestock; motorcycling, with special permits)

TRAIL SURFACE: Dirt, sand, rock

HIKING TIME: 2–3 hours (3–4 hours without gate key)

DRIVING DISTANCE: 43 miles (one way) from the I-40 and I-25 exchange

ACCESS: Year-round, but see Special Comments about gate key and racing events

LAND STATUS: BLM–Rio Puerco Field Office

MAPS: USGS San Ysidro

FACILITIES: Trailhead parking, marked trails

LAST CHANCE FOOD/GAS: Convenience store–gas station in San Ysidro

SPECIAL COMMENTS: See longer note at end of description.

GPS Trailhead Coordinates

UTM Zone (WGS 84) 13S

Easting   0335673

Northing   3937582

Latitude   35° 34' 06"

Longitude 106° 48' 48"

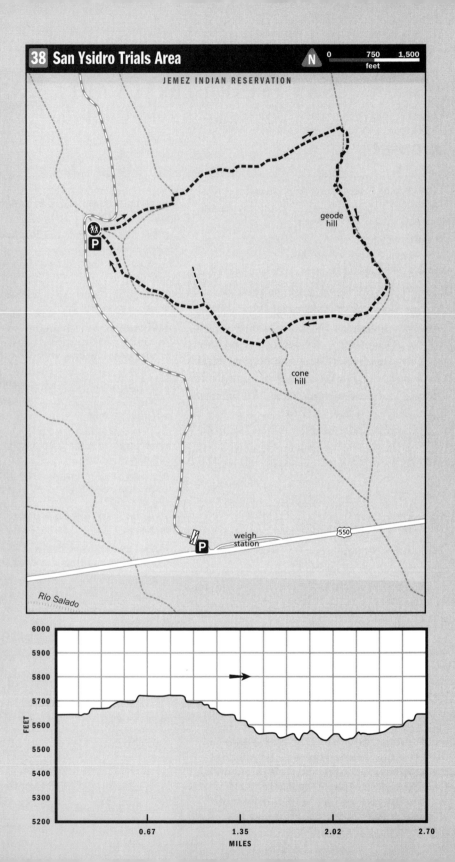

38 San Ysidro Trials Area

N

0   750   1,500
feet

JEMEZ INDIAN RESERVATION

geode
hill

cone
hill

weigh
station

550

Rio Salado

6000
5900
5800
5700
5600
5500
5400
5300
5200

FEET

0.67   1.35   2.02   2.70

MILES

sedimentary formation, it's also credited with preserving the logs in Arizona's Petrified Forest National Park.

The old granite reemerged about 75 million years ago in the Laramide Revolution, the same great compressive spasm that thrust up mountains across the American West. The Sierra Nacimiento uplifted along a north–south fault, resulting in a 50-mile range from San Ysidro to Gallina. By contrast, the eastern Jemez Mountains showed up with volcanic eruptions in just the last few million years.

The Sierra Nacimiento ("birth mountains," in reference to the birth of Christ) flank the San Juan Basin. This frontline position allows them to intercept eastbound storms. Average annual precipitation at higher elevations is nearly three feet (compared to Albuquerque's eight inches). The resulting runoff carves small but intricate canyons through the foothills, notably in the San Ysidro Trials Area.

The trials area is closed to off-road motorized vehicles, except during special-use events permitted to the New Mexico Trials Association (NMTA). They were among the first to recognize that the area's unique geologic features—namely "grippy rocks"—would enhance their motorcycle competitions and their practice events.

The NMTA hosts five events here each year. Surprisingly, the dirt bikes haven't shredded the landscape. In terms of Leave No Trace ethics, cows seem to be the worse offenders. And although tire tracks remain visible throughout much of the area, riders here are ecological saints compared to their noxious counterparts at Montessa Park (hike 8).

Small pools can become big obstacles deep in
narrow canyons.

I'm no fan of motoring through nature, but I have to admit the stunts they
pull on San Ysidro's colossal rocks are stupefying. And yet if you happen to arrive
on a day without a motorbike event, all the better. You'll probably have the whole
place to yourself, and the hiking possibilities can be overwhelming. Just look
around the parking area, and you'll spot six or seven trailheads, each marked with
a dirt-bike icon. These markers appear on trails throughout the area. All signs are
identical and hence useless for distinguishing one route from another.

The route described below is a simple combination of prominent paths
and waterways in the heart of the trials area. For a quick orientation: the hike
traverses a hilly valley bound by Red Mesa to the west, Mesa Cuchilla to the
east, and White Mesa on the far side of US 550 to the south. To narrow it down
further, it's confined to a triangular space defined by two major drainages that
merge before crossing US 550.

Start the hike by walking east, straight past the signboard. Hop across a
small wash. The wash deepens as you continue east and slightly to the north.
You can walk in it or, during wetter seasons, take the track running parallel
on the north bank. The wash gets very narrow after about 0.75 miles, so you'll
probably opt for the high road anyway.

Maintain a fairly straight path, and you'll intersect a canyon just under a
mile from the parking area. You can't miss it—some bikers have dubbed it "The
Grand Canyon." That's an enormous exaggeration. It's not more than 50 feet

across at its widest point, and it narrows down to a classic slot in places.

A cairn near to the right marks an easy entry point, though there are several to choose from. You can also look upstream for easier ways in. Be advised, however, that the Jemez Reservation lies less than 300 yards to the north. Please respect their boundaries. Also, do not enter the canyon if the forecast calls for rain. Pay special attention to the northern skies. Storms up to 10 miles away could send torrents of water and debris through this channel, and emergency exits are few over the next 0.5 miles.

That said, walk down to the canyon floor, and turn right to head downstream. The wide sandy wash narrows into sinuous chutes with polished sandstone walls. Each turn reveals marvelous details. Scoured spillways and basins hint at the furious rapids and whirlpools that follow stormy weather.

You may encounter a few ponds en route. If they're too big to cross, you'll need to backtrack for an exit from the canyon. You can reenter the canyon downstream, but the hard-rock route along the rim is just as interesting, and smaller waterways on either side of the main canyon are worth exploring as well. Also, the hill on the west bank is allegedly littered with geodes and gypsum crystals. (I didn't find any.) Or if you're confident in your sense of direction, wander off to the east—where sandstone hoodoos and ancient petroglyphs populate the ridges and gulches—then return to this canyon to finish the hike.

Once the canyon squeezes past the hill, it shallows out to a stream that trickles through dense stands of willow and tamarisk. Do not follow the stream into this wooded area. Instead, pick up the motorbike trail that curves southwest as it wraps around the base of the hill. It will lead you away from the stream and into an open meadow. Follow the track through a low pass at the far corner of the meadow.

Once you cross the ridge, you'll see two cone-shaped hills on your left, about 100 yards south. Stay on track as the path continues west and slightly to the south through a stand of tamarisk in a small wash. From there, the motorbike trail bends around the base of a ridge on your right and then aims northwest, roughly parallel to a major arroyo about 500 feet to your left. You can't see it from here, but a tree line marks the spot.

At the next fork, stay left. As the trail bends closer toward the arroyo, cross over to walk along its streambed. From here, less than 0.5 miles remains in the hike, but the wavy bedrock makes an impressive finale. As the top end of the drainage curves to your right, exit left, and walk uphill about 100 yards to the parking lot.

Note: Pick up a gate key from the BLM office at 435 Montano Road NE in Albuquerque. Though it's not usually necessary, you can also call (505) 761-8600 to reserve a key. To catch or avoid motorcycle competitions, check the events schedule posted on the New Mexico Trials Association Web site at **www.nmtrials.org.**

39 CABEZON PEAK

KEY AT-A-GLANCE INFORMATION

LENGTH: 2.4-mile balloon, plus optional summit spur

DIFFICULTY: Strenuous approach, moderate loop, insane spur

SCENERY: Views over mixed grassland steppe and volcanic fields

EXPOSURE: Mostly sunny

TRAIL TRAFFIC: Low to moderate

SHARED USE: Low (rock climbing)

TRAIL SURFACE: Dirt, rock

HIKING TIME: 2 hours, another 2–3 hours for the summit spur

DRIVING DISTANCE: 74 miles (one way) from the I-40 and I-25 exchange

ACCESS: Year-round

LAND STATUS: BLM–Rio Puerco Field Office, Wilderness Study Area

MAPS: USGS Cabezon Peak

FACILITIES: None

LAST CHANCE FOOD/GAS: Convenience store–gas station in San Ysidro

SPECIAL COMMENTS: The last 7 miles of roads and the trail can turn treacherous in wet conditions. A brochure on the Cabezon Peak Wilderness Study Area can be acquired from the BLM office in Albuquerque, or you can download it from www.nm.blm.gov

GPS Trailhead Coordinates

UTM Zone (WGS 84) 13S

Easting   0309295

Northing   3941281

Latitude   35° 35' 49"

Longitude   107° 06' 19"

IN BRIEF

This loop on the shoulders of a giant volcanic plug offers amazing vistas at every turn. A nontechnical but nonetheless harrowing spur presents the option of climbing to the top of its towering neck.

DESCRIPTION

The pedestal of Cabezon stands well over 1,000 feet high. Jutting up another 800 feet is a ribbed column of basalt that once filled the throat of a great volcano. The cinder cone has long since eroded to expose this monolithic core.

The Navajo name for it is *tse najin,* or "black rock." Their legends tell of the Twin Warrior Gods who decapitated a giant. The blood from the fatal wound spilled to the south and congealed into the lava flow at El Malpais (hike 59), and its head became what the Spaniards would later call *Cabezón,* which translates as "big head."

Spanish settlement here in the upper Rio Puerco Valley began shortly after the reconquest, but the early ranchos were soon under continual attack from Navajo neighbors to the west. Relations with eastern neighbors were strained in 1815 when the Spanish

Directions

From I-25 north, take Exit 242 at Bernalillo. Turn left on US 550 and go northwest 23 miles toward San Ysidro. Stay left on US 550 and continue another 18 miles toward Cuba. Turn left on County Road 279 to San Luis. The paved portion ends after 8.5 miles. Continue 3.8 miles straight on the dirt road. Veer left at the Y onto BLM 1114 and go south 2.9 miles. Turn left at the sign for Cabezon Peak and go east 0.9 miles to the parking area at the end of the road.

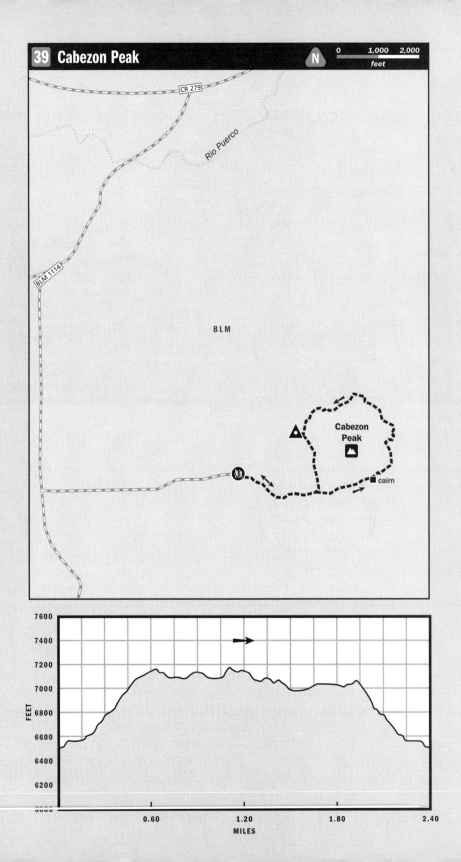

N

0   1,000   2,000
feet

CR 279

Rio Puerco

BLM 1114

BLM

Cabezon
Peak

■ cairn

7600
7400
7200
7000
6800
6600
6400
6200

FEET

0.60   1.20   1.80   2.40
MILES

Cabezon Peak

government awarded tracts of Zia, Jemez, and Santa Ana pueblo lands to Cabeza de Baca. The resulting dispute over this grant, known as the Ojo del Espiritu Santo, lasted well over a century.

Cabezon Peak straddles the western boundary, with its summit just inside the Ojo del Espiritu Santo Grant, though land on both sides is currently administered by the BLM. The property was badly eroded and overgrazed when the U.S. government purchased it in 1934. Over the past 70 years, resource-management programs have brought modest improvements to the upper Rio Puerco Valley. The once fertile farmlands have yet to return, but the terrain does support an impressive array of wildlife. Common creatures include three toad species, in addition to beaver, badger, bobcat, and porcupine. Golden eagles, great horned owls, and a variety of hawks often nest by the peak.

Cabezon is often described in some variation of New Mexico's little Devils Tower. But check the stats: Devils Tower rises 1,267 feet from the Belle Fourche River to peak at 5,112 feet, whereas Cabezon rises 2,020 feet from the Rio Puerco to peak at 7,785 feet. So why the diminutive comparison? Maybe because Devils Tower, America's first national monument, is a solitary landmark that dwarfs everything else in its empty corner of Wyoming. By contrast, Cabezon stands in the company of about 50 other plugs in the shadow of Mount Taylor, the volcano peaking at 11,301 feet about 35 miles to the southwest. Or maybe because the vertical rock on Devils Tower exceeds Cabezon's by just enough to pose a significantly more challenging climb.

Cabezon's primary summit route is not considered a technical climb, but that doesn't make it easy or particularly safe. A hardhat is well advised (a bike helmet should suffice in a pinch). If the prospect of scrambling through talus and clawing your way up a chimney sounds daunting, don't let it keep you away from Cabezon. You can enjoy a hike here without a trip to the summit.

The hike begins on the eastern side of the parking area, where an aging signboard marks the trailhead. Start up the steep trail toward the volcanic neck. After a steady climb for nearly half a mile, the trail splits. Take your pick—both branches soon cross an old barbed-wire fence that marks the western boundary of the Ojo del Espiritu Santo Grant.

The branches merge shortly thereafter. Continue around to the south side of the neck. Less than 0.25 miles past the fence, look for the marker for the summit route. Stones arranged into a ten-foot arrow point the way. There's no clear trail through the scree, so aim for the chimney. There you'll find rock ledges adequate for handholds and footholds to pull your way to the rim. Another short scramble through loose rock on the domed peak, and you're at the top. Something to remember before attempting any ascent: descents are invariably more challenging.

After several minutes of contemplating the vertical route, you might wonder if circumnavigating the peak would be more fun than scaling it. Those prone to the slightest fits of acrophobia will certainly enjoy the loop more than the climb. Hearty hikers bent on doing both should do the ascent first, while their legs are still strong. Continuing with the hike, follow the path around to the southeast shoulder. There you'll find what appears to be an easier summit route. Trust me: it isn't. From here the loop path fades as it drops into a boulder field. Few cairns mark the way, but the strategy from this point is obvious: keep the boulder fields on your left and the edge of the shoulder on your right.

Some easy boulder hopping and a short climb are necessary to round the corner to the north side. Drop back down one level to get around the boulder field there. Cross a downed fence, and continue around to the west side. An outcrop pointing due west provides a fine overlook of other plugs like Cerro Cuate ("twins hill"), 4 miles west–northwest. And just in case you forgot where you parked, look down to your left.

The final quarter of the loop is across a steep slope. Avoid drifting too far downhill or you'll face more difficulty in crossing the ridge ahead. Once over that last hump, you'll intersect the trail that brought you up here. Turn right, and follow it back down to the parking area.

NEARBY ACTIVITIES

The ghost town of Cabezon is private property, as are fenced tracts to the south and west. Just about everything else is wide open, so you can wander for miles. Use Cabezon Peak as a homing beacon, and your chance of getting lost is minimal.

40 CONTINENTAL DIVIDE TRAIL:
Deadman Peaks

KEY AT-A-GLANCE INFORMATION

LENGTH: 2.8-mile loop, longer options

DIFFICULTY: Easy

SCENERY: Mesa vistas, rock formations, burned-out coal deposits, skittish cows

EXPOSURE: Minimal shade

TRAIL TRAFFIC: Low

SHARED USE: Low (equestrians, livestock; roads are good for mountain biking, but no vehicles are permitted on this portion of the CDT

TRAIL SURFACE: Rocky trail, dirt road

HIKING TIME: 1 hour (minimum)

DRIVING DISTANCE: 73 miles (one way) from the I-40 and I-25 exchange

ACCESS: Year-round

LAND STATUS: BLM–Rio Puerco Field Office

MAPS: USGS San Luis, Headcut Reservoir

FACILITIES: None

LAST CHANCE FOOD/GAS: Convenience store–gas station in San Ysidro

SPECIAL COMMENTS: Driving the dirt road can get tricky in wet conditions. See longer note at the end of the Description.

GPS Trailhead Coordinates

UTM Zone (WGS 84) 13S

Easting   0312407

Northing 3957489

Latitude 35° 44' 37"

Longitude 107° 04' 28"

IN BRIEF

Hike the Continental Divide National Scenic Trail (CDT)—or at least a small portion of it. Access points closest to Albuquerque allow for extensive walks in Cabezon country. The loop described below uses equal parts dirt road and the CDT to circumnavigate a cluster of red hills known as Deadman Peaks. Of course, you also have the option of following the trail for many miles in either direction.

DESCRIPTION

Upon arrival at the base of Deadman Peaks, first thing everyone wants to do is check out the hoodoos. They're an odd sight, standing out there on the caliche like a colony of giant mushrooms sprouting from snowy white earth. Next they want to know where the CDT is. Fact is, they're standing right on it.

The Continental Divide National Scenic Trail, more often referred to simply as the CDT, doesn't always follow the Continental Divide. The latter, of course, is the physical ridge separating the watersheds that drain

----

Directions ⟶

From I-25 north, take Exit 242 at Bernalillo. Turn left on US 550 and go northwest 23 miles toward San Ysidro. Stay left on US 550 and continue another 18 miles toward Cuba. Turn left on County Road 279 to San Luis. The paved portion ends after 8.5 miles. Turn right here onto Torreon Road (also paved) and go north 3.7 miles. At the top of the hill, turn right onto BLM1102. (Look for a stop sign and a yellow cattle guard.) You can park here to pick up the CDT, or follow the main dirt road northeast 3.4 miles to the next CDT intersection on the south side of Deadman Peaks. Park roadside in front of the mushroom-shaped hoodoos.

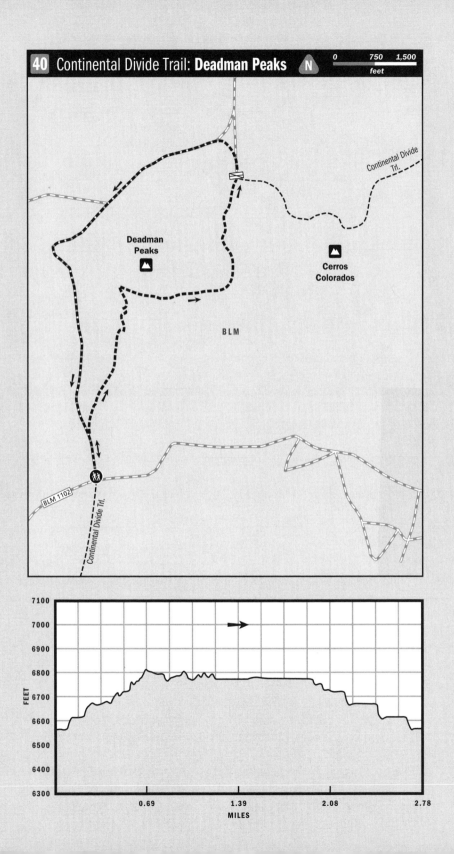

N

0   750   1,500
feet

Continental Divide Trl.

Deadman
Peaks

Cerros
Colorados

BLM

BLM 1102

Continental Divide Trl.

7100
7000
6900
6800
6700
6600
6500
6400
6300

FEET

0.69   1.39   2.08   2.78
MILES

Hoodoos stand in front of Deadman Peaks.

into the Pacific Ocean from those flowing to the Atlantic and the Gulf of Mexico. If for some reason you need to be on the actual divide, drive back to US 550, and turn left. From there it's a 35-mile drive to an unremarkable spot on the Continental Divide.

Private land issues are one reason for the CDT's deviation from its namesake, one that has proven to be the trail's biggest obstacle since Congress established it as a National Scenic Trail in 1978. An inexplicable lack of support and enthusiasm also plagued the project for its first two decades. The trail developed in fits and sputters until 1998, when the Continental Divide Trail Alliance launched its ambitious ten-year plan to complete the trail. With one year remaining, the 3,100-mile CDT was still largely a work in progress. In 2007, estimates of its usability ranged from 65 to 70 percent. At the same time, New Mexico's 740-mile portion was about 41 percent finished. One optimistic estimate has its completion scheduled for 2014.

The stretch through the Rio Puerco Valley has been operable for several years. You probably didn't notice it the first time you crossed it as you turned off the paved road, and you may not be able to identify it immediately at this second junction. Not to worry.

The hike begins at the hoodoos. Just turn your back to them, and walk straight north along the road. You should spot the cairns within a minute. Each is a pyramid stacked about knee high. Keep them in sight, and you'll never lose the trail.

About 0.2 miles from the hoodoos, the trail deviates east from the road and climbs the side of a ridge pointing south from the pedestal of Deadman Peaks. About 0.25 miles farther up is the first of six switchbacks leading to the biggest of Deadman's three peaks.

At first glance, the peaks appear as ordinary volcanoes capped with the usual rust-red cinders. A closer look reveals a shade of reddish-orange that's not quite as common in these otherwise dun mesa lands, though many roads around Torreon are the same fiery shade. This surfacing material is sometimes referred to as "red dog." Pick up a few scatters along the path, and you'll see it isn't lava. This red rock forms when heat from coal-seam fires cause low-grade metamorphic changes in the mudstones sandwiched between the coals.

The trail levels out for the next 0.6 miles as it follows the rim. On your left, the main peak rises another 200 feet. On your immediate right, the drop from the rim is 100 feet or so. The views south to Cabezon and beyond are wonderful. If you're lucky, the elements will treat you to the spectacle of a thunderstorm rolling across the valley. If you're really lucky, it'll rumble by without chasing you back to your car.

One mile into the hike, the trail turns north along the rim of a canyon that separates Deadman Peaks from the somewhat bulkier Cerros Colorados. Once the trail reaches the back end of the canyon, it turns right and joins a doubletrack. The old road comes in from the north through a drop gate and heads east into the Cerros Colorados. If you're pressed for time, it's best to leave the trail at this point. Once you turn the corner into the Cerros Colorados, you could easily lose half an hour gawking at rock formations in a 0.25-mile twist of waterways. Then there's always something else to lure you around the next bend, and before you know it you're standing on the edge of a 500-foot precipice on La Ventana Mesa with 6 miles of trail between you and your car. (Note that if you continue up toward Cuba, white-painted posts and blazes are interspersed with the rock cairns.)

So if you're in this hike for the quick 2.8-mile loop, go through the drop gate, leave it as you found it, and don't look back. Turn left on the dirt road about 200 yards ahead. From there it's about 1.4 miles back to the junction where you parked. Don't be alarmed to find a herd of ominous black cows lurking behind you. They flee like squirrels when approached.

Once back at the hoodoos, you might be tempted to see what lies along the CDT to the southwest. You'll soon run into the same problem: one hyperscenic turn after another lures you farther along the trail, dropping down into the Arroyo de Los Cerros Colorados and then quickly climbing past the 6,650-foot peak of San Luis. Next you're crossing the paved road and heading out on a high bench on the Mesa San Luis. Before you know it, you're standing on the edge of a wind-sculpted sandstone ridge, once again with 6 miles of CDT between you and your car.

Another reason for the deviation from the physical divide: scenery has a

Ascending toward the first of the three
Deadman Peaks

heavy influence on route selection. Though criteria for determining scenic value can be highly subjective, few rational hikers could disagree with the choices here in Cabezon country.

With massive cairns guiding your way, navigating this wild landscape is easy. The difficult part is knowing when to quit. One highly rated daylong hike is the 25-mile segment between Deadman Peaks and the northern end of Forest Road 239. The rescue index is fairly low, so this not a trek to undertake on a whim. It crosses breathtaking landscapes in the Ignacio Chavez Special Management Area, a rugged and remote swath of gorgeous desert wilderness.

Note: For updates on the Continental Divide National Scenic Trail, visit **www.cdtrail.org**. For a firsthand account of New Mexico's portion of the CDT, visit **matquest.blogspot.com**. Excellent maps of the Rio Puerco segment, which includes Deadman Peaks, can be downloaded from **www.nm.blm.gov**.

NEARBY ACTIVITIES

The only better way to experience the CDT is to get involved as a volunteer. For details, call (888) 909-CDTA or visit **www.cdtrail.org**.

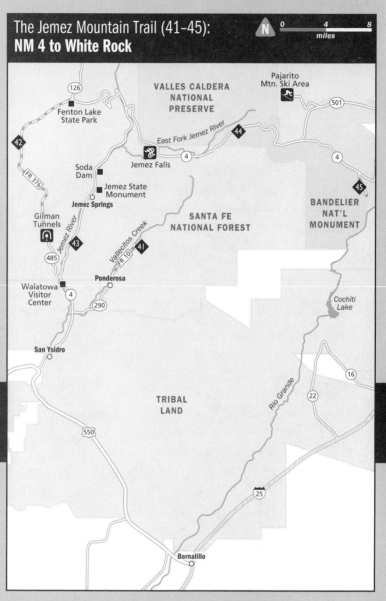

N

0   4   8
miles

Pajarito
Mtn. Ski Area

VALLES CALDERA
NATIONAL
PRESERVE

501

126

Fenton Lake
State Park

East Fork Jemez River

44

42

Jemez Falls

4

4

Soda
Dam

45

Jemez State
Monument

BANDELIER
NAT'L
MONUMENT

Jemez Springs

SANTA FE
NATIONAL FOREST

Gilman
Tunnels

43

41

485

Cochiti
Lake

Ponderosa

Walatowa
Visitor
Center

4

290

San Ysidro

16

Rio Grande

22

TRIBAL
LAND

550

25

Bernalillo

THE JEMEZ MOUNTAIN TRAIL

41 PALIZA CANYON GOBLIN COLONY

KEY AT-A-GLANCE INFORMATION

LENGTH: 4-mile out-and-back
DIFFICULTY: Easy, but exploring the goblin area can be strenuous
SCENERY: Towering ponderosa, riparian habitat, sculpted rock
EXPOSURE: Mostly shade
TRAIL TRAFFIC: Moderate
SHARED USE: Moderate (equestrians, mountain bikes; motorized vehicles)
TRAIL SURFACE: Dirt roads
HIKING TIME: 2 hours
DRIVING DISTANCE: 56 miles (one way) from the I-40/I-25 exchange
ACCESS: Year-round, but seasonal gate closures will add 0.8 miles to the hike. Though not required for this hike, entry to the Paliza Campground is $10 per vehicle.
LAND STATUS: Jemez Ranger District
MAPS: Santa Fe National Forest (West Half); USGS Ponderosa, Bear Springs Peak
FACILITIES: Camping, picnic tables, drinking water at the Paliza Campground, wheelchair-accessible restrooms
LAST CHANCE FOOD/GAS: Bar and grill in Ponderosa, usually open 2 p.m.–10 p.m.; convenience store, gas station, and visitor center on NM 4, about 2 miles north of the turnoff for Ponderosa

GPS Trailhead Coordinates

UTM Zone (WGS 84) 13S
Easting 0352770
Northing 3952880
Latitude 35° 42' 32"
Longitude 106° 37' 39"

IN BRIEF

Near the newly renovated Paliza Campground, this hike starts on a primitive road alongside a wooded creek, follows it into a ponderosa-shaded canyon to visit an assembly of standing rocks known as hoodoos and goblins, and then continues up to a ridgeline viewpoint for a look out over the canyon.

DESCRIPTION

Welcome to the famous Jemez (pronounced HAY-mess), a mountainous land so vast it would take several books to describe half of it. Allow me to recommend a few to get you started: In *Jemez Spring,* the Aztlán literary guru Rudolfo Anaya concocts a plot to blow up Los Alamos National Laboratories for the final installment in the Sonny Baca mysteries. For considerably slimmer and more practical reads, try *Guide to the Jemez Mountain Trail* by Judith Ann Isaacs and the classic *Exploring the Jemez Country* by Roland A. Pettitt.

This hike visits a spot that Pettitt

Directions ——————————→

From I-25 north, take Exit 242. Turn left on US 550 and go 23.5 miles to San Ysidro. Turn right on NM 4 (beware of speed traps) and go 6.3 miles to the signs for Ponderosa. Turn right on Forest Road 290 and go 6.9 miles, where it becomes FR 10, a maintained gravel road. Continue straight another 2.5 miles. About 0.5 miles past the paved entrance to Paliza Campground, a maintained gravel road (FR 266) starts on the right. Pull over to the left and park in the clearing ahead. The hike begins directly across the road on the primitive FR 271 heading north. During seasonal closures on FR 10, park at the gate and walk the remaining 0.8 miles to FR 271.

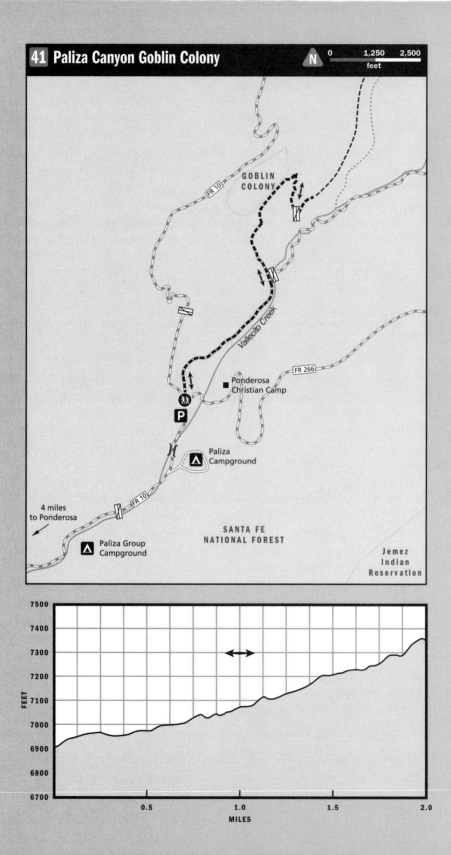

41 Paliza Canyon Goblin Colony

N   0   1,250   2,500
feet

GOBLIN COLONY

FR 10

Vallecito Creek

FR 266

Ponderosa Christian Camp

P

Paliza Campground

4 miles to Ponderosa

FR 10

Paliza Group Campground

SANTA FE NATIONAL FOREST

Jemez Indian Reservation

FEET

7500
7400
7300
7200
7100
7000
6900
6800
6700

0.5   1.0   1.5   2.0

MILES

Hoodoos lurking in the pine.

described as "the wildest half-acre in the Jemez." His comments were brief and his directions vague, which helps explain why so few people know about it today. He also underestimated the extent of the bizarre features found here: they occupy an area of at least 30 acres. However, he did an admirable job in describing the landscape: "There are gargoyles, Cleopatra's needles, backs of Triceratops and Stegosaurus dinosaurs, tents, haystacks, exploded solidified bubbles, roller coaster rides."

Indeed, these volcanic-rock formations also evoke Swiss cheese, Japanese cemeteries, and Easter Island. Add totem poles and hooded clowns to the inventory, and you begin to get the idea. And as if the rocks weren't naturally odd enough, mysterious images have been carved into some of them. Ancient petroglyphs depict antennaed humanoids and at least one creature resembling an armadillo.

The hike: To see the spectacle for yourself, walk north on the rutted red road. You'll soon cross beneath power lines, which unfortunately follow much of this route. Early in the hike you might catch a glimpse of a tent rock in the distance. It hints at the shape of things to come.

For now the trail crosses a patchwork of vegetation types, moving quickly from grassland to piñon and juniper to ponderosa. There's also a lush riparian habitat along Vallecito Creek and a smattering of Gambel oak for good measure. It's a fair sampling of Jemez Mountain flora, minus the aspen found at higher elevations.

Just under a mile, the road goes through an open gateway. An aging sign warns: "Primitive Road. Not maintained. Hazardous to public use." It should also mention that the way ahead soon becomes more creek than road.

Fortunately, this route does not go through the gate. Instead, follow the road to the left. About 0.4 miles ahead, a sandy wash and the power lines cross the road. Look up to your left, and you'll glimpse the goblin colony on the canyon wall. Fewer than 100 yards ahead, a more prominent wash crosses the road. Look up to your left again for a better view of the goblins.

They're not as big as the tent rocks at Kasha-Katuwe (hike 26) on the east side of the Jemez, nor are they as uniform. Each figure seems to have its own character. In *Dry Rivers and Standing Rocks: A Word Finder for the American West,* Scott Thybony offers no fewer than three dozen names for rocks like this. In New Mexico, "hoodoo" and "goblin" are the most common terms and perhaps the most appropriate for the majority of rocks here. But use your imagination when naming these figures. Juveniles are likely to resort to a Freudian vocabulary instead of employing architectural terms like "cupola" or "gothic spire."

Some things to keep in mind as you explore the formations: there are no developed trails in this area. Drainages provide the most convenient access corridors. Areas outside of drainages are more sensitive to erosion caused by foot traffic. Tread lightly, and avoid trampling vegetation.

Though rocks are riddled with holes ostensibly well suited for footholds, refrain from climbing on them. Many animals have already taken residence in them, including birds, chipmunks, and probably a few snakes. Also, the rock—compacted ash, really—is not as solid as it appears. In some cases, a fine balancing act is all that keeps slender goblins from toppling over.

The canyon wall is very steep, rising nearly 300 feet in less than 0.2 miles. Use caution around ledges. If you find it too difficult to return to the road below, keep ascending. FR 10 is just over the ridge. You can follow it downhill back to the parking area, but be aware that trucks from local pumice mines often use this narrow, winding road.

Getting lost in this area is unlikely. With a road above and a road below, finding either one is simply a matter of gravity awareness. However, it's easy to lose track of fellow hikers, particularly the little ones. Consider establishing a nearby meeting point in case you get separated.

Finally, don't let the rocks steal all the attention. The scaly bark of alligator juniper contributes to the variety of textures, while seasonal wildflowers add to the color palette. Petroglyphs are few and far between. It takes a good eye to spot them. (I counted four in two hours.)

When you're ready to move on, return to the road below, and turn left. That is, if you haven't exhausted yourself racing up and down the arroyos. Stick to the main road as it winds uphill. At the second hairpin turn is another open gateway. Take a moment here to enjoy the view of canyons below to the east and west.

Alligator juniper in the goblin colony

The road levels out somewhat from here for a short but pleasant walk along the ridge. Feel free to turn back anywhere along this stretch. The route ends here, but the road continues. About 0.4 miles from the gateway, it splits around a pueblo mound. You might not recognize the mound as anything of significance; only an obscured sign marks it, explaining that the area is under the protection of the Antiquities Act of 1906. The roads ahead continue to split and proliferate into a network of unauthorized roads and informal tracks. Even with the most detailed maps, it can get a bit confusing. I wouldn't recommend going farther without a GPS unit, keeping in mind that reception is spotty in Paliza Canyon.

Stroll back the way you came, watching for details you may have missed on the way up. Birdlife is abundant. Raven and red-tailed hawk frequently patrol the canyon. With an audacious call and a crest to match, Steller's jay enlivens picnic areas and campsites. The brilliant hues of the Western tanager strike a sharp contrast against the dark conifer. Burrowing owls often stake out roads and trails shortly after dark. If you happen to be out that late, revisit the goblin colony. It's a different world by moonlight.

Note: FR 10 is subject to closures due to fire or snow. Contact the Jemez Ranger District for current conditions at (505) 829-3535 or **www.fs.fed.us/r3/sfe/districts/jemez.**

STABLE MESA 42

IN BRIEF

The most scenic drive in the Jemez leads to the western base of Schoolhouse Mesa. The hike takes you to the western rim of its southern neighbor, Stable Mesa. From there you can explore windows and shelter caves in a mile-long pumice ridgeline. An optional extension ventures out to the ruins of an ancient pueblo and a historic logging camp.

DESCRIPTION

Pueblo Indians developed at least 40 settlements in the Jemez Province before the Spaniards arrived in 1541. They established many of the larger pueblos upon mesas, some as high as 8,000 feet. More recent evidence of human settlement in this area includes the townsites, camps, and cabins associated with the railroad logging period of 1922 to 1941. The road you drove up to Porter Landing is the most prominent legacy of this period. It traces the railroad grade of the Santa Fe Northwestern through the Gilman Tunnels and up the cascading Rio Guadalupe. With a population of 300, Porter was the center of operations from 1925 to 1937. Unusually high floods in 1941 washed out tracks and trestles. With the war increasing

KEY AT-A-GLANCE INFORMATION

LENGTH: 6.6-mile out-and-back, with longer options

DIFFICULTY: Moderate, with a few short, strenuous sections

SCENERY: Ponderosa forest, volcanic formations, views of the Sierra Nacimiento

EXPOSURE: Mostly shade

TRAIL TRAFFIC: Light

SHARED USE: Light (equestrians, mountain bikers; camping; limited motor-vehicle access)

TRAIL SURFACE: Dirt roads, loose rock

HIKING TIME: 3–4 hours

DRIVING DISTANCE: 62 miles (one way) from the I-40/I-25 exchange

ACCESS: FR 376 is subject to winter closures, typically December 15–May 15

LAND STATUS: Jemez Ranger District; Jemez Mountain National Recreation Area

MAPS: Santa Fe National Forest (West Half); USGS San Miguel Mountain

FACILITIES: None

LAST CHANCE FOOD/GAS: Visitor center, convenience store, and gas station located on NM 4, about 8 miles north of San Ysidro

Directions

From I-25 north, take Exit 242. Turn left on US 550 and go 23.5 miles to San Ysidro. Turn right on NM 4 (beware of speed traps) and go 9.5 miles to Cañon. Turn left on NM 485 and go north 5.7 miles. The road becomes FR 376, a narrow but well-maintained gravel road. Continue north another 7 miles to Porter Landing. A sign on a gate here reads: "Road Closed." Park alongside the barrier rail on the left, immediately before the bridge. The hike begins at a footpath on the other side of the bridge.

GPS Trailhead Coordinates

UTM Zone (WGS 84) 13S

Easting 0338475

Northing 3965268

Latitude 35° 49' 06"

Longitude 106° 47' 17"

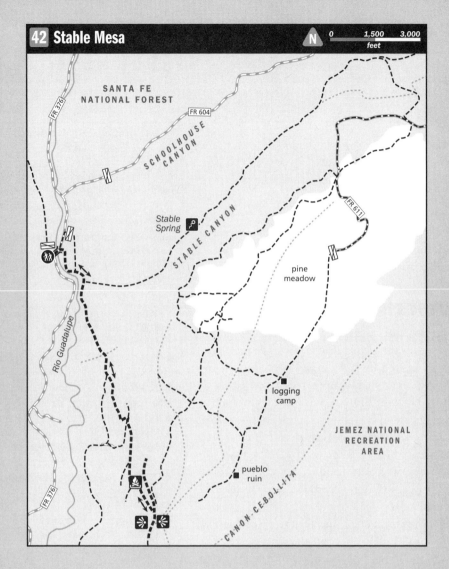

42 Stable Mesa

N

0   1,500   3,000
feet

SANTA FE
NATIONAL FOREST

FR 604

FR 376

SCHOOLHOUSE CANYON

Stable
Spring

STABLE CANYON

FR 611

pine
meadow

Rio Guadalupe

logging
camp

JEMEZ NATIONAL
RECREATION
AREA

FR 376

pueblo
ruin

CANON-CEBOLLITA

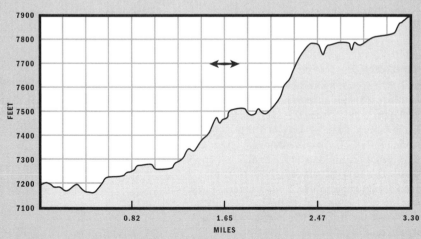

The Rio Guadalupe viewed from the Gilman Tunnels ovelook

demands for steel, the rail wreckage was quickly salvaged and sold. The last remnant standing in Porter today, a stone hearth in a clearing by the river, is the fireplace from the superintendent's lodge. Other relics remain scattered upon the surrounding mesas and throughout the canyons.

Extensive human activity also left its mark in the form of cow paths, skid trails, and logging roads. Many are permanent scars; some have faded back into the forest. For the purposes of this hike, it helps to keep in mind that the route described below uses the most obvious way to the mesa rim. Hence, if you cross something that kind of resembles a trail, it may very well be one, but it isn't part of this route.

Before setting out on the hike, look above the pines across the river, and note a forested peak less than 1 mile southeast. That's the western corner of Stable Mesa. The destination of this hike lies on the rim that seems to dip back behind the treetops.

The hike begins with a short walk up FR 376. Immediately after crossing the bridge, turn right on a footpath through a stand of trees, and walk south along the river. (If you miss the path, turn right at the gate 100 yards ahead, and follow the road down to the river.) The path soon intersects a well-defined dirt road that's closed to motor vehicles, though recent tire tracks indicate that it still gets more traffic than it should. About 200 feet ahead on the left is the fireplace from the superintendent's lodge; hidden behind scrub and trees, it's easier to spot coming from the opposite direction.

The road follows the east bank of the river. About 0.4 miles into the hike, Stable Canyon opens up on the left. Later, you might consider using its former logging road cow path to create a loop that runs about 10.5 miles. Stable Spring keeps the lower canyon fairly damp. The path is also cluttered with downed trees.

Can you find the author in this picture?

Still, it's worth exploring. Marine fossils appear in the limestone cliffs less than 0.5 miles up on the left.

For now, continue south along the main trail to a fork about 200 yards or so past the mouth of Stable Canyon. Bear left, and follow the rocky Jeep road uphill. (The more prominent road stays close to the river.) The terrain soon levels out. About 0.5 miles past the fork, shortly after dipping through an arroyo, the road forks again. Head uphill to the left. The views to the west are astounding as you ascend to the next level.

About 0.5 miles past the second fork, at the end of an S-curve, the road crosses a lesser road at a diagonal. Stick to the main road. The next fork is just under 0.5 miles ahead. A fallen tree blocks the road going straight. You'll follow the road as it bends left, but first you might want to take a short rest here.

A campfire ring sits in the middle of the road going straight. If you're in the habit of leaving trails cleaner than you found them, you could fill a few trash bags here. Feel free to take all the plastic bottles you can carry, but don't touch any tins, bottles, and other refuse dating to the logging period. If you're not sure whether it's trash or a cultural artifact, leave it alone.

Continue on the road as it bends left, then right, and then up the steepest ascent on this route. About 0.3 miles past the campsite, the steep, rocky road ends at the junction with a pronounced doubletrack. Turn right and head over a flat outcrop about 100 yards to the south. Take another break to enjoy the views to the west and get oriented.

Sitting on the western edge of the Jemez Plateau, you're now 2.5 miles into the hike. The narrow, north–south trending range to the west is the Sierra Nacimiento, the Laurel companion to the Hardy-shaped Jemez. More specifically, you're sitting on the rim near the southwestern corner of Stable Mesa. A low ridge extends about 0.2 miles south and nearly 1.5 miles north. The backbone of this ridge is volcanic rock, which appears in exposed outcrops all along the western flank. As you can see in the steep outcrop to your left, it's adorned with pocks, holes, grooves, and other intricate details.

Start by exploring the outcrops to the south. If you haven't noticed already, you're on a fingerlike extension of the mesa, with views over a gorge a few yards to the east. When you reach the end of the formations, turn around, and head to the north side of the junction to find more outcrops off the left side of the road. The designs become more elaborate, with arches and shelter caves that evoke playful shapes, like grottos and oversized fishbowl castles. Graffiti etched into the soft rock date back from a few years to several decades and perhaps many centuries. You could spend hours among these fascinating formations, and then head back the way you came—or consider racking up a few extra miles on the alternate routes outlined below.

THE RUINS AND THE LOOP

The road from the rim junction is relatively flat and easy to follow. As the map indicates, a twin road runs parallel about 0.5 miles to the east. The remains of a logging camp and a pueblo ruin are located along that road. The two sites are about a mile apart, walking distance. Numerous trees have been felled to obstruct vehicular traffic but with modest success.

The twin roads are connected by a few east–west trending tracks that are often difficult to spot. The first one to stand out noticeably appears on the right, 1.5 miles northeast of the junction. Two dirt-mound barriers obstruct this former road, which winds over a hill and across the drainage to the logging camp. Visiting both sites would add a minimum of 4 miles to the out-and-back route.

A caveat—I have yet to personally inspect the loop option in its entirety. Additional details came from reliable sources, but you're advised to proceed with an extra measure of wit and a sense of adventure. A topo map and GPS unit might be useful as well.

The road from the rim junction runs 1.6 miles northeast before entering a pine meadow. Continue straight another 1.7 miles to an intersection. Maintain your course to the northeast, traveling 0.7 miles to the far end of the meadow. Turn left at the next junction. About 100 yards or so ahead, take a right on another trail heading northeast. This 0.6-mile segment hooks west to cross the back end of a canyon spur, climbs northwest, and then bends southwest as it descends 200 feet to the floor of Stable Canyon. From there it's 2.6 miles to the mouth of the canyon, where you'll turn right on the road back to the bridge. The loop option is about 5.7 miles longer than a simple out-and-back. Add detours to the ruin sites, and you're facing a hike in the neighborhood of 12 to 14 miles.

Note: FR 376 is subject to closures due to snow or fire. Contact the Jemez Ranger District for current conditions at (505) 829-3535 or **www.fs.fed.us/r3/ sfe/districts/jemez.**

43 SAN DIEGO

KEY AT-A-GLANCE INFORMATION

LENGTH: 2.2-mile loop and spur

DIFFICULTY: Moderate to difficult

SCENERY: Pumice and sandstone formations, canyons, volcanic ash cliffs

EXPOSURE: Canyon shade; less sun in the late afternoon

TRAIL TRAFFIC: Low

SHARED USE: Low (no vehicles)

TRAIL SURFACE: Sand, rock

HIKING TIME: 2 hours

DRIVING DISTANCE: 52 miles (one way) from the I-40/I-25 exchange

ACCESS: Year-round, but the parking lot gate is locked sunset–sunrise

LAND STATUS: Jemez Ranger District; Jemez Mountain NRA

MAPS: Santa Fe National Forest (West Half); USGS Ponderosa

FACILITIES: Fishing access; paved path to riverside is suitable for wheelchairs

SPECIAL COMMENTS: High waters occasionally force the closure of the parking area and submerge the log bridge. Rains may also increase chances for rock falls and landslides. Contact the Jemez Ranger District for current conditions by calling (505) 829-3535, or visiting www.fs.fed.us/r3/sfe/districts/jemez.

GPS Trailhead Coordinates

UTM Zone (WGS 84)   13S

Easting   0343757

Northing   3952988

Latitude   34° 42' 30"

Longitude   106° 43' 38"

IN BRIEF

Starting just off the near end of the main drag through the Jemez, this freeform route relies primarily on a steep drainage to reach the saddle between two prominent mesas. The hike culminates with grand views across both San Diego Canyon to the east and Virgin Canyon to the west.

DESCRIPTION

The drive up NM 4 is a destination in itself. It starts at the 17th-century village of San Ysidro and crosses the Pueblo of Jemez (pronounced HAY-mess, a Spanish corruption of the Towa word for "people"). Eight miles up it enters the Cañon de San Diego, the Santa Fe National Forest, and the Jemez Mountain National Recreation Area. The mountainous playground is famed for hot springs, waterfalls, fishing holes, campgrounds, and of course enough hiking trails to lose yourself for days on end.

The canyon scenery is nothing short of arresting, particularly the enormous wall of two contiguous mesas flanking the west side. The first is Mesa de Guadalupe, site of the final showdown between Jemez warriors and Spanish soldiers in 1696. A local legend maintains that cornered warriors leapt from the mesa. As they plummeted toward certain death, San Diego appeared to them and

Directions

From I-25 north, take Exit 242. Turn left on US 550 and go 23.5 miles to San Ysidro. Turn right on NM 4 (beware of speed traps) and go 12.6 miles. Turn left at the sign for San Diego Fishing Access. Park in the paved lot and walk toward the river. The hike begins at the end of the paved walkway.

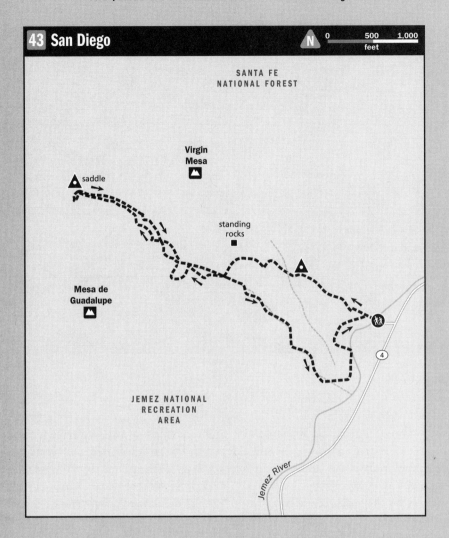

43 San Diego

SANTA FE
NATIONAL FOREST

Virgin
Mesa

saddle

standing
rocks

Mesa de
Guadalupe

JEMEZ NATIONAL
RECREATION
AREA

Jemez River

4

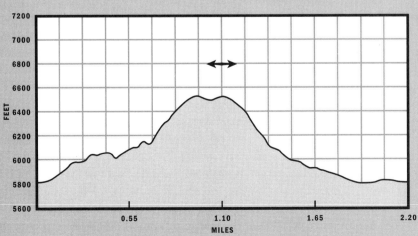

Virgin Mesa

guided them to a safe landing. (Another version reports that both the saint and the Virgin of Guadalupe appeared to them in the midst of battle, at which point the warriors fled in terror.) In any case, ruins of the warriors' pueblo can still be found on the mesa, and the saint's face still appears in the cliffs to those who stare at it long enough.

By far the larger of the two, Virgin Mesa is a seemingly insurmountable fortress of red sandstone capped with Bandelier Tuff—a tan layer of rock formed from volcanic ash. Many New Mexicans are familiar with the impressive facade, but few have glimpsed inside the secretive Virgin Canyon behind the mesas. Private-property boundaries restrict access from the south, so it seems that the only feasible access would require another 20-odd miles of driving on an eclectic assortment of roads. But look again at the mesas, or rather at the saddle ridge between them, and you'll find another way to see what's on the other side.

The hike begins innocently enough on the paved walkway to the edge of the Jemez River. The shallow, narrow stream usually contains a few pools just deep enough to hide a few trout. You can cross here using a couple of logs bolted in place. Each is about the width of a telephone pole, not half the length, and the balancing act required to get across just might be the most challenging part of the hike.

A vague footpath on the other side leads through dense vegetation, which thins out as you move away from the river. You'll soon lose sight of the bridge, so pick out a few nearby landmarks—unique rocks or trees—to help you find it when you return.

Ahead is a stepped series of embankments, red as Georgia clay and just as slick when wet. There's no path to follow, so pick your way up the slopes, aiming in the direction of the saddle. The ridges get progressively higher and steeper, with feeder drainages to cross in between. Ridge points between drainages serve as useful overlooks for scouting possible routes ahead.

More geological features emerge from the landscape, such as pavement stream-beds and cubed boulder blocks. Upon a ridge ahead stands an assembly of capped chimneys, some up to 20 feet tall. They're not too stable, and the ground beneath them is treacherously steep, so admire them from a distance. Instead of crossing over to that ridge, work your way into the main canyon below to your left.

As you start up the canyon, be aware of large rocks teetering on the edge above to your right. During my last hike here, a few dropped like cannonballs, though that was probably related to dynamiting at the Gilman Tunnels, less than 2 miles away. As an added precaution, you might consider climbing out to the left and walking the higher ground for the next 100 yards or so until the threat of falling rock subsides. There you'll locate the only major fork in the canyon. What you find in each branch may change with each heavy rain, but generally the left is a clear route up a deep, red gulch, while the right is a narrow passage choked with gray boulders. Oddly enough, the latter is the easier route.

Just for kicks, go left. The path curves around to the right and soon ends at an insurmountable red wall. Find a place to safely scramble out on the right, and then skirt the base of the cliff, back toward the gray canyon. If you come to a steep drop-off, backtrack a few yards to get around it safely.

As you continue upstream, the canyon shrinks down to a pair of runnels. The ground is still steep as you approach the saddle, but it's fairly even, making the walk relatively easy. There's scant evidence of human passage, though once I did come across an odd bit of handiwork: stacks of dead branches bound in bal-ing wire, like a coyote fence turned sideways. It formed a U-shaped corral about the size of a coffin. I first guessed it to be a shrine to San Diego but later realized it was only a hunting blind.

The terrain soon rounds out, and spectacular views open to the west. Vir-gin Canyon lies directly below with its old logging road hidden beneath the steep pitch of the lower canyon walls. Directly across the canyon is Mesa Garcia, which lines up with Guadalupita Mesa to the north. And it continues like that, ridge after ridge, as far as the eye can see.

Those of a more adventurous spirit can blaze down to Virgin Canyon Road and follow it north, deeper into the wilderness, where old logging camps and pueblo ruins remain hidden in the forest. The rest of us, content with the view, can turn back here. Look east to see the southern end of Cat Mesa and other elongated mesas, or *potreros,* radiating from the central Jemez Mountains.

To head back down to San Diego, find the northernmost runnel on the saddle and follow it downstream into the gray canyon. You'll encounter a few spillways ahead, so pick your drops carefully, and be prepared for what lies beneath. I once landed on a pumice shelf that broke apart and dropped me into a knee-deep pothole. Such awkward landings can be hard on both the ego and the ankles.

You can follow the drainage all the way out. It ends with crimson sand fanning into the bosque. From here, the log bridge is less than 0.2 miles to the north–northeast. Turn left, and work your way up the Jemez River. Depending on the time of year, you may have some fierce bushwhacking ahead. Or you might be better off climbing the embankment to avoid the dense vegetation. Keep an eye out for the landmarks you picked out earlier to find the logs. Use caution on the crossing—the Jemez River can be mighty cold.

NEARBY ACTIVITIES

If you prefer designated trails, you have several options nearby. One of the all-time favorites is the East Fork Trail (137), featuring 95°F spring-fed pools at McCauley Warm Springs. The wooded trail starts with a moderate 400-foot ascent, but most of the 2-mile hike is fairly easy. Continue hiking east from the springs another 3 miles to reach the Jemez Falls Group Picnic Area. A popular short spur from there leads to a viewing area above the 70-foot falls. The western trailhead is at the Battleship Rock Picnic Area, a 10-mile drive north from San Diego. For more details, stop by the ranger station in Jemez Springs. Located about 5 miles north of San Diego, Jemez Springs has long been a popular stopover for dining, lodging, and (of course) soaking. Call the Jemez Spring Bath House at (505) 829-3303 or (866) 204-8303, or visit **www.jemezsprings.org**.

VALLES CALDERA NATIONAL PRESERVE: Coyote Call Trail

IN BRIEF

The trail takes you up to a midlevel ridge for a glimpse of the landscapes hidden in the Baca. Peaking over 9,100 feet, it's one of the cooler summer hikes. In winter, its modest gain in elevation is ideal for beginner and intermediate snowshoeing.

DESCRIPTION

Remember the 1980 eruption of Mount St. Helens? Multiply that blast by 600, and you get an idea of what the Valles Caldera looked like about 1.2 million years ago, when it ejected 150 cubic miles of rock and sent ash as far as Iowa. This is, in the snappy parlance of telegenic scientists, a supervolcano. New Mexico's sleeping monster hasn't stirred in the past 60,000 years, but nobody knows when it will erupt again.

The giant crater once belonged to the legendary Cabeza de Baca family. In 1860 the U.S. Congress recognized a land debt to the heirs of Don Luis María Cabeza de Baca and offered them the vacant parcel of their choice. Topping their top-five countdown was a 95,000-acre tract in the northern Jemez. The property, which encompasses most of the caldera, is still known locally as Baca Location No. 1, the Baca Ranch, or simply "the Baca."

Ensuing years of livestock grazing, sulfur

KEY AT-A-GLANCE INFORMATION

LENGTH: 2.9-mile loop

DIFFICULTY: Easy

SCENERY: Cool forest of aspen, fir, and ponderosa; views across the caldera, possible sightings of bald eagles and elk

EXPOSURE: Mostly shade

TRAIL TRAFFIC: Popular

SHARED USE: Low (cross-country skiing, snowshoeing; no pets; no vehicles)

TRAIL SURFACE: Grass and dirt, or snow

HIKING TIME: 1–2 hours

DRIVING DISTANCE: 80 miles (one way) from the I-40 and I-25 exchange

ACCESS: Daylight hours

LAND STATUS: National Preserve, private management

MAPS: www.vallescaldera.gov; USGS Bland

FACILITIES: None

LAST CHANCE FOOD/GAS: Convenience store and gas station at Jemez Pueblo visitor center on NM 4, about 33 miles before the trailhead; restaurants in Jemez Springs, about 23 miles before the trailhead

SPECIAL COMMENTS: See longer note at the end of the Description.

Directions

From I-25 north take Exit 242 at Bernalillo. Turn left on US 550 and go 23.5 miles to San Ysidro. Turn right and go 41 miles on NM 4. On the left side of the road, just past mile marker 41, is a pulloff big enough for four or five cars. Park there, or if it's full, another pulloff is about half a mile ahead. Coyote Call Trail begins at the signed gate across the road from the first pulloff.

GPS Trailhead Coordinates

UTM Zone (WGS 84) 13S

Easting 0367679

Northing 3968090

Latitude 35° 50' 53"

Longitude 106° 27' 55"

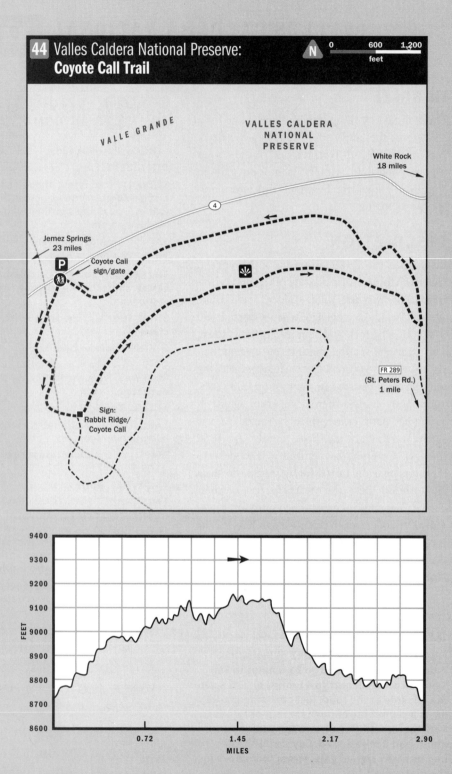

44 Valles Caldera National Preserve:
Coyote Call Trail

N   0   600   1,200
feet

VALLE GRANDE

VALLES CALDERA
NATIONAL
PRESERVE

White Rock
18 miles

4

Jemez Springs
23 miles

P

Coyote Call
sign/gate

FR 289
(St. Peters Rd.)
1 mile

Sign:
Rabbit Ridge/
Coyote Call

FEET

9400
9300
9200
9100
9000
8900
8800
8700
8600

0.72   1.45   2.17   2.90
MILES

The Valle Grande, viewed from Coyote
Call Trail

mining, and extensive logging took a toll on the land. In 1963 a third generation
oilman, James "Pat" Dunigan, bought the ravaged property for $2.5 million. A
native Texan with a master's degree from New York University, Dunigan is perhaps most fondly remembered for his environmentally balanced ranching and
caring stewardship of the Baca. When his sons sold it to the federal government
for a cool $101 million in 2000, it was in relatively sparkling condition.

This purchase, made through the Valles Caldera National Preservation Act,
would expand New Mexico's already super-sized menu of recreational opportunities. But did we really need access to another 40 miles of trout streams, 66,000
acres of conifer forest, 25,000 acres of grassland, Sandoval County's highest
peak, and the state's largest herd of elk? Absolutely. The bigger question is how
long can we keep it all unsullied?

That challenge falls to the Valles Caldera Trust, a nine-member board of
trustees that assumed management in 2002. All seem painfully aware of common recreational practices that amount to ecological mayhem for their neighbors, the Jemez Ranger District of Santa Fe National Forest, and the budget
crunches that account for the disrepair occasionally found in adjacent Bandelier
National Monument. (To be sure, both the forest supervisor and the monument superintendent serve as voting members on the Valles Caldera board. The
remaining seven trustees are appointed by the president of the United States.)

The trustees' approach to recreation has been guarded, to say the least.
Their systems of schedules and lotteries seem to be under constant revision,

An aspen bears the scars of an unprovoked knifing.

while their policies of non-changeable reservations and nonrefundable fees are firmly established. In all, they've effectively deterred the masses from swarming the caldera—except for that one weekend in the rainy summer of 2006. In a first-time showcase event that probably won't be repeated, the old ranch roads opened to private vehicles, and more than 1,500 cars showed up to slosh and skid through the preserve.

The lucky few who negotiate passage beyond the barbed-wire threshold invariably return to describe the caldera experience in superlatives reserved for the Promised Land. Recent additions to the winter schedule hint that the trustees are willing to crack the gates open a little wider. Meanwhile, all that seems certain for easy access are two "free spontaneous hiking" opportunities on the southeastern fringe of the preserve: Valle Grande Trail and Coyote Call Trail.

The hike featured here, Coyote Call Trail, begins at the pedestrian gate. There's a wooden box containing a register, a map, and some lost mittens. The map shows the trail in more detail than the one in this book does, but it's usually easy enough to follow without either.

The trail is well marked, but markers may get buried under four feet of snow. If you came here for a snowshoe hike, take a moment to study the map. Don't rely on a fresh set of tracks for navigation, or you may end up following lost tourists to the far side of Rabbit Mountain.

Start by heading south across the meadow, bearing slightly to the right along an old logging road that climbs up about half a mile to the eastern side of the domed hill ahead. Midway up the ridge behind the hill, the road turns left.

About 100 yards after rounding the corner, you'll find a sign that reads "Rabbit Ridge Scenic View," with an arrow pointing to the right, and "Coyote Call Meadow Walk," with an arrow pointing to the left. Rabbit Ridge was one of the original free trails. It may or may not reopen in the near future, though there doesn't seem to be anything to discourage anyone from exploring this ridgetop route now. A blue square tacked to a nearby tree indicates that it's more difficult for skiers, but the terrain back that way wouldn't hinder hikers.

To stay on Coyote Call Trail, continue straight past the sign, following the direction indicated by the arrow. The trail conforms to the curvature of the ridge, bowing out and back for the next mile. Near the halfway point, look for a wide break in the woods on the left. It's a good place for a short rest, as the view of the caldera from here is magnificent.

Many visitors mistake the Valle Grande for the Valles Caldera. To clarify, the Valle Grande comprises about one-sixth of the Baca Ranch and is the largest of four valleys in the Valles Caldera. The actual caldera, a collapsed volcano, measures 12 to 15 miles in diameter. The Valle Grande, about 3 miles wide from north to south, is what drivers see from NM 4. In other words, the Valle Grande is merely the crescent, whereas the Valles Caldera is the full moon.

From the overlook, the view stretches clear across to the north rim, but the other valleys remain hidden behind the hills and domes that flank the far side of the Valle Grande. The one on the left is Redondo Peak, the county's highest, at 11,254 feet. The dome on the right is Cerro del Medio. The stream snaking across the meadow in front of it is the East Fork of the Jemez River.

Continue on Coyote Call Trail another 0.5 miles or so to the junction with another old road merging from the right. Take a sharp left here, and head downhill. After another 0.5 miles, NM 4 comes into view. At that point the trail bends to the west and runs roughly parallel to the highway for the remainder of the loop.

Valle Grande Trail begins near mile marker 43, at the boundary to the preserve and Bandelier National Monument. To find it, look for a parking area on the south side, near a sign that reads "Entering Bandelier National Monument." A white sign on the north side marks the trailhead. This trail starts north along the crater rim. Cross the road, and follow the fence for the first 200 feet, then zigzag downhill through a lush forest of fir and aspen. The grassy mile-long trail takes you to the edge of the meadow in the Valle Grande.

If you can't get a close-up look at the Baca backcountry, the next best thing would be Don J. Unser's photography in *Valles Caldera: A Vision for New Mexico's National Preserve,* a handsome edition from Museum of New Mexico Press.

Note: Coyote Call is one of two trails in the Valles Caldera National Preserve that does not require reservations. Plan ahead to take advantage of the wide array of activities throughout the preserve. For an updated schedule of events and trail openings, visit **www.vallescaldera.gov,** or call (505) 661-3333; for reservations call (866) 382-5537.

45 BANDELIER NATIONAL MONUMENT:
Mid Alamo Canyon

 KEY AT-A-GLANCE INFORMATION

LENGTH: 8-mile out-and-back
DIFFICULTY: Moderate to difficult
SCENERY: Cliff dwellings, seasonal streams and wildflowers, gorges
EXPOSURE: Mostly sunny with shaded canyons
TRAIL TRAFFIC: Moderate to crowded
SHARED USE: Low (backcountry camping by permit, no pets, no vehicles)
TRAIL SURFACE: Dirt, stone
HIKING TIME: 4–5 hours
DRIVING DISTANCE: 98 miles via San Ysidro or 104 miles via Santa Fe (one way) from I-40/I-25 exchange
**ACCESS: Park and visitor center open daily, except December 25 and January 1. All day-use areas of the park open to recreation year-round at 6:30 a.m. Day-use areas must be vacated by official sunset. 7-day vehicle permit $12.00 for all persons traveling in a single, private, noncommercial vehicle; 7-day single-entry permit $6.00 per person for visitors traveling on foot or bicycle, or for individuals traveling together in a vehicle as a noncommercial, organized group. Federal Recreational Land Passes are accepted.
(SEE additional information at end of Description.)**

GPS Trailhead
Coordinates
UTM Zone (WGS 84) 13S
Easting   0385034
Northing   3960186
Latitude   35° 46' 45"
Longitude   106° 16' 19"

IN BRIEF

The extensive trail system in Bandelier National Monument allows for a wide range of hikes, from leisurely strolls among ancient cliff dwellings to weeklong treks into backcountry wilderness. The trail to Mid Alamo Canyon is geared more toward casual hikers, with a few good challenges and many rewarding views along the way.

DESCRIPTION

Architectural wonders of the 12th century include the Cathedral of Notre Dame, the Campanile of Pisa, the Citadel of Cairo, and Angkor Wat in Cambodia. During the same time, ancestral Puebloans were carving the

----

Directions ⟶

Bandelier National Monument is fewer than 40 linear miles from Albuquerque, but there are no reasonable shortcuts to its main entrance. From I-25 north, take Exit 276B to NM 599 (Veterans Memorial Highway). Go north 13.5 miles to its end at US 84. Go north 14 miles to Pojoaque and turn left onto NM 502 (Los Alamos Highway). Go west 11.2 miles and bear left on NM 4 toward White Rock. (Note that the Tsankawi section, on the left 1.4 miles past the junction, features a 1.5-mile self-guided hike through an Ancestral Pueblo village.) Drive 12 miles on NM 4 to the main entrance.
    Alternate route: From I-25 north, take Exit 242 at Bernalillo. Turn left on US 550 and go 23.5 miles to San Ysidro. Turn right on NM 4 and follow it 57 miles to the main entrance. (Note that the Ponderosa Group Campground, on the right 0.25 miles past the junction with NM 501, is a good place to set up a shuttle for longer hikes through the monument.)
    Pay at the park's entrance station and park at the visitor center.

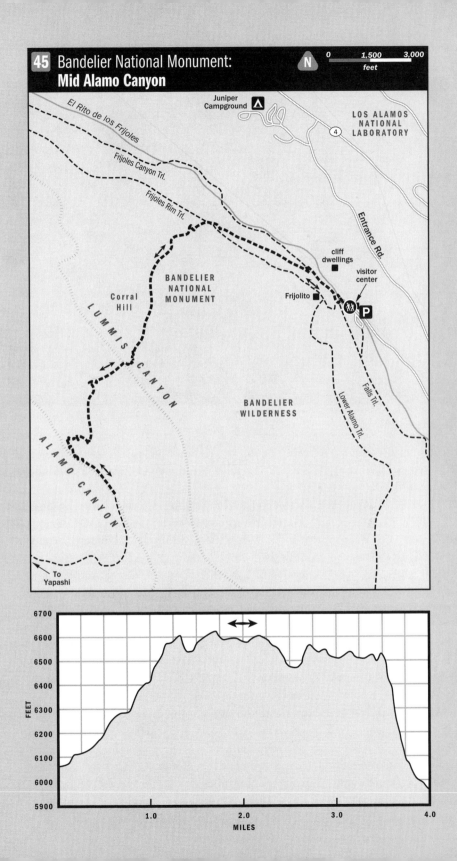

Claret-cup hedgehog blooms in May and June.

first high-rise condos into sheer cliffs of volcanic tuff on the eastern slopes of the Jemez Mountains. These cliff dwellings are the main attraction at Bandelier National Monument today.

With 70 miles of trails to choose from, picking a route in this 33,750-acre monument can be tough. The hike outlined below basically uses Yapashi Trail to reach Mid Alamo Canyon. Why stop there? Multiple canyon crossings tend to exhaust the average casual hiker. Besides, sights along this 8-mile round-trip route add up to a good sampling of Bandelier's better features. And if you need to push yourself further, the brochure map and signboards posted along the way should be sufficient to guide you a few miles deeper into the wilderness.

The main trails are easy to follow. You can't miss the stone stairways leading in and out of the canyons. Built by the Civilian Conservation Corps (CCC) in the 1930s, they seem as sturdy today as the day they were constructed. More about that project, and everything else you could possibly want to know about the monument, is available in the visitor center.

Spend at least 20 minutes with the exhibits and dioramas to prepare for any questions that might pop up on the trail. Did applicants need teeth to qualify for the CCC? How much of the monument was closed for the development of atomic weaponry? And, can I earn a Bandelier Junior Ranger patch? Those and other pertinent queries can nag you for miles if you don't know the answers.

The hike: Sated with knowledge, exit the visitor center, turn right, and follow the paved road over Frijoles Creek. At the junction ahead, turn right, and continue on the paved road to the information signboard at the Cottonwood Picnic Area. Turn left here to start on the trail to Yapashi. At the stone wall ahead, turn right, and begin the hike up the side of Frijoles Canyon. (Alternately, you can take a steeper route up to the Frijolito Ruin and then follow the rim northwest to the sign for Mid Alamo Canyon.)

You'll encounter a few signed forks as you climb toward the rim. Keep following the arrows toward Yapashi. Also, take time to view the cliff dwellings on the far side of the canyon. (The popular Main Loop Trail, an easy 1.2 miles, offers a closer inspection of the cliff dwellings, talus houses, and the Big Kiva.)

When you reach the rim, you face an older sign that doesn't mention Yapashi. A newer sign a few yards beyond it does, indicating that the distance to Mid Alamo Canyon is 2 miles. At this point, you've gone 1 mile and gained 500 feet in elevation. By now you should understand why the Bandelier trails are not to be taken lightly. They wind in and out of the numerous canyons cut through the southernmost Pajarito Plateau. Formed by the ash flow on the eastern flank of the Valles Caldera, this sloping plateau is not as flat as you might have thought.

The 2-mile stretch from here to the near rim of Mid Alamo Canyon crosses three branches of Lummis Canyon. The main branch is scarcely 100 feet deep. Compared to Frijoles and Alamo canyons, the Lummis branches are merely shaded dips in the otherwise thinly forested plateau.

Weather in the park can be unpredictable. A hike in May 2007 started in the balmy morning sun and ended with light snowfall in the afternoon. Sun exposure and thunderstorms can get fierce in the summer. Towering ponderosas bear the scars of lightning strikes and forest fires. Bandelier has a troubled history with the latter, most notably the notorious Cerro Grande Fire of 2000, a prescribed burn gone awry.

Springtime deer in the area seem indifferent to hikers, as do the low-key tarantulas that mosey about in the fall. Summer is prime butterfly season. More than 100 species have been identified in the park. Western tanagers are also summer residents, while golden-crowned kinglets seem popular among the mixed flocks of winter.

After you cross the third canyon, Alamo appears suddenly and dramatically. The trail sneaks up on the 600-foot drop, and at first a descent seems impossible. But follow the path to the right, and you'll soon find a stone staircase leading to multiple switchbacks and more stairs. The CCC's radical alterations to canyon walls don't necessarily make the journey any easier. (Ever run stadium stairs?) Their bold landscape-engineering project is in many ways just as ponderous as the cave dwellings in Frijoles. Did anyone among them object to irrecoverably altering this naturally majestic landscape? How do these changes affect the scenic value of the canyons?

As you burn your quads and glutes on the stairs, note other details that emerge in the lower canyon walls. The wavy white surface hints at future tent rocks. Fully developed versions are 10 miles to the southwest at Kasha-Katuwe

Tent Rocks National Monument (hike 26). A few freestanding tent rocks, complete with boulder caps, can be seen among the pine and box elder near the canyon floor.

At times, mainly in spring, a creek flows along the shaded path here. Outside the biting-bug season, generally limited to June, this is a fine spot to break for lunch and consider whether or not you want to trudge up the other side to Yapashi Pueblo and the Stone Lions Shrine. Keep in mind that the extra push would stretch this out-and-back hike to 11 miles. Also, Yapashi is a destination best visited as a midway point on a 13-mile shuttle hike to the Ponderosa Group Campground (see Directions). Either journey requires crossing Alamo Canyon twice.

My hiking group unanimously voted against continuing any deeper into the wilderness, preferring instead to save their dwindling energy reserves for short strolls among the ancient dwellings near the visitor center and in the Tsankawi section. In the end, they had just enough strength to stumble into the snack bar. In retrospect, it was probably best we didn't attempt Yapashi that day.

To thoroughly appreciate Bandelier National Monument, you need at least three days—your pass is good for a week. Oh, and in case you're still wondering: A CCC applicant needed at least three "serviceable natural teeth" to qualify for enrollment in the 1930s. The entire park was closed to the public for the Manhattan Project in the 1940s. And no one in my group earned a Bandelier Junior Ranger patch in 2007.

MORE KEY AT-A-GLANCE INFORMATION

LAND STATUS: National Park Service

MAPS: Brochure map available at Park Entrance Station; USGS Frijoles

FACILITIES: Gift shop, snack bar, restrooms, campgrounds, interpretive exhibits. Visitor center does not meet ADA standards but is accessible. The visitor center restrooms are not up to standard but are accessible for wheelchair users who can negotiate a 180-degree transfer. Restrooms in Loop B of Juniper Campground are accessible. The first 0.25 miles of Main Loop Trail are wheelchair-accessible; other trails may be navigable by wheelchair athletes.

SPECIAL COMMENTS: This park gets packed, especially in the late spring, in early summer, and on holidays. Arrive early or risk getting turned away at the gate. Call ahead for weather and fire conditions. For 24-hour recorded updates, call (505) 672-0343. Also visit **www.nps.gov/band**. *A Guide to Bandelier National Monument* by Dorothy Heard is a portable but comprehensive resource, complete with invaluable 3D renderings of the trails. The route to Mid Alamo Canyon is described in the section on Stone Lions Trail. The book is available at the visitor center, and from the Los Alamos Historical Society; (505) 662-6272, **www .losalamoshistory.org**.

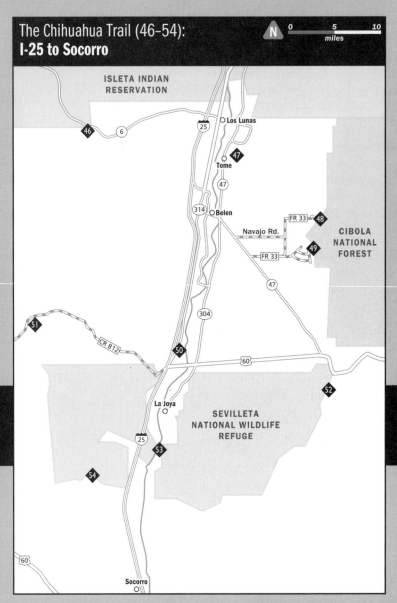

The Chihuahua Trail (46–54):
I-25 to Socorro

N

0   5   10
miles

ISLETA INDIAN
RESERVATION

46

6

25 ○ Los Lunas

47

○ Tome

47

314 ○ Belen

FR 33 48

Navajo Rd.

CIBOLA
NATIONAL
FOREST

FR 33 49

47

304

51

CR B12

50

60

52

La Joya
○

SEVILLETA
NATIONAL WILDLIFE
REFUGE

25

53

54

60

Socorro
○

THE CHIHUAHUA TRAIL

46 HIDDEN MOUNTAIN

KEY AT-A-GLANCE INFORMATION

LENGTH: 2.1-mile loop, 1.8-mile out-and-back

DIFFICULTY: Difficult loop, easy out-and-back

SCENERY: Basalt cliffs, petroglyphs, ruins, the Ten Commandments

EXPOSURE: Little shade

TRAIL TRAFFIC: Moderate

SHARED USE: Low (livestock; closed to unauthorized vehicles)

TRAIL SURFACE: Dirt road, rocky arroyos, sand, scree

HIKING TIME: 1.5 hours

DRIVING DISTANCE: 38 miles (one way) from the I-40 and I-25 exchange

ACCESS: Daylight hours; State Land Trust Recreational Permit required

LAND STATUS: State trust land

MAPS: USGS Rio Puerco

FACILITIES: None

LAST CHANCE FOOD/GAS: Full services at Exit 215. (If you're returning to Albuquerque via I-40, a Pronto Mart is about 15 miles northwest on NM 6.)

IN BRIEF

It's got a tough climb and a slippery descent, but the scenic loop reveals there's a lot more to Hidden Mountain than the unsolved riddles inscribed in Mystery Rock, also known as the Decalogue Stone of Los Lunas. But if the stone is all you came to see, then your hike is a whole lot easier.

DESCRIPTION

Hidden Mountain isn't much of a mountain, nor is it very well hidden. The naked cone rises up in full view near the convergence of NM 6, the Rio Puerco, and the BNSF railroad. Aside from the occasional train, it's a quiet junction, and evidence of human activity is nearly absent from sight.

The volcano peaks at 5,507 feet, more than 400 feet above the riverbed, where water seldom flows. The crater on top sits tilted with a chipped rim, like a discarded bowl. A crack spreads down to the north, deepening into a gulley cluttered with basalt. Tucked near the bottom of the steep chute is a boulder weighing around 90 tons. In this neighborhood, it looks like an average stone, not the kind that calls attention to itself, except maybe for the way it slumps over a dry wash as though attempting to conceal the one thing that makes it truly remarkable.

GPS Trailhead Coordinates

UTM Zone (WGS 84)   13S

Easting   0317056

Northing   3851939

Latitude   34° 47' 36"

Longitude   106° 59' 59"

Directions

From I-25 south, take Exit 215 at Los Lunas. Turn right and follow NM 6 west and north 14.5 miles. About 0.25 miles after crossing the Rio Puerco, turn left on an access road. Cross the railroad tracks and continue straight out 0.35 miles to the red gates. Park on the side of the road. Do not to block any gates. The hike begins at pedestrian gate on the left side of the road.

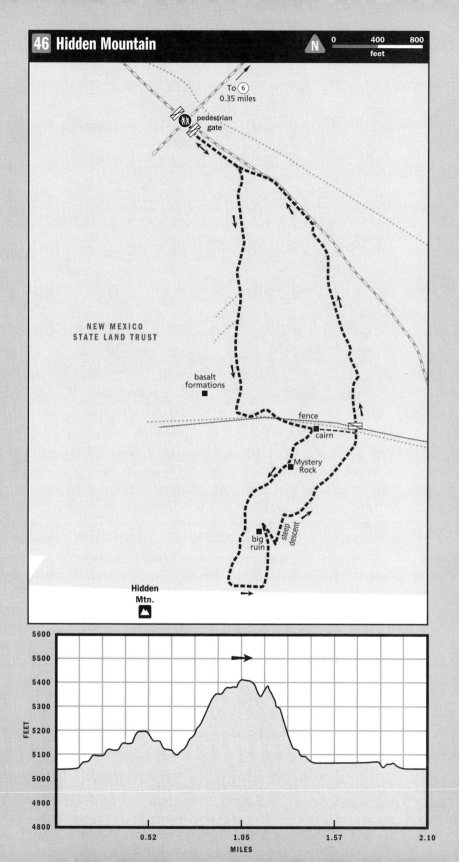

46 Hidden Mountain

N

0   400   800
feet

To 6
0.35 miles

pedestrian
gate

NEW MEXICO
STATE LAND TRUST

basalt
formations

fence

cairn

Mystery
Rock

steep
descent

big
ruin

Hidden
Mtn.
▲

Pecked into its flat patina base is a strange message. Nine lines contain a total of 216 letters from the Old Hebrew alphabet, with a few Greek letters and maybe some Samaritan tossed into the mix. The earliest known documentation of the inscription came in 1936 from Professor Frank Hibben of the University of New Mexico. Since then, every savant with a penchant for cryptograms has attempted to crack the code of Mystery Rock.

In 1949 the Harvard scholar Robert Pfeiffer advanced a Paleo-Hebrew translation that remains inconclusive after decades of academic scrutiny. In 1979 the professional calligrapher Dixie Perkins produced a Canaanite–Phoenician–Greek translation of the rock just four days after learning about it on a local TV special. Her solution also remains open to debate.

To some, the message is a 4,000-year-old memo posted by Navajo ancestors. Or a map to hidden Acoma treasure. Or it's an ancient Samaritan mezuzah, an abridged version of the Decalogue traditionally carved into a large stone slab and placed at the entrance to a synagogue. It's proof that one of the Ten Tribes of Israel passed this way, or it's a propaganda effort by Mormon Battallion soldiers who camped nearby in the 1840s. Others have cited the combination of Hebraic and otherwordly characters as evidence of an intergallactic Wandering Jew. Or maybe it's the incredibly sad story of an unfortunate Greek explorer who sailed up the Rio Puerco 2,500 years ago.

The most commonly accepted explanation: it's a hoax. The likely culprits: Hobe and Eva, a couple of UNM students armed with chisles and Semitic-language reference books swiped from Zimmerman Library. The evidence: they left their names on another stone not ten feet away, along with a date (3-19-30) that beats Hibben's initial discovery by three years.

In all the excitement to uncover the truth, the inscription has been scrubbed, chalked, re-etched, and ultimately rendered unsuitable for age-dating analysis. Further, in November 2006, someone gouged out the first line, the one that allegedly read: "I am Jehovah your God who has taken you out of Egypt" or "I have come to this place to stay. The other one met with an untimely death one year ago."

Which one of these translations provoked crypto-fascists into censoring the rock? The mysteries never cease.

The easy way to the Decalogue Stone is a mostly flat out-and-back that runs 1.8 miles round-trip. Squeeze through the pedestrian gate, and walk southeast along the dirt road. After about 0.25 miles, as you pass the first hill, a path veers off to the right and runs south 0.5 miles to a small drop gate. Go through the gate, fasten it behind you, and turn right. About 100 yards ahead on the left, you'll find a cairn. Go up the path leading into the gulley, following arrows scratched into rocks along the near side of the streambed. You'll find the Decalogue Stone about 130 yards ahead on the left. The inscription faces the streambed at the base of the stone.

The scenic loop also starts at the pedestrian gate but veers right along the *near* side of the first hill. There's no real path here, but stay close to the hill, and you'll soon wind up in a sandy wash. Follow it upstream, aiming straight for a gulley that cuts through the bigger hill ahead. (Also, notice how the gulley points up to a dark cleft in the ridgeline of Hidden Mountain. That will be your passage into its volcanic crater.)

The streambed turns rocky and the channel deepens as you head uphill. Stick to the main channel, bypassing any tributary washes merging on your right. As the channel fades out, aim slightly to the left for a sandy saddle on the ridge ahead. Once at the top, consider taking this short detour: turn right and go about 100 yards up the steep ridgeline to find tilted basalt boulders stacked up in interesting formations.

Continuing from the sandy ridge, follow the cow path curving down to the right. It's an easier descent and won't cause as much damage as trampling straight down the hillside. When you get to an old barbed-wire fence, turn left, and follow it down to the point where it crosses the wash. Here you can easily duck under it to the other side. Find the cairn about 100 yards downstream; turn right, and head up the path on the left side of the gulley, following arrows scratched into rocks along the way.

When you're done examining the rock, continue up the gulley, staying in the main channel for about 0.25 miles—but not all the way to the far side of the crater. State land ends about 100 yards shy of the south rim. That's most unfortunate because a quaint footpath follows nearly the entire curve of the crater rim, and the view from the top of the sheer black cliffs along the southern side is nothing short of dramatic (or so I'm told).

This is *not* the Decalogue Stone.

Though some anarchic hikers evidently cross the invisible boundary, you can stay in fair-play territory by cutting east at a point that seems completely arbitrary. To be more precise: at the point where the channel nearly fades into nothing, turn left. You'll intercept the path on the eastern rim in about 100 yards or so. Turn left again, and follow it north. Look for petroglyphs and shelter ruins along the way. At the fork ahead, take the left branch to check out the largest of the ruins. The circle of rocks, not much bigger than a hot tub, is a good spot to take a breather, watch the trains go by, and enjoy the wide-open views.

To get off the mountain, return to the fork, and take the other branch. The path fades as it drops down through the scree. Tack right, and carefully work your way down into a rocky wash where the terrain is a little more stable. Once the ground levels out, you'll see the gate straight ahead. Go through it, fasten it behind you, and follow the path north–northwest 0.6 miles back to the parking area.

NEARBY ACTIVITIES

If returning to Albuquerque, consider going north (left) on NM 6 for an 18-mile cruise through the southeastern corner of the Laguna Indian Reservation. It adds about 10 miles to your trip, but the scenery is spectacular. (The land is off-limits to the general public, so don't wander.) Once you reach I-40, go east to Albuquerque.

TOME HILL (EL CERRO TOMÉ) 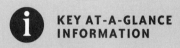 47

IN BRIEF

The terminus of New Mexico's most famous pilgrimage, Tome Hill is also a font of inspiration for great art and literature, both secular and sacred. With views of the Manzano Mountains and over the Rio Grande, the hill has a natural beauty that makes it a great place for a short hike almost any time of year.

DESCRIPTION

In the mid-17th century, Tomé Domínguez, age 90, settled in the Sandia jurisdiction with his wife, Eleña Ramírez de Mendoza. Soon after both passed away, one of their three sons, Tomé Domínguez de Mendoza, moved to Fonclara, a site at the base of this volcanic hill south of Albuquerque. In 1659 he received permission to settle the land, along with the right to "recruit" unpaid laborers from nearby Isleta Pueblo to build a hacienda. The homestead was finished by 1661 but came under attack during the Pueblo Revolt in 1680. Mendoza fled back to Spain and never saw his hacienda again.

In 1739 the Tomé Grant was awarded to the local *genízaros,* a marginalized class Hispanicized Indians and mixed-blood settlers. Ostracized by both Spanish and Pueblo societies, many genízaros developed their own customs, including religious practices based

KEY AT-A-GLANCE INFORMATION

LENGTH: 1.7-mile loop

DIFFICULTY: Easy (though some consider it hard enough to count as penance)

SCENERY: Religious iconography perched atop a solitary volcanic mass

EXPOSURE: No shade

TRAIL TRAFFIC: Moderate

SHARED USE: Low, though crowded during religious observances

TRAIL SURFACE: Dirt, rock

HIKING TIME: 1 hour

DRIVING DISTANCE: 31 miles (one way) from the I-40/I-25 exchange

ACCESS: Dawn–dusk

LAND STATUS: Private property

MAPS: Brochure map available at trailhead; USGS Los Lunas

FACILITIES: Interpretive signage, sculpture garden (wheelchair-accessible)

LAST CHANCE FOOD/GAS: All services in Los Lunas

SPECIAL COMMENTS: See longer note at end of description.

Directions

From I-25 south, take Exit 203 at Los Lunas and turn left (east) on NM 6 (Historic Route 66). Go 3.5 miles and bear right on Lujan Road. After 0.25 miles on Lujan Road, turn right (south) on NM 47. Go 3.4 miles to Tomé Hill Road. Turn left toward the hill and follow the signs to Tomé Hill Park, 1 mile ahead. Turn right on La Entrada Road, then left into the parking lot.

GPS Trailhead Coordinates

UTM Zone (WGS 84)   13S
Easting   0343855
Northing   3846812
Latitude   35° 45' 5"
Longitude   106° 42' 21"

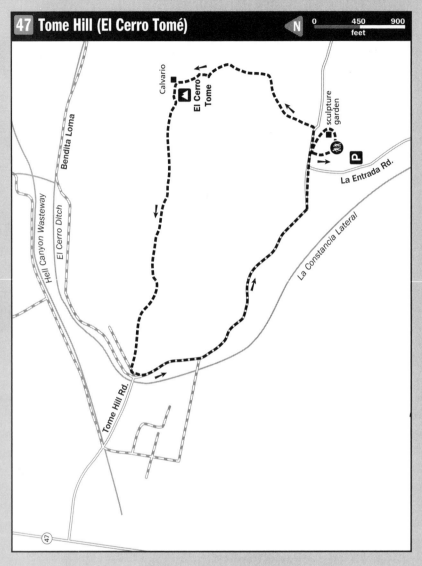

N

0   450   900
feet

Calvario

El Cerro Tome

sculpture garden

La Entrada Rd.

Bendita Loma

Hell Canyon Wasteway

El Cerro Ditch

La Constancia Lateral

Tome Hill Rd.

47

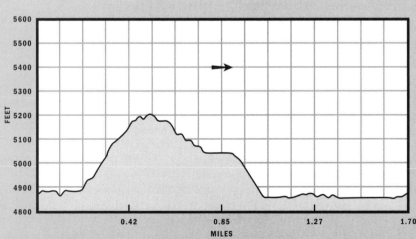

5600
5500
5400
5300
5200
5100
5000
4900
4800

FEET

0.42   0.85   1.27   1.70

MILES

Folk shrines and memorials adorn the hilltop.

largely on native beliefs and Franciscan mysticism. Their unique traditions evolved into the Penitente Brotherhood, noted for acts of mortification, flagellation, and the Good Friday crucifixion of a Penitente brother.

The annual Passion Play at Tome Hill today is said to be the same as the one described by Fray Francisco Domínguez in 1776, with one possible exception. According to a disclaimer posted in Tomé Park: "No actual crucifixion is carried out."

Credit for organizing the installation of the *calvario* on Tome Hill in 1947 goes to Edwin Antonio Berry, a World War II veteran and the son of a 19th-century Penitente leader. Berry also recorded the oral history and songs of his culture for posterity and remained the steward of Tomé Hill until his death in 2000. A stirring tribute to Tomé's most celebrated citizen can be found in Gregory Candela's locally published poetry collection, *Surfing New Mexico* (Crones Unlimited, 2001).

The route you walk here is known as Berry's Path. You hardly need a guidebook for this one. Abundant interpretive texts at Tome Hill Park spell out just about everything you could want to know about this legendary hill. But to omit this hike would be a mortal sin, for nothing else encapsulates the essence of New Mexico quite like El Cerro Tomé. The cultural significance of the hill has earned it a listing on the National Register of Historic Places.

Park literature depicts the hill as a station at the crossroads of many cultures but with an interesting slant. For instance, 1846 is recalled as "the year of the U.S. invasion and occupation of New Mexico." Fair enough. But then describing early Spaniards as mere "explorers" seems to understate the conquistadores' divine intentions. If you don't have time to read all the signs, get the equally comprehensive brochure from the black mailbox.

Begin the hike by walking around *La Puerta del Sol,* the impressive sculptural centerpiece of Tomé Hill Park. The steel and rust artwork of the artist Armando Alvarez is a complex vision of the diverse groups who have traveled El Camino Real in the past 400 years. The $100,000 piece features a 25-foot-high gateway and the life-sized likenesses of several historical archetypes. The work is often described as a celebration of cultural diversity; however, bold details evoke darker episodes of cultural conflicts.

Follow the sidewalk around a cable fence and up the road. A crosswalk ahead leads to the start of the steep South Trail. According to a sign back in the park, "The distance to the summit is over a quarter of a mile with an altitude gain of 1,200 feet." Don't worry—it's not quite that severe. The gain is a mere 400 feet. But with only two switchbacks, the rocky path takes some effort. The reward at the top is eternal salvation, along with a lovely view of the valley between the Manzano Mountains and Mesa Gallina.

Though highly discouraged now, leaving a mark on the hill is a custom that dates back 2,000 years or more. As the signs below suggest, petroglyphs appear on every flat slab of basalt on the hill. However, they're not easy to see from the trails, and the literature is a bit murky on how to find them. As a result, visitors often scour the hill in search of pecked rocks. With a good eye and better patience, you can spot a few petroglyphs from designated (though unmarked) spurs off South Trail near the top of the hill.

The calvario at the summit consists of three wood and metal crosses, each 16 feet high. A tin shrine sits at the base of the central cross, along with countless votive candles, rosaries, photographs, and handwritten prayers. It is at once a place of profound grief, joy, and hope. In addition to the permanent installation, temporary folk memorials and devotional artworks often crop up at various stations around the hilltop. There's always something new and fascinating on Tomé Hill.

Continue past the calvario on West Trail, also called Via Cruces (Crosses Way). Just over 0.25 miles downhill, a sign on the right indicates a path to the chapel. Stay on West Trail another 0.25 miles or so until it reaches the base of the hill. Turn left, and follow the road 0.6 miles back to the parking lot at Tomé Park. Or for a more scenic route, turn right, and follow the road about 3 miles clockwise around the hill.

For an enlightening and entertaining perspective on contemporary life in Tomé, read Ana Castillo's widely acclaimed novel, *So Far from God.*

Note: Tomeans (*Toméseños?*) are generally friendly, if somewhat reserved toward outsiders. Despite their ongoing efforts to preserve their traditional community, growth and development throughout the area has led to an escalating crime rate in recent years. Don't get too lulled in the pastoral setting—use the same common sense as you would when walking in an urban area.

TRIGO CANYON FALLS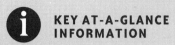

IN BRIEF

Though discontinued as an official trail, the route up Trigo Canyon remains a favorite among hikers, with most coming to visit the falls. A gentle riparian path offers plenty of opportunities for picnicking and bouldering. Enjoy the wildflowers in spring and summer and the changing leaves in autumn.

DESCRIPTION

Like the Sandia Mountains to the north, the Manzanos' western face is a steep, rugged uplift cut with wooded canyons. Though this range is much longer—stretching 40 miles compared to Sandia's 28—public access from the west is complicated, to say the least. The Manzanos' nearest peaks rise just 20 miles southeast of Albuquerque, but the Isleta Pueblo keeps them off-limits to the general public. The nearest westside trailhead then

Directions

From I-25 south, take Exit 191 to Belen. Turn left and go east 1 mile on Camino del Llano (NM 548). At the first light, turn left onto Main Street (NM 314). Drive north 0.6 miles, then turn right onto Reinken Avenue (NM 309). Go 2.4 miles east, crossing the railroad tracks and the river. Take a right onto Rio Communities Boulevard (NM 47). Your next left is 2 miles ahead on North Navajo Road. It does not have a road sign, only a green gate with a cattle guard and a stop sign. Follow this dirt road east 8.4 miles to the T-junction with another unmarked dirt road, Trigo Springs Road (FR 33). Turn left and go north 3 miles. Turn right and go through the gate with "No Hunting" signs posted on it. This road, still FR 33, gets rough as it climbs 6.2 miles east to the old JFK campground. Park near the green gate, where this hike begins.

KEY AT-A-GLANCE INFORMATION

LENGTH: 5.6-mile out-and-back

DIFFICULTY: Easy to moderate

SCENERY: Wooded canyon, rock features, springs, caves, waterfalls

EXPOSURE: Mostly shade

TRAIL TRAFFIC: Moderate

SHARED USE: Low (livestock in trailhead area; closed to motor vehicles)

TRAIL SURFACE: Packed dirt

HIKING TIME: 2–3 hours

DRIVING DISTANCE: 58 miles from the I-40 and I-25 exchange

ACCESS: Year-round

LAND STATUS: Cibola National Forest–Mountainair Ranger District

MAPS: Manzano Mountain Wilderness (South Half); USGS Capilla Peak

FACILITIES: None

LAST CHANCE FOOD/GAS: All services available in Belen, about 20 miles from the trailhead

SPECIAL COMMENTS: Though JFK Campground closed in 2005, the ranger district and local ranchers warn that the area is still a favorite haunt of persistent vandals. Trigo Canyon Trail is no longer maintained, but is still open for hiking. See additional note at the end of the Description.

GPS Trailhead Coordinates

UTM Zone (WGS 84) 13S

Easting 0365415

Northing 3838213

Latitude 34° 40' 37"

Longitude 106° 28' 09"

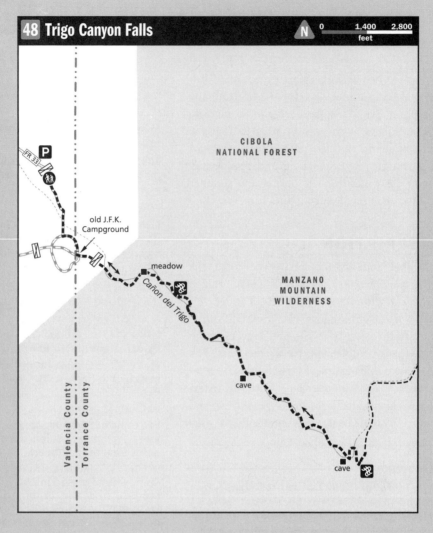

48 Trigo Canyon Falls

N   0   1,400   2,800
feet

CIBOLA
NATIONAL FOREST

FR 33

P

old J.F.K.
Campground

meadow

Cañon del Trigo

MANZANO
MOUNTAIN
WILDERNESS

cave

Valencia County

Torrance County

cave

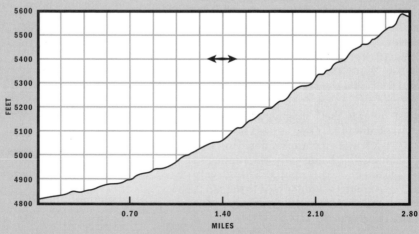

En route to Trigo Canyon

would be Encino. Forest service maps place it near the southern edge of the BLM's intriguing Manzano Wilderness Study Area. However, after negotiating jarring dirt roads through a landscape that resembled a razed favela, I found nothing but pit-mining operations. Nobody at Cibola National Forest headquarters or the Mountainair Ranger District seems to know if Encino ever existed, only that the designated trailhead never had a designated trail.

So that leaves the distant Navajo Loop, which includes FR 33, as the only viable approach to the western Manzanos. In theory, relatively few visitations help preserve the mountains' natural beauty, but that hasn't always been the case. Heavy rains washed out the original Trigo Canyon Campground in 1941. A later facility, constructed and reinforced with generous portions of concrete, was dedicated in the mid-1960s to memorialize John F. Kennedy. In the decades that followed, JFK Campground was an idyllic family retreat. Nestled at the backend of the Tomé Grant, where the mountain eases into grassy cattle lands, the site once offered above-standard campground amenities, including restrooms, picnic tables, barbeque grills, and access to the Comanche, Salas, and Trigo Canyon trails.

In more recent years, however, vandals have destroyed just about everything. Already facing a budget crunch in 2005, the forest service had no choice but to lock the gate, close the campground, and leave the site in the custody of local ranchers.

If none of this deters you from enjoying the splendors of Trigo Canyon, you're not alone. Hikers still put it to frequent use, keeping most of the old trail fairly clear. Perhaps recreational usage will continue to increase until enough people recognize that it's worth saving. Already, nearby community leaders have discussed proposals to revive the trailhead facility, and it's been rumored that the forest service may allow for a privately operated campground, now tentatively named Que Divina.

The hike begins at the green gate, which you'll likely find secured under two hefty padlocks. Use the pedestrian access, and walk up the road. The Trigo Canyon trailhead is only 0.6 miles away. Shortly after a cement dip, the road begins its loop around the old campground. Bear left to follow it clockwise through the ruins of former campsites and picnic grounds. Soon the lush green mouth of the canyon opens on the left. Walk the road through the former parking area to the brown pipe fence ahead. Crossing through the zigzag gate is like stepping into another country—the dusty back roads vanish behind you as the cool forest invites you in.

Only one trail marker remains in the area. A rusty sign for the Salas Trail (184) escaped the wrath of vandals by hiding behind pine scrub directly south of the old parking area. The Trigo Canyon Trail (formerly 185) is easier to find and, for the most part, an obvious one to follow. Just cross the stream, and commence on the broad path ahead.

You'll cross the stream often along the way, though outside of springtime and summer monsoons it's little more than a trickle. Still it's enough to sustain stands of willows and gray oak. Alligator juniper is the predominant species, or at least its reptilian bark makes it the most noticeable. Short spurs duck into the shade of dense woods. A quick detour on any one of them leads to a secluded niche, often with a campfire ring. Watch out for poison ivy.

The trail bends through a small meadow before crossing the stream again. At a fork ahead, stick to the left. (The right branch climbs up to an overhanging ledge and then presses through spindly scrub.) Both branches lead to a waterfall, just 0.2 miles upstream. Compared to the cataract farther ahead, it's not much of a waterfall, but it still counts as one by New Mexico standards. The enormous boulders surrounding it beg to be climbed, as does the giant alligator juniper nearby.

In early winter, downed foliage blankets the ground. In the summer, lower tree trunks sprout earlike mushrooms. Year-round, jagged rocks jut like monstrous incisors, dominating much of the trailside scenery, and certain places in the lower canyon could almost pass for a craggy hollow in the Ozarks.

The trail gets vague in places ahead, but you'll stay on course by sticking to the stream and maintaining your direction to the southeast. The most potentially confusing point in the hike comes less than 0.25 miles past the small waterfall. Avoid wandering up drainages on your left. Once you get past that point, steep canyon walls make it difficult to stray far from the trail.

Another 0.5 miles up, shortly before the trail crosses the stream, a short spur to the right leads up to a shallow cave. The stream kinks as it works around the massive outcrop, and the trail takes a couple of shortcuts between bends. Less than 1 mile past the first cave is another rock cliff. The cave here seems popular with local misfits, who occasionally engage in ceremonial drinking and rudimentary cave drawing. Finally, just several steps ahead, you'll arrive at a 25-foot waterfall, with smaller ones nearby in the peak-flow seasons.

This hike ends here since too few hikers press on to guarantee a clear path ahead. But if you feel compelled to continue, the trail changes direction and climbs northeast along steep switchbacks up the canyon wall. It then breaks away from the stream shortly before reaching a saddle point on the Crest Trail (170). A hike to the Crest Trail and back to the waterfall is a moderately strenuous 3 miles, pushing the overall hike to nearly 9 miles.

If that seems like too much walking for today, turn around at the waterfall, and retrace your steps the way you came. Time it right, and you might see a cattle drive rumbling through the old campground. At the end of the day, ranchers herd their snorting, stomping cows through the green gate and back to the ranch. Hunched on their horses and classically attired, they seem to be the last of the genuine cowboys in these parts.

Local ranchland is shrinking fast as Belen continues to expand. Much of the Tomé Grant is already scored for residential development. It originally stretched from the Rio Grande to the "main ridge" of the Manzanos—in all, about 122,000 acres that would have included Trigo Canyon.

Note: The last 9 miles of road to JFK Campground are poorly maintained. Four-wheel drive may be necessary in wet conditions. A high-clearance vehicle is usually not necessary, but leave the lowrider at home. For current conditions, check with the Mountainair Ranger District at (505) 847-2990 or **www.fs.fed .us/r3/cibola/districts/mountainair.**

NEARBY ACTIVITIES

For local history, and collections related to the Santa Fe Railroad, visit the Valencia County Historical Society's Harvey House Museum, located in the Harvey House Dining Room, which is listed on the National Register. En route back to I-25, after crossing the bridge over the railroad tracks, turn left on Third Street. Go two blocks south and turn left on Becker Street. Another two blocks and another left puts you on First Street. The museum is on the right at 104 North First Street. Open Tuesday through Saturday, 12:30-3:30 p.m., and available for tours. (505) 861-0581.

49 MONTE LARGO CANYON

KEY AT-A-GLANCE INFORMATION

LENGTH: 5-mile out-and-back
DIFFICULTY: Moderate
SCENERY: Broadleaf and pine forest, wildlife, caves
EXPOSURE: Mostly shade
TRAIL TRAFFIC: Low
SHARED USE: Low (equestrians, livestock; closed to motorized vehicles)
TRAIL SURFACE: Packed dirt, loose rock
HIKING TIME: 2–3 hours
DRIVING DISTANCE: 55 miles (one way) from the I-40/I-25 exchange
ACCESS: Year-round
LAND STATUS: Cibola National Forest–Mountainair Ranger District; Manzano Mountain Wilderness
MAPS: USGS Manzano Peak
FACILITIES: None
LAST CHANCE FOOD/GAS: All services available in Belen, about 20 miles from the trailhead
SPECIAL COMMENTS: The last 4 miles of dirt road can get a bit rough, especially after snow or heavy rain. Four-wheel drive is not necessary in dry conditions, but a little extra clearance might help. For current conditions, check with the Mountainair Ranger District, (505) 847-2990, www.fs.fed.us/r3/cibola/districts/mountainair

GPS Trailhead Coordinates

UTM Zone (WGS 84) 13S
Easting   0362608
Northing   3829798
Latitude   34° 36' 03"
Longitude   106° 29' 54"

IN BRIEF

Though designated as a trailhead on Forest Service maps, Monte Largo lacks a designated trail. No problem—well-worn paths facilitate hiking along its primary drainage. The lush wooded corridor is a near-perfect environment for hikes throughout most of the year.

DESCRIPTION

Don't let the approach fool you. Though the Manzanos appear as barren scarps of granite and scrub, you'll find long stretches of shaded woodland hidden behind its stark facade. The scenery in Monte Largo Canyon is much like that on the previous hike, Trigo Canyon, minus the waterfalls and vandalism. Both are densely wooded with a lush mix of oak and

----

Directions ⟶

From I-25 south, take Exit 191 to Belen. Turn left and go east 1 mile on Camino del Llano (NM 548). At the first light, turn left onto Main Street (NM 314). Drive north 0.6 miles, then turn right onto Reinken Avenue (NM 309). Go 2.4 miles east, crossing the railroad tracks and the river. Take a right onto Rio Communities Boulevard (NM 47). Go southeast 5.8 miles and turn left on FR 33. (Look for the brown Forest Access signs on the right.) Go east 6 miles, straight past the old JFK sign, and cross a white cattle guard. The road jogs slightly to the right and turns to gravel. Continue east another 0.8 miles, past the ranch house with a rail tanker in the front yard. The road then bends northeast and becomes rocky. Go straight through the first intersection ahead. One mile past the intersection, turn right (southeast) at a rock cairn and go 2.5 miles. Cross the yellow cattle guard and park on the west side of the fenced lot. A section of silver-painted fence marks the pedestrian gate. The hike begins here.

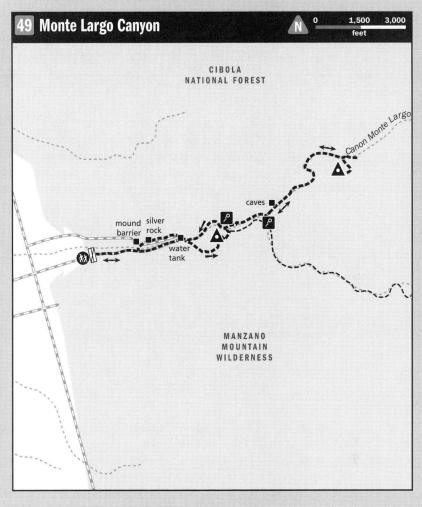

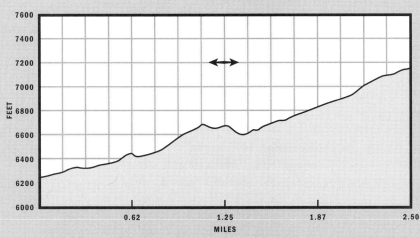

pine. But the lesser-known Monte Largo Canyon has a wilder feel to it. A good supply of acorns keeps squirrels and turkeys well fed, and summer bounties of currants attract birds and bears.

Evidence of bear activity was unusually high here, indeed throughout New Mexico, in the summer of 2007. The state's only species of bear is *Ursus americanas,* the black bear, which often appears more a shade of cinnamon brown. Their predilection for verdant mountain forests keeps them confined (usually) to wooded "islands" throughout the American Southwest. Black bears may seem cute and clumsy but can charge at speeds up to 30 mph. With that in mind, review the safety tips for hiking in bear country before entering Monte Largo Canyon. Most importantly, never try to outrun a bear. You need only run faster than the other hikers.

The hike begins at the gateway. Walk straight east along a path worn through rocky grassland. In about 0.25 miles, it bends downhill to the left. A black waterline crosses the path here. Both the line and the path descend closer to the arroyo and then turn east into the canyon. You can follow the line for a more shaded path, though dense scrub ahead will eventually coax you to cross the arroyo. Or you can cross sooner to pick up a sunny doubletrack on the north bank.

Either way, you'll pass a water tower on the north bank. About 500 feet east of the water tower, the trail splits. For a great preview of the route ahead, veer right on the more prominent branch uphill. About 0.2 miles ahead, a steel sign marks the boundary of the Manzano Mountain Wilderness. Continue uphill another 200 yards or so. The object is to climb the nearest ridge to your left, so just aim in that direction if the path fades or seems to stray elsewhere. When you reach the crest of the ridge, turn left, and walk out to the point. Cuts in the exposed rock suggest minor quarrying or mining may have occurred up here.

The Monte Largo Spring is directly below to the north, but it may be difficult to spot when foliage is full. Animals frequent the water source, making this overlook the perfect perch for watching birds and wildlife. I've seen fox and mule deer trotting below, apparently oblivious to my presence. Bring binoculars to scope out broader terrain. The dense woods stretch for about 1 mile to the northeast before disappearing into the V of the canyon. Manzano Peak, the highest in the range, stands 2 miles to the southeast.

Note that Monte Largo Canyon is one of several in a basin that spans about 2.5 miles north to south. For navigational purposes, it helps to know that all waterways in this basin eventually merge to exit through the bottleneck to the west, the way you just came in. So as long as you don't cross any major ridges, you can follow any drainage downstream to return to the trailhead.

Numerous trails are easier to spot when the trees are bare. A couple of routes that might be more suitable in wet or icy conditions are located on the arid slopes a few yards above the streambed. Geared for the rest of the year, this hike sticks to the shaded paths close to the main arroyo.

Return to the canyon floor by going down the side opposite the way you came up, and then turn right to continue following the waterline upstream. In 0.25 miles, you'll arrive at a second fork. Stay left. (For reference: the waterline goes right to the Upper Monte Largo Spring, about a minute's walk south. A steeper, sunnier trail marked with cairns continues southeast. I don't know how far it goes, but it's aimed at Manzano Peak.)

As you continue northeast, brown cliffs form vertical walls above to your left. Small caves can be seen in the sedimentary rock; pungent odors suggest that some are occupied and probably best left undisturbed. You can get a good view of them by reaching slightly higher ground on your right and looking across the arroyo.

The drainage deepens ahead, and the trail seems to split off in different directions. You may find traces of an old Jeep road or a well-worn game path meandering through towering ponderosa. You can usually switch from one to another by running a short lateral. Either way, keep the main channel nearby, usually on your right. If you find yourself bushwhacking, wandering over a barren hill, or struggling up a ridiculously steep drainage, you've undoubtedly strayed off course.

About 2 miles into the hike, the drainage curves around a bulging outcrop on the left. Immediately afterward, it hooks around a towering outcrop on the right. The trail becomes a little steeper along this S-curve.

The incline lessens as the trail runs due east for the next 0.3 miles. Primitive campsites with sturdy shelter frames and fire rings can be found at the beginning of this stretch, along with a flourish of poison ivy. For an optional detour, look for narrow switchbacks on the steep slope to your right. A short but strenuous ascent to the south may require a bit of scrambling, but it puts you atop a ridge with a commanding view of the canyon. To return to the canyon floor this time, go the same way you came up. Bushwhacking down the other side isn't worth the trouble.

You can continue up the canyon another 0.25 miles before the trail hits the wall beneath the crest, but the campsites seem as good a place as any to turn around. Follow the drainage 1 mile downstream, until you locate the waterline snaking out from the upper spring. Follow the line out of the canyon. As you approach the lower spring, the next 0.25 miles may suddenly seem unfamiliar; this is the part you bypassed on the way up when you climbed over the ridge. Continue down to the water tower, and stay on the old road. About 250 yards ahead is a large silver-painted rock. Just ahead on the left is a cairn. Turn left at the cairn to cross the arroyo. (If you encounter dirt-mound barriers on the road, you've gone about 100 yards past the cairn. Also note that the road does not lead back to the parking lot.) Once across the arroyo, continue on the trail another 0.4 miles back to your car.

NEARBY ACTIVITIES

There are a few good opportunities for geocaching in the area. One of my favorites leads to the Lone Wolf Mine near Ojo Barreras, about 1.5 miles south of the Monte Largo trailhead. To prepare for the hunt, log on to **www.geocaching.com** and, under View a Cache Listing, enter: GCV1GZ.

BERNARDO 50

IN BRIEF

Best enjoyed from November through February, the Bernardo Waterfowl Area (BWA) features three observation decks along a 2.8-mile dirt road equally suited for walking, biking, or driving. The Rio Puerco route explores a small portion of vast and undeveloped grasslands along a deep channel. Together, this pair of short loops reveals sharp contrasts in riparian environments near the confluence of the Rio Grande and a major tributary.

DESCRIPTION

The Bernardo Waterfowl Area is the second largest of the four wildlife management areas that make up the Ladd S. Gordon Waterfowl Complex. (The biggest is La Joya, briefly explored in Sevilleta [hike 53].) From November to February, about 15,000 sandhill cranes commute along the Rio Grande, with throngs of bird-watchers keeping pace on I-25. Up to 5,000 winged creatures may drop in at once on the BWA. The spectacle culminates in November with the Festival of the Cranes at the Bosque del Apache National Wildlife Refuge. But then that's a 100-mile drive south of Albuquerque, making the Gordon Complex an attractive compromise for its proximity.

KEY AT-A-GLANCE INFORMATION

LENGTH: 2.8-mile waterfowl area-hike and 3-mile Rio Puerco hike comprise two separate loops

DIFFICULTY: Easy

SCENERY: Birds, cultivated fields, marshland, grassland, ephemeral river

EXPOSURE: Some shade in waterfowl area and along the Rio Puerco riverbed

TRAIL TRAFFIC: Seasonal at waterfowl area, low at Rio Puerco

SHARED USE: Moderate (equestrians, motor vehicles, livestock)

TRAIL SURFACE: Dirt roads, cow paths

HIKING TIME: 1 hour per loop

DRIVING DISTANCE: 54 miles

ACCESS: Year-round, sunrise–sunset

LAND STATUS: NM Department of Game & Fish, BLM–Socorro Field Office

MAPS: USGS Abeytas, USGS La Joya NW

FACILITIES: Latrine at waterfowl area

LAST CHANCE FOOD/GAS: All services at Exit 191 in Belen

SPECIAL COMMENTS: For updates on winter migrations at the Bernardo Unit, call (505) 864-9187 or visit www.wildlife.state.nm.us.

Directions

From I-25 south, take Exit 175 at Bernardo, following the signs for the Ladd S. Gordon Waterfowl Management Area. The exit ramp turns loops beneath the I-25 overpass. Turn left (north) on the frontage road immediately after the northbound ramp. Drive north 1.7 miles and turn right at the sign for the Bernardo unit. You can park at the welcome sign ahead to walk the 2.8-mile loop. Directions for the Rio Puerco hike appear in the Description.

GPS Trailhead Coordinates

UTM Zone (WGS 84) 13S

Easting 0332641

Northing 3812403

Latitude 34° 26' 23"

Longitude 106° 49' 18"

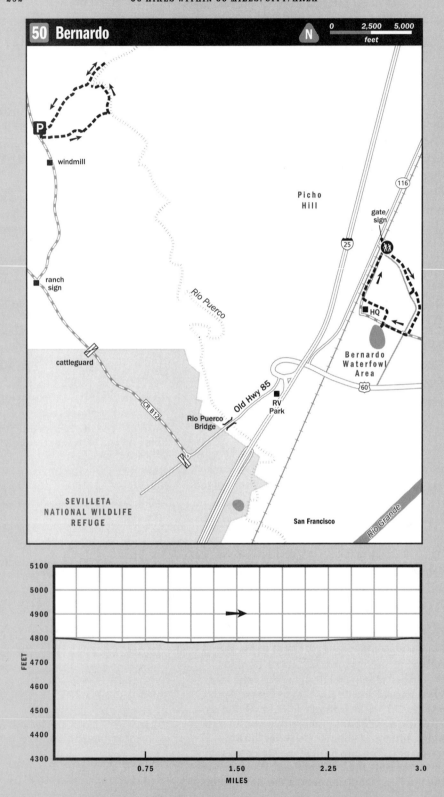

Death visits the Rio Puerco.

To catch the big show, timing is everything. On my last visit, in early February, most of the birds had just moved on to Casa Colorada, which is about 12 miles north and closed to the public. Not more than a dozen cranes lingered in the Bernardo fields. Downy clusters littered the crop stubble. There were feathers stuck to bone near the canals, with wings torn asunder. A birder with a hefty pair of binoculars explained that he'd seen hawks pouncing on small geese.

Whether you decide to walk or drive the BWA's dirt roads depends on how much time you want to spend. Traffic is another consideration. It's light most of the year, but up to 50 cars can be expected on a peak day like Thanksgiving. However you travel, signs along the way are pretty clear about where you should and should not go.

Begin scouting for birds from the first of three observation decks, located about 0.25 miles straight past the welcome sign. It's a basic viewing and photographic tower facing east for a mountainous panorama. The southern end of the Manzano range stands about 20 miles due east. Lining up to the south are the Los Pinos Mountains. The Rio Grande runs through the bosque about 1 mile out. Crop fields unfold from there to the base of the tower. Of the 1,573 acres in the BWA, 450 are cultivated for corn, sorghum, and green feed. Between the water in the irrigation ditches and the grain in the fields, migratory birds have everything they need here for a full-service refueling stop.

About 0.3 miles past the first deck, a boardwalk over an irrigation ditch and a cattail marsh leads to the second platform. The view to the west stretches over fields and out to I-25. The low ridge rising to the north is Picho Hill. The Rio Puerco runs along its base on the opposite side. Peaking about 15 miles due west are the stark, jagged Sierra Ladrones.

About 0.9 miles past the boardwalk, you'll arrive at a parking area for the third deck, which overlooks a large pond. Interpretive signs and a short path through a wooded grove are slated for installation in time for the 2007–08 birding season. The idea behind the layout is to provide birders with enough tree cover for closer looks at shy birds. The pond area is a restoration project designed to represent the Rio Grande floodplain before levees and ditches controlled its course. In its more natural state, the river tended to sprawl, creating ponds, marshes, and oxbow lakes. Stripped of its vegetation, however, it might develop characteristics of the Rio Puerco.

From the parking area at the third deck, a 1.1-mile stretch closes the loop. It's slightly shorter than backtracking, but not quite as interesting.

The Rio Puerco hike begins after an 8-mile drive toward the Ladrones. Cross back under I-25 and go up the southbound ramp. Don't miss the right turn at the sign for the RV park or you'll end up back on the interstate. Head southwest on Old Highway 85, and cross the Rio Puerco Bridge (a steel thru truss built in 1930). Half a mile past the bridge, turn right on County Road B12, and aim northwest 2.6 miles. Bear right at the Y, and go north 1.4 miles to a windmill. Just 0.4 miles past the windmill, pull off in a sandy wash to the right. Make sure you're not blocking the road, but don't go too deep into the sand.

This setting might seem more appropriate for a Max Evans novel than a nature walk. It's a basin of cattle land, much of it grazed down to bare earth. However, its low altitude and full exposure make it an attractive reserve hike for those times when you're still waiting for more conventional trails to thaw out.

With all due respect to ranchers and their delicious cows, overgrazing is at least partially to blame for the current state of the Rio Puerco basin. Although it's likely that the watershed has gone through numerous cycles of downcutting and infilling over the past few million years, historical evidence shows that overgrazing accelerated the process at the end of the 19th century.

Like the Rio Grande, the Rio Puerco once ran a shallow course through a broad floodplain. Fertile farmlands in the upper Rio Puerco Valley were then regarded as the breadbasket of New Mexico. But since the introduction of large herds in the 1880s, vegetation on the Rio Puerco watershed quickly diminished. As a result, the river began cutting downward, as did the streams that feed into it. By 1890 the changes were obvious. Deepening arroyos impeded farming in the basin, eventually leading to the abandonment of at least six agrarian towns in the upper valley.

As streams trenched into the valley floor, the riparian habitat shrank. Cottonwoods, once prevalent in the basin, are now scarce, and the main channel is choked with tamarisk, which were introduced to the valley in 1926 to mitigate erosion. If there's a bright side to any of this ecological mayhem, it's that it allows you to explore the crooked patterns cut into the earth and the bones and debitage they often yield.

Begin walking east down the dry wash. Within half a mile, you should start noticing pronounced trenching. It deepens as you approach the river, which is about 1 mile from the road. The drop to the desiccated riverbed is a sheer 15 feet or more.

Turn left, and head upstream. Watch your step—the bank is little more than a hollow crust in places, susceptible to crumbling and collapsing under the weight of a footstep. On hotter days, you may prefer to walk shaded cow paths through the forest of tamarisk below. Note that the cliff-like banks grow taller and afford fewer places to climb out upstream. Also, you may encounter deep pockets of mud, but your main concern is flash flooding. Though more often than not you'd get more water from a drooling cow than from this so-called river, flood discharges occasionally gush 5,000 cubic feet per second, with a record of 18,800 cfs monitored at the Rio Puerco Bridge.

In about 0.25 miles, you'll reach the coordinates listed in the note below. Even if you missed the satellite preview, you'll know the spot when you see it. The river has taken a sharp turn and scooped out a sizable chunk of land in the process. Caving banks along the main channel and its tributaries contribute to the Rio Puerco's high sediment loads. The river supplies an estimated 78 percent of the sediment entering the Elephant Butte Reservoir but only about 10 percent of the water. On average, only the Amazon and the Yellow River transport higher annual sediment concentrations. Put simply, the Rio Puerco, or "muddy river," is the world's third-muddiest river.

If fluvial geomorphology fails to excite you, then just wander quietly around the bend and enjoy the scenery. Before the tamarisk was considered a pernicious weed, it was a prized ornamental, and a dense red swarm of it at dusk isn't an entirely hideous sight. The Sierra Ladrones appear most ominous when cast in the gloomy silhouette of a winter sunset. Take a moment to contemplate their steely peaks if you plan to attempt the next hike in this book. When the coyotes come out to protest your presence, it's time to head back to the car.

The parking spot is less than 1 mile southwest of the outer river bend. You can go straight for it, using cow paths to get through patches of tall grass. Or just aim due west until you meet the road, and then turn left and follow it back to where you started.

Note: For the second part of the hike, an overhead preview greatly enhances your perspective. Before you go, log on to your favorite satellite image viewer (Google Earth, for example) and enter these coordinates: 34° 27' 58" N, 106° 52' 52" W. The last 4 miles of the drive to the Rio Puerco are on dirt roads that are bumpy but suitable in dry conditions.

51 SIERRA LADRONES

KEY AT-A-GLANCE INFORMATION

LENGTH: 7-mile out-and-back, 5-mile shuttle option

DIFFICULTY: Moderate to strenuous

SCENERY: Desert scrub, cacti, raptors, expansive views

EXPOSURE: Full sun

TRAIL TRAFFIC: Low

SHARED USE: Low (livestock)

TRAIL SURFACE: Sand, limestone pavements, loose rock

HIKING TIME: 3–4 hours

DRIVING DISTANCE: 72 miles (one way) from the I-40 and I-25 exchange

ACCESS: Year-round

LAND STATUS: BLM–Socorro, Wilderness Study Area

MAPS: USGS Riley, Ladron Peak

FACILITIES: None

LAST CHANCE FOOD/GAS: All services available at Exit 191 in Belen, 38 miles from the trailhead

SPECIAL COMMENTS: The last 19 miles of the drive are on a bumpy dirt road, passable to most vehicles in dry conditions.

GPS Trailhead Coordinates

UTM Zone (WGS 84)   13S

Easting   0304231

Northing   3819190

Latitude   34° 29' 45"

Longitude   107° 07' 56"

IN BRIEF

Following a game path on a long, undulating uplift, this straightforward route provides a friendly introduction to an isolated mountain range with a mean reputation. Peaks along the way allow for great views down to the foothills and canyons, and up to the toothy ridges of the Sierra Ladrones.

DESCRIPTION

Sierra Ladrones, or "thieves mountains," earned their name as a hideout for Navajo raiders who, having relieved local ranches of their stock, spirited them across the *jaral* (chaparral or scrubland) to untraceable retreats. Later banditos and rustlers continued the tradition by holing up in the range's deep canyons. Few were known to reemerge, and speculation that lost loot has yet to be found continues to this day.

Also called Los Ladrones, the dark mountains figure into local lore as the setting for Apache ambushes, disastrous treasure hunts, and encounters with ghostly

Directions ➤

From I-25 south take Exit 175 at Bernardo. Take the first left off the exit ramp and head toward the RV park. Go southwest on Old Highway 85 and cross the Rio Puerco Bridge. A half mile past the bridge, turn right on County Road B12 and reset your odometer. Basically, aim northwest on the main road for the next 19 miles, following signs toward Riley and Magdalena. However, there are a few potentially confusing junctions: At 5.5 miles and 7.2 miles, bear right at the Y. Just after the junction at 19 miles, pull over and park on the roadside. The hike begins at the tip of the ridge on your left. See Description for a shuttle option.

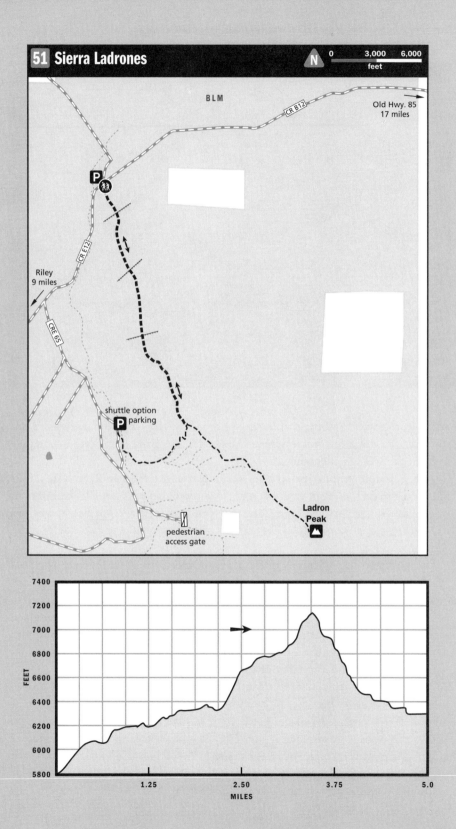

51 Sierra Ladrones

N

0   3,000   6,000
feet

BLM

CR B12

Old Hwy. 85
17 miles

P

CR E12

Riley
9 miles

CRE 65

shuttle option
P parking

Ladron
Peak

pedestrian
access gate

7400
7200
7000
6800
6600
6400
6200
6000
5800

FEET

1.25   2.50   3.75   5.0
MILES

white werewolves. Sightings of *brazas*—fireballs wheeling in the night—are not uncommon, and a few known meteor-impact sites in the area don't adequately explain the strange phenomenon.

The remote granite massif rises 4,500 feet above the Rio Puerco. It stands alone on a plain too prone to erosion to sustain reliable roads. A checkerboard of private ranchland further complicates the approach from the northeast, whereas its southeast quadrant falls in the strictly off-limits Sevilleta National Wildlife Refuge.

More than 45,300 acres in the Ladrones have been designated as a BLM Wilderness Study Area. The local wildlife population includes mule deer, black bear, mountain lion, and pronghorn. Desert bighorn sheep were reintroduced in 1992. Grasses and scrub sum up the vegetation on the lower slopes; ponderosa pine, aspen, and Douglas fir grow near the twin summits. The eastern summit, Ladron Peak, is the only named peak in the range, but the summit less than a half mile to its west is the taller of the two.

Looming on Albuquerque's southwest horizon, the range appears mono-lithic. Its complexity becomes more apparent up close. It has a longstanding rep-utation as one of the last places you'd want to hike alone. A local fireman who knows the peak well summed it up best: "It will kick your butt." An amateur mountaineer who recommended the route outlined below had used it to reach the top. He described the final ascent as a "class five scramble" through boulder fields and scree. A narrow stone scaffold between the twin summits allows for slim margins of error. "Don't try it in icy conditions" was the sage advice he offered from his hospital bed. Obligingly, I led a group up the ridge when the local forecast called for overcast skies and highs in the low 90s. A single cloud passed overhead that day, and temperatures hit 103 shortly after noon.

Don't let any of that deter you. Navigationally, this route is foolproof. You just follow a ridgeline from bottom to top or however far you want to go. Climbing becomes more difficult with distance. Each new mile begins with an incremental challenge. How far you get depends entirely on how hard you want to hike. Elevation enhances the views, of course, but you don't have to go far for wide-open vistas in all directions. So pack a lunch and plenty to drink. Above all, gringos, remember the sunscreen.

Start the hike at the side of the road by climbing south up the point of the ridge. Juniper, creosote, and cacti do their best to green the otherwise barren slopes. Limestone pavements keep the vegetation spread out, and narrow paths seem to show up wherever grasses take hold. Your only obstacles in the first 2 miles are a few barbed-wire fences, all easily crossed or circumvented.

The fence at 2 miles into the hike crosses near a peak (elevation 6,398'). It's a good spot for a quick breather because the climb is about to become somewhat more difficult. Now instead of marching directly up the backbone, you might find it easier to veer slightly to your right and aim for the saddle ahead. Once you reach that, angle back to your left for a short but steep push back up to the crest. A short rest on the 6,780-foot peak just ahead might be warranted as well.

The next mile skirts the edge of the sheer east-facing cliffs. The drop to your left is a good 300 feet in places. Your next challenge comes roughly 3.2 miles into the hike with a steep 0.25-mile push to the next peak (7,155'). From this vantage point, you should be able to make out the giant fir trees growing at the collar of Ladron Peak, in addition to the rows of enormous tiger-tooth rocks standing on its left shoulder. Also take a moment to scout out the trail ahead. The ridgeline bends to your left and assumes a relatively gentle temperament for the next 0.5 miles or so. But then, as you can see, the mountain reddens and becomes fiercely steep. That was my goal, but my group turned mutinous at the sight of it and refused to ascend the ridge any higher. In their defense, temperatures had hit 107, and our perch at 7,155' now seemed like a satisfactory accomplishment.

The shuttle option is a bit more complicated and shaves off a couple of miles at best, but it dispenses with the backtracking and varies the scenery for a more interesting hike. From the 19-mile junction, take two vehicles 1.7 miles southwest on CR 12. A junction here should be marked with a sign for Riley and another for CR E-65. Turn left, and go southeast for about 1 mile. At this point, the road bends south (right) to briefly parallel a prominent arroyo.

Continue another 0.6 miles, and turn left. In another 0.25 miles, the road returns to the arroyo and heads south again. It also gets narrow and rocky so pull over and park anywhere you can without blocking the road. If you have

Hikers negotiate the push from the saddle to the 6,780-foot peak.

a GPS unit, you might later find it useful to have taken a waypoint now. However, it's more helpful to know that all drainages on the west side of the ridge eventually lead to this arroyo. Take a moment to inspect it before leaving the vehicle so it'll seem familiar when you return this way.

From the ridge, just past the 7,155-foot peak, descend south about 300 yards, and then veer down toward the drainage on your right. Now just follow it downstream for about 1 mile. You might find walking easier on what appears to be traces of an old Jeep road near the right bank. Outside the drainage, vegetation remains fairly sparse so there's no need for bushwhacking.

The road leads into the drainage as it widens near the base. After you enter the main arroyo, climb out on the west side (your left), and turn right on the dirt road. If you parked near the second bend to the south, you'll find your car about 0.25 miles down the road.

CERRO MONTOSO  52

IN BRIEF

It's a steep climb up a lonely hill without trails, but the rewards are unmatched views of southern mountain ranges and a rare peek at inaccessible lands in the Sevilleta National Wildlife Refuge.

DESCRIPTION

The Los Pinos Mountains might be small, but don't take them lightly. They're like a scrappy little version of the Manzanos—shorter, yes, but steeper and more rugged. Colorado piñon and one-seed juniper are the dominant vegetation, with a diverse shrub component that includes scrub live oak and mountain mahogany, in addition to broom snakeweed, Apache plume, tree cholla, and banana yucca. And then there's the usual smattering of New Mexico thistle and globemallow. Bird species include bald eagle, peregrine falcon, red-tailed hawk, kestrel, and burrowing owl. Mule deer, desert bighorn sheep, pronghorn, mountain lion, and bear comprise the local animal life.

Directions

From I-25 south, take Exit 175 at Bernardo and go 20.2 miles east on US 60. (Note: NM 47 from Belen to US 60 is 10 miles shorter but adds at least as many minutes.) At Abó Pass, the road bends south. As it bends back to the east, look for an asphalt turnoff at the far end of the guardrail on the right. Take a sharp right there and go through the gate, being sure to latch it behind you. A county road sign ahead faintly spells out B115. Stay on the main dirt road, driving south 2 miles. Park on the side of the road, leaving enough room for other vehicles to pass. The hike begins about 50 yards farther down, at a sandy wash as wide as the road itself.

KEY AT-A-GLANCE INFORMATION

LENGTH: 5.2-mile out-and-back

DIFFICULTY: Moderate to strenuous

SCENERY: Piñon–juniper hills, panoramic mountain views, marine fossils

EXPOSURE: Some canyon and forest shade

TRAIL TRAFFIC: Low

SHARED USE: Low (equestrians, livestock)

TRAIL SURFACE: Sandy washes, rocky hills

HIKING TIME: 3 hours

DRIVING DISTANCE: 74 miles (one way) from the I-40 and I-25 exchange

ACCESS: Year-round

LAND STATUS: BLM–Socorro Field Office

MAPS: USGS Cerro Montoso

FACILITIES: None

LAST CHANCE FOOD/GAS: All services in Belen

SPECIAL COMMENTS: Despite obvious landmarks, navigating the return route can get tricky in places. A compass is helpful. A GPS unit with tracking features is optimal.

- -

GPS Trailhead Coordinates

UTM Zone (WGS 84) 13S

Easting 0360093

Northing 3805218

Latitude 34° 22' 44"

Longitude 106° 31' 18"

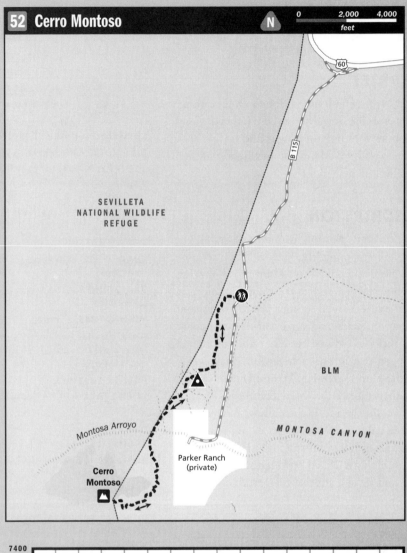

52 Cerro Montoso

N

0   2,000   4,000
feet

SEVILLETA
NATIONAL WILDLIFE
REFUGE

B 115

60

BLM

MONTOSA CANYON

Montosa Arroyo

Parker Ranch
(private)

Cerro
Montoso

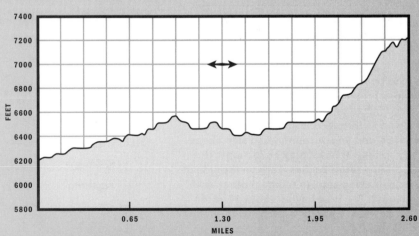

The view from Cerro Montoso

Largely absent from this otherwise familiar landscape: people.

The oft-overlooked mountains are the last in a line of uplifted fault blocks that make up the Sandia, Manzanita, and Manzano ranges. Nearly the entire Los Pinos range falls within the boundaries of Sevilleta National Wildlife Refuge, a 228,000-acre research area that's largely off-limits to the public. Only the eastern foothills extend into public land. Oddly enough, one foothill ranks among the range's highest peaks. At 7,259 feet, Cerro Montoso ("wooded hill") stands just 271 feet short of the pinnacle of Whiteface Mountain.

There are no trails leading to or up Cerro Montoso, at least not on this side of it. Most of the hill stands behind the Sevilleta fence line, ruling out access from the west. The approach is further complicated by private-ranch boundaries on its northeastern side. Fortunately, a strip of public land between the refuge and the ranch creates an access corridor from the north.

Begin the hike by walking south along the road to the sandy wash. Turn right, and head west into a small canyon. About 200 yards upstream, the wash turns to the south. Continue along the streambed another half mile or so to a major Y. At this point, you're at the southern end of a narrow basin, and the easiest way out is over a saddle on the ridge to the southwest. To get there from the Y, follow the drain on the right about 200 yards to a point where it narrows and gets thick with trees. Cross to the left bank, and continue south–southwest toward the saddle. You'll cross a deep cut about halfway to the ridge. (Pay attention to features like this or you'll end up in the wrong drain on your way back. Also be aware that large specimens of Western diamondback have been known to reside in rodent burrows near drainages.)

Take a moment on the ridge to get oriented. The first thing you might notice is the enviable estate of the Parker Ranch, situated in the valley below. To its immediate southwest is Cerro Montoso. A clear-cut boundary line neatly bisects the steep wooded hill, giving it the appearance of a zippered hood. Resurveying, fencing, and sign postings in 2006 leave little doubt as to where the Sevilleta boundaries lie. If you don't have a compass, it helps to know that the section of fence visible from here runs southwest–northeast.

Also take a moment to visualize the hike ahead: For the descent into the valley, you'll angle to the right to squeeze between the Parker Ranch and the Sevilleta fence. For the ascent, veer left to climb up the hill's eastern shoulder. Note the dense vegetation in what might be called the clavicle area. Steer wide to the left to avoid getting snagged in thick juniper. From the shoulder, it's a short walk to the top.

Now that you've got the route in your head, it's time to put it under your feet. Start downhill, stepping over veins and outcroppings of glistening white quartz. You'll soon encounter two to four narrow cuts, depending on whether you cross upstream or downstream of the nearby forks. Maintain an angle to the right, and you should be within reach of the boundary fence shortly after crossing the cuts. Follow the fence over two low ridges (more like humps, really) to find a wide, sandy wash on the far side of each one.

The ascent of Cerro Montoso begins from the second wash, which shows up on some maps as Montosa Canyon. At this point, you're about 1.5 miles into the hike. Begin veering away from the fence, aiming roughly south for just under 0.5 miles. The idea on this segment is to cross two humps at the base of the hill before turning in for the steep ascent. If you turn uphill too soon, you'll end up in one of two difficult ravines, both of which lead into the thickly wooded clavicle area.

On the steep mid to upper slopes, limestone outcroppings and scree are loaded with marine fossils. Widespread imprints of bivalve and nautilus shells range in size from fingernails to silver dollars. The BLM does not discourage visitors from picking up common fossils, but you might want to wait until you're heading back downhill before filling your pockets with rocks.

As the grade lessens, start aiming for the peak. The true summit, Parker Peak, is about 150 feet west of the fence, but you can still legally squeak above the 7,200-foot contour line and peer into the Sevilleta. Somewhere down there, researchers might be coaching Mexican gray wolves for release into the wild, discovering a cure for plague in Gunnison's prairie dogs, or analyzing trophic cascades among banner-tailed kangaroo rats. The scientific possibilities are as broad as the land itself.

Views to the north and east include the Manzano and Gallinas mountains, respectively. These two ranges comprise the Mountainair Ranger District of Cibola National Forest. Fewer than 50 miles to the south, Oscura ("dark") Peak stands at 8,732 feet. The Trinity Site, ground zero for the first atomic bomb, lies 2.75 miles to the west of it. Had you been standing here on Cerro Montoso at dawn on July 16, 1945, you would've seen a mushroom cloud reaching six times higher than the rise of Oscura Peak.

To return to the car, bolder hikers bent on creating a loop might try circling around the eastern side of the ranch. I haven't tried it, but I expect such a route

would easily double the length of the overall hike, with a 100-foot-deep canyon to cross midway. Otherwise, follow the directions in reverse, and keep count of the drainages. One that's easy to forget is the first cut *after* overlook ridge. Make sure you cross it before you start following any washes back out. Otherwise you'll likely end up in a wash that leads toward the Parker Ranch. On the plus side, you can't get too lost. All drainages eventually flow to the road, B115, so a wrong turn would add no more than 2 miles to the overall hike.

NEARBY ACTIVITIES

Abó Ruins–Salinas Pueblo Missions National Monument: The unique buttressed walls of the Franciscan mission church of San Gregorio de Abó still dominate the Tompiro Pueblo of Abó. To visit this remarkable site, return to US 60, turn right, and drive 8 miles east. Turn left on NM 513, and go 0.5 miles north. Open daily from 9 a.m to 6 p.m., Memorial Day through Labor Day, and from 9 a.m. to 5 p.m. the rest of the year. (505) 847-2400; **www.nps.gov/sapu.**

53 SEVILLETA NATIONAL WILDLIFE REFUGE

KEY AT-A-GLANCE INFORMATION

LENGTH: 7-mile out-and-back; shorter and longer options

DIFFICULTY: Easy

SCENERY: Birds and wildlife along irrigation canals and wetlands

EXPOSURE: Mostly sunny

TRAIL TRAFFIC: Low

SHARED USE: Moderate (dogs must be leashed, mountain bikes, equestrians, motor vehicles)

TRAIL SURFACE: Dirt and gravel roads

HIKING TIME: 2–3 hours

DRIVING DISTANCE: 60 miles (one way) from the I-40/I-25 exchange

ACCESS: Year-round, 1 hour before sunrise to 1 hour past sunset

LAND STATUS: U.S. Fish & Wildlife, NM Department of Fish & Game

MAPS: Brochure map at visitor center; Sevilleta NWR Hunting Areas; USGS La Joya

FACILITIES: Interpretive exhibits, restrooms, water at visitor center, limited wheelchair accessibility in Unit A

LAST CHANCE FOOD/GAS: All services at Exit 191 in Belen, 26 miles from the trailhead

SPECIAL COMMENTS: See longer note at the end of the Description.

- -

GPS Trailhead Coordinates

UTM Zone (WGS 84) 13S

Easting   0329578

Northing   3797509

Latitude   34° 18' 17"

Longitude   106° 51' 07"

IN BRIEF

An overlooked jewel in the south, Sevilleta National Wildlife Refuge contains miles of seldom-traveled dirt roads that meander along an irrigation ditch between the BNSF Railroad and the Rio Grande. Even in the height of winter migrations, most birders bypass the wetlands here for the Bosque del Apache Wildlife Refuge farther south, allowing for secluded walks and bicycle rides most of the year.

DESCRIPTION

The refuge gets its name from a military post established nearby in the 16th century. "New Seville" was later included in the Sevilleta de la

- -

Directions ⟶

From I-25 south, take Exit 169. At the bottom of the off ramp, pull a U-turn around the fence to the right and proceed 0.4 miles, following signs to the Sevilleta NWR Visitor Center.

A brochure at the visitor center details directions for the 4-mile drive to Unit A. If the center is not open when you arrive, look for the brochure in the Plexiglas box to the left of the front entry. If it's empty, head to Unit A by driving back down toward I-25 and through the underpass. Immediately after the northbound off ramp, reset your odometer and turn right. Drive south 0.4 miles. The road curves east and becomes dirt. Area regulations are posted ahead at 0.7 miles. Continue straight east to a T-junction at 1.2 miles. Turn right and go south to a junction at 2.3 miles. Turn left, using caution on the steep crossing at the railroad tracks, and go to the junction at 2.4 miles. Take the first right and drive south along the west side of the ditch. The parking area is on the right at 4.0 miles. The sign there reads: "No parking for next mile." About 200 yards beyond that is a parking area for physically challenged hunters.

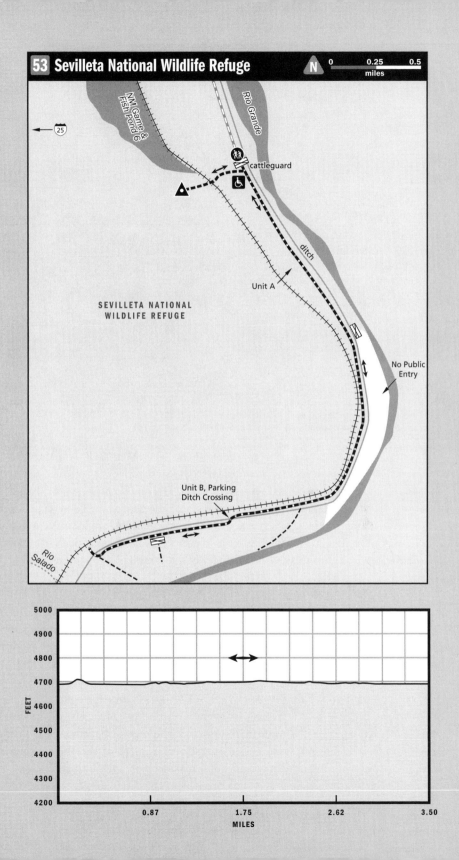

53 **Sevilleta National Wildlife Refuge**

N   0   0.25   0.5
        miles

NM Game &
Fish Pond 6

Rio Grande

25

cattleguard

SEVILLETA NATIONAL
WILDLIFE REFUGE

ditch

Unit A

No Public
Entry

Unit B, Parking
Ditch Crossing

Rio
Salado

5000
4900
4800
4700
4600
4500
4400
4300
4200

FEET

0.87   1.75   2.62   3.50
                    MILES

A shy slider in Unit A's seasonally dry Cornerstone Marsh

Joya Land Grant, awarded by the governor of the New Mexico Province to the community of Sevilleta in 1819. A century later, the State of New Mexico accepted the land from the community heirs in lieu of taxes. The land later served a 30-year stint as the Campbell Ranch before achieving national refuge status in 1973.

Several major biotic zones meet within Sevilleta NWR, including conifer woodland, Colorado Plateau shrub steppe, and Great Plains grassland. This hike skirts a bosque riparian forest within a finger of Chihuahuan desert that extends north to Albuquerque.

Sevilleta National Wildlife Refuge is managed primarily for the study of natural processes such as flood and fire, but it is perhaps best known for its role in the Mexican Gray Wolf Reintroduction Program. Aside from special tours and guided hikes offered one to three times a year, most of the 360-square-mile ecological research facility is strictly off-limits. However, two areas in the heart of the refuge remain open to the general public. Add to those the adjacent La Joya Waterfowl Area, and you have about 4,000 acres where you're usually free to roam.

Start the hike by walking south from the first parking area. Cross a cattle guard, and turn right on the old dirt road before the second parking area; this is the entrance to Unit A Corner Stone Marsh. As in most of the Rio Grande floodplain, water here is controlled through a system of irrigation ditches, or acequias. Wheel valves, such as the one that bridges the ditch ahead, are opened in the late fall, creating ponds for a variety of waterfowl and shorebirds, including pintails, herons, pelicans, and sandpipers. In all, 225 species of birds have been sighted in the refuge. The ponds are drained in January, allowing weedy fields to overtake the wetlands for the remainder of the year. Pronghorn, elk, bighorn sheep, bobcat, and mountain lion are known to frequent the area.

Continuing along the road as it bends left, you'll find the Unit A boundary ends at the railroad tracks. Walk across the tracks and into the La Joya Waterfowl Area. Just before a triangle barrier gate, a path to the left leads up a hill. It's a short climb, but as the highest point in the hike, it offers the only overlook of the area. You'll also get a great view of the BNSF as it comes around the bend and thunders down the tracks below.

Beyond the gate, the road tends to get choked with pigweed as it continues between a ditch full of cattails on the right and a series of ponds on the left, which are also subject to seasonal flooding.

When you're done with La Joya, cross back through Unit A, and turn right on the main road. (Or, if pressed for time, you can drive to the next parking area.) From here the way is pretty straightforward. The ditch is on the left; thick vegetation is on the right.

Though beautiful, particularly when blazing autumnal colors, tamarisk releases salt into the soil, killing off native plants. Many attempts to rid it from Sevilleta have failed, but one program launched in the spring of 2006 shows promise. Armed with chainsaws and herbicides, inmate work crews from the Central New Mexico Correction Facility managed to eradicate the tree from two acres of Unit A in as many months.

Unit B begins just over 2 miles downstream from the Unit A parking area. The road bends west before widening into a gravel lot. You'll find a low railroad trestle on the north side and a parking area on the south. It's also your first opportunity on this hike to cross the ditch. (Driving on either side south of this point can get a bit dicey due to bad road conditions.)

On the east side, two roads run parallel to the ditch. If you want to wander down to the Rio Grande, see the map for access trails. Whether they're open or closed depends on the nesting whims of certain protected species. Roadside signage tends to be both current and clear on the matter of places you can't go.

The road ends at a wire fence about 0.8 miles past the Unit B parking area. Beyond the fence is the Rio Salado ("salty river"). Its shallow bed spans more than 600 feet and is usually dust dry. In this barren expanse the only exceptional feature is the old iron railroad bridge, which creates a stunning image when cast in silhouette against a Technicolor sunset.

Note: Access varies by season. Call Sevilleta NWR for details on Units A and B, (505) 864-4021. Call the New Mexico Department of Fish & Game Albuquerque office for details on the La Joya Waterfowl Area, (505) 222-4700. Birders can get a comprehensive checklist from the visitor center. Also, Sheryl Mayfield's *Sevilleta National Wildlife Refuge Field Guide to Flowers,* an outstanding primer on local plant life, is available as a free download from **www .fws.gov/southwest/refuges/newmex/sevilleta/ecosystem.**

54 SAN LORENZO CANYON

KEY AT-A-GLANCE INFORMATION

LENGTH: 4-mile out-and-back
DIFFICULTY: Easy, with moderate to severe options
SCENERY: Sandstone canyon, slots, caves, hoodoos, springs
EXPOSURE: Some canyon shade
TRAIL TRAFFIC: Moderate
SHARED USE: Moderate (livestock; equestrians; stagecoaches, motor vehicles permitted in lower canyon)
TRAIL SURFACE: Sand, rock
HIKING TIME: 2–4 hours
DRIVING DISTANCE: 70 miles (one way) from the I-40/I-25 exchange
ACCESS: Year-round
LAND STATUS: BLM–Socorro Field Office; Sevilleta National Wildlife Refuge
MAPS: USGS Lemitar, San Lorenzo Spring
FACILITIES: None
LAST CHANCE FOOD/GAS: Exit 191 in Belen, 36 miles from the trailhead
SPECIAL COMMENTS: Depending on recent weather conditions, a 4WD vehicle with high clearance may be necessary for the last 2 miles of the approach to the canyon. Do not attempt to drive the arroyo when heavy rains are expected. For local conditions and other info, contact the BLM Socorro Field Office at (505) 835-0412, or online at www.nm.blm.gov.

GPS Trailhead Coordinates

UTM Zone (WGS 84) 13S
Easting 0316662
Northing 3790987
Latitude 34° 14' 38"
Longitude 106° 59' 27"

IN BRIEF

Here's the challenge: hike 2 miles of San Lorenzo Canyon without getting lured into any caves, slots, or scrambles to the rim. To accomplish such a task would require a dead-ened sense of natural curiosity or perhaps the unwavering determination of San Lorenzo himself (Saint Lawrence to the Anglos).

DESCRIPTION

First, if you managed the drive to the mouth of the canyon, you may notice that the road continues around the bend. In fact, the road ends in a box about 1 mile up. Sure you could drive to it, but then you'd be a nuisance to those here for the canyon's serenity—and besides, you'd miss the best details.

San Lorenzo Canyon thrives with life typical of Chihuahuan desert: fourwing salt-bush, rabbitbrush, yucca, tree cholla, and prickly pear cacti. In the warmer months, col-lared lizards run amok—on their hind legs, when frightened. Cattle sometimes saunter

Directions ⟶

From I-25 south, take Exit 163 at San Acacia. Turn left, cross over the interstate, then turn right and go 2.3 miles south on the frontage road. Turn right onto C94, or B90 on some maps. (Either way, it's unmarked, so just turn right before a small trailer park and drive through a narrow underpass.) When the pavement ends, keep on the main dirt road that goes west. When in doubt as to which is the main road, bear right. Sooner or later you'll end up in the arroyo. Follow the tire tracks in the sand to the mouth of the canyon. The shortest drive from the underpass to the mouth is 4.4 miles. The "official" route is 4.7 miles. Park on the left side of the arroyo and walk into the canyon.

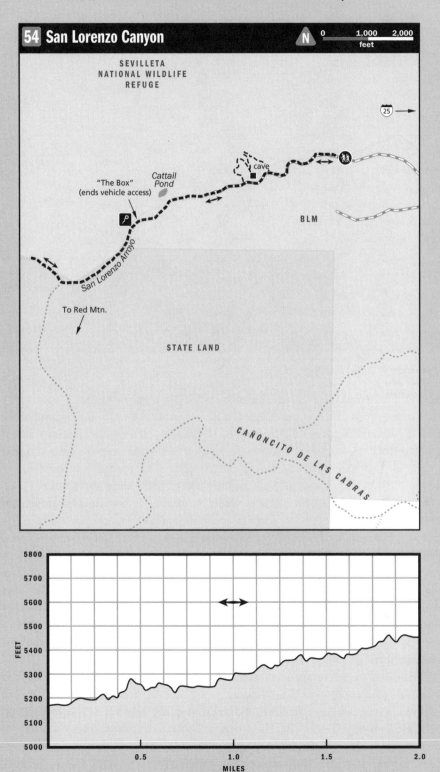

54 San Lorenzo Canyon

N   0   1,000   2,000
feet

SEVILLETA
NATIONAL WILDLIFE
REFUGE

25

cave

Cattail
Pond

"The Box"
(ends vehicle access)

San Lorenzo Arroyo

BLM

To Red Mtn.

STATE LAND

CAÑONCITO DE LAS CABRAS

Formations in the lower canyon

up to the box and stare in bewilderment at the apparent dead end.

The canyon also contains arches, pillars, springs, caves, hoodoos, and other classic Western features. It's the kind of landscape you'd expect to see in an old cowboy flick. A stagecoach would fit right in with the scenery, and you just might see one careening around an outcropping. The road is a favorite haunt of the New Mexico Carriage Club and the Rio Grande Mule and Donkey Association. (You can find their event schedules online at **www.nmcaequine.com** and **www.rgmda.com**.) Both seem to favor the coldest months for rides in the canyon. Lorenzo, or Lawrence of Rome, achieved martyrdom by roasting on a gridiron. Summertime in his canyon can feel the same way.

Aside from the obvious route up the throat of the main canyon, there are many side canyons, slots, niches, and crevices begging for exploration. Possible detours are too numerous to list, so my best advice is this: hike the route as outlined below and explore the most alluring side options on your return. If you start by wandering into every crevice that catches your eye, you'll never make it halfway through this hike.

Some detours are apparent before entering the canyon. If you can't resist wandering off in another direction, be aware that the fenced land to the north is closed to the public. (For more about that area, see hike 53, Sevilleta National Wildlife Refuge.) Technically, the refuge boundary runs down the center of the arroyo, but the entire canyon is open to the public. Also, while the area directly south of San Lorenzo Canyon is popular with hikers, most of it is state land, with some leased parcels. "No trespassing" signs are rare but should be observed when encountered.

Start hiking up the canyon. Sculpted formations are nearby and impossible to miss. Look closely for the small details as well. For example, the canyon walls seem to be leaking in places. The water source isn't exactly certain, but a few plump cottonwoods farther up the canyon suggest it was more plentiful in past years.

The largest of the shelter caves shows up on the right about 0.5 miles into the hike. One potential side hike involves scrambling up through a narrow passage on the west side of the cave and traversing the cliff above it to a point on the outcropping on the east side. After enjoying the view from there, head for the back of the alcove farther east and choose carefully among a number of steep ways down. This roughly M-shaped detour, noted on the map, requires modest climbing abilities.

Note: In 2007 a university student on a stargazing hike slipped off a cliff and fell to his death. The BLM now discourages climbing on the cliffs because of their loose composition.

About 300 yards past the cave is the first of the aforementioned cottonwoods. From here the canyon widens as steep cliff walls fall away from the road. Look toward the back of a clearing that opens on the right—a white crescent appears on a rock wall. The mysterious marking, clearly visible from 500 feet away, seems to point to a cattail pond. A ranch that once stood nearby has since collapsed and vanished beneath thick tangles of creosote. The white mark will soon follow, one hopes, as it is apparently the handiwork of modern idiots with a surplus of enamel paint.

At 1 mile into the hike, the canyon narrows again and seems to end in a box. Algae-laden water trickles from the rock only to vanish into the sand. A second spring is just around the corner, next to a cave about the size of a broom closet. This cave has a kind of sunroof but remains sufficiently dark to hide a recess big enough to crawl through. No telling how far back it goes because it's soaking wet inside and the smell is horrendous.

Climb over the boulders on the left side of the box at the lowest point and follow the emerald spring. The narrow canyon soon opens to a wide, sandy wash. The upper canyon ahead is chock-full of grand features similar to those in the first half, but here's where the small details get fascinating. Look closely at the porous basalt boulders, particularly those that have tumbled away from the canyon walls on the right side. At first glance, some appear as though caught in the crossfire of a multicolored paintball battle. These red, white, and green splotches are agate veins that have filled joints and other types of pore spaces in the basalt. Fine-crystalline forms of silica (quartz) mixed with various impurities show up in striking colors. Iron and copper impurities, for example, produce green colorations. Although it's obvious that amateur rock hounds have chipped away their own souvenirs, much still remains for other visitors to enjoy.

Continue following the spring's sinuous route. At 1.4 miles into the hike,

the canyon takes a right. A prominent arroyo opens up just past the outer corner of the turn. It flows from Red Mountain, about a 2.5-mile hike to the south, but it contains several steep pour-offs, some about 30 feet high. Proceed with caution if you venture up in that direction.

About 0.5 miles past the big arroyo opening on the left, a downed boundary fence marks the official turnaround point for this hike—or so I'm told. In truth, I never made it that far. My personal best for resisting diversions along the way currently stands at 1.5 miles—considerably better than past efforts that fell short of the box.

NEARBY ACTIVITIES

Cañoncito de las Cabras ("little canyon of the goats") runs roughly parallel to lower San Lorenzo Canyon, about 1 mile to the south. It's possible to cut across higher ground, visiting homestead ruins along the way. But it's easier to drive back down C94 to the underpass, turn around, and then drive back up again, this time veering to the left after 2 miles.

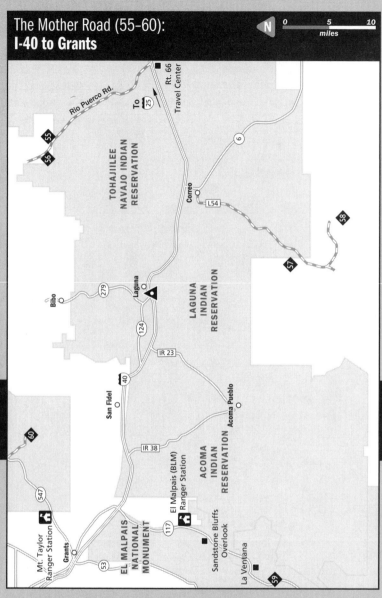

THE MOTHER ROAD

55 HERRERA: Oh My God

KEY AT-A-GLANCE INFORMATION

LENGTH: 6.3-mile balloon

DIFFICULTY: Easy to moderate

SCENERY: Sculpted sandstone domes, bluffs, dunes, slot canyon

EXPOSURE: Mostly sunny

TRAIL TRAFFIC: Low

SHARED USE: Low (livestock; equestrians, mountain bikes; motorized vehicles)

TRAIL SURFACE: Rugged dirt roads, sand, rock

HIKING TIME: 2–3 hours

DRIVING DISTANCE: 33 miles (one way) from the I-40 and I-25 exchange

ACCESS: Year-round

LAND STATUS: BLM–Rio Puerco Field Office

MAPS: USGS Herrera

FACILITIES: None

LAST CHANCE FOOD/GAS: All services are available at the Route 66 Travel Center at Exit 140, on the south side. (See Herrera Mesa, hike 56.)

SPECIAL COMMENTS: It's a rough dirt road, but most cars can handle the 14.5-mile stretch between Exit 140 and the gate if they take it slowly.

GPS Trailhead Coordinates

UTM Zone (WGS 84) 13S

Easting   0310070

Northing   3896104

Latitude   35° 11' 24"

Longitude   107° 05' 10"

IN BRIEF

Navigate arroyos and abandoned dirt roads to explore a seldom-visited landscape tucked between the Navajo and Laguna reservations. This hike takes you to one corner full of mystical formations, but plenty more await rediscovery by those prepared to wander.

DESCRIPTION

If you think the road coming out here was rough, try driving beyond the gate. On second thought—don't. Only in the broadest sense of the word do these rutted imprints qualify as "roads." A few years ago, Southwest Off-Road Enterprises used them for an annual dirt-bike rally called the Oh My God 100. Oddly, contenders didn't find the course challenging enough, so SORE moved the rally to a locale near Cuba, New Mexico.

Today, few surviving roads overlap their designated lines on the old racecourse maps. Many seem to be transient apparitions, prone to vanishing and reappearing elsewhere. The road running north from the windmill is an example: It was there the first time I passed. A few hours later, it was gone.

Aside from the near-complete disintegration of the old racecourse, very little has

Directions

From I-40 west, take Exit 140 and follow the frontage road 0.6 miles. Turn right at the intersection ahead to go northwest on Rio Puerco Road (CR 334). After 14.5 miles on this rugged dirt road, cross a cattle guard and pull off to the right where the road bends to the left. Don't block the road or the gate entrance on the right. Driving beyond the gate is allowed but not recommended for most vehicles.

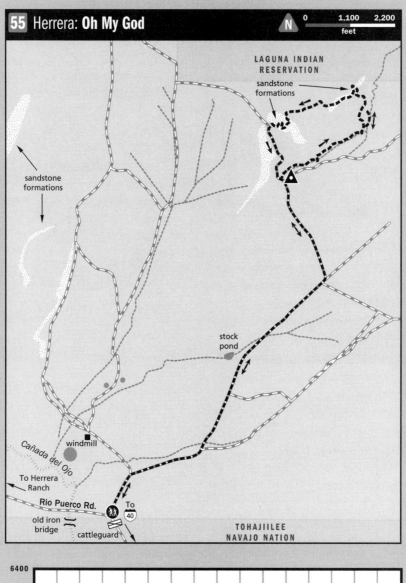

N

0   1,100   2,200
feet

LAGUNA INDIAN
RESERVATION

sandstone
formations

sandstone
formations

stock
pond

windmill

Cañada del Ojo

To Herrera
Ranch

Rio Puerco Rd.

To
40

old iron
bridge

cattleguard

**T O H A J I I L E E
N A V A J O   N A T I O N**

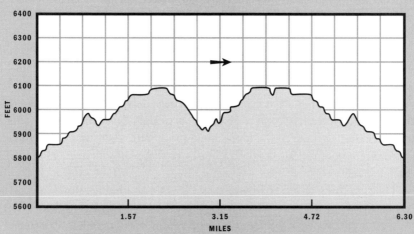

6400						
6300						
6200			→			
6100						
6000						
5900						
5800						
5700						
5600						

FEET

1.57   3.15   4.72   6.30
MILES

since happened on this land, which is why those who know of it (and few do) still refer to it as the Oh My God. The name seems most appropriate. It's also known as T–11, in reference to its township, but that doesn't quite capture the magnificence of the place.

The southeastern corner of the OMG drops off into spectacular badlands. In 2004, claimholders planned to mine it for humate, a kind of Jurassic compost that makes an environmentally sound alternative to chemical fertilizers. However, their focus seems to have shifted to uranium interests elsewhere, and the OMG has remained quiet. If you do happen to find a freshly bladed road running east from the gate, that probably means the humate operations are up and running. Aside from the possibility of extra traffic at the gate, it shouldn't affect this hike, which loops around formations to the northeast.

The road to the loop, as described below, is neither the shortest nor the most scenic—it merely follows the most reliable track. Start from the drop gate—be sure to latch it behind you—and head northwest along the road. At the first Y, less than 0.25 miles ahead, bear right. Alternately, those with an unerring sense of direction can attempt to maintain a straight line for a slightly shorter and more colorful route to the loop, while those with a GPS unit can wander at their leisure and report at their convenience to these coordinates: N35° 12' 43"; W107° 04' 16".

Those sticking to the road will pass a stock pond hidden down on the left at the end of the first mile. From there the road bends slightly right. Follow it another 0.6 miles to a well-defined junction, where you'll turn left. Continue 0.5

miles to another junction. The road to the right follows a cliff line. Go straight past it, heading downhill to an overlook for a preview of the loop ahead.

The loop starts at the base of the cliff at its lowest point. Turn right off the road, and follow the arroyo eastward. At first glance it seems perilously littered with broken glass. These frosty shards are acicular gypsum crystals. No point in collecting them; they'll just crumble in your pockets. But try this scientific demonstration: expose a piece to a flame. The crystal turns opaque white as it loses moisture. Now it is essentially a fragment of drywall.

As you continue downstream, the cliffs on your right don't rise higher so much as the arroyo runs deeper. Evidence of churning floodwaters reveals itself as washtub-sized potholes in the exposed bedrock. About 0.5 miles from the road, the arroyo drops away in a dry waterfall. It's not too difficult to climb down here, but you'll find an easier way down from the bank ahead. Angle down to the streambed, and continue another 200 feet or so, until you see a narrow canyon merging from the left. Follow it upstream to an impressive little slot canyon.

Those with limited climbing abilities might need a boost to get into the slot—and more importantly, a trusted spotter to help them down later. The reward for the effort is a brief passage between sinuously sculpted walls, some just barely shoulder-width apart. You can explore the slot from end to end in less than ten minutes, but allow more time to appreciate the details. Evidence of past visitors appears on the walls as black smudges from campfire smoke, and as cattle brands etched into the sandstone. Look for an "H" with curly serifs and a lazy pitchfork. (Incidentally, flash-flooding hazards make slot canyons unwise spots to pitch your camp.)

Climbing out of the back end of the canyon is difficult and potentially dangerous. Instead, return to the arroyo, and climb out at the point through which you came in. Once on the upper bank, head north, passing the back end of the slot on your right. About 200 yards ahead you'll see the first of many spectacular sandstone formations, namely big cliffs, small caves, and various hoodoos. In early spring, snake tracks follow mouse prints over a sugary dune. Nearby domes appear to be constructed from the hides of white elephants. Other formations take the shape of giant monteras, chupacabras, and other oddities.

The main road is less than 0.5 miles west of the easternmost formations, so your best strategy for exploring this amazing terrain is to meander predominantly in that direction. Steep cliffs and the Laguna boundary fence should keep you from straying too far off course. Once you reach the road, turn left, and follow it south about 0.3 miles to close the loop—or wander off the west side of the road to explore more formations. When you get back to the junction with the cliff-line road, continue south–southeast to return to the gate by the way you came. Or if you're feeling adventurous, try exploring roads and arroyos farther west. A word of caution: there are far more of them on site than I could fit on a map, so keep your bearings. A GPS unit wouldn't hurt either.

56   HERRERA MESA

KEY AT-A-GLANCE INFORMATION

LENGTH: 3-mile out-and-back; 4 miles if walking from the main road
DIFFICULTY: Moderate
SCENERY: Jurassic rock formations, grasslands, homestead ruins, views
EXPOSURE: Mostly sunny, though shaded by mid-afternoon
TRAIL TRAFFIC: Low
SHARED USE: Low (livestock, equestrians, mountain bikes; closed to all motorized vehicles)
TRAIL SURFACE: Rugged dirt roads, sand, loose rock
HIKING TIME: 2 hours
DRIVING DISTANCE: 36 miles (one way) from the I-40/I-25 exchange
ACCESS: Year-round
LAND STATUS: BLM—Rio Puerco Field Office
MAPS: USGS Herrera
FACILITIES: None
LAST CHANCE FOOD/GAS: All services available at the Route 66 Travel Center at Exit 140, south side
SPECIAL COMMENTS: Most cars can handle the 15-mile stretch of corrugated dirt road between Exit 140 and the junction of Route 54. An alternate route running north from Exit 131 is about 9 miles longer and would require a detailed road map but is said to be a smoother, more scenic ride.

GPS Trailhead
Coordinates

UTM Zone (WGS 84) 13S
Easting   0307260
Northing   3896153
Latitude   35° 11' 56"
Longitude   107° 07' 02"

IN BRIEF

Near a lonely corner of the Tohajiilee Navajo Reservation, a forgotten trail scraped into rocky ledges presents one of the few routes to the upper tiers of Herrera Mesa. Views along the way overlook equally impressive mesas, outcrops, and canyons.

DESCRIPTION

The road you took out here is usually devoid of traffic, but that could change. It continues on to several uranium sites, including a mining town developed by the notorious Kerr-McGee Company. Completed just in time for the uranium bust, it has drawn more vandals than miners. But with uranium prices on the rise since the new millennium, traffic along this road could get busy soon.

The uranium prospector Rod Peterson came to Herrera Mesa in the 1960s. His search

----

Directions

From I-40 west, take Exit 140 and follow the frontage road 0.6 miles. Turn right on Rio Puerco Road (CR 334). Stay on this main road northwest 14.5 miles, then cross a cattle guard and follow a bend to the left. Continue another mile to the next junction. (Route 54, unsigned, merges from the south.) Bear right and drive northwest 0.9 miles. Look for a dirt road on the left. (If you pass through a wire fence, you've gone about 50 yards too far.) Park nearby, being sure not to block either road. Alternately, you can drive on the dirt road, but be aware that it gets bumpy and there's room enough ahead to park only one vehicle. Follow it as it crosses a shadow road and curves around to the south. After 0.4 miles, it reaches a T-junction. A green gate blocks the road on the right and a dirt barrier blocks the shadow road on the left. Pull up to the barrier and park there. The hike begins at the gate.

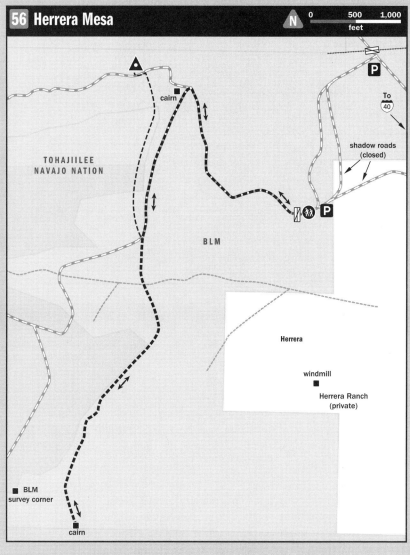

N

| 0 | 500 | 1,000 |

feet

TOHAJIILEE
NAVAJO NATION

cairn

BLM

shadow roads
(closed)

To
40

Herrera

windmill

Herrera Ranch
(private)

BLM
survey corner

cairn

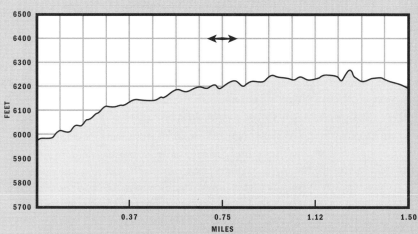

6500
6400
6300
6200
6100
6000
5900
5800
5700

FEET

0.37   0.75   1.12   1.50

MILES

The remains of an iron bridge point to Herrera Mesa.

led him to a quarry of dinosaur bones, which contain uranium. Since then, well over 100 bones have been pulled from the site, including several from a large tyrannosaur and some from an allosaurus; additionally, the partial skeleton of a 40-foot sauropod has been uncovered.

The Peterson Quarry is New Mexico's first Morrison Formation dinosaur-bone bed and likely the state's most prolific source of Jurassic material. Excavations are expected to continue through 2010 or until the last bone is unearthed. Volunteers trained by the New Mexico Museum of Natural History assist in the digs, and increasing public interest has the BLM evaluating the potential for site tours.

In the meantime, preservation efforts include discouraging people from visiting. It seems that excavation and collection by amateur boneheads elsewhere have ruined a considerable volume of scientific research and resources. Fossils without contextual data have no value, yet people still collect them. Though the bones at the Peterson Quarry are too big to steal, all it takes to destroy potentially significant remains is one souvenir hunter with a garden spade and a pathological affection for *Jurassic Park*. Maybe he'll score a bone fragment or a rock that looks like one. And then maybe he'll find an agitated mob of paleontologists armed with shovels and picks. In these rugged and remote lands, Nature has a way of striking a balance.

To summarize: avoid the quarry until the BLM says it's ready for visitors.

Most of the approximately 12-square-mile Herrera Mesa stands on Navajo land. Formerly known as the Cañoncito, the Tohajiilee is one of three Navajo bands outside the Big Rez farther west. Their reclaimed name translates to "water dippers," referring to their ancestors' renowned survival strategy of harvesting water from catch basins in the rocks.

The ranch at the base of Herrera Mesa is privately owned and remains active. Even though the house and barn evoke a sense of hopeless abandonment, and ruts and cacti have rendered their long driveway impassible, the corrals and stock tanks are still in good use. Herrera Ranch boundaries aren't always apparent on the ground, but for a general idea, the shadow road mentioned earlier is on the ranch, whereas the corrected route to the gate is on public land.

Herrera Mesa displays the distinctive banding of the Morrison Formation, a group of sedimentary rock layers of the late Jurassic (161–145 million years ago). From a distance, the eastern face appears as an insurmountable wall. Closer inspection reveals that the wall is stepped. Think of it somewhat like a tiered cake. Old trails follow the edge of each tier, each leading to a point where you can easily walk up to the next level.

Information about these old roads is scant. They may have started as Indian trails, later used by ranchers leading livestock to mesa-top pastures, and perhaps still later enhanced by uranium prospectors. All that's certain is that someone put a tremendous amount of effort into clearing rocks and stacking them into walls to create a semblance of roads that don't seem to lead to anything but wonderful views.

The hike begins at the gate. In contrast to the ledge trails, the road from the BLM gate is clearly defined. Follow it uphill for less than 0.5 miles to a fireplug-sized cairn on the left. But before making the turn onto an ill-defined trail, consider staying on the main road another 200 yards or so. As the road begins to curve around an outcrop and lead into a wide canyon, fantastic vistas open up to the north. Unusual formations in the valley below might be described (albeit inadequately) as a series of small mesas tilted at a 45-degree angle. Also just around the bend, a steep, faded path starts on the left and follows a ledge above the trail that begins at the cairn. The two run parallel for about 0.25 miles before the lower trail rises to merge with the high one. Keep it in mind as an option on the return route.

Now go back to the cairn and head south up the old trail. It may be little more than a slight indentation, but it becomes clearer as its rock edges stack up higher and it gradually climbs to the next tier. After 0.25 miles or so, the decrepit remains of a wire fence lean over the trail. The equally antiquated ruins on Herrera Ranch can be seen far below to the left. At this point, you have little choice but to step up to the next level. A short climb to the right puts you in a sunken portion of the mesa top, a kind of triangular cove. The walls ahead and on your right delineate the boundary between public land and the Navajo reservation. From this perspective, it may seem as though only the top tiers of the mesa belong to the Navajo. Actually, aside from a few small bits of the northern and eastern sides, it's all theirs.

The upper path mentioned earlier merges in from the north. Again, keep it in mind for the return route. Do not follow it in either direction now. (For

reference: It curves west, toward the back of the cove to cross a shallow point in the arroyo ahead. It then cuts back southeast to climb through a cleft in the wall. From there it joins up with a double-track that looks as though it serves more mule-drawn wagons than motorized vehicles. Overall, it's a long hike you might enjoy another day.)

For this hike, continue south, keeping the mesa rim on your left. Cross the arroyo and pass the eastern end of the cove wall to pick up the old trail. It squeezes along a narrow ledge for about 0.25 miles before arriving at a fence much like the last one. Again, step up to a slightly higher level. This upper ledge soon widens, giving acrophobes a bit more breathing room. At this point you're directly behind the old Herrera home, and about 400 feet above it.

Continue south along the rim to a small cairn. It marks the Navajo boundary, as does a fence below, which stretches due east to the horizon. You're now in the southwesternmost corner of public land on Herrera Mesa. At this juncture, it helps to know that Tohajiilee officials neither encourage nor discourage visitors from hiking on the reservation. Accordingly, the route description ends here, indecisively, at an otherwise arbitrary spot. A more natural terminus might be the mesa point in plain view just 0.25 miles ahead. Whether you proceed to that lovely overlook or turn back at the cairn is up to you.

GREATER PETACA PINTA: Volcano Hill  57

IN BRIEF

It's a volcano. It's a hill. It's Volcano Hill. This improvised route climbs the southern flank and circumnavigates the crater rim to provide an overview of immense but little-known public lands in the lower Rio Puerco Valley. Rich with wildlife and geologic wonders, Greater Petaca Pinta is a handsome candidate for the state's next designated Wilderness area.

DESCRIPTION

In 2003 the New Mexico Wilderness Alliance completed a four-year study of public wildlands throughout the state to assess their suitability for Wilderness designations. One major focus area was Greater Petaca Pinta, a 74,000-acre confederation of public lands about 40 miles southwest of Albuquerque.

With Laguna Pueblo to the west, Acoma Pueblo to the north, and a checkerboard of private, BLM, and state lands to the east and south, access to the complex can get a bit perplexing. Rugged roads pose further challenges to traveling its interior. But what seems to keep most outdoors enthusiasts away is the

----

Directions ⟶

From I-40 west, take Exit 126 and go 2 miles south on NM 6. Turn right on Old US 66 and go 1.5 miles west (over the railroad). Turn left on the road signed L 54 (IR 55 on some maps) and drive 13.8 miles south–southwest to a cattle guard and a sign for the Cerro Verde Ranch. Continue about 200 yards straight past the cattle guard and look for a doubletrack on the right. Follow it 0.4 miles northwest, toward the volcano, and park off to the right. As a courtesy to ranchers and their cattle, don't park within 300 yards of the stock pond.

KEY AT-A-GLANCE INFORMATION

LENGTH: 2.7-mile balloon
DIFFICULTY: Moderate
SCENERY: Grasslands, cinder cones, mesas
EXPOSURE: Full sun
TRAIL TRAFFIC: Low
TRAIL SURFACE: Lava rock
SHARED USE: Low (livestock; hiking route impassible for vehicles)
HIKING TIME: 2 hours
DRIVING DISTANCE: 51 miles (one way) from the I-40/I-25 exchange
ACCESS: Year-round
LAND STATUS: BLM–Rio Puerco Field Office
MAPS: USGS Cerro Verde
FACILITIES: None
LAST CHANCE FOOD/GAS: Pronto Mart on NM 6, about 1.5 miles southeast of Old US 66
SPECIAL COMMENTS: In theory, a right-of-way has been established across pueblo land as described in the directions below. Still, there's a remote chance you'll encounter local officers who say otherwise. A polite explanation of your intent to hike solely on public land should suffice. (Citing a guidebook to challenge their jurisdiction, on the other hand, may prove counterproductive.) Also, despite significant road improvements in late 2006, it's still unpaved and can get ugly after heavy rain.

GPS Trailhead Coordinates

UTM Zone (WGS 84) 13S
Easting   0288105
Northing 3853001
Latitude   34° 47' 50"
Longitude 106° 18' 58"

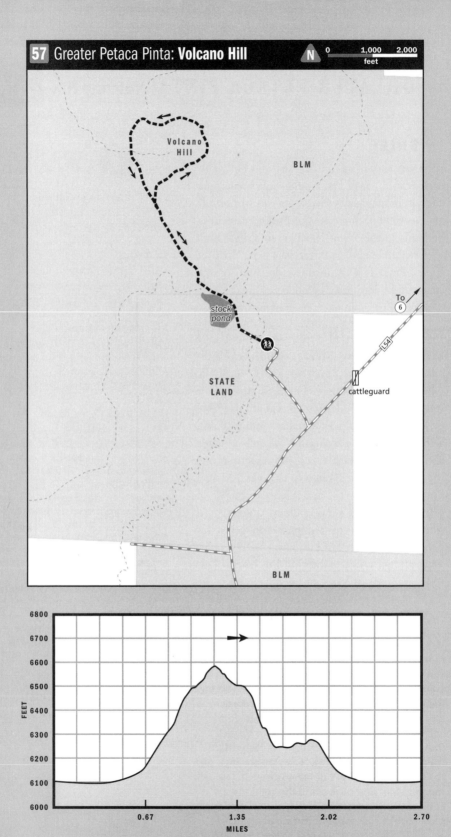

N

0   1,000   2,000
feet

Volcano
Hill

BLM

To
6

154

stock
pond

cattleguard

STATE
LAND

BLM

6800

6700

6600

6500

6400

FEET

6300

6200

6100

6000

0.67   1.35   2.02   2.70

MILES

The approach to Volcano Hill

fact that few are aware it even exists. Such a vast playground won't likely remain hidden much longer.

The Petaca Pinta Complex comprises three units: Petaca Pinta, Volcano Hill, and Sierra Lucero. The most easily accessed is the 27,000-acre Volcano Hill unit. Its namesake cinder cone rises 500 feet above a basalt lava flow and nearly 800 feet above the grasslands at the base of the escarpment to the immediate northwest.

The route set for this hike is fairly simple, and there's no particular reason to follow it precisely. There are no formal trails, and it would take a far longer hike to fully appreciate just the centerpiece feature of this vast unit.

The hike: Start by walking around the right side of the stock pond; its high bank makes a clear path through the tall grass. Cross the arroyo that feeds into it. As you approach the volcano, larger chunks of lava rock make walking somewhat tricky. It can be a real ankle twister, so watch your step. A couple of junipers ahead indicate a small black-sand wash, which creates another clear path toward the volcano. Note two points rising on the left flank, and aim for the base beneath the one on the right. From there, the remnants of a constructed path cut a relatively clean diagonal track up to the low end of the ridge.

The view from the ridge reveals that Volcano Hill is shaped more like a croissant than like a cone. When it erupted about 3 million years ago, the blast opened up the west side. The remainder of the route is pretty clear: follow the rim

counterclockwise. When you run out of ridge on the far side, return straight to this point, and then go back out to your vehicle the same way you came in.

For now, just climb up to the peak. The brick-red lava is more exposed at higher elevations. Orange, green, and yellow lichens thrive on the craggy rock, which is pocked with all sizes of vesicles, cavities that were formed by expanding steam and gas bubbles as the lava cooled. The lava solidified quickly, resulting in jagged edges, and it'll cut you up pretty good if you're not careful.

Because Volcano Hill is the central unit, its peak offers an excellent vantage point for a quick survey of the surrounding complex. In the western portion, Petaca Pinta is the smallest, though arguably the most scenic, of the three units. Likewise, it is by far the most difficult to access. Driving to that unit via BIA 541 requires permission from both the Laguna and Acoma pueblos.

The namesake feature of Petaca Pinta is an isolated finger-like extension from Blue Water Mesa at the southern end of the escarpment—the 1,000-foot cliffs on the far side of the plains—though it's difficult to distinguish one monumental feature from the other at this distance. If you're facing due west, Petaca Pinta is at 11 o'clock, about 10 miles out. The colorful escarpment exposes almost the entire 180 million years of the Mesozoic era. The basalt lava that caps the Mesozoic rocks is relatively fresh, having flowed from Cerro del Oro just 3 million years ago.

Nearly the mirror image of Volcano Hill, Cerro del Oro stands at ten o'clock, 14 miles out. Eye-catching features located outside the complex include Badger Butte, the lone plug at one o'clock, 4.5 miles out, and the 11,301-foot summit of Mount Taylor at two o'clock, 35 miles out.

The Petaca Pinta unit also includes juniper-dotted foothills and canyons that drop down to badlands and lava-capped mesas. Pronghorn, prairie dogs, and badgers inhabit the grasslands in the area. The unit's eastern boundary falls a few miles shy of the Arroyo Colorado—the dark scar that cuts through the plains below. It flows (sometimes) to the north to meet the Rio San Jose. Everything that drains out of this area goes into the Rio Puerco, which in turns runs south to join the Rio Grande.

On the near side of the arroyo, a vague road marks the Volcano Hill unit's western boundary. Closer in, scattered springs and numerous natural depressions that retain water are located in the lava flow around Volcano Hill. Though not easy to find, both petroglyphs and cave shelters have been noted around Volcano Hill. The caves are now home to several species of bats, including big-eared bats. You can help protect their health, and your own, by staying out of the caves.

Although the name "Volcano Hill" sounds uninspired, the caves' names read like the premise for an Abbot and Costello routine: Who Cave, What Cave, Which Cave, That Cave, This Ain't That Cave, and so on. Collectively they comprise the Pronoun Cave Complex, designated as an Area of Critical Environmental Concern. Fossils found in the caves provide a rare record of species that no longer range in New Mexico. The cave complex extends through the Sierra Lucero unit to Cerro del Oro.

The closest major feature in the neighboring Sierra Lucero unit is Cerro Verde. Peaking at 7,132 feet just 3 miles to the southeast, the "green hill" nearly doubles the climbing challenge of Volcano Hill. Directly behind it are the conjoined mesas, Cimarron and Gallina. Featured in the next hike, Gallina boasts the highest elevation in the complex: 7,855 feet. The high caps on this and other prominent rises catch enough moisture to support dense piñon–juniper woodlands, making Sierra Lucero not only the largest of the three units but also the most ecologically diverse.

Resuming the hike at hand, follow the ridge as it curves around to the west. Use caution: it narrows to the width of a sidewalk, and winds strong enough to knock you off balance are not uncommon. As you approach the end of the northern flank, you'll find a more gradual descent by veering right. As the ground levels out, aim left to cut across the mouth of the crater. Climb straight up the ridge ahead. Your car should be visible just 0.75 miles to the southeast.

NEARBY ACTIVITIES

Now that you've got an overview of the terrain out here, plan on a full day of biking and hiking. The Sierra Lucero unit is well suited for beginner to intermediate levels of mountain biking. Starting 1 mile past the Cerro Verde Ranch cattle guard, contiguous sections of public land stretch 5 miles south and 7 miles east. Factor in additional contiguous sections, and it adds up to about 40,000 acres of public land. Park on the side of the road, and ride off into the rolling hills. A detailed map with compass and/or a GPS receiver with tracking functions are highly recommended for navigating Greater Petaca Pinta.

58   GREATER PETACA PINTA: Mesa Gallina

KEY AT-A-GLANCE INFORMATION

LENGTH: 6-mile out-and-back, 7.8-mile balloon

DIFFICULTY: Strenuous

SCENERY: Piñon–juniper forest, geologic features, wildlife, views

EXPOSURE: Some canyon and woodland shade

TRAIL TRAFFIC: Low

SHARED USE: Low (canyon route impassable for vehicles)

TRAIL SURFACE: Sand, gravel, loose stone, bedrock

HIKING TIME: 5 hours

DRIVING DISTANCE: 59 miles (one way) from the I-40/I-25 exchange

ACCESS: Year-round

LAND STATUS: BLM–Rio Puerco Field Office

MAPS: USGS Mesa Gallina

FACILITIES: None

LAST CHANCE FOOD/GAS: Pronto Mart on NM 6, about 1.5 miles southeast of Old US 66.

SPECIAL COMMENTS: Regular cars should be OK on the back roads in dry conditions. Watch for naturally occurring speed bumps in the last 6 miles. In theory, a right-of-way has been established across pueblo land as described in directions. Still, you might encounter local officers who say otherwise. A polite explanation of your intent to hike solely on public land should suffice.

- -

GPS Trailhead
Coordinates

UTM Zone (WGS 84)   13S

Easting   0295491

Northing   3847419

Latitude   34° 44' 54"

Longitude   107° 14' 03"

IN BRIEF

As a basic out-and-back, the round-trip hike would be a mere 6 miles, almost all of it in a deep, rocky arroyo. Extra miles add up fast when you explore the top of Mesa Gallina, the highest point in the Petaca Pinta Complex. From the top, survey a fascinating landscape where the Rio Grande Rift meets the Colorado Plateau.

DESCRIPTION

It's a straight shot south—road to rim in just 3 miles. What could be easier? But in retrospect, I'd say this route easily ranks among the top five most difficult hikes in the book. Maybe it was the 1,200-foot gain in elevation over loose rock and sand, or maybe it was the extra 2 miles of wandering the mesa top, but my

- -

Directions ⟶

From I-40 west, take Exit 126. Turn left and drive 2 miles south on NM 6. Turn right on Old US 66 and go west (over the railroad) 1.5 miles. Turn left on the road signed L54 and continue 16.4 miles south–southwest on the main dirt road. (At this point, two stone blocks mark a new dirt road on the right.) Continue south past the blocks another 0.4 miles and turn left on a dirt road. From here, stay on the main track for the next 6.1 miles. More specifically, at 2 miles is a drop gate with an erroneous sign. (See Nearby Activities for details about the sign.) At 3.5 miles, the road bends east. At 5.3 miles, go right at the Y and cross the Arroyo Lucero ahead. The road soon splits again. Go left through the hairpin turn. The road soon bends back to the east and runs along the northern side of the Arroyo Lucero for the next half mile. Pull off the road and park right before it begins to bend north away from the arroyo.

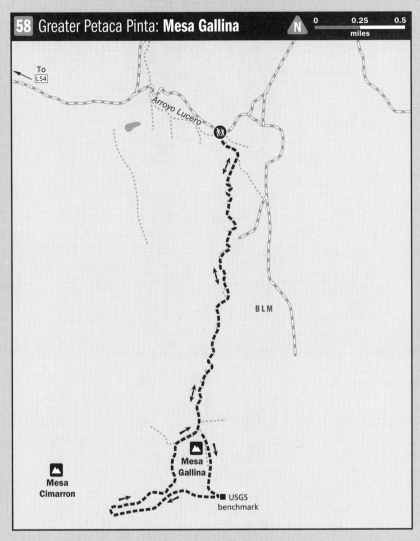

Arroyo Lucero

BLM

Mesa Cimarron

Mesa Gallina

USGS benchmark

To L54

N

0   0.25   0.5
miles

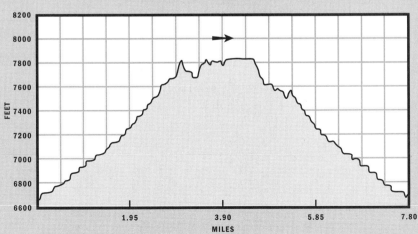

Crotalus molossus

hiking buddy and I returned from the hike feeling inexplicably fatigued.

Was it worth it? Absolutely. The deep Arroyo Lucero provided ample shade on an otherwise sizzling spring afternoon, and storms brewing over the badlands to the west sent cool breezes to the mesa top. Hawks keened above. Paintbrush, yucca, and cacti bloomed in electric colors. And every so often, crystals sparkled from geodes in the charcoal-colored sand. We were also treated to a rattlesnake encounter—my first in nearly a decade. This three-foot pit viper was a black-tailed rattlesnake, *Crotalus molossus,* one of the least aggressive species. Cornered against a solid rock wall, it gave us ample warning. Its steady buzz seemed to indicate that it preferred a good 15 feet of personal space. We respectfully obliged and passed without incident the first time—but we didn't count on crossing the same snake twice.

That's just a small sampling of the wondrous assortment of animals, plants, and minerals to watch for as you climb Mesa Gallina. Also keep in mind that since the majority of this hike traverses a steep waterway and the mesa is just high enough to snag rain clouds rolling off the Colorado Plateau, you should pay special attention to weather conditions.

The hike begins in a relatively shallow wash about 200 feet south of the road. Follow the wash upstream to the southeast for the first 200 or 300 yards and then to the south; stay to the right to avoid straying up tributary channels merging from your left. For the next mile, there's little doubt as to which

Scial negotiates the south side of the mesa.

drainage to follow. At the next notable fork, the arroyo merely splits around an island—take your pick. Once past the island, you're back to a single channel and halfway to the rim.

Another mile ahead, a channel comes in on your left, followed by another on your right—go up the middle. The Lucero benchmark is less than half a mile straight ahead. However, you'll probably drift slightly west as the terrain levels out in that direction. In that case, when you reach the rim, turn left, and follow it to the southeastern corner of the mesa.

A standard U.S. Geological benchmark, stamped Lucero 1952, is set in outcropping bedrock about 50 feet north of the mesa's highest point and 14 feet west of a bluff. Two reference marks from a 1958 survey are nearby.

You can go back the way you came or explore the mesa. Unless you have an unerring sense of direction, do not stray far from the rim. The inner meadows and wooded areas can be somewhat disorienting.

About 0.25 miles west of the benchmark, on the far side of a few low hills, the rim is a jumble of boulders with gaps that form seemingly bottomless shafts. Take an extra measure of caution in this area. To the immediate west and down one level, a shelf affords unobstructed views of ranges to the south. The nearest major peak is Ladron, about 20 miles to the southeast.

Climb back to the upper rim, and go to the mesa's southwestern corner for views over the Petaca Pinta Complex. As mentioned in the previous hike at

Volcano Hill, this area is composed of three units: Petaca Pinta, Volcano Hill, and Sierra Lucero. Mesa Gallina stands in the easternmost unit, roughly in the center of a north–south trending escarpment known as the Sierra Lucero.

Approximately 30 place names in New Mexico honor Pedro Lucero de Godoy and his descendants. The Mexico City native arrived in Santa Fe in the early 1600s and became an established religious and political figure before the Pueblo Revolt in 1680. His sons and grandsons were prominent in the reconquest of 1692, and many residents of New Mexico and Colorado today embrace their Lucero lineage.

By comparison, about 45 place names in New Mexico pay tribute to *gallina*, which means "chicken," though it more often refers to *gallina de la tierra*, "wild turkey." A point of slight distinction: Chicken Mountain, the 7,826-foot peak 5 miles to the southwest, falls just 29 feet shy of Mesa Gallina's great height.

When you're ready to return to the road, aim east–northeast. All drains flow into the basin that forms the head of Arroyo Lucero. It's all downhill from there.

As for the rattlesnake, it was where we left it when we returned several hours later and well past dark. We'd forgotten about it, and it didn't bother to remind us of its presence until we passed within a step or two of its rattle. Had it been a Mojave rattler, I might be missing a hiking buddy right now. But then you won't find snakes that mean within 60 miles of Albuquerque.

NEARBY ACTIVITIES

Two miles down the dirt road, just past the wooden frame of what was once Virgils Windmill, a new sign at the drop gate reads: Keep Out. Certainly, the Major Cattle Company had a good reason for posting it. Their ties to the land go back some 70 years. But whether or not they had the right could be a matter of dispute. According to the most recent BLM Edition maps, the sign stands at the gateway to 15,000 acres of public land in the Sierra Lucero.

If you prefer to obey the sign, pull off the road, and take an alternate hike up nearby Cerro Verde. Rising about 750 feet to peak at 7,132 feet just 2 miles north of the gate, the "green hill" doesn't pose the same challenge as Mesa Gallina, but it's a pleasantly vigorous stroll all the same. You can also park on the main dirt road about 1 mile north of the stone blocks and approach it along the arroyo flowing from the east.

EL MALPAIS: Narrows Rim Trail 59

IN BRIEF

A gradual ascent on a cliffside trail culminates with a grand view of the largest accessible arch in New Mexico. Numerous overlooks along this designated trail reveal the stark expanse of black lava that dominates El Malpais National Monument.

DESCRIPTION

First, a confession: this trail lies 6 miles beyond the prescribed 60-mile radius. However, El Malpais is just too spectacular to omit because of a minor technicality like that.

El Malpais (pronounced mall-pie-EES, though sometimes without the last syllable) refers to both the national monument and the national conservation area, administered by the National Park Service and the Bureau of Land Management, respectively. Between the two, El Malpais comprises 377,000 acres of public badlands.

Generally speaking, the terms *malpais* and *badlands* are used to describe any land that's inhospitable to humans. In New Mexico, there's usually a lava flow involved that makes them extra bad. Likewise, the lava flow of El Malpais National Monument is a most brutal terrain. And like most dangerous things in nature, its allure is irresistible.

The land wasn't always so bad. Its shale and sandstone bluffs quietly emerged from a

KEY AT-A-GLANCE INFORMATION

LENGTH: 7.8-mile out-and back
DIFFICULTY: Moderate
SCENERY: Sandstone bluffs, lava fields, natural arch, wildflowers, cacti
EXPOSURE: Minimal shade
TRAIL TRAFFIC: Moderate
SHARED USE: Low (pets must be leashed; closed to bicycles and all motorized vehicles)
TRAIL SURFACE: Sand, rock
HIKING TIME: 3 hours
DRIVING DISTANCE: 92 miles (one way) from the I-40/I-25 exchange
ACCESS: Year-round
LAND STATUS: National Conservation Area (BLM), Cebolleta Wilderness Area
MAPS: Brochure maps in visitor centers; USGS North Pasture
FACILITIES: Picnic tables and restroom at trailhead. No water.
LAST CHANCE FOOD/GAS: Convenience store—gas station at Exit 89.
SPECIAL COMMENTS: El Malpais (BLM) Visitor Center, 9 miles south of Exit 89, is a highly recommended stop en route to the trailhead. See Nearby Activites at end of description.

GPS Trailhead Coordinates

UTM Zone (WGS 84) 13S
Easting 0233721
Northing 3858745
Latitude 34° 50' 10"
Longitude 107° 54' 43"

Directions ⟶

From I-40 west, take Exit 89 and turn left on NM 117. Go south 21.7 miles to the Narrows Picnic Area. Turn left on the gravel drive. Several yards ahead on the right, a wooden sign marks the start of Narrows Rim Trail.

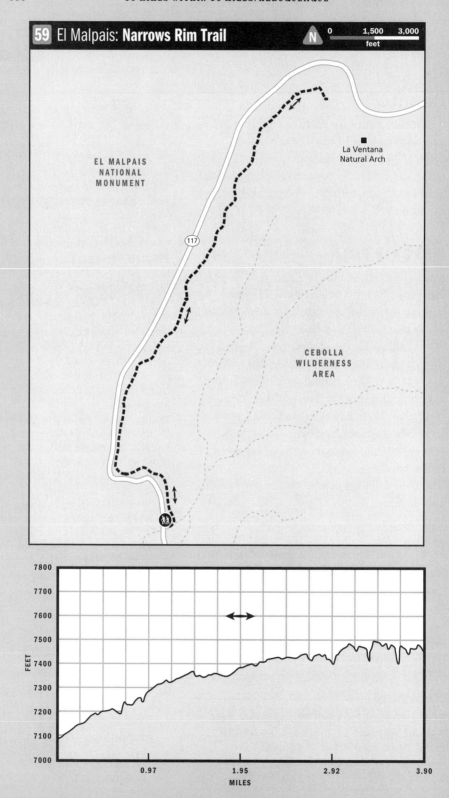

La Ventana, an alcove natural arch

receding ocean 70 million years ago. Sedimentary layers are obvious today in white, tan, and rust-colored bands running the length of the escarpment like bathtub rings.

Then, about 120,000 years ago, the floor cracked open and unleashed a riot of molten lava. A series of eruptions would follow, about five major flows in all, until the valley was filled with a river of lava 40 miles long and 5 miles wide. Some geologic studies peg the latest outburst at 1000 BC, though eyewitness reports from ancestors of the nearby Acoma Pueblo suggest it could've been as recent as AD 1200.

Much of the lava cooled to form edges as sharp as steak knives. Jagged ridges and deep sinkholes further inhibit recreational opportunities. A rugby scrum is out of the question. Hiking is advised only in designated areas and only with the sturdiest footwear.

If you arrived in sneakers, you still have no shortage of places to explore, including the terrain of this hike. The flow stopped a few yards shy of the cliffs south of La Ventana, leaving room for a narrow passage between the jagged lava bed and the steep wall. Hence the name, The Narrows (or *La Angostura*, as it appears on Spanish maps).

NM 117 now occupies this corridor, through which you pass to reach the trailhead. Narrows Rim Trail runs 500 feet above it to provide glorious views at every turn. The vastness of enigmatic black fields adds credence to legends of lost treasure, including gold looted in train robberies, in addition to tales of a private jet said to have crashed and vanished out there with a hefty cash cargo. If nothing else, it's a land of strange phenomena. For one, it's the only place I've seen snow falling while temperatures hovered at 58°F.

The hike starts on a sandy trail. Look to the left for a cave—water jugs stashed inside are for thirsty souls traveling the Continental Divide National Scenic Trail. The Continental Divide itself crosses over the Chain of Craters, 18 miles due east, on the far side of the lava flow. (For more information, visit www.cdtrail.org.)

Pass the cave, and begin ascending the mesa. This is the steepest part of the hike, and it's no more strenuous than a flight or two of stairs. For the remainder of the hike, the ascent is almost imperceptible. The only difficulties are the sandy pockets that can slow you down and the rocks that may trip you up. Also, the grade is more noticeable on the descent.

Once atop the mesa, you will find that, well above the back end of the Narrows Picnic Area, the trail bends west (left) and then slightly south. Before it starts north again, carefully approach the cliff's edge where it curves inward. Stand on the near point, and find the most prominent crack in the wall below. Trace it down to the rocky ledge. Two petroglyphs appear on the left side, about six feet above the undercliff. One is a spiral, probably representing the sun; the other appears to be a bighorn sheep. It takes a good eye to spot them, but once you do, you'll know how to find more ahead.

The trail soon runs a straight course north, never diverging more than a toss from the rim. The next cairn is always in sight, and painted rocks report your mileage almost every half mile. Stray east, and you'll be wading through scrub, where you might stumble over an ancient ruin buried under a mound of sand. Wander to the west, and you'll plummet from a cliff. In short, you can't get lost.

About 3.5 miles into the hike, the trail forks around a cluster of six or so yuccas. Go right. A stone ahead marks the terminus at 3.3 miles, but I measured it as closer to 4 miles, not counting frequent detours to the rim. Either way you'll know when you've reached the prow when you see La Ventana ("the window"), an alcove natural arch on the far side of the pasture below. With a height of 80 feet and a span of 165 feet, it's considered the second-longest arch in New Mexico. (The state record goes to the inaccessible Snake Bridge in San Juan County.)

The trail curves around for a closer view of the arch from the backside. Few continue that way, so the extra mile may require some bushwhacking. Your time would be better spent on other nearby trails.

Though amazing overlooks are the dominant feature, take time to notice details closer at hand as you make your way back to the trailhead. Lichen growing on the sandstone takes on shades of neon lime, and it's the catalyst for reducing these fossilized sand dunes back into sand. The red and pinkish tones in the sandstone indicate a high iron content.

Be on the lookout for approaching storms. Strikes are frequent along the rim, as graveyards of trees seem to testify, though much of it is just blowdown. High winds twist and gnarl pines in krummholz contortions, while the feathery seeds of mountain mahogany shiver in the breeze. Not many animals show themselves on the trail, but footprints left in sandy patches confirm their presence. Look for signs of elk, bobcat, black bear, and mountain lion.

Note regarding wheel-chair access: El Malpais (BLM) Visitor Center and restroom facilities through-out the area are wheelchair-accessible. The lower trail to La Ventana Natural Arch is accessible, and one picnic

table at the Narrows Picnic Area will accommodate wheelchairs. Access is on packed dirt. Part of the Sandstone Bluffs Overlook is wheelchair-accessible, as is a short loop trail at the Zuni–Acoma Trailhead.

NEARBY ACTIVITIES

For a walk in the lava fields, try the Zuni–Acoma Trail, an ancient trade route about 6 miles north of the Narrows Picnic Area. For other destinations—including ancient pueblo ruins, abandoned homesteads, miles of tunnels, bat caves, cinder cones, and perennial ice—El Malpais (BLM) Visitor Center has all the details and occasionally offers guided programs. Interpretive exhibits and literature provide a thorough orientation to the area's complex features. For more information, call the Grants Field Station at (505) 287-7911, or visit **www.nps.gov/elma** or **www .nm.blm.gov.**

60 MOUNT TAYLOR:
Gooseberry Spring Trail

GPS Trailhead
Coordinates

UTM Zone (WGS 84) 13S

Easting   0259992

Northing   3900627

Latitude   35° 13' 12"

Longitude   107° 38' 13"

IN BRIEF

Often snow-capped into mid-spring, Mount Taylor is the massive volcano on Albuquerque's sunset horizon. A classic hike on a designated trail winds through woods and meadows to culminate on the rim of the caldera.

DESCRIPTION

Our final destination stands just 54 miles west of where we began, though at an elevation some 6,300 feet higher. The Navajo know this volcanic peak as *Tsoodzil*, "turquoise mountain." According to their tradition, it's the mountain of the south, one of four sacred peaks that mark the boundaries of *Dinetah,* the Navajo homeland.

Thong trees further indicate a history of local Indian activity. Also called trail trees, water trees, and buffalo trees, they began as flexible saplings that were notched and bent at right angles. The "thong" refers to a

----

Directions ⟶

From I-40 west, take Exit 85 and veer right toward Grants. (Note the classic Route 66 motels and diners on Santa Fe Avenue.) About 2.5 miles from the exit, turn right on First Street (NM 547). Go about 1 mile and bear right onto Roosevelt Avenue. Go 0.4 miles and turn left onto Lobo Canyon Road. Follow the road (still NM 547) about 12 miles up Mount Taylor and turn right onto Forest Road 193. (Do *not* turn at the Lobo Canyon Campground, which is about 4.5 miles too soon. And if you run out of paved road, you've gone about 100 yards too far.) Stay on FR 193, a maintained dirt road, 5 miles. The trailhead is on the left. Look for a hiking icon on a green sign, and a brown post labeled Trail 77. Park in a small lot on the right. (If you see the signed junction of FR 193 and FR 501, you've gone about 200 yards too far.)

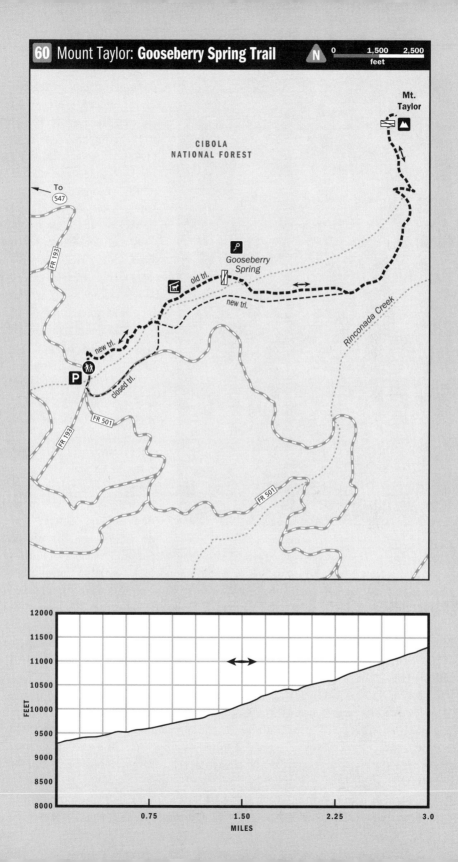

N

0   1,500   2,500
feet

Mt.
Taylor

CIBOLA
NATIONAL FOREST

To
547

FR 193

Gooseberry
Spring

old trl.

new trl.

new trl.

closed trl.

P

FR 501

FR 193

FR 501

Rinconada Creek

12000
11500
11000
10500
10000
9500
9000
8500
8000

FEET

0.75   1.50   2.25   3.0
MILES

Y-shaped stick or leather strap, which prevented the tree from growing out of the contorted position. Their distinct stair-step trunks pointed the way to nearby resources, such as water, food, or medicinal herbs. Subtler modifications coded the details. In short, thong trees are like pages from an old guidebook. Many still stand out among regiments of pencil-straight aspens on Mount Taylor, particularly on north-facing slopes.

The mountains show up on early Spanish maps as *Sierra de la Zebolleta,* or "range of the little onion." Later settlers renamed them in honor of San Mateo. In 1849 an army lieutenant dubbed the central peak for President Zachary Taylor, who soon repaid the favor to New Mexicans by preventing Texas from expanding its state boundaries into the New Mexico Territory. The Anglo name stuck for the mountain, but the range is still referred to as both the Cebolleta Mountains and the San Mateo Mountains.

The area has an extensive history of logging, grazing, and mining, as evidenced by an endless web of roads. Yet the Mount Taylor Ranger District, a 520,000-acre corner of Cibola National Forest, contains only two maintained hiking trails: the Strawberry Canyon Trail at McGaffy Campground near Fort Wingate and Gooseberry Spring Trail, featured here. Together they total nearly 4 miles. An alternate route for the Continental Divide National Scenic Trail is gradually emerging as a third trail. So far, the segment from Lobo Canyon Road to the top of Horace Mesa—a good 2 miles—is in solid shape and adequately marked. However, the same cannot always be said for the Gooseberry Spring Trail.

The hike begins on the north side of FR 193, in a patch of quintessential American woodland. Bluebirds, squirrels, and chipmunks frolic. Aspens bear the paired initials and heart-shaped scars of adolescent affections. To the south, runoff from Gooseberry Spring sometimes streams from the draw and tunnels under the road. You'll see this stream (or its dry bed) again often throughout the hike ahead. and if you miss a right turn on your way down from the peak, you'll end up following it back to the road.

Start north on a pale gravel trail that climbs quickly into denser woods. Gravel soon gives way to a carpet of pine needles. The first 0.5 miles of this new trail holds its form as it winds around rock formations near the edge of the draw, which by this point has assumed the proportions of a canyon. The trail then descends into a meadow and crosses the streambed, where you might find a trickle of water. An arrow on a sign close ahead points to the junction of the new trail, the old trail, and a swath of erosion.

This is where the way can get a little murky. Perhaps a bit of maintenance will help clarify it in time for your hike. If not, it helps to know that the new trail supposedly angles uphill to the northeast as it begins its gradual climb to the ridge, thus avoiding livestock facilities farther up the canyon. Conversely, the old trail approaches the junction from the south and stays close to the arroyo as it bends northeast. In terms of navigational ease, the old arroyo route may still be the better way to go. Whichever way you choose, pick a nearby landmark that you'll recognize later because you probably won't notice the backside of the arrow sign on your return.

This hike continues up the arroyo, crossing it an odd number of times. An old corral lists on the left bank, and the canyon meadow widens as you approach a drop gate. Go through it and leave it as you found it. You're now about 1 mile into the hike, and it's about to get a bit more strenuous. On the plus side, staying on the right track is a cinch from here to the peak. You can see the trail climbing into a stand of aspen on the north-facing slope of the canyon. Cross over to the right side of the arroyo, and begin the steep ascent to the ridge.

The old and new trails merge near the edge of the meadow on the other side of the aspen woods, where it becomes less a path than a rut. As you follow the tracks uphill, your destination peak comes into view on the left. At this point, you're about halfway there. The rest of the hike is high and exposed so keep an eye out for storm clouds.

At 1.8 miles, the trail slumps over a saddle on the ridge and curves left. Enjoy a brief stretch of flat terrain while it lasts. Far below to your right, Rinconada Creek begins its winding 14-mile course to the Rio San Jose. The trail eases back over the ridge and crosses the uppermost cut of the arroyo. Note the Z-shaped switchbacks ramping up the southern slope of the peak. Once you get through those, you'll arrive at the gateway in an old fence. From there it's less than 0.25 miles to the peak.

Upon the sacred summit of Tsoodzil, the head of Pogo the Possum is mounted on a steel pole, along with a sign reading: MT. TAYLOR ELEV. 11,301, and a box containing a logbook and a thermometer. Take a moment to read past entries, and enjoy the view. On a clear day, you can see into both Arizona and Colorado. Closer in to the northeast, a road splits from FR 453 to drop over the rim and slither down to the floor of the caldera. Trekkers should take advantage of the bird's-eye view to scout out potential routes below.

You can extend your hike another mile on a steep, narrow path that winds down to FR 453 near La Mosca Lookout. Otherwise, retrace your steps to the parking area.

Note: Check with the Mount Taylor Ranger Station or the Northwest New Mexico Visitors Center for road conditions and possible closures. The ranger station is located en route at 1800 Lobo Canyon Road and can be reached at (505) 287-8833 or **www.fs.fed.us/r3/cibola/districts/mttaylor.** To reach the Northwest New Mexico Visitors Center, turn left from the end of the ramp at Exit 85, and follow the signs about 0.25 miles to the parking lot on the left. You can call them at (505) 876-2783.

NEARBY ACTIVITIES

The Mount Taylor Ranger District's biggest drawback is the long ride to its primary access road, but adventurous hikers can cut nearly 30 miles of driving by starting their hikes from the southern end of Rinconada Canyon. To get there from Albuquerque, take Exit 100 north to San Fidel. Turn left on Old Route 66 (SR 124), and go 2 miles west. (From Grants, take Exit 96, and drive 1.4 miles east.) Turn north on FR 400 (CR 16). The first 4.7 miles are usually maintained well enough for most cars, but be sure to check with the ranger station or the visitor center for current conditions and instructions for crossing private boundaries.

For those who don't mind a long drive, consider a scenic route back to Grants via San Mateo and Milan. FR 239 and FR 456 are usually suitable for most cars. Numerous old tributary roads present infinite possibilities for impromptu hikes.

Finally, I couldn't end this book without mentioning Bibo, the revived ghost town on the east side of Mount Taylor. Visit Our Lady of Loretto, an adobe mission built by Jewish settlers in the 1880s (Mass is held on the second and fourth Fridays at 7 p.m.) Get a burger and suds at the historic Bibo Bar, established in 1913. Hours are generally from 11 a.m. to 2 a.m. Call (505) 552-9428 or visit **www.bibobar-nm.com.** To get there, take Exit 114 at Laguna, and go west about 1.2 miles to the turnoff for Paguate and Seboyeta. Turn right, and drive about 11 miles north to Bibo.

APPENDIXES
AND INDEX

APPENDIX A:
PUBLIC LANDS

Public Lands Information Center
www.publiclands.org
1474 Rodeo Road
Santa Fe, NM 87105
(505) 438-PLIC
Billing itself as "Your One-Stop Source for Recreation Information," the PLIC is a handy resource for planning outdoor activities in the western states. Their site includes links to road conditions, weather, fire alerts, and an online museum that details the history of public lands with an interactive timeline and virtual scrapbooks.

STATE AND LOCAL AGENCIES:

Albuquerque Open Space Division
www.cabq.org/openspace
3615 Los Picaros SE
Albuquerque, NM 87105
(505) 452-5200
The OSD manages more than 28,000 acres in and around Albuquerque to conserve natural and archaeological resources, provide opportunities for outdoor education, provide a place for high and low impact recreation, and define the edges of the urban environment.

Middle Rio Grande Conservancy District
www.mrgcd.com
1930 Second Street SW
Albuquerque, NM 87102
(505) 247-0234
The MRGCD oversees 1,200 miles of ditches and canals to ensure that the Middle Rio Grande Valley is full of farmlands, wildlife, and recreational opportunities.

New Mexico Department of
Game and Fish
www.wildlife.state.nm.us
3841 Midway Place NE
Albuquerque, NM 87109
(505) 222-4700
The New Mexico Department of Game and Fish manages 56 areas that provide primarily for fishing and hunting, though many include camping, picnicking areas, and trails for hiking and wildlife viewing.

New Mexico State Land Office
www.nmstatelands.org
310 Old Santa Fe Trail
Santa Fe, NM 87501
(505) 827-5760
The New Mexico State Land Office manages some 22 million acres. Hiking, hunting, and horseback riding is allowed by permit on publicly accessible and noncommercial land. Permit applications can be downloaded from their Web site.

New Mexico State Parks
www.nmparks.com
1220 South St. Francis Drive
Santa Fe, NM 87505
(505) 476-3355 or (888) NMPARKS
With 34 (soon to be 36) parks throughout the state, the New Mexico State Parks Division manages more than 117,000 acres, not including water surface area in 17 reservoirs. Annual day use passes and camping permits are available to purchase online.

Bureau of Land Management
www.nm.blm.gov
The BLM manages more than 12 million
acres, most of which is open to outdoor
recreation activities including backpacking,
hiking, biking, whitewater boating, fishing,
caving, wildlife viewing, and cultural site
touring.

Rio Puerco Field Office
435 Montano NE
Albuquerque, NM 87107
(505) 761.8700

Socorro Field Office
901 South Highway 85
Socorro, NM 87801
(505) 835-0412

Taos Field Office
226 Cruz Alta Road
Taos, NM 87571
(505) 751-4710

National Park Service
www.nps.gov
The NPS manages 14 sites totaling
391,031 acres in New Mexico, including
visitor centers and trails to historic, cultural, and natural and scenic sites visited
by over 1.5 million people annually.

U.S. Fish and Wildlife Service
www.fws.gov
The USFWS manages five National
Wildlife Refuges that are open for
wildlife viewing.

U.S. Forest Service
The USFS manages about 9 million acres
of New Mexico's most ecologically diverse
lands ranging in elevation from 4,000 to
more than 13,000 feet.

Cibola National Forest
www.fs.fed.us/r3/cibola
2113 Osuna Road NE, Suite A
Albuquerque, NM 87113
(505) 346-3900

Sandia Ranger District
11776 Highway 337
Tijeras, NM 87059
(505) 281-3304

Mountainair Ranger District
40 Ranger Station Road
Mountainair, New Mexico 87036
(505) 847-2990

Mount Taylor Ranger District
1800 Lobo Canyon Road
Grants, NM 87020
(505) 287-8833

Santa Fe National Forest
www.fs.fed.us/r3/sfe
1474 Rodeo Road
Santa Fe, NM 87505
(505) 438-7840

Española Ranger District
1710 North Riverside Drive
Española, NM 87532
(505) 753-7331

Jemez Ranger District
Highway 4
Jemez Springs, NM 87025
(505) 829-3535

Pecos/Las Vegas District
Highway 63
Pecos, NM 87552
(505) 757-6121

APPENDIX B:
EVERYTHING ELSE YOU NEED TO KNOW ABOUT NEW MEXICO

GET INVOLVED

Audubon New Mexico
www.newmexicoaudubon.org
(505) 983-4609
Four chapters of the New Mexico
Audubon Council offer programs and field
trips throughout the year. Visit the scenic
headquarters and hiking trails at the
Randall Davey Audubon Center at 1800
Upper Canyon Road in Santa Fe.

New Mexico Wilderness Alliance
www.nmwild.org
(505) 843-8696
The New Mexico Wilderness Alliance is
a grassroots environmental organization
dedicated to the protection, restoration,
and continued enjoyment of New Mexico's
wildlands and Wilderness areas. Check their
events calendar for hikes and other outings.

Sierra Club
www.sierraclub.org/nm
(505) 243-7767
With a mission to "explore, enjoy and protect the planet®" the Sierra Club has four
chapters dedicated to New Mexico. The
Santa Fe–based Rio Grande Chapter hosts
the best outings.

JOIN THE CLUB

Albuquerque Double Eagle Hike
and Bike Club
members.aol.com/abqdoubleeagles
(505) 298-1256

A good source for local urban routes and
sanctioned volkssporting events.

Albuquerque Hiking and Outdoor Meetup
hiking.meetup.com/204
Launched in 2006, this sociable group for
hiking enthusiasts hosted more than 100
events for nearly 300 members in its
inaugural year.

New Mexico Mountain Club
www.swcp.com/~nmmc
Founded in 1952, the NMMC hosted more
than 500 outings for nearly 1,000 members
in its 55th year.

GEAR UP

Albuquerque:

REI
www.rei.com
1550 Mercantile Avenue NE
(505) 247-1191

Sport Systems Ski & Bike
1605 Juan Tabo NE, Suite Z
(505) 296-9111

Sportz Outdoorz
6915 Montgomery NE
(505) 837-9400

Stone Age Climbing
www.climbstoneage.com
4201 Yale Ave NE
(505) 341-2016

Santa Fe:

Alpine Sports
www.alpinesports-santafe.com
127 Sandoval Street
(505) 983-5155

Sangre de Cristo Mountainworks
www.sdcmountainworks.com
328 South Guadalupe Street
(505) 984-8221

Travel Bug
www.mapsofnewmexico.com
839 Paseo de Peralta
(866) 992-0418

VIRTUAL NEW MEXICO

Arts, entertainment, and the inside dirt:
www.alibi.com

Dining recommendations:
www.nmgastronome.com

Interactive maps:
landstatus.nmstatelands.org

Outdoors and recreation news:
www.abqjournal.com/go

USGS topographic maps:
sar.lanl.gov/topo_maps

Oddities and peculiarities:
www.mystrangenewmexico.com

VISITOR INFORMATION

Albuquerque Convention & Visitors Bureau
www.itsatrip.org
(800) 284-2282

Santa Fe Convention & Visitors Bureau
www.santafe.org
(800) 777-2489

New Mexico Tourism Department
www.newmexico.org
(800) 733-6396

For information on just about everything
else in Albuquerque, dial 311 from any
local phone or visit cabq.gov/a-z

INDEX

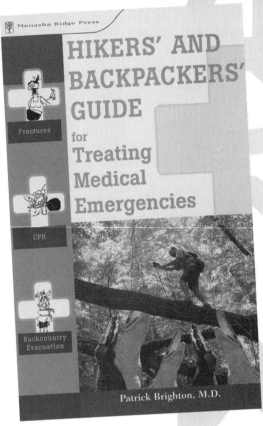

HIKERS' AND BACKPACKERS' GUIDE FOR TREATING MEDICAL EMERGENCIES

by Patrick Brighton, M.D.
ISBN 10: 0-89732-640-7
ISBN 13: 978-0-89732-640-7
$9.95
116 pages

By keeping descriptions and remedies for injury and illness simple, this book enables participants in a particular sport to be informed, stay calm, and appropriately treat themselves or fellow participants. Reading this book before initiating the activity also enhances awareness of potential problems and fosters prevention of accidents and disease. With a refreshing splash of humor, this guide is as informative as it is entertaining.

GPS OUTDOORS

by Russell Helms
ISBN 10: 0-89732-967-8
ISBN 13: 978-0-89732-967-5
$10.95
120pages

Whether you're a hiker on a weekend trip through the Great Smokies, a backpacker cruising the Continental Divide Trail, a mountain biker kicking up dust in Moab, a paddler running the Lewis and Clark bicentennial route, or a climber pre-scouting the routes up Mount Shasta, a simple handheld GPS unit is fun, useful, and can even be a lifesaver.

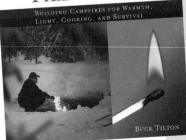

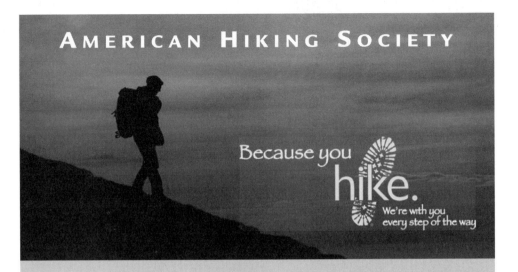

DEAR CUSTOMERS AND FRIENDS,

SUPPORTING YOUR INTEREST IN OUTDOOR ADVENTURE, travel, and an active lifestyle is central to our operations, from the authors we choose to the locations we detail to the way we design our books. Menasha Ridge Press was incorporated in 1982 by a group of veteran outdoorsmen and professional outfitters. For 25 years now, we've specialized in creating books that benefit the outdoors enthusiast.

Almost immediately, Menasha Ridge Press earned a reputation for revolutionizing outdoors- and travel-guidebook publishing. For such activities as canoeing, kayaking, hiking, backpacking, and mountain biking, we established new standards of quality that transformed the whole genre, resulting in outdoor-recreation guides of great sophistication and solid content. Menasha Ridge continues to be outdoor publishing's greatest innovator.

The folks at Menasha Ridge Press are as at home on a white-water river or mountain trail as they are editing a manuscript. The books we build for you are the best they can be, because we're responding to your needs. Plus, we use and depend on them ourselves.

We look forward to seeing you on the river or the trail. If you'd like to contact us directly, join in at www.trekalong.com or visit us at www.menasharidge.com. We thank you for your interest in our books and the natural world around us all.

SAFE TRAVELS,

Bob Sehlinger

BOB SEHLINGER
PUBLISHER